MANDELSTAM,
BLOK, AND THE
BOUNDARIES OF
MYTHOPOETIC
SYMBOLISM

MANDELSTAM, BLOK, AND THE BOUNDARIES OF MYTHOPOETIC SYMBOLISM

STUART GOLDBERG

THE OHIO STATE UNIVERSITY PRESS | COLUMBUS

Copyright © 2011 by The Ohio State University.
All rights reserved.

Library of Congress Cataloging-in-Publication Data

Goldberg, Stuart, 1971–
 Mandelstam, Blok, and the boundaries of mythopoetic symbolism / Stuart Goldberg.
    p. cm.
 Includes bibliographical references and index.
 ISBN 978-0-8142-1159-5 (cloth : alk. paper)—ISBN 978-0-8142-9260-0 (cd)
  1. Russian poetry—20th century—History and criticism. 2. Symbolism in literature. 3. Mandel'shtam, Osip, 1891–1938—Criticism and interpretation. 4. Blok, Aleksandr Aleksandrovich, 1880–1921—Criticism and interpretation. I. Title.
 PG3065.S8G65 2011
 891.71'3—dc22
                        2011013260

Paper (ISBN: 978-0-8142-5635-0)
Cover design by James A. Baumann
Text design by Juliet Williams
Type set in Adobe Minion Pro

*Диночке
с любовью*

CONTENTS

Acknowledgments		ix
Note on Transliteration		xiii

PART I

Chapter 1	Introduction	3
	Immediacy and Distance	3
	"The living and dangerous Blok . . ."	6
	Symbolism and Acmeism: An Overview	8
	The Curtain and the Onionskin	15
Chapter 2	Prescient Evasions of Bloom	21

PART II

Chapter 3	Departure	35
Chapter 4	The Pendulum at the Heart of *Stone*	49
Chapter 5	Struggling with the Faith	56
	Ambivalent Irony and the Word	57
	Inverting the Symbolist Heresiography	64
	Stumbling into a New Poetics	71
	Stealing the Sanctuary	79

PART III

Chapter 6	Bedside with the Symbolist Hero	85
Chapter 7	The Superficial and the Profound	100
	Fodder for Parody	100
	Modernist Time Poetics	105
	The Mythopoetics of Tristia	109
Chapter 8	Blok's Theater Poems	130
Chapter 9	Boundaries Erected, Boundaries Effaced	147
	Masquerade Bounded	148
	Theatrical Wonder Breaks Free	153

PART IV

Chapter 10	"To Anaxagoras" in the Velvet Night	167
	Visions Apart	172
	"To Anaxagoras" in the Velvet Night	176
Chapter 11	From Theatricality to Tragedy	185
Chapter 12	Of Badgers and *Barstvennost'*	197
Chapter 13	Conclusion: Whence (and Whither) Authenticity?	211

Appendix	217
Notes	221
Selected Bibliography	277
Index of Works by Mandelstam and Blok	291
Subject Index	297

ACKNOWLEDGMENTS

This book has been a long time in coming, and there are many who have helped me along the way. First among them is David Bethea, my dissertation advisor at the University of Wisconsin–Madison, who has been stalwart supporter, wise mentor, critic, and friend, and to whom I turned for advice at every stage of this project. Judith Kornblatt has also gone far and above the call of duty, both during my years in graduate school, as a reader on my dissertation committee, and beyond. I would like to thank Andrew Reynolds, who joined the faculty at the University of Wisconsin only during the semester of my defense but found time to give my thesis a very thorough and helpful reading. I offer thanks to professors Alexander Dolinin, Clare Cavanagh, Yuri Shcheglov, and Halina Filipowicz for helping to form me as a scholar, and with me this book.

I would like to thank Lada Panova, Alexander Zholkovsky, Oleg Lekmanov, and Sergei Vasilenko for their generous advice and support. I thank Nikolai Bogomolov, Lazar Fleishman, Georgii Levinton, Dina Magomedova, Alexander Mets, and Omry Ronen for their valued input and suggestions on various portions of this book. I thank Bettina Cothran for her consultations on German texts. A special debt of gratitude is reserved for Mikhail Gasparov, on whose invitation I came for my Fulbright year to work at the Institute for Advanced Study in the Humanities of the Russian State University of the Humanities (RGGU), and with whom, to my great sadness, I arrived too late to study. I thank Irene Masing-Delic, the "anonymous reader" mentioned in the endnotes, who scrupulously reviewed my book for The Ohio State University Press, as well as the second reviewer who remains anonymous. I thank Sandy Crooms and Maggie Diehl, my excellent editors. I thank Martin Boyne who worked on the index. Of course, all shortcomings are my own.

The lion's share of the research for this book was funded by a graduate fellowship of the Dolores Zohrab Liebmann Society and a faculty Fulbright research grant. I am deeply indebted for this support, without which this book, in its present form, simply would not exist.

I thank the archivists and librarians at the Mandelstam Archive in Princeton, Pushkinskii dom and the Russian National Library in Petersburg, and the Russian State (Lenin) Library and State Literary Museum in Moscow for their openness and assistance. I thank the Mandelstam Society for their support. Though it came too late to impact this book, I thank Sergei Vasilenko for an authorial tour of the wonderful literary museum dedicated to Mandelstam that he has single-handedly built in the Moscow suburb of Friazino.

Several portions of this book have appeared in other form in previous publications. These are "Bedside with the Symbolist Hero: Blok in Mandel'shtam's 'Pust' v dushnoi komnate'," *Slavic Review* 63.1 (Spring 2004): 26–42; "Blok's Living *Rampa:* On the Spatial and Conceptual Structuring of the Theater Poems," *Slavic and East European Journal* 49.3 (2005), 474–89; "Preodolev*aiushchii* simvolizm: Stikhi 1912 g. vo vtorom izdanii 'Kamnia' (1916)," in *"Sokhrani moiu rech'* . . ." 4/2 (Moscow: RGGU, 2008): 487–512; "'Kak trudno rany vrachevat' . . .': Mandelstam's 'Prescient' Evasions of Bloom," in *Russian Literature and the West: A Tribute to David M. Bethea* (Stanford: Stanford University Press, 2008), 27–43; "Sootnoshenie iskrennosti-podlinnosti (authenticity) v poetike Mandel'shtama i Bloka," in *Miry Osipa Mandel'shtama. IV Mandel'shtamovskie chteniia: materialy mezhdunarodnogo nauchnogo seminara* (Perm: Izd. PGPU, 2009): 271–85; and "'To Anaxagoras' in the Velvet Night: New Considerations on the Role of Blok in Mandelstam's 'V Peterburge my soidemsia snova'," *Russian Review* 69 (April 2010): 294–314. My thanks go out to the editors of these publications.

I thank Phil McKnight, Director of the School of Modern Languages at Georgia Tech, for his support, mentoring, and friendship. Though I cannot thank all friends by name, I would like to mention particularly Alyssa Gillespie and Martin Daughtry, who were always there to lend an ear, and often regarding this project.

My greatest debt is to my family, to my wonderful children Sophia and Lilia, and especially to my wife Madina, who has supported me in so many ways and who, twenty years ago almost to the day, first introduced me to the poetry of Osip Mandelstam.

NOTE ON TRANSLITERATION

Russian quotations and bibliographic citations, as well as the names of contemporary scholars publishing primarily in Russian, are transliterated according to the simplified U.S. Library of Congress system. Names of Russian cultural icons, as well as those of Russian scholars broadly publishing or well recognized in the West, are given in the text in commonly used forms (e.g., Mandelstam, Gogol, Bely, Lydia Ginzburg).

PART I

CHAPTER 1

INTRODUCTION

IMMEDIACY AND DISTANCE

Osip Mandelstam was a poet renowned for the breadth of his culture and the seeming ease with which he navigated this self-designated "blessed inheritance, / The wandering dreams of other bards."[1] But he was also, through no choice or fault of his own, a younger contemporary of Russian Symbolism. Transplanted as a small child from Warsaw to St. Petersburg, one of two centers of Russian Symbolism, he received his secondary education at the Tenishev School, where his teacher of Russian literature was Vladimir Gippius, a poet and aficionado of Symbolist verse with personal ties to the movement. In 1909, Mandelstam first participated in the poetry workshops of Viacheslav Ivanov, one of the Symbolist *maîtres*, and he continued to attend Ivanov's "Academy" often, if not constantly, as late as 1911.[2] Mandelstam's own first published poetry was written contemporaneously with the beginning of the decline of Russian Symbolism, and the period of his poetry through 1911 has long been recognized, with some qualifications, but fundamentally accurately, as his "Symbolist" period.

Such a uniquely non-elective connection to Russian Symbolism—among all the manifold artistic phenomena that would later sound in the poet's "thousand-barreled reed pipe, animated at once with the breath of all ages"— demands special consideration.[3] Mandelstam's overarching strategy for incorporating Western culture into his poetry was "licenced thievery," i.e., complete freedom to choose or pass over the gifts of the past.[4] Symbolism, however, could not be freely chosen because it had, in a sense, already been given.[5]

At the same time, the "confessional mode" and prophetic stance of the Symbolist poet were not open to Mandelstam as a Jew and a newcomer. The poetry of the "second generation" of "mythopoetic" Symbolists had been dominated by the quest for an all-transforming, mystical union with the Divine Feminine or Russia as Bride.[6] Mandelstam, the young and somewhat awkward Jew, was, as Gregory Freidin has pointed out, no suitable bridegroom for Russia.[7] At the same time, as the movement aged and journals became ever more inundated with the work of epigones, the late-coming Symbolist poet no longer had access to the charismatic aura necessary to maintain the crucial tension of the diaphanous word, simultaneously relating to this-worldly and otherworldly reality.[8] As Mandelstam himself was to put it a little over a decade later, "Russian Symbolism shouted so much and so loudly about the 'ineffable' [neskazannoe] that this 'ineffable' passed hands like paper money" (II, 423).[9]

So what was *given* could not be *taken*; nor could it be effectively employed. In a poetics that would be dominated by "distanced reiteration," Mandelstam first had to generate distance from Symbolism in order to create the aesthetic tension required for an effective and palpably new return.[10]

In his earliest essay, "François Villon" (Fransua Villon, 1910), Mandelstam describes how Paul Verlaine "smashed the *serres chaudes* [hothouses] of Symbolism," which contained the protective atmosphere allowing that movement's embodied allegories to flourish. Verlaine in this sense repeats the feat of Villon, who freed French poetry from the medieval "rhetorical school," the "Symbolism of the 15th century" (II, 301). It is inevitably implied that Mandelstam can be a Villon/Verlaine on Russian soil.[11] However, Mandelstam, the poet, "learns from everyone and speaks to everyone."[12] After the initial Acmeist polemics of 1912–14, Mandelstam is more concerned with incorporating the Symbolist legacy as an enriching element of his verse than in "smashing" it. As Omry Ronen notes, "In accordance with its stated aims, acmeism subordinated all cultural codes, as material, to the tasks of poetry as such, considered to be the most universal of models."[13]

At the same time, Symbolism was more to Mandelstam than simply a raw material, interchangeable with any other. One has a sense that the chaotic, Dionysian element foregrounded in Symbolism fed Mandelstam's own worldview, that it was necessary to his art. After the too staid poetic cosmos of his first book, *Stone* (Kamen', 1916), the poet, faced with the turmoil of the Great War, felt an inner call to reintroduce the Symbolist chaos to his poetry.[14]

However, by 1911–12, the Symbolist poetics had in many ways spent its charge. As noted above, lofty words had undergone "inflation" and hemorrhaged the value that was once perceived in their relation to a higher reality. A major question I will be asking on these pages is *how* does Mandelstam "reinvigorate" those elements of the spent Symbolist poetics that he actively needs? As I intend to show, his main tactic is to generate productive ambivalence of tone through a distinctive play with immediacy and distance. Mythopoetic Symbolism represents a historical stage in the development of Russian verse and of Mandelstam's own poetry, with its own characteristic set of motifs, *topoi*, and narrative structures. As these elements of Symbolist poetics enter Mandelstam's poetry, the fluid boundaries characteristic of the Symbolist worldview—between this world and the other world, biography and history, the world of art and the world beyond its frame—become mirrored within his poems. However, the Symbolists' metaphysical boundary-crossings and conflations of distinct spheres were in the eyes of the Acmeists "unchaste." When Mandelstam depicts such "encroachments," as when the spiritual other enters his poetry, particularly in terms borrowed from the Symbolists themselves, there is always an open question as to the author's attitude toward them and as to their ontological "reality," both within and beyond the world of his verse.

The angle of refraction at which Symbolist *topoi* enter Mandelstam's poetry—which is to say, the tone and the pragmatics of the text—is ultimately the key to meaning. However, tone is a notoriously difficult thing to pin down. Therefore, while Mandelstam's oeuvre contains varied and often antithetical approaches to almost every problem, it is fortunate that his poems often hold the structural cues through which we can begin to question this angle. For instance, within two poems written in 1920 lurk elements of the Symbolist worldview. However, in "Venetian life, morbid and barren" (Venitseiskoi zhizni, mrachnoi i besplodnoi), boundary-dissolving masquerade—a fine analogue for one major element of the Symbolist worldview—is paradoxically contained by manifold non-permeable frames of paintings and mirrors. Remove is inscribed in the poem's structure and imagery. In contrast, in "The spectral stage barely glimmers" (Chut' mertsaet prizrachnaia stsena), with its permeable theater curtain and semiotically unified space of theater and vestibule, the transcendent, otherworldly realm of art, which Mandelstam depicts in terms reminiscent of the Symbolists' vision of their Ideal, leaks out—from stage to hall to vestibule to street—by analogy contaminating, if only temporarily, the world beyond the text. Not aesthetic distance, but immediacy of experience is implied.

At the end of the Introduction, in "The Curtain and the Onionskin," I explore two of Mandelstam's own "metadescriptions" of this play with immediacy and distance, two metaphorical embodiments within his writings of the productively unstable boundaries at the poet's command.

"THE LIVING AND DANGEROUS BLOK . . ."

One major goal of this study is to delineate Mandelstam's diverse strategies for writing and rewriting his relationship with the Symbolist heritage, primarily on the cusp of and after his "conversion" to Acmeism in 1912, and to seek out the visible traces of Mandelstam's ephemeral play with the boundary between two poetics. As an upper chronological limit for the study, I take, roughly, the period after Blok's death in the early 1920s. This encompasses Mandelstam's most active overcoming and assimilation of the Symbolist legacy. During this time, Symbolist authors were still active on the literary scene in Russia, however they may have come to be overshadowed for posterity by the emergence of the new movements of Acmeism and Futurism. Moreover, the literary shadow of the poet's own genesis within the Symbolist womb had not yet dissipated to be replaced by the shadow of history, paradoxical as that may seem in 1910s Russia. Within this time frame, I focus particularly on those strategies that are not reducible to an Acmeist/Symbolist dichotomy but continue to actively engage the Symbolist tradition.

My second major goal is to present, for the first time, a coherent narrative of Mandelstam's relation to Alexander Blok, far and away the most compelling poetic voice among the Symbolists, and the only Symbolist poet who presented Mandelstam with any apparent creative anxieties.[15] Mandelstam was perceptive enough to note that the rival poetic movement, Futurism, "should have directed its attack [ostrie] not against the paper fortress of Symbolism, but against the living and truly dangerous Blok" (II, 348). Blok loomed large, even from the face of postcards,[16] and his high-Romantic stance, which maintained its tragic essence even when outwardly undermined by irony, was in many ways antithetical to that which Mandelstam would cultivate.

Blok's poetry projected a cult of the Romantic persona. Mandelstam, in the period we are considering, claimed that his memory was "inimical to all that is personal" (II, 99). In 1921, after Blok's death, Yury Tynianov would write:

> [A legend] surrounded [Blok's lyric hero] from the very beginning; it seemed even that it anticipated the very poetry of Blok, that his poetry only developed and supplemented the postulated image.
>
> In this image [people] personify the whole art of Blok; when they speak of his poetry, almost always behind the poetry they inadvertently substitute *a human face*—and it is this *face*, and not the *art*, that everyone loved.[17]

In contrast, the sensitive critic Boris Bukhshtab, writing in 1929, which is to say, without access to either the as-yet-unwritten poetry of the 1930s or Mandelstam's early unpublished Symbolist verse, could assert, "a portrait accompanying Mandelstam's poetry would be artistic tactlessness."[18]

In addition, Blok's rather uncharitable view of the young poet surely had some effect on their personal relations. Mandelstam intersected with Blok in the 1910s, as might be expected, at St. Petersburg/Petrograd cultural gatherings, but he also spent at least some time with Blok in close company, thanks to their common friend, Vladimir Piast. The attitude of Blok, who despised pretense in personal relations, could not have been entirely masked, and these feelings are documented in his diaries. A. L. Grishunin catalogs most of Blok's derogatory and often anti-Semitically tinged remarks about the younger poet.[19] He omits one particularly telling entry: "In the evening, the 'Academy'—Piast's talk, his old article about the 'canon,' Viacheslav Ivanov's verbosity [mnogoglagolanie] put me to sleep entirely. In the evening, we drink tea at 'Kvisisana'—Piast, I and Mandelstam (eternal [vechnyi])" (29 October 1911).[20] "Eternal" nicely situates Mandelstam among the other tiresome presences that oppress Blok, while simultaneously, through a nod at the Wandering Jew (*Vechnyi* Zhid), hinting at both the younger poet's ethnic identity and one widely noted element of his character (that of a wanderer).[21]

For Mandelstam, Blok's poetry stood at the boundary between tragedy and tragic pose, which was, for him, its inherent travesty. Russian Symbolism struck the mature Mandelstam with its theatricality, and Blok possessed the voice that either could transcend this theatricality or was its most dangerous siren. Moreover, Blok's often unpalatable and sometimes "maximalist" stances on social issues and history were foreign to the younger poet. And ultimately, Mandelstam was to find in Blok a repellent personal *barstvennost'* (lordliness), judging by the subterranean jabs in Mandelstam's prose. All these elements combined to make Blok a deeply problematic figure, demanding much inner struggle on the part of Mandelstam.

In the context of Western literary scholarship, such a state of affairs brings to mind Harold Bloom's theories on the anxiety of influence. In chapter 2, I set Bloom's theories in the context of turn-of-the-century Russia. I demonstrate the awareness of Russian poets, long before Bloom, of the mechanisms and anxieties of influence, analyze Mandelstam's ingenious and seemingly prescient dialectical evasions of Bloom, and finally, following David Bethea and Andrew Reynolds, consider the adjustments necessary to Bloom's theories for application to Russian poetry, with its unique emphasis on word as deed and the lived life of the poet. Thus placed in proper perspective, Bloom indeed turns out to be useful for examining certain aspects of Mandelstam's relation to Blok.

The heart of the narrative of Mandelstam's relation to Blok is to be found in the chapters beginning with chapter 6, "Bedside with the Symbolist Hero." Of course, it is not always possible or desirable to separate Mandelstam's coming to terms with Blok from his assimilation of Symbolism more broadly.

SYMBOLISM AND ACMEISM: AN OVERVIEW

Russian Symbolism emerged in the 1890s under the influence of European, and particularly French, Symbolism and as a reaction to the positivist aspects of Russian literary realism and the social directedness of Russian literary criticism.[22] These dogmas had exerted an almost suffocating dominance in the development of Russian poetry from the 1840s on, marginalizing aesthetic concerns and those poets who were given over to them. Early Russian Symbolist poets—for instance, Dmitry Merezhkovsky, Valery Briusov, Zinaida Gippius, Konstantin Bal'mont, Fedor Sologub—were importers of recent European cultural developments and proselytizers of a pan-aestheticizing worldview, megalomaniacal, amoral individualists and seekers of the new religious consciousness. Often, they combined these seemingly contradictory impulses in complex and paradoxical amalgams.

The second "generation" of Symbolists, whose literary debuts came shortly after the turn of the twentieth century, were deeply influenced by such contradictory forces as Friedrich Nietzsche, on the one hand, and Vladimir Solov'ev's Sophiological theology and messianism, on the other.[23] Drawing upon Orthodox religious philosophy, a variety of mystic traditions, German Romanticism, and the theories of the nineteenth-century Ukrainian linguist Alexander Potebnia, they developed a Neoplatonic understanding of the nature and function of the word and artwork, the value of which lay in its connection to the greater reality of the ideal realm.[24] Thus emerged an eschatologically oriented poetics, weighted toward tragedy (both personal and national), which viewed art from within a religious-teleological framework and valued Dionysian rapture and transcendence of the self.

These poets believed in the inseparability of life and art and the importance and the possibility of life-creation (*zhiznetvorchestvo*)—both on a personal-artistic plane and also on a cosmic scale, which demanded that the artist be a theurgist, that is, act upon the world through the connection of his or her art to a higher reality. Their ultimate goal, arising from these precepts, was, at least theoretically, collective creation—myth-creation (*mifotvorchestvo*).[25] At the same time, artists such as Blok and Andrei Bely could not help experiencing doubts as to the reality—or at least imminence—of all these things. Doubts generated more whirlpools of tragedy (heroic pessimism) and irony, disillusionment and rebirth, stoic renunciation of the poet-prophet's path, and "heretical," at times carnivalesque, aestheticism.

"Mythopoetic" (myth-creating) is a potentially problematic term, and I want to make clear that I have no intention of implying an *adequacy* of the Symbolists' works to the nature of myth in archaic cultures. The term is no more nebulous or inaccurate than the more broadly used "younger," however, and it certainly speaks more profoundly, even if demanding corrections and qualifications, to the nature of the younger Symbolists' art.[26] In any case, we can speak of a striving toward myth, which perhaps, strictly speaking, "devolved" into the generation of narratives, but narratives that were latent in these poets' works from the very beginning because of their investment in certain archetypal situations, which lent their works structure and commonality.[27] Hence, the mythopoetic Symbolists' works exhibit not only retrospective descriptions and rearrangements of their own earlier poetry into narrative form,[28] but also anticipations in their early poetry of later developments, precisely because these developments are structured into the initial problem.

Blok's poetic path, in particular, struck contemporaries with its apparent organicity, its semblance of natural generation from its roots. Modest Gofman, writing in 1908, highlights an important aspect of Blok's poetry:

[*Blok*] *starts* from wavering and doubt in the existence of the World Soul as a Prekrasnaia Dama.

> Но страшно мне: изменишь облик Ты,
> И дерзкое возбудишь подозренье,

Сменив в конце привычные черты.
О, как паду и горестно, и низко,
Не одолев смертельныя мечты.

And I fear: You will change Your appearance,
And will excite a brazen suspicion,
Having changed, in the end, Your familiar features.
O, how I will fall bitterly, and low,
Not having overcome the mortal reverie.

Gofman continues, "And the whole first romantic period of Alexander Blok's work (ending with "The Snow Mask" [Snezhnaia maska, 1907, S.G.]) can be characterized as an unfolding of these lines."[29]

In terms of narrative, we might even speak, within the movement, of an overarching Romantic plot encompassing vision, loss, and circuitous return, enriched by memory.[30] Blok imagined this inner history of the Symbolist poet's path as a Hegelian triad ("On the Current State of Russian Symbolism" [O sovremennom sostoianii russkogo simvolizma, 1910]), Bely in terms of the unearned, and hence sacrilegious, insight of the neophyte, leading to spiritual death and resurrection ("In Place of a Foreword" [Vmesto predisloviia] in *Urn* [Urna, 1909]).[31] The third major mythopoetic Symbolist poet and the movement's most prominent theorist was Viacheslav Ivanov. His perspective seems, from the outset, all-encompassing and immutable, as if from above and beyond the drama.[32] However, the same "myth" informs Ivanov's early works on a different scale. On the one hand, this is the historical scale of humanity's falling away from a direct experience of the deity, the need to seek paths back to closeness or communion in the present, and the expectation (*chaianie*) of universal community and a reborn archaic-religious tragedy as the ultimate goal of art in the future.[33] On the other hand, it is the ongoing and infinitely repeated drama of the individual soul's path *back* to the deity, as depicted, for instance, in the poem "Maenad" (Menada, 1905).[34]

The impulse to subjugate all other structures to the mythopoetic narrative is eloquently attested in poet Sergei Solov'ev's review of *All Melodies* (Vse napevy, 1909), a late volume by Briusov, as noted above, one of the major Symbolist poets of the older generation:[35]

The imperial quiet of fall has descended on the poetry of Briusov:

And ever more calmly, ever more submissively
I walk toward some Bethlehem.

With these words he ends his book. The poet heads for Bethlehem, carrying the gold of his poetry as a gift to the unknown god. It is pure and imperishable: the poet has turned to gold the tears of Orpheus, pining for his lost Euridice.[36]

Briusov saw *All Melodies* as the end of an epoch in his poetry. His poem "Star" (Zvezda, 1906) is indeed written in the mythopoetic mode, summing up certain key themes of his poetry and submitting them all to an overarching narrative of mystical revelation and humble pilgrimage and expectation. However, "Star" is not the end of the book; it is one of four poems that, in their symmetry, make up the final section of *All Melodies*—"Conclusion." "Star" is not even the last of these, each of which is a summation of Briusov's poetry from a different perspective, stressing the many faces of his art. Solov'ev, however, has a need to see the mythopoetic narrative as the *telos* of Briusov's poetry as a whole.

It is surely not coincidental that Mikhail Gasparov, supremely aware of Mandelstam's writings and skeptical of the religious content of the Symbolists' art, challenges the mythic status precisely of Don Juan and Carmen, those two archetypal plot kernels that Mandelstam, on the basis of Blok's poetry, asserts have recently attained "civic equality" with myth.[37] Mandelstam himself, as we see, chooses these words carefully, even as he accords Blok this grandest achievement among his contemporaries. Still, Mandelstam is receptive not only to Blok's myth-making, but also to Ivanov's claims to mythological thinking (in the archaic sense) and also applies the concept of contemporary myth-making in his own work.[38] At the same time, Mandelstam is careful not to repeat the errors of Ivanov, who, despite the authenticity of his archaism—"never for a minute does he forget himself, speaking in his barbaric native tongue"—"unbelievably overloaded his poetry with Byzantine-Hellenic images and myths, significantly devaluing it" (II, 343, 341).

A sense of the power of myth-creation, at least within the artistic realm, is, in fact, one of the more profound aspects of the younger Symbolists' influence upon Mandelstam. In his programmatic essay "Pushkin and Skriabin" (Pushkin i Skriabin, 1916–17?), Mandelstam writes about the "myth of forgotten Christianity." This myth, the generative power of which is precisely in its occlusion of truth—Christianity has been forgotten, allowing us to search for it anew—is the gift, in large part, of the Symbolists themselves. Their anguished searchings betray their failure to recognize the redemption. Mandelstam's *Tristia* demonstrates how this myth can become a fertile conceptual model, spreading through and organizing, to varying degrees, individual poems.[39]

The diachronic Symbolist macroplot takes its inner dynamism at any given point from the striving of the poet—treated with seriousness or ironically undermined—to break down the walls of rational, three-dimensional, historical existence, traversing, through theurgy and life-creation, the boundaries between "this world" and the "other world," art and life. As Briusov notes, "Art is only there, where there is audacious striving [derznovenie] to get beyond the limit, where there is a thrust beyond the boundaries of the knowable, in the thirst to draw even a drop of the 'alien, otherworldly element' [stikhii chuzhdoi, zapredel'noi]."[40] Acmeism originated in the wake of the Symbolists' own "crisis" and debates on the nature of art, and not least from a desire to re-establish these boundaries, which the poets and their epigones had often too cheerfully vanquished. "The first condition of successful building," wrote Mandelstam, "is sincere piety toward the three dimensions of space—to look at the world not as a burden and an unfortunate accident, but as a God-given palace" (II, 322).

Still, it was clear even from the beginning—at least to the Acmeists themselves—that this respect for boundaries should not exclude religious feeling. Nikolai Gumilev: "To always remember the ineffable, but not insult one's thought about it with more or less likely conjectures—this is the principle of Acmeism."[41] Mandelstam: "The Middle Ages are dear to us because they possessed to a high degree a sense of boundaries and partitions. They never mixed different planes and related to the otherworldly with enormous restraint. A noble amalgam of rationality and mysticism and a perception of the world as a living equilibrium binds us to this epoch [. . .]" (II, 325).

The sense of boundaries and equilibrium in early Acmeism led, particularly in the poetry of Mandelstam, to the magnificent graphic and architectural poetry that to this day underlies some studies of Acmeist poetics.[42] But the rigor of this distance between poet and world, subject and object, was precisely what was necessary in order to lay the foundation for more subtle play with, and sometimes assaults on, boundaries.[43] As Sergei Averintsev wrote, "Mandelstam's path to the infinite [. . .] is through the taking serious of the finite as finite, through the firm laying of a sort of ontological boundary."[44]

As has been noted many times, Acmeism defies easy or precise characterization in terms of chronology, adherents, or poetics.[45] In a compelling synthesis, Oleg Lekmanov, in *Kniga ob akmeizme* (1998), defines the movement as a series of concentric circles. On the outside, there was the loosely allied Poets' Guild, organized by Gumilev and Sergei Gorodetsky in October 1911, which included a fairly broad variety of mostly younger poets. Their meetings consisted of reading by each participant and grounded, detailed discussion and criticism. Many of these poets published in the substantially Acmeist journal *The Hyperborean* (*Giperborei*), edited by the substantially Symbolist Mikhail Lozinsky.[46] The middle circle consisted of those six poets who named themselves Acmeists, and whose collective publications, together with Gumilev and Gorodetsky's manifestoes, presented the face of the new movement in early 1913.[47] These were Vladimir Narbut, Mikhail Zenkevich, Gorodetsky, Gumilev, Anna Akhmatova, and Mandelstam. They still represented very broadly differing poetics, ranging from the more staid and classical to the more earthy and grotesque. (As Lekmanov and others have noted, Mandelstam himself leaned at times to the "left" wing, and even courted Futurism.) The innermost circle was defined by the "semantic poetics" and ongoing subtextual dialogue of those three poets, still varying broadly in temperament, the sum of whose works have largely defined our picture of the movement *ex post facto*: Gumilev, Akhmatova, and Mandelstam.

Victor Zhirmunsky, in his classic first analysis of the new movement, summarized Gorodetsky and Gumilev's program: "the exiling from art of mysticism as a mandatory topic and the fundamental goal of all poetic creation," "instead of a complex, chaotic, isolated individual—the variety of the outside world, instead of emotional, musical lyricism—precision and graphic visuality in the combination of words."[48] Generalizing, we can speak of a series of contrasts of emphasis, differentiating Symbolism and Acmeism in the Acmeists' writings: music vs. architecture, the Dionysian vs. the Apollonian (chaos vs. cosmos), religious initiates vs. a guild of medieval craftsmen (but also Masonic builders), impressionism vs. clarity/precision, the otherworldly vs. the culturally distant and the extrapersonal (the interlocutor, the precursor) as the source of art's seeking outside of itself.

Mandelstam noted, however, that "not the ideas, but the tastes of the Acmeists" dealt a mortal blow to Symbolism. "The ideas turned out to be adopted in part from the Symbolists, and Viacheslav Ivanov himself aided much in the construction of Acmeist theory" (II, 257).[49] The Acmeists' new tastes were connected, first and foremost, to a sense of balance—balance in worldview, balance in approach to the individual (*lichnost'*), and balance in the development of and attention to all aspects of poetic language, in a way that does not favor any one factor or distinguish between form and content.[50]

Still, Acmeism also arose as a reaction against the hypertrophic musicality and vagueness of Symbolism. "For the Acmeists, the conscious sense of the word, Logos, is just as beautiful a form as music for the Symbolists," wrote Mandelstam (II, 321). Later, Mandelstam would call the Acmeists "smysloviki" (senseworkers), and one of the most influential studies of the poetics of Acmeism finds its essence precisely in its "semantic poetics."[51] This semantic poetics was not neutral but tended toward the compounding of "ambivalent antitheses" and the multiplication of semantic vectors.[52] Mandelstam had a deep affinity for the writings of Pavel Florensky, perhaps in part because, for Florensky too, "both thesis and antithesis, in their contradictory simultaneity, are essential to 'truth.'"[53]

This perception of truth as the simultaneous presence of contradictory perspectives and a feeling for the exponentially expansive associative potential of language underlie the dialogism of Acmeism—its renowned subtextual poetics.[54] In the Acmeists' poetry, the voices of others are not subsumed in the monolithic voice of the poet (as in Blok's allusions to other poets, for instance) but remain a simultaneously composite and organic whole, a fugue of perceptibly competing voices and impulses, which is nonetheless transcended in the organic voice of the poet.[55]

Competing and coexisting components of truth are also visible in the interrelation of humor and seriousness in Acmeism and in the nature of Acmeist irony. For Blok, irony was a destructive force, a seductive, derisive nihilism, which he himself applied to consummate artistic effect in the poetry and drama of his "antithesis."[56] The other Symbolists' irony was more diverse and more constructive.[57] However, it was hardly comparable in tone to the Acmeists' "luminous [svetlaia] irony, not undermining the roots of our belief."[58]

Similarly, Acmeism was characterized by the sting of inside jokes, and in its early period, by a certain cabaret atmosphere, which can inform *in absentia* even the most serious of the Acmeists' works.[59] One did not hamper the other, and even existentially sustained it. In Mandelstam, the beautiful and serious—even lofty—"slow whirlpool" [medlennyi vodovorot] of "Sisters—heaviness and tenderness" (Sestry—tiazhest' i nezhnost', 1920) can reappear, transformed into the "funnel of a urinal" [voron(ka) pissuara] in a 1925 translation from Jules Romains's *Les Copains* (1913), with no perceived threat to the integrity of the original context.[60] In Blok's poetry, such transformations, for instance, that of the transcendent Fair Lady into a prostitute or cardboard doll, are perceived as an attack on the ontological reality of the original revelation or, at the least, as a ridiculing of the poet's earlier naïveté.[61]

The expression "ambivalent antithesis" emphasizes the irreconcilable and unreconciled in Acmeism: "I'm a double dealer, with a dual soul, / I am friend of night, I'm day's champion" [Dvurushnik ia, s dvoinoi dushoi, / Ia nochi drug, ia dnia zastrel'shchik].[62] However, Acmeist poetics can, as Omry Ronen demonstrates, also often be perceived as dialectical synthesis or sublation.[63] The second wave of influence of Symbolism in Mandelstam's poetry, first visible in "Ode to Beethoven" (Oda Betkhovenu, 1914) and palpable throughout the poetry of the *Tristia* period (1916–early 1921), is just such a sublation of Apollonian and Dionysian, masculine and feminine impulses in a tonally ambivalent and entirely new synthesis worthy of the "hermaphroditic" lyric poet ("François Villon").

Another powerful example of Acmeist sublation is Mandelstam's understanding of the nature of the word.[64] As we see in "On the Nature of the Word" (O prirode slova, 1922), the word, for Mandelstam, is freed of its connection to a Platonic idea, of its realism, in that counterintuitive medieval-philosophical sense that underlies Ivanov's usage in the term "realistic Symbolism." Hence, he is in his rights to speak of Russian nominalism (referring to the competing strain of thought, which saw meaning as deriving from linguistic convention). However, it is specifically the word's "inner freedom"—its freedom from the bonds of reference and from utilitarianism, even (or especially) the utilitarianism of "mystic intuition"—which makes it akin to Christ, the Word, makes it "active flesh, resolving itself in an event" [plot' deiatel'naia, razreshaiushchaiasia v sobytie] (II, 246). Mandelstam thus comes to a remarkably deep and original synthesis between linguistic rationalism and a "mystic presumption" about the nature of the word.[65]

THE CURTAIN AND THE ONIONSKIN

In Mandelstam's works we encounter two images that most emphatically demonstrate, even embody, the poet's play with the productively unstable boundaries between discrete spheres of existence: in one case, temporal planes, and in the other, poetry and life. As such, the curtain and the onionskin are fine models for the shifting and ambiguous state of remove at which the Symbolist heritage finds a place in Mandelstam's poetry.

In the final paragraph of "In a Fur Coat above His Station" (V ne po chinu barstvennoi shube), the last essay of Mandelstam's autobiographical *The Noise of Time* (Shum Vremeni, 1923-24), Mandelstam writes, "With trepidation do I lift [slightly, tentatively, S.G.] the film of onionskin covering the winter hat of the writer" [S trepetom pripodnimaiu plenku voshchennoi bumagi nad zimnei shapkoi pisatelia] (II, 108). The raising of the corner of the fine sheet of translucent paper that shielded portraits and engravings in the era's books visually evokes the poet's play with immediacy and distance. Moreover, the image that had been shielded by the layer of onionskin itself represents both immediacy—the writer's unmediated contact with the frigid night of Russian reality, "where terrible statehood is like a stove, piping with ice" [gde strashnaia gosudarstvennost', kak pech', pyshushchaia l'dom] (II, 108)—and remove—the aristocratic "fur" that the writer of the nineteenth century "grew" in order to protect himself from the cold: "Night thickened his coat. Winter clothed him" (ibid.).

The essay's overarching theme is the poet's transition from vicarious witness of Symbolism as a child, experiencing contact with literature through the mediation of books and Symbolist "house servant" Vladimir Gippius, to Russian Poet in the present. This shift, echoed metaphorically in the poet's initial stepping out into the cold together with Gippius, engenders ambivalence on several levels. Partly, this ambivalence is connected to issues of class, nineteenth-century Russian literature's perceived *barstvennost'* (aristocracy, lordliness), which will be at the center of our attention in terms of Mandelstam's relation to Blok in chapter 12. But also, contact with reality is fraught with real dangers. The writer in the main stream of the Russian tradition is a writer in the world.[66] As Bethea once put it, "the lived life of the poet" becomes "a record of the authenticity of the text."[67] And Mandelstam himself had seen in the death of the artist a final, transformative creative act (II, 313).

The onionskin thus represents the translucent, tissue-fine boundary between the writer as writer and the writer as social actor, between word as art and word as deed—in essence, between literature and life.[68] Not surprisingly, this final image of *The Noise of Time* possesses a rich dualism. On the one hand, the present-tense "pripodnimaiu" [I lift] can convey past action, the perspective of the child, who, raising the corner of the onionskin together with Gippius, gets his first intimations of the exhilarating and frightening presence of the Russian poetic tradition. Mandelstam the child lifts the onionskin from the book-bound portrait of the writer cautiously, and he very well may let it fall in fright. On the other hand, the mature poet, in the 1920s, is forced to raise the onionskin in earnest, for the deaths of Blok, Gumilev, and Velimir Khlebnikov serve as an undeniable affirmation of the potent and, in fact, deadly relationship between literature and life. Still, there is an aesthetic pleasure to be derived from this play with perspective, a pleasure that one clearly senses in this passage as well.

Another locus of play with immediacy and distance, this time taken from Mandelstam's poetry, is the "theater" curtain of "I will not see the celebrated *Phèdre*" (Ia ne uvizhu znamenitoi "Fedry," 1915), the poem that closes the canonical 1916 edition of Mandelstam's first book, *Stone*:

Я не увижу знаменитой «Федры»
В старинном многоярусном театре,
С прокопченной высокой галереи,

При свете оплывающих свечей.
И, равнодушен к суете актеров,
Сбирающих рукоплесканий жатву,
Я не услышу, обращенный к рампе,
Двойною рифмой оперенный стих:

— Как эти покрывала мне постылы...

Театр Расина! Мощная завеса
Нас отделяет от другого мира;
Глубокими морщинами волнуя,
Меж ним и нами занавес лежит:
Спадают с плеч классические шали,
Расплавленный страданьем крепнет голос,
И достигает скорбного закала
Негодованьем раскаленный слог...

Я опоздал на празднество Расина!

Вновь шелестят истлевшие афиши,
И слабо пахнет апельсинной коркой,
И словно из столетней летаргии
Очнувшийся сосед мне говорит:
— Измученный безумством Мельпомены,
Я в этой жизни жажду только мира;
Уйдем, покуда зрители-шакалы
На растерзанье Музы не пришли!

Когда бы грек увидел наши игры...

I will not see the celebrated *Phèdre*
In a venerable, many-tiered theater,
From the high, soot-smoked gallery,
By the light of guttering candles.
And, indifferent to the bustle of the actors,
Gathering a harvest of ovations,
I will not hear addressed to the footlights,
A verse plumed with double rhyme:

How these veils weary me . . .

> Theater of Racine! A mighty curtain
> Divides us from another world.
> Agitating with deep furrows,
> Twixt them and us a curtain lies:
> Classical shawls drop from shoulders,
> A voice molten with anguish strengthens,
> And the diction, inflamed by indignation,
> Strikes a mournful temper . . .
>
> I am late to Racine's festivities!
>
> The crumbled programs rustle once again,[69]
> And the scent of orange rind faintly wafts,
> And my neighbor, as if awakened
> From a hundred-year lethargy, says to me:
> —Tortured by the ravings of Melpomene,
> In this life I thirst for only peace.
> Let us hence, while the jackals of the audience
> Have not yet come to tear the Muse asunder.
>
> If only could a Greek observe our games . . .

Outwardly, the poem affirms the inaccessibility of a cultural heritage that will forever remain in the past.[70] The shift from the alexandrine couplets of Racine's *Phèdre* to this poem's blank verse seems to subtly reinforce the concept of a barrier that makes a perfect translation from one cultural idiom to another impossible. However, even in the first octave, as Gregory Freidin was first to note, Mandelstam quite vividly brings to life that very same theater of Racine, which his hero "will not see."[71] What is more, in the first monostich, Phèdre appears almost to empathize with the hero, to similarly suffer from the mutual impenetrability of their worlds.

"How these veils weary me!" she laments. And though, in the world of Racine's tragedy, her words refer to the oppressive splendor that surrounds her in her shame,[72] in Mandelstam's poem the mention of these coverings (*pokryvala*) immediately precedes the theme of the "mighty curtain," which, "agitating with deep furrows," separates Racine's theater from the present. Phèdre's words, we are told, are directed at the footlights, that sublime boundary that forms the very essence of theater and is the natural locus of the invisible, but weighty, curtain. "Plumed," like an arrow, or a swallow, Phèdre's line, which is to say Racine's poetry, tests the powerful dividing curtain from the opposite side.[73]

The description of the curtain is followed in the second octave by a pronounced crescendo—not quite conveyed in the translation, where the syntax has forced me to reverse the last two lines. Here, the poet mentally enters and seems on the verge of embodying in the present the space of Racine's theater. The structure of the poem primes us to expect that the "voice molten with anguish" will belong to Phèdre. However, Racine's heroine unexpectedly, but judiciously, fails to materialize in the second monostich, supplanted by the voice of the poet: "I am late to Racine's festivities!" I say judiciously because it was, after all, the dividing curtain that "agitated," provoking this "diction, inflamed with indignation."[74]

Though the lyric persona once more laments having missed the performance, the third octave even more openly asserts the re-emergence—even resurrection—of Racine's era in the present: "Vnov' shelestiat *istlevshie afishi*" [The *crumbled* (decayed) programs rustle once again]. In the final monostich, the poet again seems resolved to the firm delineation of cultural strata—twentieth-century Russia, seventeenth-century France, and the ancient Greece of Euripides. Mandelstam's attempts to breach the boundary between epochs are accorded the status of play, "games."

However, in the next poem, which opens the poet's second collection, *Tristia*, all curtains are raised.[75] Racine's Phèdre now declaims her role in proper alexandrine couplets. She is answered by a voice that speaks as part of an archaic tragic chorus and seeks to appease the god-like black sun, which has risen as a result of her guilt.[76] Still, a consciousness of the fact that there was and is a curtain, and that it has been raised, remains. This consciousness serves as a prerequisite, allowing, in the end, for the more "Symbolist" poetics of *Tristia* as a whole, in which chronological and spatial boundaries are often wiped away, taboos subverted.[77]

The poet's words in "Pushkin and Skriabin" about how the pre-existing salvation of the world by Christ frees the Christian artist to "wander the footpaths of mystery" *in play* (II, 315) are a similar logical "loophole." They allow the poet not to renounce the footpaths of mystery—that is, the central theme of mythopoetic Symbolism—while at the same time not implicating himself in the Symbolists' hubris. (The Symbolists of course believed that they were wandering or straying from these paths in earnest.)

Applied to Symbolism, play with the curtain or the onionskin, the translucent and dynamic barrier that separates the two poetics, amounts to play with the pragmatics of the text, the relation of the text to its audience and to extratextual reality. In a variety of ways, not the last of which is a special sort of ambiguous and almost weightless irony, Mandelstam establishes one degree of separation between the "author" and renewed and reactivated motifs, ideas, and poetic devices borrowed from Symbolism. However, this paper-thin and always ambiguous separation often allows not so much for the dismissal or ridicule of Symbolist claims—for instance, to the transcendent power of word and name—as for their underhanded affirmation, with a renewed force, which proceeds from an infusion of conceptual complexity and healthy, self-deprecating doubt.

Mandelstam came to understand this power of ambiguous denial very early. So he concluded his earliest essay, on that "thieving angel" François Villon, and with it, later, his collection of essays, *On Poetry* (O poezii, 1928):[78]

> "I know well that I am not the son of an angel, crowned with the diadem of a star or another planet," said about himself a poor Parisian schoolboy, capable of much for the sake of a good dinner.
>
> *Such* denials are equivalent to a positive conviction. (II, 309)[79]

CHAPTER 2

PRESCIENT EVASIONS OF BLOOM

What happens when, rather than testing the applicability of Harold Bloom's theories of poetic influence to Mandelstam's poetry, one instead uses the works of Mandelstam and other turn-of-the-twentieth-century Russian poets to test Bloom himself, to put to question the inevitability of what Bloom represents as universal mechanisms of authorship and literary evolution?[1] By looking at these poets, and especially Mandelstam, we may observe that the issues Bloom raises are in fact real, and, indeed, of importance to Russian poets, but, at the same time, that they are not hidden from view, as Bloom would have it, expressed only at the level of a Freudian repression and compensation. Moreover, we will see that Mandelstam demonstrates a range of compelling strategies not only to circumvent these anxieties, but to obviate them on a plane that represents a dialectical revision of Bloom's theories.

Bloom, in 1973, when he was publishing *The Anxiety of Influence*, probably did not know Mandelstam or his works.[2] Moreover, one senses that he would be little concerned with the results of the present research—for he is far more invested in the creative force of his own theoretical narrative. However, it is nonetheless instructive to juxtapose these two very distant authors: Bloom, the poetically minded theorist of late-twentieth-century America, and Mandelstam, the early-twentieth-century Russian poet.[3]

Mandelstam seemed to Anna Akhmatova a poet uniquely without influences. "Mandelstam has no teacher," she wrote, "I don't know a similar instance in world poetry."[4] At the same time, Nadezhda Mandelstam noted the poet's openness to the work of others: "I learn from everyone—even from Benedikt Livshits," he is reported to have said.[5] Mandelstam indeed presents at least the appearance of having completely escaped poetic anxiety. Still, he clearly did experience some degree of anxiety before Alexander Blok, and his "superhuman chastity" in regard to Alexander Pushkin (noted by Akhmatova) also points to latent anxieties.[6] The need to sidestep anxiety goes to the heart of what is Bloomian, and it is the poet's struggle precisely with the most powerful precursor or precursors that typically draws Bloom's interest. And yet Mandelstam appears to me to be a "strong latecomer" in a sense both unforeseen by Bloom and anticipating him—the poet presciently aware of the mechanisms and psychology of influence. His success in side-stepping verbal anxiety is attributable particularly to his ingenious positioning of his poetry vis-à-vis the concepts of influence, priority, and originality.

Bloom's Anxiety of Influence theory centers on the concept that poetic influence, rather than expressing acceptance of the poetic father figure through direct borrowing, is a process of repulsion from the past through acts of creative "misprision" (misreading). The poetic present is progressively narrowed as ever-diminished poets search for their own space in a universe divested of priority. Strong poets are those who are able to take up the struggle with the father figure and emerge as individual poetic voices. Bloom's post-Freudian approach to the psychology of poetic creation is centered around the image of the "Family Romance," with its latent tension between son and father (precursor); Bloom represents this Oedipal struggle as the core narrative of *any* strong poet's genesis as poet.[7]

Mandelstam's immediate literary context as a beginning poet and the source, positive or negative, of much of his conceptual framework as a thinker about poetry is to be found in Russian Symbolism and, in particular, in Viacheslav Ivanov.[8] Michael Wachtel, in his study of the influence of Goethe and Novalis on Ivanov, argues that the Russian Symbolists defy the Bloomian model altogether, as a result of their lifelong emphasis on poetry as reception. A single, synthetic tradition, and cults of memory and simultaneity, lead to a poetics that celebrates, rather than resists, the poetic past. "Rarely," he writes, "has a creative movement so eagerly and energetically looked backwards."⁹ Still, the Russian Symbolists, while affirming the continuity of the tradition, provided vivid examples of strong misprision. Consider, for instance, Bely's reading of the Nietzsche of *Thus Spoke Zarathustra* as a Christ figure.¹⁰ Continuity meant that every great artist was a Symbolist and ought to be read as such.

The Symbolists, it should be noted, displayed a demonstrable awareness of issues of originality, priority, and influence. Briusov, for instance, wrote, in 1920:

> Often places not at all similar in terms of outward content more deeply reveal the influence of another writer than those that are almost identical. In the very insistency with which one or another method is repudiated, one can sometimes more accurately trace influence than in imitations.¹¹

It would be hard to get closer, in the rationalist language of Briusov, to the underlying principle of Bloom's Anxiety of Influence, stripped of its Freudian and Romantic-metaphorical vestments. Even among the younger Symbolists, with their religious/mystical bent and striving for collective (*sobornoe*) creativity, there reigned a *de facto* code of originality. Consider the following letter, written by Blok to Sergei Solov'ev in December 1903, shortly after the publication of Briusov's *Urbi et orbi*:

> Your last name is pasted onto *your* poems... In my opinion, in ["Korolevna"] there is no imitation of Bely. I hurry to assure you that you never seemed to me a "humble worker" ... Is it possible to write: "Mal'chik na gorku uzh vvez sanki s obmerzloi verevkoi?" It's already written in "U<rbi> et O<rbi>!" I will not suffer such a usurpation from Briusov, and I will take revenge on you with a dagger—in my time. Incidentally, one should think that soon I myself will write poems which will all turn out to be duplicates of Briusov.¹²

First, Blok seems to answer concerns, apparently voiced earlier by Solov'ev himself, that the latter poet may be too dependent on Bely, even that all of his last poems are imitative (that his name is pasted onto *others'* poems). Then, he playfully criticizes Solov'ev for repeating Briusov, himself incorporating a paraphrase from Briusov's epistle to Bely in *Urbi et Orbi*, and, finally, unerringly foretells his own coming dependence on Briusov's poetry. We can see, then, that for Solov'ev and Blok, originality (hence priority) is a concern and a valid criterion for evaluating poetry, if, for Blok at least, it is apparently not a matter of great anxiety.

Blok the Symbolist appears largely free of poetic anxiety—and, in fact, the ease with which he borrowed led to certain disingenuous comments by Mandelstam:

> Beginning from a direct, almost pupil-like dependence upon Vladimir Solov'ev and [the late Romantic poet Afanasy] Fet, Blok did not completely break with a single one of the obligations he had taken upon himself, did not cast off a single piety, did not trample a single canon. He only complicated his poetic credo with more and more pieties [. . .]. (*SS*, II, 273–74)

Blok's poetry, perhaps because of his great "receptiveness," provides some excellent examples of Bloom's *apophrades*, an opening of one's poetry to the spirits of the dead, with the "uncanny effect [. . .] that the new poem's achievement makes it seem to us, not as though the precursor were writing it, but as though the later poet himself had written the precursor's characteristic work." Bloom later writes, "When I read [Stevens's] *Le Monocle de Mon Oncle* now, in isolation from other poems by Stevens, I am compelled to hear Ashbery's voice, for this mode has been captured by him, inescapably and perhaps forever."[13] Similarly, in some of Fet's poetry of the late 1880s, when one reads it now, one cannot help hearing to an uncanny extent strains of Blok. What was an incidental strand in the former has become central to the latter.[14]

In Mandelstam's poetry, we can sense, if not anxiety, then an awareness of poetic latecoming as a problem that demanded overcoming. His most eloquent statement on poetic belatedness is "The bread is poisoned and the air drunk up" (1913):

> Отравлен хлеб и воздух выпит.
> Как трудно раны врачевать!
> Иосиф, проданный в Египет,
> Не мог сильнее тосковать!
>
> Под звездным небом бедуины,
> Закрыв глаза и на коне,
> Слагают вольные былины
> О смутно пережитом дне.
>
> Немного нужно для наитий:

Кто потерял в песке колчан;
Кто выменял коня — событий
Рассеивается туман;

И, если подлинно поется
И полной грудью, наконец,
Все исчезает — остается
Пространство, звезды и певец!

The bread is poisoned and the air drunk up.
How difficult to heal the wounds!
Joseph, sold into Egypt,
Could not more mightily languish.

Beneath a starry sky the Bedouins,
Eyes closed and on horseback,
Compose unconstrained lays
Of a vaguely experienced day.

Little is needed for inspiration:
Who lost a quiver in the sands;
Who bartered for a horse—the fog
Of events dissipates.

And if it is sung authentically
And with a full chest, at last,
All vanishes—remain
Space, stars and singer.

It is well known that air is a frequent symbol of poetic freedom and poetic creation in Mandelstam's poetry, recurring regularly almost from his first poems to his last.[15] In "The bread is poisoned," the air has been drunk, used up. Moreover, to take our cue from the poet's namesake, Joseph, the biblical dream reader, it has been used up by his jealous and ungifted brothers.[16] This image of poetic deprivation is contrasted to the final three stanzas' depiction of a poetic golden age, displaced from the "poet" not chronologically, but culturally, in the improvisatory and oral creation of the Bedouins, who are *uninhibited* latecomers.[17] These free artists exist in a space of unstifled creation (their "*free* lays" contrast with the image of Joseph, sold into slavery), a space where one can breathe and sing "with the whole chest." It is finally this uninhibited, but, for the "poet," unattainable, freedom that can produce a transcendence of all spatial boundaries and a face-to-face meeting with the eternal stars.

It is more than tempting to read this account as an expression of anxiety of influence with regard specifically to the Russian Symbolists. The younger generation, with the exception of Ivanov, are, by age, more accurately described as elder siblings than poetic fathers. Their proximity, in both time and place—down to a frequenting of the same cultural gatherings and publication in the same journals—makes them prime candidates to steal the "poet's" air. Their jealous stinginess in recognizing Mandelstam's talents equates them with Joseph's brothers.

Moreover, in the poem's finale, Mandelstam's lyric "I" lays claim, through the surrogate Bedouins, and over the heads of the also latecoming Symbolists, to the stars. Stars, while a natural association for the once Sabaean Bedouins, were a central symbol particularly for the younger generation of Symbolists, led by Ivanov, whose first books of poetry and theory were entitled *Pilot Stars* (Kormchie zvezdy, 1903) and *By the Stars* (Po zvezdam, 1909), respectively.[18] It is a trick of Mandelstam's virtuosity that the overall impression derived from the poem is one of absolute freedom, rather than the latecomer's suffocation. This impression is not only a result of the poem's composition—the preponderance of strophes dealing with the Bedouins. Mandelstam, who, like the horsemen of the second stanza, was noted for reading his poetry with his eyes closed, subtly interpolates—in fact, almost sublimates—himself into the picture of poetic uninhibitedness.[19]

In addition, the concept that "little is needed for inspiration" challenges the Symbolists' valorization of universal themes.[20] Priority, for Mandelstam, does not depend either on chronology or on scale, as it clearly does for Bloom. Creative space ("Prostranstvo, zvezdy") can emerge suddenly from the infinitesimal (a pathway more fully explored in Mandelstam's poetry of the 1930s).[21] Finally, it gives some satisfaction to note that, in Mandelstam's "Bloomian" poem *avant la lettre*, the family feud of literary succession is expressed without resort to the Freudian crudities of the "Family Romance," with its accidental Oedipalism.[22]

Mandelstam has an array of strategies for actively defusing the threat of anxiety of influence. In the larger scope of the poet's creative life, "The bread is poisoned" is an early poem, written during what he would later call the "Sturm und Drang" [buria i natisk] of Acmeism. Just a year later, Mandelstam would stake out one of his quintessential positions regarding the shape of poetic tradition in "I have not heard the tales of Ossian" (Ia ne slykhal rasskazov Ossiana, 1914).

"Poetry is property," avers Bloom.²³ Mandelstam's "answer":

Я получил блаженное наследство —
Чужих певцов блуждающие сны;
Свое родство и скучное соседство
Мы презирать заведомо вольны.

И не одно сокровище, быть может,
Минуя внуков, к правнукам уйдет;
И снова скальд чужую песню сложит
И, как свою, ее произнесет.

I received a blessed inheritance—
The wandering dreams of other bards;
We are free of course to scorn
Our kin and boring neighbors.

And more than one treasure, maybe,
Will, passing the grandchildren, to the great-grandchildren go;
And once again the skald will compose another's song
And pronounce it like his own.

As Clare Cavanagh encapsulated the ethos of this poem, "culture and poetic tradition become a kind of licensed thievery. They leave the poet free to ransack history for its treasures, to pick and choose among pasts."²⁴

Mandelstam thus challenges the concept of poetic propriety.²⁵ The better part of a decade later, he openly challenges the concept of poetic priority as well:

> Often one comes to hear: that's good, but it is yesterday. But I say: yesterday has yet to be born: it still hasn't happened for real. I want Ovid, Pushkin, Catullus again, and I am not satisfied with the historical Ovid, Pushkin, Catullus. [. . .]
>
> So, not a single poet has yet been. We are free from the burden of memories. But how many rare premonitions: Pushkin, Ovid, Homer. [. . .] (II, 224–25)

Here chronology is set on its head.²⁶ Not only does Mandelstam emerge as precursor of the "real" Ovid, Catullus, and Pushkin, but he also can be the imaginative will that generates these "ancestors" to his own specification ("I want"). It is too little, for Mandelstam, like Bloom's strong poet, to create himself, to beget himself incestuously on the precursor's Muse. Mandelstam will also re-beget the precursor's poetry, as it ought to be.

This rewriting might be seen to exemplify the Bloomian/Nietzschean "will to power,"[27] were it not for Mandelstam's statements circumscribing the role of the individual creative will. It is the pre-existing form of the poem, its "audible cast" [zvuchashchii slepok]—which the poet must "hear" and "divine"—that defines the category of "imperative" or "ought to be" for Mandelstam.[28] The individual creative will (Pascal's reed, in the quotation below) is subverted to a greater power, which, not contained within the poet, also cannot be subsumed in the reflected solipsism of the Romantic poet's "Muse":

> Не у меня, не у тебя — у них
> Вся сила окончаний родовых:
> Их воздухом поющ тростник и скважист,
> И с благодарностью улитки губ людских
> Потянут на себя их дышащую тяжесть.
> Нет имени у них. Войди в их хрящ,
> И будешь ты наследником их княжеств [. . .]

> Not mine, not yours—but theirs
> Is all the power of gendered [or ancestral] endings:
> The reed sings and is cleft with their air,
> And with gratitude the snail spirals of human lips
> Will pull onto themselves their breathing weight.
> They have no name. Enter into their gristle,
> And you will be heir to their princedoms [. . .][29]

This rewriting of the precursors' poetry, as it should be, *for the first time*, might also be considered a Bloomian *clinamen* (a "swerve"), were there any element of psychological repression involved. Instead, Mandelstam is supremely conscious of his own relation to the poetic past, present, and future.

A differing relation to the past accords with a differing conceptualization of "new" and "old." Romantics and Symbolists strive after *new* experience. In Mandelstam, the highest joy of poetry is that of recognition—achieved through iteration, distanced both chronologically and in artistic realization—of archetypal situations and motifs. The new vision that, for the English Romantics as well as for the Russian Symbolists, is called upon to transform the world—as M. H. Abrams puts it, "a revolution in seeing which will make the object new"[30]—is, for Mandelstam, a new vision of an old scene: "the poet does not fear repetitions and easily becomes drunk on classical wine. [. . .] Classical poetry is the poetry of the revolution" (II, 225, 227).

The reader's experience of distanced iteration is bound up in the phenomenon of intertext. Mandelstam's intertextual poetics, already mature in *Tristia*, might be seen, taking some liberties with Bloom's terminology, as a sort of *apophrades*, a controlled welcoming of the shades of the unthreatening dead, especially given the consonant imagery of the collection. Ivanov is perhaps the most important influence in the transformation of Mandelstam's poetry as he moves from *Stone* to *Tristia*. However, one can discover little real anxiety in relation to Ivanov or almost any other of the many poets whose voices resound in Mandelstam's second collection (the key exception being Blok). Furthermore, intertextuality, in the broadest sense, leads Mandelstam to an answer to the problem of self-creation, that fundamental need of all poets upon which Bloom's argument, to a great extent, rests.[31] In his most powerful (and natural) sublation of Romantic categories, Mandelstam defines the "organic poet" as a ship "all [. . .] hammered together out of salvaged boards," but with "its own build" (III, 34).[32] The poet's originality and organicity exist in harmony with his composite nature and indebtedness to the past.[33] As we can see, Mandelstam's poetics represents a dialectical revision of the very Romantic mindset that exacerbates, if not generates, the burdens of influence and the anguish of foregone priority.

So far, my observations have related to how Mandelstam ingeniously obviates anxiety of influence on a specifically verbal plane. However, as David M. Bethea, Anna Lisa Crone, and Andrew Reynolds have shown, in the Russian context, poetic anxieties can be overshadowed by extra-poetic ones. In a context in which speech acts entail real and not just psychological dangers, the Poet as Poet cedes his place to the Poet within History. In Russia, confrontation with history often meant censorship, censure, isolation, starvation, exile, or execution; however, history also preserves models of courageous inner freedom. For the Poet within History, the tsar or state can function, in Bloomian terms, as the obstructive father figure, in the tension of the struggle with whom the strong poem is generated.[34] This type of anxiety played an important role in Mandelstam's development. The shadow of an increasingly intolerant state was enough to silence the poet in the second half of the 1920s and to provide a powerful counterweight to his creativity in the 1930s.[35]

At the same time, the poet's potential anxieties may relate not only to the state, but also to those individuals who lived in its shadow, accepted the mortal stakes involved, and emerged as strong poets.[36] For these, the lived life of the poet becomes an element of the poetic record. Moreover, if it is indeed "ontological *rhymes*" (Bethea) that may be observed within and between the lives of Russian poets in the Pushkinian tradition, then this implies the conscious, or at least intuitive, *structuring* of life and art, of poetic past and present. Not Bloomian blindness, but an uncanny ability to look the past and potential future face on and not flinch, despite intimations of violent and untimely death—this is what is demanded of a Pushkin or a Mandelstam.[37] Given the stakes, anxiety before the precursor's word, deed, and fate is only natural. However, I do not see in Mandelstam's anxiety before Pushkin the ache of belatedness and deficiency, the original wound implied by Bloom— which can be assuaged only by a *reduction* of the precursor. Rather, in that finding of "evidences of election that will fulfill his precursors' prophecies by fundamentally re-creating those prophecies in his own unmistakable idiom" (Bloom)—well-demonstrated by Reynolds in regard to "To the empty earth" (K pustoi zemle, 1937)—Mandelstam appears to express, instead, awe and love for Pushkin and to savor the honor of participating in the ongoing conversation of poetry, of joining its table, having finally *earned* his place as an equal.[38]

In Russian literature we may also observe more traditionally Bloomian anxieties, situated, however, not surprisingly, at the crossroads of poetic and extra-poetic reality. Blok himself once shared an anxiety of this sort with Anna Akhmatova. She writes:

> I mentioned in passing that the poet Benedikt Livshits complains that he, Blok, through his very existence [odnim svoim sushchestvovaniem] gets in the way of him writing verse. Blok didn't laugh, but answered with complete seriousness: "I understand that. Lev Tolstoy prevents me from writing."[39]

In the case of Livshits, it is Blok the "person" who prevents him from writing—"through his very existence." In the case of Blok and Tolstoy, the same is true, and the contrast between Tolstoy the writer and Tolstoy the man is amplified by the fact that Blok's anxiety crosses the boundary between prose and poetry.

For Mandelstam, the key precursor, whose mix of poetics and persona necessitated a "Bloomian" response, was Alexander Blok. As noted above, Gregory Freidin has written on the ways in which the charismatic expectations attached to the Symbolist poet, of whom Blok was the paragon, effectively excluded the young, Jewish Mandelstam from the position of "Russian poet" until he could generate his own poetic mythology and write himself into that tradition. However, the young Mandelstam also defines a new relation between author and text that circumvents those expectations. Rather than take up, more or less unmodified, the charismatic role of the Symbolist poet *qua* prophet/martyr, Mandelstam, in the second half of *Stone,* banishes the Symbolist *lyric hero* from his poetry.[40] Having done so, Mandelstam's entire poetic stance performs a Bloomian kenosis in relation to Blok's poetry. Through a casting off of the Symbolist-theurgist's manifest role in the drama of salvation, Mandelstam deflates Blok's overstated tragic-prophetic stance. What is more, his resulting, more subtle spokesmanship ultimately regains an element of the charismatic power that he divests from the Symbolists.

Mandelstam's struggle with Blok is a struggle with the lyric hero who is most representative of the Symbolist tradition and, ultimately, with the man behind the mask of that lyric hero. It is also a struggle to reshape, or sublate, the Romantic expectations of these two poets' common readership.

Ultimately, Mandelstam's evasions of the yet-to-be-born Bloom are as precise and prescient as they are because his poetic development is in large part a dialectical transformation of Symbolism (antithesis–synthesis), while both Bloom and Symbolism grow out of the same precursor: the Romantic tradition. Mandelstam is, paradoxically, both before and *after* Bloom.

PART II

CHAPTER 3

DEPARTURE

The various editions of Mandelstam's first book, *Stone,* represent artistic visions of the poet's development, not divorced from his actual trajectory, but rather shaped by his creative will in each new period.[1] The 1913 edition of *Stone* takes the formed poet as a "given." "A body is given me, what shall I do with it" [Dano mne telo, chto mne delat' s nim], the collection begins, and later in the same poem, Mandelstam intones, "On the panes of eternity has already lain / My breath, my warmth" [Na stekla vechnosti uzhe leglo / Moe dykhanie, moe teplo").[2] In each of the later editions, however, a six-poem preamble precedes this tender, but unequivocal, assertion of the poet's self-awareness as poet.

The canonical 1916 edition opens, to be precise, with an informal cycle of three four-line iambic-tetrameter miniatures, ostensibly fragments, each marked 1908 and displaying the same, relatively infrequent enclosing rhyme (m-F-F-m). These poems depict in iconic form three stages of the poet's development:

(1) *Genesis:*[3]

Звук осторожный и глухой
Плода, сорвавшегося с древа,
Среди немолчного напева
Глубокой тишины лесной…

The sound, cautious and muffled,
Of a fruit, fallen from the tree,
Amidst the unceasing melody
Of the deep forest quiet …

(2) *Childhood, with its irrational fears, obliquely linked to Christianity (see chapter 5):*

Сусальным золотом горят
В лесах рождественские елки;
В кустах игрушечные волки
Глазами страшными глядят.

In the forests Christmas trees
Burn with tinsel gold;
In the bushes toy wolves
Gaze with frightening eyes.

(3) *Youth:*

Из полутемной залы, вдруг,
Ты выскользнула в легкой шали —
Мы никому не помешали,
Мы не будили спящих слуг…

From the half-lit hall, suddenly,
You slipped in a light shawl—
We hindered no one,
We did not wake the sleeping servants …

The 1923 and 1928 editions reorganize this three-poem opening, while retaining its thematics. Growth is now reinforced formally, as Mandelstam reinstates the second stanza of "In the forests" and replaces "From the half-lit hall, suddenly" with the nostalgic, three-stanza "To read only children's books" (Tol'ko detskie knigi chitat', 1908). Also, Mandelstam highlights, through the poems' dominant subtexts, three early influences on his poetry: Pushkin, Romantic poet Fedor Tiutchev (a transparent allusion to whom was elided in the one-stanza version of "In the forests"), and Symbolist Fedor Sologub.[4]

In the canonical 1916 edition, the image of the young woman in "From the half-lit hall, suddenly" provides a natural transition to "More tender than tender" (Nezhnee nezhnogo, 1909). This poem is, through its creative re-embodiment of one key *topos* and discursive reference frame of mythopoetic Symbolism—poetry to the mysterious female "ty" (you, fam.)—perhaps as good a starting point as any for a discussion of the ways in which Mandelstam subtly manipulates the tone of his earliest poems to draw tension from the Symbolist heritage, while not succumbing to its gravitational pull.[5]

Нежнее нежного
Лицо твое,
Белее белого
Твоя рука,
От мира целого
Ты далека,
И все твое —
От неизбежного.

От неизбежного —
Твоя печаль
И пальцы рук
Неостывающих,
И тихий звук
Неунывающих
Речей,
И даль
Твоих очей.

More tender than tender
Is your face,
Whiter than white
Your hand,
From the whole world
You are distant,
And all that is yours—
From the inevitable.

> From the inevitable—
> Your sadness
> And the fingers of hands
> Which do not grow cold,
> And the quiet sound
> Of speech
> Which is not despondent,
> And the distance
> Of [i.e., in] your eyes.

The poem's originality lies largely in its tone—delicate almost to the point of ethereality. A host of subtle formal achievements bring to fruition experiments from "The noiseless spindle" (Besshumnoe vereteno) and "Your vivacious tenderness" (Tvoia veselaia nezhnost'), unpublished poems written in the same year. (We should keep in mind that it was the Symbolists—Ivanov, Briusov, Bely, and others—who introduced more aggressive formal, and particularly metrical, experimentation to Russian poetry.)

"Your vivacious tenderness," in particular, reads like an etude of "More tender than tender." Like its more successful cousin, it is configured on the backdrop of what was, by this time, the rather worn narrative, canonized in Symbolism, of the meeting between the poet and a mysterious or otherworldly woman:

> Твоя веселая нежность
> Смутила меня.
> К чему печальные речи,
> Когда глаза
> Горят, как свечи
> Среди белого дня?
>
> Среди белого дня...
> И та — далече —
> Одна слеза,
> Воспоминание встречи;
> И, плечи клоня,
> Приподымает их нежность.

> Your vivacious tenderness
> Disconcerted me.
> What sense in sorrowful speech

When eyes
Burn like candles
In broad daylight?

In broad daylight . . .
And she [that one, fem.]—is far away—
One tear,
The memory of a meeting;
And, bowing shoulders,
Tenderness lifts them up.

The woman's "vivacious tenderness," her human warmth, contrasts with the "poet's" "sorrowful speech." The description of her eyes, which "Burn like candles / In broad daylight," while clearly evocative of the hieratic diction of the younger Symbolists, is instead made to describe her connection with life. Still, the mythopoetic Symbolist context is sufficiently strong that this natural language association ("eyes / Burn" [glaza / Goriat] = liveliness, "*vivacious* tenderness" [*veselaia* nezhnost']) is not immediately sensed. The second stanza, which takes place after her exit, also evokes the younger Symbolists' mythopoesis—specifically, the moment of loss after the initial vision (perceived, after Baudelaire and Solov'ev, as a meeting). However, the woman's human tenderness has been enough to reverse the sense of loss that is expected, and that receives a self-ironic jab in "One tear."

"Your vivacious tenderness" has an unusually complex, even fanciful, strophic structure. Its rhyme scheme is a perfect mirror (AbCdCb bCdCbA), with nearly tautological lines at the center, differing only in punctuation and hence in intonation. The elaborate metrical structure is a near mirror as well.[6] The combination of this highly structured form and the skittish and elliptical syntax of the second stanza makes it feel somewhat forced.[7]

"More tender than tender" betrays a more elegant design. Its two stanzas consist of 16 lines of iambic dimeter, but with the penultimate verse split into two one-foot lines, thus introducing an extra line and rhyme. In the first stanza, a quatrain of alternating rhyme is encased in two layers of enclosing rhyme—a distorted mirror of sorts that is itself mirrored and distorted in the second stanza: AbCdCdbA AefGfGheh. This scheme is highly productive in terms of the phonic, rhythmic, syntactic, and semantic tensions generated. The poem opens in a static, almost iconic, close-up of face and hand, in lines seemingly unrhymed and in an oddly unfamiliar meter: "NizhNʲEye NʲEZHnəvə / LiTSO tvaYO, / BiLʲEye BʲElǝvǝ / TvaYA ruKA." The next two lines ("At MIrə TSElǝvǝ / Ty daliKA") introduce movement, through alternating rhyme and the concept of the heroine's "distance." But then the stanza resolves in stasis and apparent completion with two enclosing rhymes: "I VS'O tvaYO / At ni-izBʲEZHnəvə."

The second stanza opens with a combination of tautological rhyme and semantic destabilization, as the syntax of the closing lines of the first stanza is reinterpreted. Her sorrow has its source in the inevitable, rather than (or in addition to) being distant from it. Lines 10–15, which mirror lines 2–7 metrically, also present a complex semantic mirroring, coursing back from demeanor to hand to face (as the source of sound) and complicating the postulates of the first stanza. ("From the inevitable—Your sadness"—"From the whole world / You are distant"; "And the fingers of hands / Which do not grow cold"—"Whiter than white / Your hand"; "And the quiet sound / Of speech / Which is not despondent"—"More tender than tender / Is your face.")

Most powerfully, Mandelstam overcomes the elaborate mirror structure's gravitation toward stasis through the introduction of the hyper-stanzaic rhyme "rechei." A passage in a draft to "François Villon" concerning the latter's *huitains* (ababbcbc) and *dizains* (ababbccddc) provides insight into how Mandelstam likely understood this rhyme's function: "The introduction of a new rhyme 'c' in Villon has a special meaning. It is as if the strophe receives a push, comes alive, and resolves itself in the final line with an energetic or witty outburst."[8] Here too, the strophe and poem receive an unexpected stimulus with the introduction of the 'h' rhyme and resolve with great satisfaction in the final line.

The poem also has a tendency to compile rhythmically into longer units of two lines based on its syntactic structure. This places additional emphasis on "Rechei," as the only line that frustrates the syntactic/metric coincidence of line pairs. The first three and the fifth of these pairs form composite lines of iambic pentameter, with a caesura after the third foot and a dactylic ending before the caesura. In other words, they feel, perhaps, like a clipped alexandrine. (Traditionally, iambic pentameter in Russian poetry has had either no stable caesura or a caesura after the fourth syllable.) At one of his lectures on versification, which Mandelstam attended on 23 April 1909, Viacheslav Ivanov had spoken about the opposite tendency, the potential of regular internal rhyme to split into shorter lines a series of long iambics, making reference specifically to alexandrines.[9] Notably, Mandelstam's intense formal experimentation in 1909 more or less coincided with these detailed lectures by Ivanov on prosody (with much attention to fixed strophic forms).

The leitmotif of rhythmic insufficiency in "More tender than tender" is also repeated on a larger scale, as the first stanza has a total of 40 syllables, while the second stanza has only 38. The difference is slight, but it is palpable to the reader as the absence of the dactylic rhyme that would complete the mirror. The entire poem seems formulated rhythmically, on the deepest level, to create a feeling of quiet loss, which is balanced by the subtle uplift of the unexpected masculine rhyme in the final line. This formal brilliance, redolent of the more radical experiments of the youthful Bely ("World Soul" [Dusha mira, 1902]) and the youthful Vladimir Mayakovsky ("Down the Cobblestones" [Po mostovoi, 1913]), remains, in Mandelstam's poem, wonderfully understated. It is remarkable that a poem in which 17 of 35 words are rhymed can sound so fragile.

In theme, "More tender than tender," as I have noted, is a variation on the Symbolist genre, which might loosely be termed "verses to *you*" (not necessarily capitalized). The phenomenon I am speaking of is at once broader than and narrower than the tradition of Sophiological poetry, the topology of which has been charted by Lada Panova.[10] It is narrower in that I segregate—perhaps somewhat artificially—one discursive framework used in poetry dedicated to the mystic Sophia (i.e., I—You—reader, but not I—She—reader),[11] but broader because not all appeals by the Symbolists to the mysterious feminine "you" were intended to address the Eternal Feminine. In fact, a primary rationale for a broader approach is that play with the boundaries of the Sophiological tradition was a key element in the genre's poetics. Surely an ambiguity inscribed in the poem itself underlies Blok's misconstruing of Briusov's Baudelaire-influenced "To Her, Close at Heart" (K Blizkoi, 1903) as a poem in the Solov'evian, Sophiological mold. (Blok, as is well known, quotes from "To Her" alongside Solov'ev for the epigraphs to the 1905 edition of *Poems about the Fair Lady*.)[12]

A prime example of this type of play in Mandelstam himself is the poem "You passed through a cloud of fog" (Ty proshla skvoz' oblako tumana, 1911). Here, Mandelstam achieves an exquisite balance between the image of a physical woman, implied particularly in the intimations of a threatening sexuality/sensuality in the second stanza, and an evocation of the World Soul as revealed in nature. The *topos* of the heroine's appearance in nature, striding from behind a veil of fog, is combined with one of "Her" most characteristic features, the flush of her cheeks, which, later in the poem, is openly equated with the dawn or sunset. This may also, however, be understood as a sort of pathetic fallacy: "How your flush *plays on everything!*" [Kak *na vsem igraet* tvoi rumianets!] (my emphasis). *Tanets-rumianets*, moreover, is a typical Blokian rhyme.[13] The picture is filled out by an eschatologically (or, more likely, a quasi-eschatologically) charged ending: "How the shining wound of bright days / Shows even through the cloud of fog!"

[Kak skvozit i v oblake tumana / Iarkikh dnei siiaiushchaia rana!]. (Blok had written, "Through the former clouds glanced / A bright unworldly gleam" [Proglianul skvoz' tuchi prezhnye / Iarkii otblesk nezemnoi] [I, 171].) Penned eight years earlier, Mandelstam's poem would surely have resonated as a Sophiological poem, but, as Mandelstam himself well understood, poems exist in a historical context within the ever-changing poetic tradition.[14]

This "genre," which is of particular importance to the mythopoetic Symbolists through the (often ambivalent) identification of the poem's addressee with the Eternal Feminine, but which also marks the poetry of the older Symbolists, for instance, Briusov and Sologub, takes its roots in the poetry of Vladimir Solov'ev, Afanasy Fet, and the French Symbolists. These authors are, in turn, influenced by the poetry of Goethe, Dante, and Petrarch and by the tradition of courtly love poetry that influenced them.[15] In other words, it is a tradition with the deepest cultural roots in European poetry and many antecedents in Russian poetry as well.

For ease of discussion, however, and also because I believe there is some degree of psychological validity to the association with Blok, I will consider "More tender than tender" against the backdrop specifically of Blok's poetry. Other than perhaps Solov'ev, no Russian poet is as strongly associated as Blok is with this tradition of courtly love poetry and its descendants, since for no other Russian poet does it play such an enduring and central role.[16] For no other Symbolist poet is orientation toward the female "You" such an integral element of the poet's voice.[17]

The possibility of a Blokian contrastive model is hinted at in the specific traits of the heroine. Tenderness, whiteness, and distance from (and simultaneous presence in) the world are all marked characteristics of Blok's heroine of the period of *Poems about the Fair Lady*. The *disembodied* face, hand, and speech are also typical of Blok. This is of course not to say that these features are not broadly employed throughout Symbolist poetry, and world poetry for that matter. In Blok's early poetry, it is precisely these abstracted, clichéd features and epithets that have a high degree of semioticization. Therefore, it is paradoxically these "nondescript" features of the heroine of "More tender than tender" that are evocative of Blok's early poetry—if not of Blok's poetry exclusively.[18]

Most importantly, Mandelstam's "distance / Of your eyes" [dal' / Tvoikh ochei]" recalls what is possibly the single most memorable feature of Blok's Stranger: "I look beyond the dark veil, / And see an enchanted shore / And the enchanted distance" [Smotriu za temnuiu vual', / I vizhu bereg ocharovannyi / I ocharovannuiu dal'] (II, 212). This distance in the Heroine's eyes is analogous to the spiritual vistas accessible through the eyes of an icon.[19] Mandelstam's heroine, however, is also imbued with a striking, human warmth qualitatively different from the earthly side of Blok's heroine—"the fingers of hands / Which do not grow cold, / And the quiet sound / Of speech / Which is not despondent." This humanity is underscored by the complexity of her character: "The heroine is 'enveloped in *sadness*,' but her speech is *not despondent*."[20]

The overall effect is a *humanizing* of the heroine, while maintaining her connection to that which is beyond human comprehension ("the distance / of your eyes"). Rather than attempting to subvert the Symbolist model, as in "Your vivacious tenderness," Mandelstam allows its echo to continue sounding, providing depth to his portrait. Without making any transcendent claims for his heroine (and, in fact, while guarding her humanity), he is able to bask her in the afterglow of the Symbolist heroine's ambiguous divinity.

The power of "More tender than tender," visible particularly in comparison with "Your vivacious tenderness," grows out of its sophistication and sure-footed unity of tone. In contrast, the strength of the sixth poem of *Stone*, "There are chaste charms" (Est' tselomudrennye chary), also written in 1909, is precisely in its tonal ambivalence:

Есть целомудренные чары:
Высокий лад, глубокий мир;
Далёко от эфирных лир
Мной установленные лары.

У тщательно обмытых ниш,
В часы внимательных закатов,
Я слушаю моих пенатов
Всегда восторженную тишь.

Какой игрушечный удел,
Какие робкие законы
Приказывает торс точеный
И холод этих хрупких тел!

Иных богов не надо славить:
Они как равные с тобой!

И, осторожною рукой,
Позволено их переставить.

There are chaste charms:
A lofty mode, a deep serenity;
Far from the ethereal lyres
Are the lares I have set.

At the painstakingly washed niches,
In the hour of attentive sunsets,
I listen to my penates'
Always ecstatic stillness.

What a toylike domain,
What timid laws
Are proclaimed by a lathed torso
And the cold of these fragile bodies!

Some gods one needn't laud:
They are as equals to you!
And, with a cautious hand,
You are permitted to rearrange them.

Omry Ronen gives the classic interpretation of this poem, on the basis of subtextual analysis, as a quintessential proto-Acmeist statement of Mandelstam's new "attitude toward the poetry of the past, the 'careful rearrangement' and 'justification' of its lasting values." Clare Cavanagh, in contrast, sees the poem as an embodiment of the young poet's failure, in domesticating the great figures of the past, to make those poets speak, to create a poetry of living and dynamic voices.[21]

Despite the subtextual evidence linking Mandelstam's penates to past poets and the validity of *both* of these above approaches, these figurines may be seen not only as the poets of the past, but also as a deflated image of the deified Ideal(s) of the mythopoetic Symbolists. The poem's context, on this plane, is to be sought in a debate progressing at the time within the Symbolist camp. Sergei Gorodetsky, in his article "Idol-creation" (Idolotvorchestvo, 1909), having adopted Ivanov's definition of "realistic" (essentially Neoplatonic) and "idealistic" (freely associative) Symbolism, accuses Bely and Blok of trading in their divine idea/Ideal for idols, in the form of poetic images:

Idea (ens realissimum) or *eidōlon*? For many poets this question is a fateful one. Where should one direct one's creative energy: toward heralding the essential [sushchee], or toward the transformation of appearances [vidimosti], toward the creation of fragile [khrupkie] images . . . ? How can one prefer a feminine, quiet receptiveness to superficially flashy, independent creation? Is it not better to sing one's own ditty [pesenka], no matter what sort, than to sing another's—even a divine other's—song [pet' s chuzhogo, khotia by i bozhestvennogo golosa]?[22]

Gorodetsky's purpose is, of course, to denigrate the individualist's "ditty." Mandelstam, while accepting the terms of Gorodetsky's argument, comes to a diametrically opposed conclusion. A ditty is held at least outwardly preferential to the divine song, and the Idea(ls) of the mythopoetic Symbolists are exchanged for the prosaic figurines of household deities.

The second stanza is particularly crucial to establishing the poem's double-voicedness. The "painstakingly washed niches" evoke, in particular, Blok's patient service at the altar of his Ideal ("A youth, I light the candles, / I guard the incense flame" [Ia, otrok, zazhigaiu svechi, / Ogon' kadil'nyi beregu] [I, 209]); "attentive sunsets"—the Argonauts' (Bely's circle) and Blok's beloved sunset vigils.[23] "Ecstasy" [vostorg] was a key concept, particularly for the Argonauts, and listening to the Ideal's quiet is yet again evocative of the mythopoetic Symbolists: "To you, Whose Half-light was so bright, / *Whose Voice calls through stillness*" [Tebe, Chei Sumrak byl tak iarok, / *Chei Golos tikhost'iu zovet*] (Blok, I, 333, emphasis mine). In other words, the lyric persona's care for his *penaty* is imagined through a contrast to the Symbolists' worship of the Eternal Feminine, as it is represented in their poetry.[24]

This second stanza, then, interposes a palpable distance between the speaker and mythopoetic Symbolism, whether we take the *penaty* as the poets themselves (Symbolists as a subset of the greater tradition) or as the Symbolists' gods.[25] In stanza three, Mandelstam underscores his transfer of the mythopoetic Symbolists' Ideal to the realm of play within the art work:

Какой игрушечный удел,
Какие робкие законы
Приказывает торс точеный
И холод этих хрупких тел!

What a toylike domain [also "inheritance," "lot"],

> What timid laws
> Are proclaimed by a lathed torso
> And the cold of these fragile bodies!

As S. N. Broitman has noted, in Mandelstam's early poetry the theurgic strivings of mythopoetic Symbolism are often redirected inward, into the world of the poem.[26] In "There are chaste charms," the Symbolists' Ideal is reduced to a series of possibly metaphorical domestic idols, standing in "painstakingly washed niches." And it turns out that in this small, precisely delimited poetic world, the boundary between "here" and "there" is no more binding than in a children's game: the poet can touch (and even rearrange) his gods. The lyric persona's assertion of his equality with these "gods" in the fourth stanza ("They are as equals to you!") sounds a bit disingenuous, given his power to "rearrange" them. At the same time, however, the "poet" and his penates are made equal in their smallness.

Interestingly, Gorodetsky in his article criticizes as a blatant example of self-absorbed aesthetic excess Bely's poem "The Wilderness" (Pustynia, 1907): "Ether; into the ether— / An ethereal way. / And, here— / The royal purple path of sunrise / Splits / The sapphire of the sapphire / Chamber" [Efir; v efir— / Efirnaia doroga. / I, vot— / Zari porfirnaia stezia / Sechet / Safir safirnogo / Chertoga].[27] "Here," writes Gorodetsky, "is that meager little song, which to the idealistic Symbolist is dearer than apprehension of the Extant [Sushchego]; *efir, efir, efir, safir, safir.*"[28] In Mandelstam's poem, the "ethereal lyres" are contrasted with the penates, patrons and muses of his little ditty, and returned to their rightful status as a marker of "realistic" Symbolism. Compare, from a large number of examples, "And the blueing velvet of the ether / Drew close and caressed us" [I zalastilsia k nam / Golubeiushchii barkhat efira], from the first poem of Bely's *Gold in the Azure* (*Zoloto v lazuri*, 1904), or Ivanov's programmatic "Artistic Creation" (Tvorchestvo): "The ether is full of unperceived visages, / And above the azure midnight / New luminaries, to the strumming of harmonious lyres, / Sail through the stormless ocean" [Ispolnen oblikov neprózrennykh efir, / I nad polunoch'iu lazurnoi / Svetila novye, s briatsan'em stroinykh lir, / Plyvut chrez okean bezburnyi].[29] Indeed, the "ethereal lyres" in Mandelstam's poem can refer at once to both types of excess characteristic of the Symbolists—artistic and epistemological.[30]

In order to understand the ultimate sense of Mandelstam's evocations of Symbolism here, we must consider the question of pragmatics that is latent in the conflict between Ronen's and Cavanagh's readings, as they, respectively, elevate and diminish the poet. Are Mandelstam's deflated Symbolist gods primarily a gesture of irony toward the Symbolists ("the Symbolists' gods are material for my little ditty") or a gesture of irony toward the self ("the Symbolists' Gods, on entering the small world of my poetry, are reduced to idols/playthings")? It is impossible to speak with certainty about the poet's vantage point in relation to Symbolism, and this uncertainty becomes an important characteristic of the poem. "There are chaste charms" is full of tenderness for the penates and the "poet's" domesticated world, infused with self-deprecating irony. However, at the same time, the poem hints at the possibility of equality with the great poets of the past, or even superiority over them. We are ultimately left asking: Is the speaker small, looking out, or huge, looking in?

In the period 1909–11, "purely" Symbolist poems are interspersed in Mandelstam's writings with poems displaying varying degrees of individuation from Symbolism. Consider the poem "A meager beam, with chill measure" (Skudnyi luch, kholodnoi meroiu, 1911), which the poet valued enough to include in the exceedingly slim, 23-poem first edition of *Stone*. It was written two years after "More tender than tender" and "There are chaste charms," yet it bears distinct tonal echoes of Blok's poetry and a unity of individual voice characteristic of Symbolism:

> Скудный луч, холодной мерою,
> Сеет свет в сыром лесу.
> Я печаль, как птицу серую,
> В сердце медленно несу.
>
> Что мне делать с птицей раненой?
> Твердь умолкла, умерла.
> С колокольни отуманенной
> Кто-то снял колокола,
>
> И стоит осиротелая
> И немая вышина
> Как пустая башня белая,
> Где туман и тишина.
>
> Утро, нежностью бездонное
> Полу-явь и полу-сон,

Забытье неутоленное —
Дум туманный перезвон.

A meager beam, with chill measure,
Sows light in the damp forest.
I carry sorrow, like a gray bird,
Deliberately, in my heart.

What shall I do with the wounded bird?
The firmament has gone silent and dead.
From the fog-shrouded belltower
Someone has taken down the bells.

And the height stands
Orphaned and mute,
Like an empty white tower,
Where there is fog and silence.

Morning, bottomless with tenderness,
Half reality, half dream,
Unslaked oblivion—
The foggy peal of thoughts.

There are several *topoi* here that the early Blok frequently uses, though none could be distinguished as a specific reference to Blok among the greater body of Symbolist poetry. These include "sorrow"; bells; the mute heavens; an empty white tower, fog, and silence; and "Half reality, half dream."[31] In any case, however, foreign elements are fully integrated within Mandelstam's lyric "I," betraying no sense of distance or dissonance. "A meager beam" remains a whole and vital expression of Mandelstam's poetic voice, the confession of a—in this "minute of poetic consciousness"—Symbolist poet.[32]

CHAPTER 4

THE PENDULUM AT THE HEART OF *STONE*

In histories of early-twentieth-century Russian literature, particularly those focusing on the Acmeists, the year 1912 has taken on almost legendary dimensions. On New Year's Eve 1912, the illustrious Stray Dog cabaret—home away from home for bohemian Petersburg—opened its doors. This was the year that Ivanov and Bely retreated to the isolated bastion of the journal *Works and Days* (Trudy i dni),[1] the year of Ego-Futurism and Igor Severianin's first notoriety, and, in December, of Cubo-Futurism's audible *Slap in the Face of Public Taste* (Poshchechina obshchestvennomu vkusu). In 1912, Gumilev took over the literature section of the premier art journal of the day *Apollo* (Apollon) and the poetry journal *The Hyperborean* began its short-lived print run. Under the imprint of the Poets' Guild were published Akhmatova's first book *Evening* (Vecher) and Zenkevich's *Wild Porphyry* (Dikaia porfira), while almost the entire print run of Narbut's *Hallelujah* (Alliluiia) was confiscated for "pornography." The book's scandalously earthy poems had been set using a Church Slavonic typeface.[2] This was also the year that the work of Gumilev and Gorodetsky's Poets' Guild distilled, in late fall, into the more coherent movement

49

that would announce itself to the world in the publications of the Acmeists in early 1913.[3] And this of course was the year of Mandelstam's much-flaunted "conversion" to the new movement, the year he would write such early masterpieces of Acmeism as "Hagia-Sophia" (Aiia-Sofiia) and "Notre Dame."

Zhirmunsky, in 1916, penned the classic definition of the Acmeists as *preodolevshie simvolizm* (they who have overcome Symbolism).[4] However, it would perhaps be more accurate to call them *preodolevaiushchie* (they who are overcoming). The Acmeists of course had their moments of bravado: "From this day forth, not a single line by Sologub, Briusov, Ivanov or Blok will be printed in *Apollon*," Mandelstam is said to have boasted around town in January 1913, raising the ire of Sologub's wife, A. N. Chebotarevskaya.[5] Still, Mandelstam at least once referred to the members of the new movement in print as "younger Symbolists" [mladshie simvolisty] (II, 341–42). This is a nomenclature that feels almost paradoxical after the strongly anti-Symbolist memoirs of Nadezhda Mandelstam and Anna Akhmatova.[6] Mandelstam noted too that "Viacheslav Ivanov himself aided much in the formulation of Acmeist theory" (II, 257). In his book *Kniga ob akmeizme*, Oleg Lekmanov presents convincing evidence for an overarching balance between the this-worldly and the otherworldly in Acmeism, and even proposes that the choice by Gumilev and Gorodetsky of six so distinct and disparate poets may represent a conscious attempt at *collective* balance.[7] On the trembling scales of Acmeist balance, Mandelstam's poetry of 1912, particularly as he chose to organize it in his collections beginning in 1915, consciously represents a process of prolonged and elusive "overcoming."

A. G. Mets, following Nikolai Khardziev, remarks on the arrangement of poems by year but without regard to month and day in the second edition of *Stone* (1916; released Dec. 1915).[8] This structure makes the need to search for a compositional principle within each year apparent. Even if we are to assume that the poems are arranged in the closest approximation of chronological order, we must take into account the following: the reader acquainted with the first edition of *Stone*, which was constructed on different compositional principles, would have sensed the new ordering as a shift; and the exclusion of four previously published poems written in 1912—two are precisely dated and the dating of the other two is highly likely—certainly had an impact on the overall composition.[9] What is more, we have precise dates for only three of the 12 poems included in *Stone* (1916) under the year 1912. Therefore we have no serious foundation to assume that these poems are arranged specifically in chronological order (though we have no information refuting such a supposition either).[10] Careful analysis of the poems marked 1912 in the second edition of *Stone* will show that the general principle of grouping poems by year (and only by year) allowed the poet to create a dynamic and sophisticated compositional structure, at the same time leaving intact the general picture of his development.

Within the year 1912, the poems of *Stone* can be divided into six contrasting but connected pairs:

1. "Ia vzdragivaiu ot kholoda"
2. "Ia nenavizhu svet odnoobraznykh zvezd"
3. "Obraz tvoi, muchitel'nyi i zybkii"
4. "Net, ne luna, a svetlyi tsiferblat"
5. "Peshekhod"
6. "Kazino"
7. "Paden'e—neizmennyi sputnik strakha"
8. "Tsarskoe selo"
9. "Zolotoi"
10. "Liuteranin"
11. "Aiia-Sofiia"
12. "Notre Dame"

1. "I shudder from the cold"
2. "I hate the light of the monotonous stars"
3. "Your image, agonizing and unstable"
4. "No, not the moon, but a radiant clock face"
5. "Pedestrian"
6. "Casino"
7. "Falling is the constant companion of fear"
8. "Tsarskoe selo"
9. "Gold Ruble"
10. "Lutheran"
11. "Hagia-Sophia"
12. "Notre Dame"

This structure (in any case immanent within the book's composition) is given a particular visual boost in the pairing of these poems, through to the beginning of "Tsarskoe selo," on facing pages.[11] As Sergei Averintsev has noted, a similar compositional structure, juxtaposing poems on facing pages, was used by Paul Verlaine in his book *Parallèlement*. Averintsev, in fact, contrasts Mandelstam's compositional principles to this "obvious, i.e. somewhat mechanical" structure.[12] Nonetheless, it seems that Mandelstam from time to time takes advantage of this technique in the 1916 edition of *Stone,* and not only among the poems marked 1912. What is more, a clear tendency toward more frequent and pronounced pairings marks the later editions of *Stone* (1923, 1928). This is most readily apparent in the edition of 1923, in which no dates of poems are given. There, Mandelstam places

"Onto the mother-of-pearl shuttle" (Na perlamutrovyi chelnok, 1911) right after "Inexpressible sadness" (Nevyrazimaia pechal', 1909). (Both poems feature rays of sun filtering into a room and delicate fingers presented in close-up; both are in the same meter and have an enclosing rhyme scheme and the same number of strophes.)[13] There, "That evening the lancet forest of the organ did not hum" (V tot vecher ne gudel strel'chatyi les organa, 1917) meets "Bach" (Bakh, 1913); "Europe" (Evropa, 1914) meets "The Hellenes mustered for war" (Sobiralis' elliny voinoiu, 1916); a vision of a French "Abbot" out of the novels of Flaubert or Zola (Abbat, 1915) meets a fragment of an Old French epic ("Aymon's Sons" [Synov'ia Aimona, 1922, from the twelfth- or thirteenth-century *Les quatre fils Aymon*]). Each of these is clearly a meaningful pairing.

It is not at all surprising that Mandelstam paid special attention to the compositional pairing of his poems. As has been noted many times, a rich "dualism" characterizes his poetry on all levels, from oxymoronic turns of phrase to compositional reversals and ideological double-voicedness in individual poems or the genetic splitting of the famous twin poems (*dvoichatki*).[14]

The group of poems marked 1912 in the edition of 1916 begins with two four-quatrain poems about stars, consisting of four stanzas each, "I shudder from the cold" and "I hate the light." In the first, the lyric persona, not without some irony, accepts the Symbolist concept of "connection" (*sviaz'*) and submits to the orders of the stars, which threaten to mortally wound him, piercing his *heart* with a *pin/ray* descended from above.[15] In the second, he expresses his hatred for the "monotonous"—an epithet easily readable here as "Symbolist"—stars and himself threatens to wound the *breast* of the now not "mysterious," but "empty," heavens with the upwardly thrust *needle* of his thought and verse.[16] The first poem is written in three-ictus *dol'nik,* a meter with strong Symbolist, and especially Blokian, associations. The second is in a logaoedic meter. Rhythmically they are similar, but the musical freedom of the first meter contrasts with the more rigid structure of the second, and if in the first we sense a dancing syncopation, in the second we feel the rhythmic force of repeated blows.[17]

These poems are followed by two short, two-stanza poems constructed upon verbal anecdotes ("'Lord!' I said by accident, / Myself not thinking to say it" ['Gospodi!' skazal ia po oshibke, / Sam togo ne dumaia skazat']; "What time is it, they asked him here— / And he replied to the curious: 'eternity!'" [Kotoryi chas, ego sprosili zdes'— / A on otvetil liubopytnym: 'vechnost'!']). The first poem continues Symbolist debates surrounding the living "word-symbol" and the dead "word-term."[18] Its opening ("Your image, agonizing and unstable, / I couldn't perceive in the fog" [Obraz tvoi, muchitel'nyi i zybkii / Ia ne mog v tumane osiazat']) evokes the early poetry of Blok, in which the agonizing struggle of the lyric hero to hold on to the image of the heroine, often hidden by fog and constantly threatening to alter her appearance ("izmenish' oblik Ty!" [I, 99]), is a leitmotif. The second poem was long considered the poetic credo of Mandelstam as Acmeist.[19] Incidentally, already Clarence Brown saw in the two tercets of "No, not the moon" the ending of a nonexistent sonnet.[20] In *Stone* (1916), they were printed opposite the two quatrains of "Your image, agonizing and unstable."

These are followed by a pair of sonnets united by the image of the abyss. The first of these remains within the sphere of influence of Symbolism (about which see chapter 5 below), while, in the second, the poet demonstrates a bold freedom in manipulating Symbolist clichés, transforming them and infusing them with new content.[21] The next pair—"Falling is the constant companion of fear" and "Tsarskoe selo"—encompasses a radical contrast in tone, composition, and theme.[22] Thus, "Falling is the constant companion of fear" might be considered the quintessential transitional poem, the last "Symbolist" poem of the collection.[23] It should be noted that, in this pairing, tension and alarm are supplanted by ironic playfulness, just as, in the previous two poems, the "light intoxication" of "modest life" [op'ianen'e legk(oe) [. . .] zhizni nebogatoi] takes the place of drama and "insurmountable fear" [nepobedimyi strakh].

After "Tsarskoe Selo," we encounter two genre scenes. The first, "Gold Ruble," depicts a typically Symbolist milieu.[24] The second, "Lutheran," sketches a staid funeral scene. It is the more Acmeist for its Protestantism, reinforced through a rejection of "chosenness" and immediacy of connection to the deity. However, the final image, of humanity as candles, burning, invisible, in the stark light of day, accrues on the poem's backdrop of this-worldly religiosity a remarkable spiritual depth and power:

И думал я: витийствовать не надо,
Мы не пророки, даже не предтечи,
Не любим рая, не боимся ада,
И в полдень матовый горим, как свечи.

And I mused: no need for oratory,
We are no prophets, not even forerunners,
We don't love heaven, don't fear hell,
And burn in the blanched noonday like candles.

Finally, this portion of *Stone* comes to a singular climax with the two cathedral poems. The first, "Hagia-Sophia," bears certain distinctly Symbolist traits, even given the overarching Acmeist associations of the poetry of architecture (see below); the second, "Notre Dame," is among the most striking poetic manifestoes of Acmeism.[25] The general principal of composition within each pair, excluding "Falling" and "Tsarskoe selo," appears to be thematic and compositional similarity and tonal and "ideological" contrast.[26] In addition, the first poem of each pair displays a greater pull upon the poet of the Symbolist poetics and worldview.

Moreover, while the poems "I shudder from the cold" and "Your image" in important ways challenge the poetics and theory of Symbolism, they, along with the other poems situated in our Symbolist column, unquestionably demonstrate a greater gravitation toward Symbolism than those with which they are paired. One might say that these poems, with the exception perhaps only of "Hagia-Sophia," continue the conversation of the Symbolists themselves about poetry, taking, however, an ever more radical "reformational" stance, something that clearly cannot be said about the poems to which they are contrasted. In any case, in moving to the left-hand side of our diagram—and, more often than not, the left-hand page of the open book—we time and again confront the necessity of recapturing poetic territory in which the poet had already seemed firmly ensconced on the previous page.

In this sense, the poems of 1912 in *Stone* (1916) can be visualized as a pendulum, swinging between the poles of Symbolism and Acmeism, with each full swing moving gradually further toward the Acmeist pole. The first edition of *Stone* (1913) presents another structure entirely: here, "No, not the moon" does serve as the fulcrum upon which the book turns, separating Acmeist from Symbolist texts. In this earlier edition, "Your image" and "Pedestrian," both poems from what we have called the "Symbolist" side of the later edition's pendulum, fall on the Symbolist side of this divide. Notably, "Pedestrian" is located *before,* rather than after, "No, not the moon" (as in the later edition). In addition, "I hate the light," which comes before any of those poems but on the "Acmeist" side of the pendulum in the later edition, is placed in the second half of the earlier edition, among the Acmeist poems. The nature of this reshuffling strongly buttresses our hypothesis about the pendulum composition at the center of *Stone* (1916).

Gumilev, in his review of *Stone* (1913), notes the division of Mandelstam's book into two "sharply divided sections: up to 1912 and after that year."[27] Later, in his review of *Stone* (1916), he inaccurately (from a strict, compositional standpoint at least) continues to call "No, not the moon" the breaking point: "from this time forward, the poet becomes an adept of the literary movement known as Acmeism."²⁸ As I will demonstrate more fully in the next chapter through an analysis of four poems located at the Symbolist "backswing" of the pendulum, in *Stone* (1916), Mandelstam presents not a miraculous conversion to the faith of Acmeism, but a prolonged struggle between Acmeism and another artistic system with a continuing pull on the poet. This likely made sense from Mandelstam's vantage point at the end of 1915. By then, the triumphantly Acmeist "Notre Dame" could no longer function as even a conditional end-point in his poetic development, and the poet's new openness toward elements of the Symbolist poetics was becoming more and more apparent.²⁹

The swinging pendulum at the center of *Stone* (1916) represents the poet's inner struggle—torn between two poetics. However, this compositional arrangement is just as much an aesthetically reconstructed view of his poetic evolution as is the sharp turn from Symbolism to Acmeism depicted in the 1913 edition. Therefore, in the pendulum structure at the heart of Mandelstam's collection, we observe not only struggle, but also aesthetic play with the poet's own distance from, and connection to, Symbolism.

CHAPTER 5

STRUGGLING WITH THE FAITH

In this chapter, I will more closely examine four poems falling on the Symbolist pole of Mandelstam's pendulum. Not surprisingly, given that "Symbolism is unthinkable without its religious pretensions,"[1] those of Mandelstam's poems that demonstrate an active overcoming of Symbolism reflect religious thematics in a variety of ways. In these poems, metaphysics is often intimately tied to narrative structures, the poetic realization of which is mediated by a species of light-handed irony that gains its force through questioning—but not discarding—the hierarchies and dichotomies that organize the Symbolist worldview.

Thus, in "Your image, agonizing and unstable," the Symbolist doctrine of the "living word" is "tested" in the crucible of accidental blasphemy and "ambivalent irony." In "Pedestrian," Mandelstam inverts the Symbolists' own "heresiography," exposing their distortions of the "faith." In "Falling is the constant companion of fear," an exploration of the poet's own real struggle with religious faith, while sacrificing none of its surface resonance, simultaneously serves as an extended conceit for the poet's struggle with Symbolism and leads the way to a renewal of the older poets' worn lexicon of symbolic concepts. Finally, in "Hagia-Sophia," Mandelstam appropriates for Acmeism the Symbolist sanctuary and "inner abyss" it safeguards into the present and future.

AMBIVALENT IRONY AND THE WORD

If the poetic word of the younger Symbolists exists ideally in the tension between "here" and "there," the tension in certain of Mandelstam's poems, particularly in 1912, is generated through their ambiguous situation in a new binary that posits the Symbolist diaphanous word at one pole and a word free from the possibility of otherworldly representation at the other. This new orientation allows the poet effectively to challenge the system's hegemony from within. Simply to write this-worldly poems would be to remain within the sphere of Symbolist conceptions about art—to be a pseudo-realist. To write ironic poems travestying Symbolist ideals would be, at best, to work squarely within the Symbolist mode and, at worst, to be regarded as a poor epigone of the Symbolists' own ironic masterpieces. Instead, Mandelstam engenders a shift in the axis through which the word's tension is generated, deploying a characteristic "ambivalent" irony.[2]

As Irina Paperno has shown, "Your image, agonizing and unstable" challenges the Symbolists' dualist conception of the living "word-symbol" and dead "word-concept" through engaging the then-current debate surrounding the heresy of *imiaslavie* [Name-glorifying].[3] The Orthodox monks of Mount Athos understood the name of God to be God himself, "so that its recitation brought about his immediate presence."[4] One was to recite the Jesus prayer—"Lord Jesus Christ, Son of God, have mercy on me, sinner!" [Gospodi Iisuse Khriste, Syne Bozhii, pomilui mia greshnogo!][5]—over and over again until the name "loses its external shell, ceases to be pronounced aloud, and then even to oneself and, 'having merged with breath,' is silently present in the heart of the worshiper."[6] Here is the text of Mandelstam's poem:

Образ твой, мучительный и зыбкий,
Я не мог в тумане осязать.
«Господи!» сказал я по ошибке,
Сам того не думая сказать.

Божье имя, как большая птица,
Вылетело из моей груди.

Впереди густой туман клубится,
И пустая клетка позади…

Your image, agonizing and unstable,
I could not grasp in the fog.
"Lord!" I said by accident,
Myself not thinking to say it.

God's name, like a large bird,
Flew forth from my chest.
Ahead a thick fog billows,
And an empty cage is behind . . .

Paperno gives a lucid explanation of the metaphysical content:

> The impossibility of directly grasping the image of God drives the "I" to the unintended pronunciation of the divine name ("by accident"), i.e. to the violation of a prohibition. Thus is created, even if unintentionally, the situation of the "Jesus prayer." "The divine name" acts in this poem in the form of an independent entity, the real living force which the *imiaslavtsy* saw in it. However [its] pronunciation leads to a disunion with the divine name, present [prebyvaiushchee] in the heart (in the rib "cage"): the name-bird flies from the chest. One can explain this as a depiction of death: . . . the word-bird abandoning the body-cage is drawn from the mythological motif of the bird-soul, flying away from the body. In the last lines, the position of the "I" changes: the "I" as if flies from the chest with the bird-soul (noted by A. K. Zholkovsky). In this way, the pronunciation of the divine name, or the speaking of a "living word," breaking the law of silence, leads to death.[7]

In Paperno's conception, Mandelstam thus polemicizes with the unambiguously positive, theurgic valuation given to pronunciation of the living "word-symbol" in the theoretical works of Bely and Ivanov. However, the poem's dialogue with the Symbolists is more complex, in terms of both its sources and its tone.

The first two lines are plainly Blok-oriented:

Образ твой, мучительный и зыбкий,
Я не мог в тумане осязать.

Your image, agonizing and unstable,
I could not grasp in the fog.

Omry Ronen notes that "Clouds and mist are . . . a conventional symbol of transient events as phenomenon and appearance which obscure the immutable higher truth."[8] However, the first two lines betray a distinctly Blokian approach to this *topos*. They re-enact, in miniature, the archetypal master plot of the "Motionlessness" (Nepodvizhnost') cycle of Blok's *Poems about the Fair Lady*. In that work, the oft-suffering poet strains to grasp and hold onto an image of the Eternal Feminine that is in constant danger of changing and betraying his hopes. This feminine image is simultaneously this-worldly and otherworldly. Similarly, in "Your image, agonizing and unstable," the image of a presumptively female "you," shrouded in fog, pains the poet with its ephemerality. The female gender, while contested by associations with "Gospodi" (Lord) in line three, is strongly implied by the Blokian underpinnings of the entire context and reinforced by a resonance with Mandelstam's poem "You [fem.] passed through a cloud of fog" (Ty proshla skvoz' oblako tumana, 1911), which the poet had intended to publish alongside "Your image, agonizing and unstable" in the journal *The Hyperborean*.[9]

Compare the following examples from Blok, which anticipate the lexicon of "Your image" (*tuman, zybkii*) more precisely than is reflected in these idiomatic translations: "You were veiled by mists" [Tebia skryvali tumany] (I, 200); "Irreparably fog-like—you" [Bezyskhodno tumannaia—ty] (I, 191); "You will read on my brow / About a love unfaithful and unsteady" [Ty prochtesh' na moem chele / O liubvi nevernoi i zybkoi] (I, 242); "I waited in vain . . . Ill, rebellious and morose . . . *I greedily gazed into the mists // But you walked [ever] past*" [. . . tshchetno zhdal . . . Bol'noi, miatezhnyi i ugriumyi . . . *V tumany vsmatrivalsia zhadno. // No mimo prokhodila ty* . . .] (I, 131, my emphasis). And note that, here, Blok, like Mandelstam in "Your image," gives the pronoun in lowercase.

These surface echoes point us toward some deeper connections between "Your image" and the structurally emphasized first and last poems of Blok's original cycle, "Poems about the Fair Lady," published in the almanac *Northern Flowers* ("Severnye Tsvety." Tretii al'manakh knigoizdatel'stva "Skorpion") in 1903. The cycle opens with the poem "I enter dark churches" (Vkhozhu ia v temnye khramy, 1902), in which the lyric "I," awaiting the appearance of his Fair Lady among the flickering of icon lamps, is greeted instead only by a silent icon (*obraz*): "Just an image [or icon], but a dream of Her" [Tol'ko obraz, lish' son o Nei] (I, 240).[10] In the final stanza, however, doubt is cast aside:

О, Святая, как ласковы свечи,
Как отрадны Твои черты! —
Мне не слышны ни вздохи, ни речи,
Но я верю: Милая — Ты.

O, Holy One [fem.], how affectionate are the candles,
How joyous are Your features!—
I hear neither sighs, nor speech,
But I believe: the Sweet One is You.[11]

Blok's ambiguous word flickers on the boundary between this-worldliness and otherworldliness. On the one hand, there is "*But* an image" of Her; on the other, the words "How joyous are *Your* features!" imply a complete identity between the icon (features) and the reality behind it. The "image" that Mandelstam's speaker contemplates stands in an ambiguous and possibly ironic relationship to Blok's prototype, since we do not know whether that which he strives to grasp has divine or secular content, nor, likely, does the speaker himself.[12]

The implicit contrast between these two "images" is amplified through the parallels between "Your image" and the tenth and final poem of Blok's cycle. "I await a call, I seek an answer" (Ia zhdu prizyva, ishchu otveta, 1901) begins, like "Your image," in a state of heightened anticipation. The first stanza represents the plot in a misleadingly condensed form:

Я жду призыва, ищу ответа,
Немеет небо, земля в молчаньи,
За желтой нивой — далёко где-то —
На миг проснулось мое воззванье.

I await a call, I seek an answer,
The sky is mute, the earth in silence,
Past the ochre field—far off somewhere—
For an instant my calling awakened.

The crux of the poem comes in the third stanza:

Я жду — и трепет объемлет новый,
Всё ярче небо, молчанье глуше —
Ночную тайну разрушит слово...
Помилуй, Боже, ночные души!

> I wait—and a new trembling will embrace me,
> The sky is ever brighter, the silence deeper—
> The secret of night will be destroyed by a word . . .
> Have mercy, God, on night souls! (I, 113)

As anticipation lengthens, the silence grows deeper. The speaker feels that a word will destroy the night's secret. However, the tension is too much and he speaks. That spoken word is none other than the divine name: "Have mercy, *God*, on night souls!" In fact, this line may be seen as a bridge between Mandelstam's "Gospodi" and the Jesus prayer: "*Gospodi* Iisuse Khriste, Syne Bozhii, *pomilui* mia greshnogo!" [Lord Jesus Christ, Son of God, have mercy on me, sinner!].¹³ The unfortunate result of that spoken prayer is the non-materialization of the divine call. The lyric "I's" speech returns to him from afar only as an echo of his own words: "beyond the field, somewhere, awoke / As a distant echo my calling" [prosnulos' za nivoi, gde-to, / Dalekim ekhom moe vozzvan'e] (I, 113).

Mandelstam's and Blok's poems thus represent essentially the same scenario. The speaker, unable to withstand the tension and uncertainty of expectation in the dusk/fog, invokes God's name. In Blok's poem, the consequence is a missed opportunity for divine revelation or consummation and a continuation of the "poet's" state of suffering and expectation. Mandelstam's speaker invokes the divine name more unexpectedly and, apparently, with more dire consequences, if indeed the final lines represent, from the soul's perspective, his death.

Mandelstam's image of the Divine as a bird that flies from the poet's chest bringing death is also evocative of Andrei Bely's *The Silver Dove* (*Serebrianyi golub'*, 1910). Throughout Bely's novel, an expectation is developed that the book's hero, Dar'ial'sky, will be killed by a dove-spirit pecking its way out of his chest. (The Dove-child instead emerges from the chest of the sectarian leader, Kudeiarov: "from the chest, just like an egg, a white bird's head is pecking its way out; look—from the bloody, torn up chest, seeping crimson blood [purpurovuiu krovushku tochashchei], a doveling flitted out, as if woven of fog.")¹⁴

Bely's novel, however, lacks a strong connection between the divine spirit, which will burst forth from the chest, killing its host, and the pronunciation of the divine name, the act of taboo speech.¹⁵ In Mandelstam's poem, we have a hint of that direction, which Acmeism will take in its prioritizing of names and elevation of the "word" as "god term." Hence, in Mandelstam's 1915 poem "And to this day at Mount Athos" (I ponyne na Afone), deification of the Name by the *imiaslavtsy* will be called the "beautiful heresy": "The word is pure joyousness, / Healing from world-weariness!" [Slovo—chistoe vesel'e, / Istselen'e ot toski!]. However, as the "image" in Mandelstam's earlier poem retains the *possibility* of an otherworldly referent, so, in this poem, does the author's placement of the word "slovo" [word] at the beginning of a line seem calculated to maintain a potent ontological ambiguity. Is the word capitalized or not, the Word or every word?[16]

In its first publication, on page 21 of the inaugural issue of *The Hyperborean* in 1912, "Your Image" is clearly placed by the editors into dialog with modernist peasant poet Nikolai Kliuev's contemporaneous "Woodsong" (Lesnaia), which was printed on pages 15–19. Kliuev's poem transposes certain Symbolist *topoi* into a peasant-forest context and stylistics. (Note, for instance, the lyric persona as "vitiaz'-skhimnishche" [hero-hermit; the Russian peasant styling and augmentative are untranslatable] or the "gray-haired pine wood" [sedovlasyi bor] that "guards the maiden's tower" [terem storozhit]).[17] However, Kluev's poem retains the semantic matrices and plot mechanisms of Symbolism, particularly apparent in the ending. This finale, which can also be seen as a reworking of Pushkin's "Prophet" (Prorok, 1826), demonstrates well what Mandelstam forewent in "Your Image":

Тут взмахнул мечом светозарный гость,
Рассекал мою клеть телесную,
Выпускал меня словно голубя
Под зенитный круг, в Божьи воздухи,

И открылось мне: Глубина глубин,
Незакатный Свет, только Свет один,

Только громы кругом откликаются,
Только гор альтари озаряются,
Только крылья кругом развеваются.

И звучит над горами: «Победа и Мир!»
В бесконечности духа бессмертия пир.

Here the radiant guest swept up his sword,
Cleft open my corporeal cage,
Released me as if a dove
Up under the circle of the zenith, into the divine airs,

And revealed to me was: the Depth of depths,
Never setting Light, solely Light alone,

Only thunders around me are answering,
Only the altars of the mountains are illuminated,
Only the wings all around flutter and wave.

And over the mountains resounds: "Victory and Peace!"
In the infinity of spirit immortality's feast.[18]

Mandelstam's revision of the Symbolist model is both more subtle and more radical.[19] But what is it that Mandelstam hopes to say in the debate over the nature of the word? The whole truth is in the tone, and the tone, as ever, is tricky.[20] In the first two lines of "Your image," Mandelstam plays upon the "wornness" of Blok's *topoi*, harnessing the failing tension of the Symbolist word to generate tonal ambiguity.[21] Does his "you" belong *only* to this earthly world? Despite the lowercase letter, we cannot be sure.

The ironically intoned third and fourth lines ("'Gospodi!' skazal ia po oshibke, / Sam togo ne dumaia skazat'" ["Lord!" I said by accident, / Myself not thinking to say it]) appear to dissipate the poem's tension, just as the speaker's words had dissipated the night tension in Blok's "I await a call, I seek an answer."[22] For a moment, it seems that the scene is entirely grounded in this world and the word "Gospodi!" is an interjection devoid of its original, in this case, divine, content—precisely the dead shell of a word.[23]

Lines 5 and 6, however, represent yet another reversal. The apparently idiomized "Gospodi" is labeled "divine name" [Bozh'e imia], and, truly alive as in the beliefs of the *imiaslavtsy*, flies forth from the poet's chest of its own volition.

The penultimate line of the poem ("Vperedi gustoi tuman klubitsia") initially appears to return us to the state of expectation experienced at the beginning of the poem, as occurs so often in Blok's poetry of the first book (as well as, specifically, "I await a call"). It would seem that nothing has happened. However, the final line once more defies our expectations. However we choose to read them, the words "And an empty cage is behind" imply a significant change. Whether the emptiness is physical or metaphysical, whether the cage is a rib cage or the world-cage, this line appears to confirm the real, theurgic power of the word. How much more so if this word is fatal! And yet—the speaker is not dead, or at least the awkwardness of positing a ventriloquist-speaker relating his own death is enough to sow a measure of doubt regarding the ontological status of what has just occurred. Cannot emptiness be emotional, death metaphorical? Is the poet not still playing with us?

"Your image, agonizing and unstable" is, of course, serious and ironic simultaneously—hung in the balance between the Symbolist and post-Symbolist word.[24] As I noted in the Introduction, Mandelstam's irony serves to preserve the power of the word in the face of a declining Symbolist poetics. After the destructive irony of the Symbolists' antithesis, direct affirmation of the ideal becomes impossible. However, hints and possibilities become stronger than affirmation. Alongside a "safely" rational, metaphorical reading, analogous to the material explanations given in Romantic fantastic tales, Mandelstam's "Your image, agonizing and unstable" presents the *possibility* of a truly potent and dangerous word. Moreover, it maintains and even advocates for this possibility precisely through only ambiguously undermining the ontology of this "talismanic" word.

INVERTING THE SYMBOLIST HERESIOGRAPHY

> All the permanent—that is only a parable. And the poets lie too much.
> —Friedrich Nietzsche, *Thus Spoke Zarathustra*

While in "Your image, agonizing and unstable" Mandelstam entertains the possibility of a theurgic *word* that can bridge the gap between divine and earthly, in "Pedestrian" he comes down squarely against Symbolist claims to overleap that same precipice *in life*. Instead, on these grounds, Mandelstam, would-be apostate from the Symbolist faith, turns the tables on the *maîtres* and confronts in Symbolism a "religious" heresy.[25] Not surprisingly, since the younger Symbolists' writings bear the distinct mark of Vladimir Solov'ev's theology, Mandelstam's fault finding reads like an inversion of that author's heresiography.

Solov'ev sees the source of all anti-Christian heresies in a denial of the Godmanhood (*bogochelovechestvo*) of Christ: "Such a denial of the God-man, as a true mediator between the divine and creation, lays between these two an impassible abyss."[26] Some heresies recognize only the godly element, others recognize only the flesh, and yet others posit a relation between them other than that which "retains the strength of both conjoining elements at the same time as the completeness of their internal connection."[27]

Godmanhood was understood by Solov'ev as a "dynamic process of reconciliation between creation and Creator, leading to 'spiritualized matter' and 'embodied spirit.'" Through Solov'ev's teachings this implicitly Christological concept, transformed to describe a "creative tension leading to, but not synonymous with *theosis* [deification of humanity, S.G.]," had a formative impact on the nature of Symbolist gnosis and life-creation and on how the younger Symbolists, including Blok, conceived the relationship between the this-worldly and the otherworldly.[28]

When Ivanov came to define "heresy" in "On Sect and on Dogma" (O sekte i o dogmate, 1914), he was to use as his quintessential example the recognition, by the Church Fathers at the first Ecumenical Council, of the related doctrine of consubstantiality (*homoousia*, the belief that the Son is "of the same substance" as the Father) and the repudiation of the opposite, heretical doctrine, *homoiousia* (like essence).[29] For the mythopoetic Symbolists, the consubstantiality and two-in-one-ness of Christ provide the model for the coexistence of the divine and the mundane in the phenomenal world. Hence, disjointedness (*bessviaznost'*) is the directing essence of the contemporary, infirm soul,[30] and mimesis, analogous to *homoiousia*, is "the original sin of art."[31]

For Solov'ev, the most complete of heresies is that anti-Christian religion, Islam, which recognizes a prophet in Christ but denies the incarnation and affirms instead "a God alien to humanity, an inhuman [*beschelovechnyi*] God."[32] Islam betrays a "deep internal connection" to Christian heresies, and particularly the heresy of iconoclasm, which, according to Solov'ev, implicitly denies the material element of the incarnate divine (icons of Christ) and the possibility of flesh taking on divinity (*obozhenie*) (icons of the saints).[33]

> Believing in a Christian God and recognizing Christian law, the majority of eastern Christians all their lives tended toward another pole. They did not live by the law of their faith. [Solov'ev refers to their failure to fuse the divine and material in life, S.G.] Islam concludes from this the bankruptcy of the law itself and gives another, more executable law. In light of our impotence to bring into being the God manly life, Islam doesn't even have pretensions to internal unification with the deity . . .[34]

These last lines could easily describe, from a Symbolist perspective, the Acmeists' distaste for Symbolism's attempts to breach the divide between the divine and the worldly.

Mandelstam's discourse on the Symbolist heresy in "Peshekhod" turns out to have an entirely fortuitous connection to Islamic heresiography, which is founded, like Acmeist doctrine, on archetypal principles diametrically opposed to those of Solov'ev—namely, the mutual separation of divine and worldly spheres in a post-prophetic age. One influential heretical group among Muslims of early modern Iran

> envisaged divinity as incarnated (*hulūl*) in humans, with each believer an earthly god who is able to connect with the holy personally through pro-

phetic inspiration, illumination or permeation. They believed in the dual and yet integrated existence of spirit and matter and in the human potential to transcend matter and access the divine while on earth.[35]

This dispute is clearly distant from the Russian context and would not merit a mention, especially given the similarity of the orthodox Islamic position to Protestant views of the post-revelation world (as in Mandelstam's "Lutheran"), were it not for a particularly apt turn of phrase. Islamic heresiographers referred pejoratively to these ecstatics as "exaggerators" (*ghulāt*).[36]

Exaggeration turns out to be a highly productive category for looking at "Pedestrian," in which the Symbolist "crosser-over" is depicted as a teller of tall tales. The title, "Peshekhod," does double service, referring both to the striding wayfarer of the second stanza and to the lyric hero, who is content to walk, rather than fly. The translation, "Pedestrian," should be understood in the context of an earlier English usage, for instance: "Professor Blackie in his younger years was a great pedestrian, and he used to boast that there was not a mountain in Scotland on top of which he had not been" (1895).[37]

Пешеход
М. Л. Лозинскому

Я чувствую непобедимый страх
В присутствии таинственных высот;
Я ласточкой доволен в небесах
И колокольни я люблю полет!

И, кажется, старинный пешеход,
Над пропастью, на гнущихся мостках,
Я слушаю — как снежный ком растет
И вечность бьет на каменных часах.

Когда бы так! Но я не путник тот,
Мелькающий на выцветших листах,
И подлинно во мне печаль поет;

Действительно лавина есть в горах!
И вся моя душа — в колоколах —
Но музыка от бездны не спасет!

Pedestrian
M. L. Lozinskii

I feel an insurmountable fear
In the presence of mysterious heights;
I'm happy with a swallow in the heavens,
And it's the bell tower's flight I love!

And, it seems, old-time pedestrian
Above the abyss, on boards that give,
I listen as a snowball grows
And a stone clock strikes eternity.

If only! But I am not that wayfarer,
Flitting by on faded pages,
And genuinely sorrow sings within me;

Truly there is an avalanche in the mountains!
And all my soul is—in bells—
But music will not save from the void!

With the exception of the concluding line, Mandelstam's differences with Symbolism in this poem can be categorized as differences of degree. The bell tower of line 4, even if it is firmly planted on the ground, still probes the heavens' substance ("it's the bell tower's *flight* I love!"). Nor is it likely coincidental that both of these images—the swallow and the bell tower—betray subtle connections to the otherworldly.[38] In addition, the exaggerated drama of the second stanza is cast as something nominally desirable, if impossible. "If only!" exclaims the speaker.

Most importantly, the speaker contrasts the reality of his own metaphysical existence with "that wayfarer" [putnik tot] in terms that belie specifically the latter's dishonesty or exaggeration: "And *genuinely* sorrow sings within me; / *Truly* there is an avalanche in the mountains!" [I *podlinno* vo mne pechal' poet; / *Deistvitel'no* lavina est' v gorakh!; emphasis mine]. Symbolist sadness is alive and well in Mandelstam. The mountains do threaten an avalanche, but not the doomsday chime of eternity, nor the immense snowball, which mark the traveler as an exaggerator, or simply a teller of tall tales.[39]

Ivanov sees as a prerequisite of creation, "which we call Symbolist," that state "when 'there is no barrier' between us and 'the bared abyss,' opening—

in Silence."[40] This foundation of Symbolist creation, the unmediated experience of the abyss, is still a part of "Pedestrian." The abyss that threatens the speaker, while not physical, is quite real, in stark contrast to that which gapes from the opposite page in "Casino," and which serves only as a sort of Symbolist misnomer for the physical ocean outside the window.[41]

Even the speaker's insistence that "music will not save from the void" does not imply a rejection of Symbolist theory. Why should music bring salvation *from the abyss* if music is tied to Dionysian ecstasy and anti-individuation?[42] What has changed is rather the desirability of this encounter. In fact, in these final two lines, Mandelstam underscores his own connection with the Romantic poet Fedor Tiutchev, Ivanov's prototypical Symbolist, as Ivanov himself reads him: "But Dionysus is more powerful, in Tiutchev's soul, than Apollo, and the poet *must save himself from his enchantment at the altar of Apollo.*"[43] In "Pedestrian," the poet turns away from Symbolism as artistic method not because he doubts the verity of the fundamental postulates of Symbolist theory, but because the Symbolists themselves have not followed these postulates to their logical conclusions, have not been honest in the face of their "abyss," and because he himself is not capable of such a feat.

Dimitrii Segal notes the possibility that Mandelstam polemicizes in "Pedestrian" against Mikhail Lozinsky's poem "Wayfarer" (Putnik, 1908). Lekmanov, while analyzing the more compelling echo of Mandelstam's poem in Lozinsky's apparent reply, "There is in the world a music of windless heights" (Est' v mire muzyka bezvetrennykh vysot, 1913), repeats this claim in passing, calling "Pedestrian" "an attempt to convert Lozinsky to Acmeism."[44] However, one can hardly consider "Pedestrian" a polemic against or even a dialogue with Lozinsky's poem, and one should not seek in Lozinsky the prototype of Mandelstam's traveler.[45] Certain evidence hints rather forcefully that if Mandelstam addresses Lozinsky here, he addresses him only indirectly—through a polemic against some third person, whom he has depicted in his wayfarer.[46] The epithet "faded" [vytsvetshie] for "pages" [listy], used to refer to the as-yet-unpublished poetry of his friend, would sound rather like derogatory dull (*bleklye*), while the phrase "*that* wayfarer" [putnik *tot*] implies a third party. True, the poet Vladimir Shileiko associated Lozinsky with things antiquated, but this was in texts written later than "Pedestrian."[47]

In "Dva soneta Mandel'shtama i dve interpretatsii," Ronen sketches the poem's cultural backdrop, citing a whole collection of "thematic subtexts" united by the "motifs of avalanche and landslide as answer to heroic religious quest." Among these texts, Henrik Ibsen's *Brand* stands out. *Brand* clearly deserves our most scrupulous attention, particularly given the echoes of this play in Mandelstam's "Falling is the constant companion of fear."[48] It should be noted that Brand's desire to erase the boundaries between religion and life, his austerity and unwillingness to compromise, his preaching of sacrifice and aspiration for physical ascension to the ideal made him a paragon for many at the turn of the century, particularly among the mythopoetic Symbolists, who attempted to emulate precisely these traits.[49]

Ronen also mentions as a potential model for the wayfarer of "Pedestrian" Mandelstam's contemporary Pavel Nikolaevich Batiushkov, whose mundane mysticism is described by Bely in his memoirs *The Beginning of the Century* (Nachalo veka). However, it seems likely that in Mandelstam's wayfarer we see the shadow not of Batiushkov, but of Bely himself, whom Mandelstam here confronts with Bely's own pervasive subtext—Friedrich Nietzsche.[50] Note that Mandelstam later underscores the insincerity of Bely in his review of the latter's *Notes of an Eccentric* (Zapiski chudaka, 1922), where he writes that "a lack of measure and tact, a lack of taste—is falsehood" and that "if a person experiences colossal spiritual catastrophes three times a day [. . .] we have the right not to believe him" (II, 423). Lekmanov notes an allusion in this same review to nineteenth-century prose master Nikolai Gogol's paradigmatic liar, Khlestakov.[51]

The primary subtext of Mandelstam's dialogue with Bely is the poetic cycle "To Briusov" (Briusovu) from Bely's *Urn* (1909). The poem "Meeting" (Vstrecha), depicting a clash with magus-Briusov on an icy peak, begins: "Mists, chasms and grottoes . . . / As into the air, I ascend to insurmountable heights" [Tumany, propasti i groty . . . / Kak v vozdukh, podnimaius' ia / V nepobedimye vysoty]. These final words are transformed by Mandelstam into "insurmountable fear / In the presence of mysterious heights" [nepobedimyi strakh / V prisutstvii tainstvennykh vysot]. In the same poem by Bely, an avalanche (*lavina*) and snowball (*kom*) also make an appearance:

И катится над головой —

Тяжеловесная лавина,
Но громовой, летящий ком
Оскаленным своим жерлом
Съедает мертвая стремнина.

And over head rolls—

A weighty avalanche,
But the thundery, speeding mass of snow [snowball]

> Is swallowed up by the maw
> Of the dead slope.⁵²

The image of the poet's passage over the abyss, borrowed from Nietzsche's *Thus Spoke Zarathustra*, was one of Bely's favorites. It appears as the deflated image of the epigones of Symbolism in "Stamped Galosh" (Shtempelevannaia kalosha, 1907), but also in an elevated form in "Symbolism as a Worldview":

> *Eternity* [Vechnost'] will bare its teeth. Its maws will gape, threatening to swallow. The blinding gold of Nietzscheanism, *a striding along the summits* [shaganie po vershinam], is something wild, *ancient* [drevnee], which calls the Titans from Tartarus.⁵³

Indeed, it is not out of the question that Mandelstam's main target in "Pedestrian" was in fact the following specific swat at the Petersburg literary scene by Bely in "Stamped Galosh" (republished in *Arabesques* in 1911): "An abyss is the necessary condition of *comfort* for the *Petersburg* writer. Ah, this delightful abyss! It frightens only *Muscovites* and provincials who are used to taking *seriously* the chasms of the spirit."⁵⁴ One might imagine how Mandelstam, in "Pedestrian," defends the honor of the Petersburg Symbolists, a group to which not only he, but also Lozinsky, belongs, parrying: the abyss *scares* me, I take it *seriously*—but *you*?!

In his essay "F. Nietzsche" (F. Nitsshe, 1907), Bely directly quotes the magician from the "Song of Melancholy" in *Zarathustra* and appropriates the images of bridge and abyss. Mandelstam reunites these images with that element of Nietzsche's conception which Bely ignores—falsehood:

> "Suitor of truth?" they mocked me; "you?"
> "No! Only poet!
> An animal, cunning, preying, prowling,
> That must lie,
> That wittingly, willingly must lie [. . .]
> *This*, the suitor of truth?
> No! Only fool! Only poet!
> Only speaking colorfully,
> Only screaming colorfully out of fools' masks,
> Climbing around on mendacious word bridges,
> On colorful rainbows,
> Between false heavens
> And false earths . . .⁵⁵

In "Pedestrian," the Symbolists are unmasked as "exaggerators," false theurgists, scrambling across rickety word bridges. However, the metaphysical longing that drives them forward retains its hold on the poet. Is it not the danger of this attraction and the abyss that gapes beyond it that push Mandelstam to seek, in the nascent, Apollonian faith of Acmeism, a foundation that can structure the chaos of his soul?[56]

STUMBLING INTO A NEW POETICS

The remarkable edifice of Mandelstam's "Notre Dame" (1912) and the prose of "The Morning of Acmeism" (1913–14?) present the reader with a harmonious and inherently dynamic vision of the Gothic. However, if we look at Mandelstam's earlier essay "François Villon" (1910), we see two competing aspects of Gothic art, which is characterized not only by the dynamic equilibrium seen in architecture (physical and social), but also by a detachment of poetry from life, an artificial "hothouse atmosphere" of fragile allegory, which links medieval poetry to French Symbolism.

"Falling is the constant companion of fear" (1912) is at the nexus of this clash. Like the Gothic, images and conceptions such as stone, flame, and eternity function in the poem at an ambivalent crossroads between Mandelstam's Symbolist and Acmeist poetics. Later, and less charitably than in "François Villon," where he makes clear that they are not simply "dead abstractions," Mandelstam will characterize these concepts thus:

> The last five or six Symbolist words, like five evangelical fish, weighed down the basket: among them a big fish: "Existence."
>
> You couldn't feed hungry time with them, and one had to ditch [. . .] all five, and with them the big, lifeless fish "Existence."
>
> At the end of a historical era, abstract concepts always reek of rotten fish. (II, 104)

Rather than discarding these abstractions, however, Mandelstam transforms them, generating for them new roots and new associations. "Falling" is a record of this dynamic process:

> Паденье—неизменный спутник страха,
> И самый страх есть чувство пустоты.
> Кто камни к нам бросает с высоты —
> И камень отрицает иго праха?

И деревянной поступью монаха
Мощеный двор когда-то мерил ты —
Булыжники и грубые мечты —
В них жажда смерти и тоска размаха...

Так проклят будь, готический приют,
Где потолком входящий обморочен
И в очаге веселых дров не жгут!

Немногие для вечности живут;
Но, если ты мгновенным озабочен,
Твой жребий страшен и твой дом непрочен!

Falling is the constant companion of fear,
And fear itself is a feeling of emptiness.
Who throws us stones from on high—
And a stone denies the yoke of dust?

And with the wooden gait of a monk
You measured the paved courtyard—
Cobblestones and crude dreams—
In them are thirst for death and a pining for abandon ...

So, be damned, Gothic refuge,
Where he who enters is befuddled by the ceiling,
And merry logs aren't burned in the hearth!

Few live for eternity;
But if you are preoccupied with the momentary,
Your lot is frightening and your house unsound.

In this poem, one entirely consistent and meaningful semantic plane serves as an extended conceit for a second, equally profound one. To truly understand Mandelstam's discourse of struggle with Symbolism in "Falling," we must first explore the poem's primary discourse of ambivalent faith.

While only Margolina has attempted to look at "Falling" as an essentially religious poem, Ronen also comments on the religious sense of the first stanza, noting a matrix of biblical and other subtexts for the *topos* of the stone in Mandelstam's early poetry. I will breach this well-traveled material again, and briefly relate the poetic evidence of the poet's earlier struggle with faith both because this context is crucial to understanding the poem and in hopes of further clarifying some of the inherent logical and semantic ties.⁵⁷

By Mandelstam's own admission, he was "raised in a nonreligious environment (family and school)" and had long "striven toward religion, hopelessly and platonically—but more and more consciously of late."⁵⁸ Those words were written in 1908 to Vladimir Gippius, himself the representative of an "antagonistic essence"—"religious culture, I don't know whether Christian or not, but in any case religious."⁵⁹ The climax of the poet's crisis of faith appears to have come in 1910, the year before his conversion to Methodism.⁶⁰ In a triptych of poems from this year united around the figure of a reed sinking into or rising out of a deep pool, Mandelstam cryptically depicts the conflict between his Jewish roots and his adopted Christian, Russian culture.⁶¹ In other poems from the same year, the lyric persona compares himself to a snake, crawling to the foot of the cross in an empty church ("When the grasses of the mosaics droop" [Kogda mozaik niknut travy]) and is "annihilated, deafened" by the bells of ancient churches, left without prayers or words ("When the bells' reproach" [Kogda ukor kolokolov]).

Among the poems of 1910, "Falling" is most profoundly anticipated by "A black crucifix on the headboard" (V izgolov'e chernoe raspiat'e), in which the poet's ship-soul, raised on breakers of evangelical Latin, is threatened by Fedor Tiutchev's "submerged rock of faith" [podvodnyi kamen' very]. Confronted with the cross, a symbol of belief, the lyric persona finds itself empty:

В изголовье черное распятье,
В сердце жар и в мыслях пустота —

A black crucifix [hangs] on the headboard,
[There is] fever in the heart and emptiness in the mind—

However, he is drawn to the church through its aesthetic and sensual manifestations:

Ах, зачем на стеклах дым морозный
Так похож на мозаичный сон!
. . .
И слова евангельской латыни
Прозвучали, как морской прибой.

Oh, why is the frosty mist on the windows
So like a mosaic dream!

. . .
And the words of the Gospels' Latin
Resounded like the crashing of the sea.⁶²

This results in the uplift of belief:

> И волной нахлынувшей святыни
> Поднят был корабль безумный мой…
>
> And on a surging wave of sanctity
> My mad ship was raised . . .

However, faith constructed upon emptiness leads to fear (as we will see below, not unwarranted): "I fear the 'submerged rock of faith.'" Thus, Mandelstam establishes the (corner)stone as an emblem of the threatening call to faith, connects it explicitly to Tiutchev (emphasizing its dialogic character with quotation marks and the only authorial footnote in his early poetry) and transfers it from a poem spoken from a position of faith to a poem spoken in crisis.⁶³

In light of this longstanding personal drama, the first two lines of "Falling" read not as platitudes, but as an axiom tested in the waters of personal experience:⁶⁴

> Паденье — неизменный спутник страха,
> И самый страх есть чувство пустоты.
>
> Falling is the constant companion of fear,
> And fear itself is a feeling of emptiness.

Faith built upon emptiness entails fear, which leads inexorably to falling.

The final line of the first quatrain is marked by a crucial ambivalence of tone upon which the whole sense of the poem depends:

> Кто камни к нам бросает с высоты —
> И камень отрицает иго праха?
>
> Who throws us stones from on high—
> And a stone denies the yoke of dust?

This line can be read, on the one hand, as confirmation of the redemptive potential of the cornerstone, the "'stone which the builders rejected' that 'is become the head of the corner,'"—that is, as a continuation of the preceding line. There, the unexpected collocation "Who throws *us* stones from on high" [Kto kamni *k nam* brosaet s vysoty]—"k nam" ([to] us), not "v nas" (at us) or "na nas" (onto us)—transforms the threat naturally associated with stones thrown from on high, and they begin to sound like life buoys or a rope. However, it is also possible to read the fourth line in a contrasting tone—of mild or strong incredulity as to this potential ("And a stone *denies* the yoke of dust?" [I kamen' *otritsaet* igo prakha?]).[65]

As is apparent in "A black crucifix," Mandelstam sees the cornerstone as much from the perspective of unbeliever (stumbling block) as believer (sanctuary): "Everyone who falls on that stone will be broken to pieces, but he on whom it falls will be crushed" (Luke 20:18). It is only through the mediation of 1 Peter that Mandelstam ultimately arrives at a new "Acmeist" understanding of the word-stone:[66]

> Like newborn babies, come to love the pure verbal milk [vozliubite chistoe slovesnoe moloko], so that by it you may grow up into salvation [. . .] As you come to Him, the living stone [. . .] build of yourselves too, like living stones, a spiritual house [i sami, kak zhivye kamni, ustroiaite iz sebia dom dukhovnyi] [. . .] And so, for you, believers, this Stone is precious. But for the faithless [. . .] "a stumbling block and rock of temptation," on which they stumble, not submitting to the word [pretykaiutsia, ne pokoriaias' slovu] [. . .]. (1 Peter 2:2–8, literal translation of Russian Synodal text)

Those *who love the pure verbal milk,* who *submit to the word,* will be formed into a spiritual house, the living stones of which presage the image of the medieval *socium* in "François Villon":

> He, who first proclaimed in architecture the dynamic equilibrium of masses and built a groined arch, brilliantly expressed the psychological essence of Feudalism. Medieval man considered himself just as indispensable and integral to the world's edifice as any stone in a Gothic construction, bearing with dignity the weight of its neighbors and entering, as an unavoidable calculation, into the common play of forces. (II, 308)

This image of human stones in the socium links 1 Peter to Mandelstam's mature conception, in "The Morning of Acmeism," of words as stones in the dynamic equilibrium of a "groined arch." Those word-stones, in turn, have as their prototype a Word-Stone that is indeed understood as Tiutchev's stone from "Problème" (as Mandelstam directly states), but only after "Problème" has been strongly re-read (in the Bloomian sense) through the prism of the Book of Daniel, which previously existed as a potential reading but is now raised to a dominance not consonant with the tone of Tiutchev's poem.[67] In "Falling," we see not a reflection of this intensely idiosyncratic reading of Tiutchev's "Problème," but a synchronic snapshot of the development of this semantic field in Mandelstam's poetry.

In the figure of the monk in stanza two, Mandelstam embodies the contradictions of weak faith. The traditional, emblematic pose of a pacing monk is with head bowed. This downward gaze ("Cobblestones and crude dreams") is contrasted to the properly upward direction of a monk's thoughts. But, even when looking up, faith is not reaffirmed, for in the Gothic refuge, "he, who enters, is befuddled by the ceiling." As Gogol wrote,

> Stepping into the sacred darkness [mrak] of this church ... having raised one's eyes upward, where one above another, one above another, the lancet arches are lost, intersecting, and there is no end to them—it is perfectly natural to feel in one's soul the involuntary terror of the presence of sanctity, which the bold mind of man dares not even touch.[68]

Not only vertiginous height but also pictorial representations of the last judgment, adorning the ceiling, may have obfuscated one unsure of his beliefs.[69] The warming, worldly flames of Mandelstam's longed-for hearth (line 11) bear an implicit contrast to the purifying or, worse yet, damning flames of biblical judgment.

The first line of the last tercet effectively confirms the fact that the lyric hero does not set himself among those who are able to live for the sake of eternity.[70] To live for the moment, however, is also bankrupt. The answer to this predicament is to be sought outside of the dichotomy of belief and unbelief. It lies in Tiutchev's stone and the gay flames of the hearth, in the transformation of religion into culture.

Symbolism too, however, can be understood as a religion, another faith that generates complicated feelings of attraction and doubt in Mandelstam. A letter from Mandelstam to Viacheslav Ivanov, written in August 1909, provides us with a basis to understand the words "Gothic refuge" in the first tercet as a reference not only to a physical structure (church), but also to Symbolism itself, and, in particular, to that philosophy of Symbolism systematically expounded in Ivanov's *By the Stars*. "Allow me first a few words about your book," Mandelstam wrote:

It seems to me it can't be challenged—it's captivating—and destined to win hearts.

Can it be that stepping under the vaults of Notre Dame, one ponders the truth of Catholicism and does not become Catholic simply by force of his presence under these vaults?

It's just that it seemed to me that the book is too—how should one put it—round, without corners.

You can't get at it from any side, to smash it or smash oneself on it.[71]

In this light, the richly suggestive "obmorochen" [befuddled], from the first tercet of "Falling," should be understood in the sense of having a spell put on one, being under someone's deceptive charms.[72] To enter Notre Dame is to be a Catholic; to read *By the Stars* is to be a Symbolist. With the oath "So, be damned" [Tak prokliat bud'], Mandelstam attempts to break the spell, since to smash the system, as did Villon and Verlaine, is impossible: "You can't get at it from any side, to smash it or smash oneself on it."

Virtually every element of the poem reads quite naturally as a reference to the poetry of the Symbolists. In the first stanza, this referentiality is perceptible in the image of falling,[73] the emptiness which is its cause,[74] and the apocalyptic and theurgic pathos with which the "yoke of dust," imposed upon mankind by God in Genesis 4:19, is rejected. The image of the monk also lends itself to interpretation as an allusion to the Symbolists.[75] The younger Symbolists often referred to themselves as monks,[76] and Mandelstam himself calls Ivan Konevskoi and Alexander Dobroliubov, members of the older generation, "militant young monks of early Symbolism" (II, 99). In "Falling," the younger Symbolists' "faithful gait" [pokhodka vernaia],[77] the necessarily repetitious faithfulness of their vigil, is transformed into a mechanical circling of the monastery courtyard ("wooden stride" [dereviannaia postup']).

The expression "Cobblestones and crude dreams" [Bulyzhniki i grubye mechty] can be seen as an almost allegorically exact re-encoding of "kamen' pretykaniia i soblazna" (literally, a stone of stumbling and temptation). At the same time, in the Symbolist-monastic context, "crude dreams" evokes the *topos* of sinful desire for the Virgin Mary. The "monk's" downward gaze seeks to avoid the tripping stone of faith at the same time that his desire defiles his sanctuary. Finally, while a "thirst for death" characterizes much of early Symbolism, one cannot help also being reminded, in the line "a thirst for death and pining for abandon" [zhazhda smerti i toska razmakha], of Blok's Gypsy motifs—"Smash life like my wine glass!" [Zhizn' razbei, kak moi bokal!].[78]

The Symbolists are implicated in the tercets, as well. For the Symbolists, fire was always the carefully tended flames of hieratical devotion, the flames of universal conflagration, or the sacrificial pyre.[79] Mandelstam implicitly contrasts these flames of mandatory martyrdom with the merry warmth of the hearth.

The love affair of the younger Symbolists with eternity hardly needs illustration. They are implicitly contrasted in the final tercet to the older Symbolists, bearers of a similar affection for the instant, which embodied "the highest degree of life's intensity."[80] It is of course no surprise that the house of these older *decadent* poets is doomed to fall. As Lekmanov has noted, the key point of reference here is Edgar Allan Poe's "The Fall of the House of Usher," which, it should be noted, allegorizes the demise of an effete and degenerate aristocracy.[81]

In relation to the Symbolist faith, as in the purely religious reading above, line 4 of "Falling" can take on a distinctly separate, incredulous, or ironic tone. In addition, the interplay between the plural "stones" [kamni] in line 3 and the singular "stone" [kamen'] in line 4—both scan identically—reinforces the sense of paradox already implicit in "a *stone* denies the yoke of *dust?*" Our senses send us multiple revelations, a meteoric shower of impressions, inspirations, and fears, yet we are called on to believe in one absolute and unchangeable Logos. This contrast of variegation and unity is a fine analogy for, on the one hand, the contradiction between the vague religious feelings described in Mandelstam's letter to Vladimir Gippius of 14 (27) April 1908 ("worship of 'Pan,' i.e. an uncomprehended [nesoznannyi] God") and the threat to accept the revealed God; and, on the other, the conflict between the variegated and multivalent world of Acmeist poetics and the unidirectional pull of the Symbolist worldview and image system (as the Acmeists saw it).[82]

In the end, it is the poem's composition that provides the strongest argument, other than Mandelstam's subsequent remarks in "The Morning of Acmeism," for finding in lines 3–4 of "Falling," alongside the author's incredulity, a positive conception of the word-stone as a potential source of relief from "the yoke of dust." "Pedestrian" and "Falling" are constructed on almost identical compositional principles: a two-line introduction outlining a problem, followed by what is, in "Pedestrian," clearly a constructive, if not entirely unambiguous, solution in the next two lines; a negative second quatrain that expands the problem introduced in the first two lines through its portrayal of a personage of ambiguous relation to the lyric "I"; a strongly voiced four-syllable objection that opens the tercets; and a conclusion voicing the speaker's still ambivalent position. The apex of constructive thought in "Pedestrian" comes in lines 3–4. We are free to expect it in the same place in "Falling."

Ultimately, the lyric "I" in "Falling" remains within the grasp of the irreconcilable contradictions of the Romantic/Symbolist consciousness—torn between faith and doubt, the eternal and the momentary, the uplifting and the base. These extremes are contested in the poem only by Tiutchev's stone and the flame of the hearth. This, however, is enough for Mandelstam to set about building the solid edifice of a new poetic system, which will transform the language of his predecessors.

In "Falling," Mandelstam salvages at least two of the Symbolist "evangelical fish." Vladimir Gippius's beloved rhyme, *plamen'*—*kamen'* [flame—stone] ("In a Fur Coat above His Station"), tantalizingly hidden between the lines of Mandelstam's poem, points the way to a new, as yet untested, poetics.

STEALING THE SANCTUARY

In "Falling," Symbolism retains a tight hold on the poet—so tight, it seems, that only with a curse can he break free. "Hagia-Sophia," the final poem at the Symbolist reaches of the pendulum's swing, presents a stark contrast to this enduring dependency. To conclude this chapter, I will very briefly consider Mandelstam's poem in the context of his struggles to transcend the Symbolist "faith."

Айя-София

Айя-София—здесь остановиться
Судил Господь народам и царям!
Ведь купол твой, по слову очевидца,
Как на цепи, подвешен к небесам.

И всем пример — года Юстиниана,
Когда похитить для чужих богов
Позволила эфесская Диана
Сто семь зеленых мраморных столбов.

Куда ж стремился твой строитель щедрый,
Когда, душой и помыслом высок,
Расположил апсиды и экседры,
Им указав на запад и восток?

Прекрасен храм, купающийся в мире,
И сорок окон — света торжество;
На парусах, под куполом, четыре
Архангела прекраснее всего.

И мудрое сферическое зданье
Народы и века переживет,
И серафимов гулкое рыданье
Не покоробит темных позолот.

Hagia-Sophia

Hagia-Sophia—here the Lord ordained
Peoples and emporers to halt!
Your dome is, after all, in the word of a witness,
Dangled from the heavens as on a chain.

The years of Justinian are an example to all,
When Ephesian Diana allowed
One hundred seven columns of green marble
To be abducted for foreign gods.

But whither strove your generous builder
When, lofty of soul and of design,
He laid out the apses and exhedras,
Having directed them West and East?

Beautiful is the church, bathing in the world,
And forty windows—a triumph of light;
On the spandrels, under the cupola, four
Archangels most beautiful of all.

And the wise, spherical building
Will outlive peoples and ages,
And the resonant wailing of the seraphim
Will not warp the dark gilding.

There are many elements tying "Hagia-Sophia" to what might be termed an abstract, conditionally Symbolist pole in Mandelstam's art. To those two explicitly mentioned in Clare Cavanagh's elegant reading (the cathedral's name, connected with Solov'evian thought, and its spherical shape, evoking Mandelstam's description of Viacheslav Ivanov's *By the Stars*) one might add a number of additional connections easily extrapolated from her analysis: a disjunction from history and connection to eternity, the "disembodied flight" of seraphim and archangels, the function of the cathedral's dome as analogue to and microcosm of the heavenly dome, and the "chain" that links Hagia-Sophia, in a simile, to the heavens—a metaphorical embodiment of the Symbolists' concept of "connection" *(sviaz')*.[83] These elements are balanced by opposing tendencies in the poem but still stand to distinguish "Hagia-Sophia" from the essentially Acmeist "Notre Dame," in which "style as a system of antitheses" corresponds to "the description of the Gothic as a system of counterforces."[84]

Inside Hagia-Sophia, the lyric hero finds not a system of counterforces, raising to impossible heights the monstrous mass of the cathedral's walls at the will of the architect-creator, but rather ancient wisdom and "the resonant wailing of seraphim" [serafimov gulkoe rydan'e].[85] Still, Mandelstam, while not parting with the expansiveness and profundity of the Symbolist inner abyss, frames this abyss within the bounds of an Acmeist poem.[86] Inside these tightly constructed verses, with their classical form and elegant exposition, stand the firm walls of the church. And this girding is sound: "the resonant wailing of the seraphim / Will not warp the dark gilding" [serafimov gulkoe rydan'e / Ne pokorobit temnykh pozolot].

Symbolist Wisdom (Sophia) has been kidnapped and is now forced to serve Acmeism, providing the new poetics with inner depth, just as the columns of the temple of Ephesian Diana, "kidnapped" by Justinian, serve as the structural support for a Christian cathedral (and later still for a mosque). The Symbolist heritage is not devalued and will continue to retain its place in Mandelstam's poetics. The assuredness of the poem's tone makes it possible to speak here not of criticism of Symbolist poetics, or of competing claims, but of the outright appropriation of the Symbolist sanctuary.

PART III

CHAPTER 6

BEDSIDE WITH THE SYMBOLIST HERO

> You will say . . . that Aratov's dark passion grows, that here is a whole tragedy . . . Oh, no—it is a mirage. Not passion grows, but sickness . . .
>
> —Innokenty Annensky, "The Dying Turgenev"

> Сонет, несущий смерть
> [A sonnet bearing death]
> —Konstantin Bal'mont

"[. . .] Futurism should have directed its attack [ostrie] not against the paper fortress of Symbolism, but against the living and truly dangerous Blok" (II, 348), wrote Mandelstam.[1] It is tempting, in interpreting this statement, to echo the oft-repeated truism that Mandelstam's critical prose speaks as much of the poet as of his professed subject. But Mandelstam did direct his poetic rapier, his Acmeist point, against Blok in a series of poems from 1912.[2] These include "I shudder from the cold," "Your image, agonizing and unstable," "Barrel Organ" (Sharmanka) and, especially, "Let, in the stuffy room where there are clumps of gray cotton" (Pust' v dushnoi komnate, gde kloch'ia seroi vaty), published in *The Hyperborean* no. 8 (1912) and not included in the poet's collections during his lifetime.

"Let, in the stuffy room" can be read as Mandelstam's attempt to do away with the overpowering presence of Blok's lyric hero, the source of the older poet's charismatic power.³ Mandelstam accomplishes this through an intricate juxtaposition, at the level of subtext, of competing models of death and a deflation of that model flaunted by Blok:

> Пусть в душной комнате, где клочья серой ваты
> И стклянки с кислотой, часы хрипят и бьют —
> Гигантские шаги, с которых петли сняты, —
> В туманной памяти виденья оживут.
>
> И лихорадочный больной, тоской распятый,
> Худыми пальцами свивая тонкий жгут,
> Сжимает свой платок, как талисман крылатый,
> И с отвращением глядит на круг минут...
>
> То было в сентябре, вертелись флюгера,
> И ставни хлопали — но буйная игра
> Гигантов и детей пророческой казалась,
>
> И тело нежное — то плавно подымалось,
> То грузно падало: средь пестрого двора
> Живая карусель без музыки вращалась!

> Let, in the stuffy room, where there are clumps of gray cotton
> And phials of acid, the clock wheeze and strike—
> Giant steps from which the loops are stripped—
> In foggy memory, visions will come to life.
>
> And the feverish patient, crucified with grief,⁴
> Thin fingers twisting a fine braid,
> Squeezes his kerchief like a winged talisman,
> And looks with disgust upon the circle of minutes . . .
>
> That was in September. Weathervanes twirled
> And shutters banged—but the raucous game
> Of giants and children seemed prophetic,
>
> And the tender body now smoothly rose
> Now cumbrously fell: amid the motley courtyard
> A living carousel spun without music!

"Let, in the stuffy room" is yet another sonnet, a form Mandelstam used extremely rarely, but at least five times in 1912, in poems as critically important to his poetic path as "No, not the moon" (most likely the tercets of a sonnet),[5] "Pedestrian," and "Casino." *All* of the sonnets of 1912, in one way or another, dramatize Mandelstam's "overcoming" of the Symbolist heritage.

The key image that explains the connection between the portrait of the ill figure in the quatrains of "Let, in the stuffy room" and the scene that is played out in the tercets is the *gigantskie shagi*—that is, a fair attraction or yard game that consists of "a contraption in the shape of a pole with a spinning toppiece, to which are attached long ropes with loops on the ends."[6] "Holding onto them, those at play run up and swing around the pole."[7] Presumably, the impression of the striking clock provokes in our ill hero the details of the scene played out in the tercets, which depict the visions that issue forth from foggy memory in expanded form. Once we begin to picture children leaping around a carnival pole, these last two stanzas are not difficult to decode. However, the unusual syntax of the first stanza implies an equality between the *gigantskie shagi* and the striking clock. There are two levels at which the comparison potentially takes place.

On the one hand, the clockface, with its spinning hands, perhaps resembles this contraption, with ropes extended (the clock hands) but without the loops.[8] As Georgii Levinton has pointed out, however, this visual association is rather absurd: clock hands don't *visibly* spin; the ropes of *gigantskie shagi* don't rise to a horizontal position while spinning; if the loops have been removed, no one is spinning, and the ropes, consequently, if separate from the loops and present at all, are hanging vertically.[9] Still, regardless of the visual barriers, the speed of spinning, or the angle of the ropes to the pole, the fact of circular motion *per se*, around an axis and on spoke-like extensions, does make the association possible. As we will see below, such circular motion bears important philosophical associations for Mandelstam. At the same time, we must consider the possibility that the giant steps are equivalent to the clock, not—or not only—through their visual mimicry of the clockface and conceptual imitation of the circling hands, but also through their echo of the *sound* of its striking.[10] Of course, this implies a rather different sort of "giant steps," not taken in the idiomatic sense related above. One might imagine, in fact, that this latter association may sometimes have come to even the contemporary reader first, given the almost absurdly difficult image of the clock as a children's yard game and the rather sinister-sounding conglomeration of giant steps, striking clock, awakening visions, and nooses (*petli*).

Mandelstam treats the ill figure and his childhood memories with what seems to be a tone of light irony. On a literal level, there is nothing in the poem to prove to the reader that the hero is mortally ill. While Mikhail Gasparov sees in the line "Squeezes his kerchief like a winged talisman" the ever-at-the-ready handkerchief of a tubercular, its corners splayed, this same line, if read in a different tonality, might also describe a hapless subject, clutching his handkerchief and suffering at the hands of a very bad cold. Cotton batting and acid may initially sound more serious, but they would not have to a contemporary of Mandelstam. Gasparov notes that cotton batting and vials with sulfuric acid were placed between double windowpanes to keep the glass from freezing in winter.[11] Still, there are more deeply embedded hints that this illness may indeed be fatal. The first is a possible Pushkinian subtext. "I s otvrashcheniem gliadit na krug minut . . ." [And looks with disgust upon the circle of minutes . . .] recalls Alexander Pushkin's "I s otvrashcheniem chitaia zhizn' moiu" [And reading my life with disgust] from "Remembrance" (Vospominanie, 1828), while certain elements of the scene recall Vasily Zhukovsky's "Pushkin's Last Minutes" (Poslednie minuty Pushkina, 1837), the most prominent account of the poet's last days following his fateful duel with Georges d'Anthès. As Zhukovsky notes, Pushkin had a "small general fever" and "suffered less from pain than anguish [toska]." "Oh, the anguish [Akh, toska]," he is supposed to have said. The poet "himself put poultices on his stomach." "Once he asked, 'what time is it?' And, in answer to Dal''s reply continued with a cracking voice: 'Will . . . I . . . suffer so . . . for long? . . . Please . . . let it be soon! . . .' This he repeated several times [. . .]" It was as if Pushkin "listened to the steps of approaching death [podslushival shagi priblizhaiushcheisia smerti]." Finally, "the [clock] struck two in the afternoon [udarilo dva chasa po-poludni] and only three-fourths of an hour of life remained in Pushkin."[12]

"Let, in the stuffy room" was written approximately three months after the seventy-fifth anniversary of Pushkin's death, so Zhukovsky's text is likely to have been recently refreshed in Mandelstam's memory. "The description of the last days and death of Pushkin, given by Zhukovsky with such heart-rending poignancy and simplicity in [his] letter to the poet's father, is too well-known to the reader for us to repeat or retell it here," intoned Nikolai Lerner in an article dedicated to the anniversary and published in the popular weekly *The Field* (Niva).[13] The full purport of these seemingly tenuous coincidences will become clearer after we examine the Blokian layer of the poem. In any case, we witness in Mandelstam's poem not a portrait of Pushkin's death, but a montage of details that may call that scene into passive memory.

Even more than Zhukovsky and Pushkin's "steps of approaching death," the combination of "chasy khripiat i b'iut" [the clock wheezes and strikes] and "gigantskie shagi" [giant steps] evokes "Steps of the Knight Commander," which, after a two-year gestation, Blok completed only two months before Mandelstam wrote his "Let, in the stuffy room." (The full text of Blok's poem may be found in the Appendix.)

> Тихими, тяжелыми шагами
>   В дом вступает Командор...
>
> Настежь дверь. Из непомерной стужи,
>   Словно хриплый бой ночных часов —
> Бой часов: «Ты звал меня на ужин.
>   Я пришел. А ты готов?..»

> With quiet, heavy steps
>   The Knight Commander enters the house...
>
> The door flung wide. From the inordinate cold,
>   As if the hoarse striking of a night clock—
> The striking of a clock: "You called me to dinner.
>   I've come. But are you prepared?.." (III, 93–94)[14]

Blok did not publish "Steps of the Knight Commander" until that fall, in *Russian Thought* (Russkaia mysl'), no. 11. However, not only is it likely that Mandelstam had heard Blok's masterpiece before he wrote "Let, in the stuffy room," but also I would contend that it is specifically Blok's presumptive reading of his poem that inspired Mandelstam's, with its stark contrast between high tragic anticipation and banal reality.

On 21 April 1912, Mandelstam was present at a reading by Blok at Peter's Academy (Petrovskoe uchilishche). We know he spoke with the older poet,[15] and Blok's diary entry for 18 April gives us an idea of what, among other things, Mandelstam may have heard from him: "All day at home, at night I caught cold from the *fortochka* [an independently opening small inset window], in these frosts . . . the cursed apartment has again become unbearable." On 21 April, the day of the reading, Blok wrote, "A terrible cold, I've become hoarse, I barely read at the evening [of poetry] at Peter's Academy."[16]

Of the works that comprise Alexander Blok's myth of retribution, few are so powerful and evocative as "Steps of the Knight Commander." Having inherited from Alexander Pushkin the mask of Don Juan, Blok subtly interpolates the story onto the present, merging it fully with his own personal mythology, and in doing so creates what is perhaps the most inspired vision in Russian literature of the Symbolist intellectual's sacrificial death at the dawn of the new age. Echoes of Blok's masterpiece dot the works of his contemporaries.

The comic effect of Blok, twentieth-century Don Juan, celebrated declaimer of his poetry, barely reading the high tragic lines of "Steps of the Knight Commander" in a completely hoarse voice, cannot be overestimated.[17] It seems almost certain that Mandelstam wrote "Let, in the stuffy room" under the immediate impression of that reading, sometime during the final ten days of April.[18]

In fact, Blok's presence permeates "Let, in the stuffy room." Throughout, the poem's images evoke and comment upon Blok's poetry, his poetic stance, and his worldview. On the most superficial level, in addition to the above resonances, one might point to the phonic resemblance to, and the semantic deflation of, "Pusto v pyshnoi spal'ne" [The luxurious bedchamber is empty] in "Pust' v dushnoi komnate" [Let, in the stuffy room]. In addition, the cryptic phrase "S kotorykh petli sniaty" [from which the loops/nooses/hinges are removed], in the absence of a clear referent, might call to mind the phrase "Sniata s petel'" [slipped from the hinges], evoking the image of the wide-flung door in "Steps of the Knight Commander." Several allusions to Blok's poem are thus potentially packed into the dense opening quatrain of Mandelstam's.[19]

The eighth line ("I s otvrashcheniem gliadit na krug minut . . ." [And looks with disgust upon the circle of minutes . . .]) also alludes to the Symbolist aesthetics. A subtext from Innokenty Annensky makes this particularly clear. In "∞" ("The emblem of the Mysterious resembles" [Deviz Tainstvennoi pokhozh]), a thoughtful dialogue with the younger Symbolists, we find the lines "V krugu emalevykh minut / Ee svershaiutsia obety" [In the circle of enamel minutes / Her vows are consummated].[20] The boundless feminine unknowable of the Symbolists (and here grammatical gender is crucial to establishing the cultural context) is worshipped from within the circle of worldly time. It is this symbolic clockface that reappears to taunt the ill figure in "Let, in the stuffy room."

In Blok's poetry and essays, the poet's thirst for an end to time (in the vein of the Apocalypse) struggles with a sense of *bezvremen'e* (the contentlessness of present time), and the horror of our terrible world (*strashnyi mir*) is intimately linked with images of eternal return and eternal circling: "let the beautiful violet eyes [. . .] eternally gaze through the swamp fog [. . .]

let the happiness of the horseman, circling in the swamp on a tired horse, flow silently [. . .] May it not be so."²² Images of circling and of cyclical time abound in Blok's poetry of the second and third books. The image of the clockface, with its meaninglessly, endlessly circling hands (which ostensibly show the time), is a highly successful compacting of this *topos*. Mandelstam himself, in an unpublished prose fragment from the early 1910s, wrote, "One might consider the movement of a clock-hand across the face to be the archetype of the absence of an event."²³

The first of the tercets is also intimately tied with Blok's poetry. Wind that calls to the poet to break his seclusion is featured prominently in the opening of *Song of Fate* (Pesnia sud'by, publ. 1909), and as far back as 1905, Blok had written "To My Mother" (Moei materi), one possible source of Mandelstam's weathervanes:

Тихо. И будет всё тише.
Флаг бесполезный опущен.
Только флюгарка на крыше
Сладко поёт о грядущем.

Ветром в полнебе раскинут,
Дымом и солнцем взволнован,
Бедный петух очарован,
В синюю глубь опрокинут.
...
Смолы пахучие жарки,
Дали извечно туманны...
Сладки мне песни флюгарки:
Пой, петушок оловянный!

Quiet. And it will be still quieter.
The useless flag is lowered.
Only the weathervane on the roof
Sings sweetly of the future.

Thrown by the wind across half the sky,
Agitated by smoke and sun,
The poor rooster is charmed,
Toppled into the dark blue depths.
...
The pungent saps are hot,

> The distance eternally foggy...
> *The songs of the weathervane are sweet to me:*
> *Sing, little tin rooster!* (II, 87, emphasis mine)

The "poet" interprets the weathervane (or more precisely weathercock) as a sign that *bezvremen'e* may some day end. But these seem to be false hopes: "Quiet. And it will be still quieter." The rooster is only a *petushok oloviannyi*—a tin toy.[24] Its calming melodies, in the larger context of Blok's poetry, continually sedate the lyric hero and prevent his venturing out into the world and history.

In addition, throughout Blok's poetry we are confronted with images of the poet alone in his room or behind closed windows:

> Хожу, брожу понурый,
> Один в своей норе.
> Придет шарманщик хмурый,
> Заплачет на дворе...
> . . .
> О том, что ветер в поле,
> И на дворе весна.
> . . .
> И свечка догорела,
> И маятник стучит.

> I pace, I wander downcast,
> Alone in my burrow.
> A gloomy organ grinder will come
> And start weeping in the yard . . .
> . . .
> That the wind is in the field,
> And in the yard it's spring.
> . . .
> And the candle has burnt out,
> And the pendulum knocks. (II, 226)

In "Let, in the stuffy room," the wind, which should show the poet his path, is again a source of false hope. The wind is forever changing. (Compare Blok's fears regarding his Fair Lady.)[25] The weathervanes spin meaninglessly, prefiguring the hands of the despised clock. Still, the children do not notice this fact.

In the first tercet of "Let, in the stuffy room," "September" clearly signifies the absence of spring. Spring, understood in an apocalyptic-allegorical sense, was of central concern to the Symbolists, as can be seen in Bely's "the sacred spring's / always thoughtfully sad children" [sviashchennoi vesny / vse zadumchivo grustnye deti][26] or Merezhkovsky's "Our speech is daring, / But condemned to death / Are too early forerunners / Of a spring too long in coming" [Derznovenny nashi rechi, / No na smert' osuzhdeny / Slishkom rannie predtechi / Slishkom medlennoi vesny] from "Children of the night" (Deti nochi, 1896), a well-known poem that likely had a formative impact on "Steps of the Knight Commander."[27] References to the desired spring are ubiquitous in Blok's poetry.

In addition, in "Let, in the stuffy room," the very use of the word "stuffy" hints at the ill figure's pining for spring. As noted above, cotton batting and vials with sulfuric acid were placed between double windowpanes to keep the glass from freezing. The fact that the cotton is gray implies that the winter is old.[28] Thus, in Mandelstam's poem, the situation of Fet's "Convalescent" (Bol'noi, 1855)—written in the same iambic hexameter and descriptive third person as "Let, in the stuffy room"—is imitated:

Просиживая дни, он думал всё одно:
«Я знаю, небеса весны меня излечут...»
И ждал он: скоро ли весна пахнёт в окно [...]?

Sitting out the days, he thought one thought:
"I know that the skies of spring will cure me . . ."
And he waited: would the smell of spring soon waft through the window
[...]?[29]

Mandelstam later wrote that Blok started from "a direct, almost schoolboy dependence on Vladimir Solov'ev and Fet" (II, 273), and it is characteristic that his composite portrait of the Blokian lyric hero might bear a trace of Fet's convalescent.

At the same time, September refers us to the Symbolist system of Zodiacal signs. Before the revolution, under the Gregorian calendar, the ascendency of Libra began on 11 September.[30] *Libra* (Vesy—Scales) was the name of the leading Symbolist literary journal. From the outset, the journal's name would have been interpreted as a reference to the Zodiac, given that the Symbolists' publishing house was already called Scorpio (Skorpion). The series of autumn Symbolist signs also implicitly includes—certainly for the younger Symbolists—Virgo, that is, *Deva,* the Virgin, and by extension, the

Eternal Feminine, a sign that would still have been dominant during the first third of September. Blok was later to give the name "Under the Sign of Virgo/ the Virgin" (Pod znakom Devy) to a cycle of old poems from the "epoch of sunsets," which he published for the first time in *Russian Thought* only in 1914. The title underscored his distance from the earlier mood. September, the month of Virgo and Libra, is the time of the youthful vigor and sanguine hopes of the Symbolists.[31]

On the whole, then, the first tercet depicts the false hopes and mistaken signs that deceive the Symbolist children (the plural implicates them as a group) and lead them to expect spring in September: "the game . . . seemed prophetic." The second tercet describes the motion of the *gigantskie shagi*. This motion, up and down in a perfect circle, synthesizes two types of movement that Mandelstam deploys in his sonnets of 1912. In "Barrel Organ," the Symbolists' art (and more specifically Blok's) is an old, sentimental song, which goes round and round but never gets anywhere,[32] while in "Falling" the iterative sense of this word takes hold. Symbolist attempts to fly, based as they are on emptiness, inevitably result in falling.[33] Not only are the *gigantskie shagi* a visual representation of this vicious circle of attempted flight and inevitable falling—a recognizable, if not entirely fair, summation of the younger Symbolists' art—but that flight turns out to be a fiction, a child's make-believe.[34]

The final line, "A living carousel spun without music!" [Zhivaia karusel' bez muzyki vrashchalas'!], can be seen as the nails in the coffin of Blok's worldview. At the center of that worldview, Mandelstam later asserted, music finally came to occupy the place of a Copernican sun (II, 275).[35] In "Let, in the stuffy room," Mandelstam thus denies Blok the reality of that nucleus around which his poetic world revolves. What is more, the carousel recalls lines from "Her Songs" (Ee pesni, 1907) in "The Snow Mask": "I will twirl you / On an aerial carousel" [Na vozdushnoi karuseli / Zakruzhu]. "Her Songs" begins, "Not in a stuffy earthly prison / do I kill" [Ne v zemnoi temnitse dushnoi / Ia gubliu] (II, 251). "Let, in the stuffy room" seems to say resoundingly, "not so": your fate is to die not crucified in the snow pyre, but imprisoned in a stuffy room.

The image of the rooster, thrice evoked in Blok's "To My Mother," is repeated in "Steps of the Knight Commander": "From a blessed, unfamiliar, distant country / The singing of the cock is heard" [Iz strany blazhennoi, neznakomoi, dal'nei / Slyshno pen'e petukha" (III, 93). In Blok's poem, this singing heralds the onset of a qualitatively new reality, which is to coincide with the moment of the hero's tragic death: "*Donna Anna will rise at your mortal hour*" [*Donna Anna v smertnyi chas tvoi vstanet*] (III, 94). The *absence* of this rooster is hinted at subtly in three places in "Let, in the stuffy room": first, in the image of the spinning weathervanes; second, in the "*winged* talisman"; and, third, phonetically, in line 3 (*petli*), which evokes the archaic, but familiar, *petel* (rooster).[36] In "Let, in the stuffy room," the anticipated crowing of the rooster—which promises the transcendence of worldly time in an event—never materializes. It is supplanted by the implacable clockface.

One final image remains to be explicated. "Children" [deti] is ubiquitous Symbolist shorthand for the poets themselves, but who are the giants? And why the plural? One superficial answer might be to look to Bely's "Images" (Obrazy) cycle in *Gold in the Azure* and his *Northern Symphony* (Severnaia simfoniia, 1900), which together provide a rich stock of giants (*velikany*). More pointedly, however, it seems that the answers to these questions return us to the Pushkinian substratum of the poem. Through a simple plural, Mandelstam forces us to recognize a connection he clearly feels between "Steps of the Knight Commander" and not only Pushkin's Don Juan text, "The Stone Guest" (Kamennyi gost', 1830), but also Pushkin's statuary myth in its entirety. This connection clearly explains the appearance of Evgeny from "The Bronze Horseman" (Mednyi vsadnik, 1833) in Mandelstam's "Petersburg strophes" (Peterburgskie strofy, 1913), breathing in the gas fumes of motorcars borrowed from "Steps of the Knight Commander." What is more, Pushkin's statuary myth comprises a third figure connected with the concept of retribution—the golden cockerel weathervane of "Tale of the Golden Cockerel" (Skazka o zolotom petushke, 1834).[37] In connection with the Symbolists, the "play / Of giants and children" then might imply these poets' literary (i.e., unserious) challenges to oppressive government and fate, their flirtation with these dangers from within their art.

All this, it seems, is more than enough for the poem to be read as a deflation of Blok. However, the Symbolist hero's mundane death is brought into sharper focus through a series of intersecting contexts and subtexts. We have already noted allusions to Pushkin and Fet. Mandelstam's poem also strongly evokes Semyon Nadson's "I dreamed I was ill, that my brain burned" (Snilos' mne, chto ia bolen, chto mozg moi gorit, 1884).[38] Mandelstam wrote, in the essay "The Sinani Family" (Sem'ia Sinani, 1923), that during his school years, years that included friendship with Boris Sinani, "modernism and Symbolism cohabitated" in his head "with the most virulent *nadsonovshchina* and doggerel from [the populist journal] *Russian Riches* (Russkoe bogatstvo).[39] Blok was already read, including *The Fair Booth* [his metatheatrical, ironic masterpiece], and he got along spendidly with civic motifs and all of that poetic drivel [tarabarskaia poeziia]. He wasn't antagonistic to it; after all, he himself came out of it" (II, 95).

In Nadson's poem, the lyric hero dreams of himself, dying, delirious and feverish, in his familiar room, of the pity lavished on him by a young woman, and of the pity he himself would feel for her. Upon waking, he regrets that he is not dying (at least not yet—Nadson himself would die of tuberculosis in 1887). Sadly, he is forced to return from this beautiful, sentimental dream to life, with its monotony and vulgar, petty concerns. Nadson's "Somewhere wheezily the clock wails and strikes" [Gde-to khriplo chasy zavyvaiut i b'iut] is forcefully echoed in Mandelstam's "the clock wheezes and strikes" [chasy khripiat i b'iut]; his hero is stricken with "alarmed grief" [trevozhnaia toska]. "Capricious shadows, like hands, creep, extending from everywhere" toward the lyric hero, anticipating Mandelstam's hero's alarming, indeterminate vision of "giant steps, from which the loops are slipped" [gigantskie shagi, s kotorykh petli sniaty]. The ending, with its distaste for everyday life, is reminiscent of the hero's disgust for the "circle of minutes" in "Let, in the stuffy room." Even the structure of the poem, in which the hero's dream gives way to the present (taking place in autumn), is reminiscent of and complexly inverted in Mandelstam's, where the depiction of the ill figure in the present gives way to a vision of the past, also taking place in autumn. It is likely that Mandelstam sensed an inner kinship between Blok's and Nadson's heroes—a common thread of pathos and *theatricalized* "tragedy."

Finally, the Symbolist hero's imaginary death is implicitly contrasted to the real death of Mandelstam's closest childhood friend, Boris Sinani. A. A. Morozov suggested to Mikhail Gasparov that the poem was written in reminiscence of Sinani, who, "'born for heroic feats,'" died of tuberculosis in 1911.[40] "'The raucous game of giants and children'" for Morozov "'is a prophecy of SR terrorism.'"[41] The powerfully charismatic and precocious Sinani, son of an important insider in Socialist-Revolutionary circles, drew Mandelstam—then a Marxist—to Socialist-Revolutionary thinking, and the two of them tried to join the military/terrorist wing of the party together. They were turned away because of their age. The seductiveness of such an approach derives from its simplicity. The poet recalls the suffering of his tubercular friend, dying in his stuffy room and reminiscing in a half-delirious state about the childhood games, in which the pair imagined, in play, their future challenge to the giants (reactionary forces oppressing society), a challenge tragically unrealized.

However, the forceful non sequitur, "Gigantskie shagi, s kotorykh petli sniaty"—in fact, the difficulty of reading into the first stanza at all, given its syntax, an image of the yard game so clearly represented in the final tercet—can only mean that the reader's mind will explore other possibilities and that the poem's meaning does not stop here. True, certain elements of Sinani's death appear to have found a reflection in the poem (as per Mandelstam's later description in *The Noise of Time*): "Boris *raved* about Finland, moving to Raivola [where the two witnessed a meeting of the military wing of the Socialist Revolutionary party] and some ropes for packing. Here we played at *gorodki* [a game in which one must strike figures of pins with a thrown bat]" (II, 97). And there is the fact that the fever, thin fingers, and handkerchief likely do hint at tuberculosis. Still, the details are subtly transformed. Late fall becomes September. Whipping rain becomes wind ("The soaked wings of glory beat against the window [. . .] The night sun in a Finland, blind from rain" [ibid.]). The game of *gorodki* is replaced by *gigantskie shagi*. The implication—as I see it, at least—is that the memory of Sinani's death informs the poem, rather than amounting to its function.

Mandelstam describes the period of Sinani's influence thus:

> All around strange currents rushed—from a thirst for suicide to a desire for the end of the world. The gloomy, reeking literature of problems and ignorant universal questions had just marched past, and the dirty, hairy hands of the merchants of life and death made repellent the very name of life and death. That was a truly ignorant night! Writers in Russian peasant shirts [kosovorotki] and black blouses traded, like shopkeepers, in God and the Devil, and there wasn't a house where they didn't tap out with one finger the thick-headed polka from [Andreev's] *Life of a Man*, which became the symbol of the vile Symbolism of the street. Too long the intelligentsia was fed on university songs. Now it was nauseous from universal questions: that same old philosophy out of a beer bottle!
>
> All of this was scum when compared to the world of the Erfurt Program, communist manifestoes and agrarian debates. [. . .] and in the meager party polemics there was more life and more music than in all of the writings of Leonid Andreev. (II, 98)

In these lines, one cannot help hearing a hint of a polemic with Blok, who strongly praised Andreev's *Life of a Man* (Zhizn' cheloveka, 1907)[42] and famously descended, in the period of his "antithesis," to the revelation "You're right, drunken monster! / I know: the truth is in wine" [Ty pravo, p'ianoe chudovishche! / Ia znaiu: istina v vine] (II, 213).

So, on one side of the scales, Mandelstam sets Pushkin's very real life building through very real death[43] and Sinani's extra-literary demise; on the other, he sets the sentimental pathos of the dying Nadson and the historiosophic rhetoric and magnificent, but hollow, "tragedy" of Blok.[44] Blok's hero, needless to say, does not win from this matrix of comparisons. True, Blok himself had thoroughly deflated his lyric hero in any number of poems, including "To My Mother" above. Yet even the deflated Blokian hero retains a modicum of tragedy. This Mandelstam denies him in "Let, in the stuffy room."

Still, Mandelstam's good-natured assault remains far from the destructive irony described in Blok's 1908 essay.[45] It affirms even as it deflates, since a worthy adversary is a necessary element. The best gauge of the stingingly playful tone of "Let, in the stuffy room" may, in fact, be Mandelstam's own words in his autobiographical prose vignette "In a Fur Coat above His Station" (like "The Sinani Family," from *The Noise of Time*):

> Literary malice! If not you, with what would I eat [my] earthly salt?
> You seasoning for the bland bread of understanding, you merry consciousness of incorrectness, you conspiratorial salt, passed with an ironic bow from decade to decade in a cut-glass shaker with a towel! That's why I so love to extinguish the fever of literature with frost and prickly stars. Will it crunch the snow? Will it cheer up on a frosty Nekrasov street? If it's real—then yes. (II, 103)

In "Let, in the stuffy room," through colliding narrative and subtext, literary myth and biographical anecdote, and, more broadly, life and art, Mandelstam unmasks Blok's high tragic stance. I suspect that the poem also functions in Mandelstam's oeuvre as a ritual burial of the older poet, a dispersing of his immense shadow and a severing of the bonds that tied Mandelstam's own lyric hero to Blok's poetry.[46] As we have seen, Blok plays a surprisingly persistent, although never dominating, role in Mandelstam's poetry of 1909 to 1912.[47] Freed from the stifling encroachment of the Symbolist lyric hero and the expectations he generated, Mandelstam was then able to open up his poetics to other more amenable elements of the Symbolist system, as we will see in the following chapter. In at least one area—modernist time poetics—Blok himself was to be a most compelling model.

That Mandelstam chose to efface this crucial turning point in his official narratives of poetic development in the 1913 and 1916 editions of *Stone* is not altogether surprising. If we exclude the possibility that Mandelstam himself suffered from the excessive piety toward Blok of which he accuses the Futurists in "Storm and Stress," it is of course possible that he did not value the poem as highly as his other sonnets. His choice of *The Hyperborean* as a venue to publish and his apparent plans to include "Let, in the stuffy room" in a later, unrealized edition of *Stone* argue against this, however.[48] It seems more likely that Mandelstam, at least within the context of these early editions, did not want the record of a *struggle* with Blok to mar the surface of a poetic edifice constructed upon the unshakable assertion of free choice of poetic ancestry and affiliation. It also may be that "Let, in the stuffy room" simply did not find a place within the strict compositional architectonics particular to the 1916 edition.

Although Mandelstam would come to acknowledge the power of Blok's historical vision by 1922, in 1912 he could not help distrusting the older poet's maximalism and lofty posture. "Steps of the Knight Commander," it appears, provided Mandelstam with much-needed ammunition for a poetic confrontation—one-sided, it is true. On one level, "Let, in the stuffy room" reflects the struggle of a whole generation of poets to find a distinct voice in the aftermath of the crisis of Symbolism, and Mandelstam's playful deflation of Blok's poetic myth is a natural stance for the polemically sober early Acmeist in reaction to Blok's Symbolist/Romantic "overstatement." On another, the poem is a highly individual record of a key moment in the inevitably lonely and unique effort of a great poet to free himself from the pull of the dominant lyric voice of his times.

CHAPTER 7

THE SUPERFICIAL AND THE PROFOUND

In the first two sections of this chapter, I examine the influence of Symbolism and Blok on Mandelstam after his conversion to Acmeism, but before his intense re-examination of Blok beginning in 1920. On the one hand, Blok provides material for parody; on the other, Blok's metaphorical poetics and embodiment *in poetry* of anachronistic modernist time structures are of the first importance in Mandelstam's renewal of his poetics in *Tristia*, which can rightfully be seen as a new synthesis of Acmeism and Symbolism. In general, however, Blok as an active *problem* seems to recede from Mandelstam's poetry, only to reappear with renewed urgency in 1920.[1] At the same time, the renewed Symbolist influence in Mandelstam's poetry in *Tristia* is connected to the figure of Viacheslav Ivanov, who provided Mandelstam with the organizing myth of his second book, the "myth of forgotten Christianity."[2] This is the topic of the final section of the chapter.

FODDER FOR PARODY

Among the works that make up Mandelstam's parodic "portrait gallery" of 1913—"Cinema" (Kinematograf), "Tennis" (Tennis),

"American Girl" (Amerikanka), "Dombey and Son" (Dombi i syn), "American Bar" (Amerikan bar)—is one poem that clearly plays upon the transformation of Symbolist imagery and diction, and, more specifically, the writings of Blok.

Старик

Уже светло, поет сирена
В седьмом часу утра.
Старик, похожий на Верлэна,
Теперь твоя пора!

В глазах лукавый или детский
Зеленый огонек;
На шею нацепил турецкий
Узорчатый платок.

Он богохульствует, бормочет
Несвязные слова;
Он исповедоваться хочет —
Но согрешить сперва.

Разочарованный рабочий
Иль огорченный мот —
А глаз, подбитый в недрах ночи,
Как радуга цветет.

Так, соблюдая день субботний,
Плетется он — когда
Глядит из каждой подворотни
Веселая нужда;

А дома — руганью крылатой,
От ярости бледна,
Встречает пьяного Сократа
Суровая жена!

Old Man

It's already light, a siren sings

Just after 6 A.M.
Old man, who resembles Verlaine,
Now is your time.

In [his] eyes is a cunning or childlike
Green fire;
On [his] neck he has pinned a Turkish
Patterned kerchief.

He blasphemes, mutters
Disconnected words;
He wants to give confession—
But to sin first.

A disenchanted worker
Or embittered spendthrift—
And [his] eye, struck in the depths of the night,
Blossoms like a rainbow.

Thus, observing the Saturday,
He stumbles on—while
From every gateway watches
Cheerful indigence;

And at home—with winged chastisement,
Pale from rage,
A severe wife
Meets the drunken Socrates!

Lada Panova cites "Old Man" as an example of eternal return in its cultural aspect, underscoring the contrast with the Symbolists' more typical, pessimistic interpretation of the Nietzschean concept.[3] Cyclicity is introduced through a series of comparisons. The old man bears a resemblance to Verlaine—a wink between author and reader. After all, the "disenchanted worker / Or embittered spendthrift" can hardly be imagined to perceive, through intoxication, pain and chastisement, his kinship to Verlaine.[4] Mandelstam's old man is also likened metaphorically to Socrates, a comparison—motivated by the tales of Socrates' shrewish wife—that functions on the surface level as a "calque" for "drunken philosopher." At the same time, the poem activates the traditional comparison, on the basis of physical resemblance, between Verlaine and Socrates.⁵ This circle of culture, however, also embeds a pattern of "deflations," which the author does not necessarily look upon negatively. These are the deflations of the image of Socrates in Verlaine—despite the poetic gift of the latter—and of Verlaine in the old man, in whom we presuppose no such gift. The poetic gift of Verlaine is instead implicitly shifted outside of the bounds of the poem to the author, who, as we have seen, subtly hinted at his own kinship to Verlaine in his first article, "François Villon."

G. G. Amelin and V. Ia. Morderer have proposed as prototype of the old man Nikolai Kul'bin, futurist artist, autodidact art theorist, and organizer, whom Mandelstam would have known from the Stray Dog cabaret and whose physical resemblance to Verlaine and Socrates was "paid witness to by contemporaries."⁶ However, having acknowledged that "this doesn't help make sense of the poem itself," Amelin and Morderer conclude that "the intentional disembodiment of the image of the old man and collapsing of the plane of reference does not allow one to directly relate him to anyone."⁷

There is, however, yet another prototype, which, when revealed, becomes of primary importance, unveiling an entirely new stratum of the poem's plot. This layer is a parody on one of the most characteristic plot motifs of mythopoetic Symbolism, and especially its Blokian embodiment—the meeting with Sophia, the Divine Feminine, at sunrise.

The first element to catch the reader's eye in this connection might be the collocation "glaz . . . tsvetet" (eye . . . blossoms) in lines 11–12. Blooming eyes are a characteristic marker of Blok's idiolect: "And under the mask—so calmly / [Her] eyes blossomed" [I pod maskoi—tak spokoino / Rastsveli glaza] (II, 277); "Enamourment blossomed in curls / And in the early sadness of eyes" [Vliublennost' rastsvela v kudriakh / I v rannei grusti glaz] (II, 152).⁸ I. I. Shkuropat has proposed looking at the same set of lines as a "parodic allusion to the typically Symbolist image of the rainbow."⁹ Mandelstam clearly evinces Symbolist diction here.

The multicolored blooming of the old man's black eye occurs as a result of that which took place "in the depths of night" [v nedrakh nochi], a time of Symbolist anticipation. The events of the poem are presented in implicit contrast to that which ought to have taken place at the dawn ("It's already light, a siren sings / Just after 6 A.M."). In the typical early mythopoetic Symbolist or Blokian poem, the poet anticipates at this hour the appearance of, or meeting with, Sophia.

The old man's wife is "severe" [surovaia]. Blok's Heroine is described, in *Poems about the Fair Lady,* as both "strict" [strogaia] and (less often) "severe" [surovaia]: "Always haughty and severe" [Vsegda nadmenna i surova] (I,

229), "You are white, impassive in [Your] depths / In life—strict and irate" [Belaia Ty, v glubinakh nesmutima / V zhizni—stroga i gnevna] (I, 190). The final word of the poem, *zhena* (wife, but also woman [biblical, archaic]), is, of course, one name for the Symbolists' ideal: "Vsë nevesta—i vechno zhena" [Ever bride—and eternally woman] (I, 330). Thus we can see in the morning meeting of this drunk "Socrates" and his shrewish wife a burlesque shadow of the Symbolist hero's anticipated rendezvous with the Eternal Feminine at a more than simply daily dawn.

The secondary meanings of the word "sirena" reinforce this impression of betrayed hopes. The siren, "a beautiful, seductive, but heartless woman" (Ushakov), can be understood as the Fair Lady, enticing but deceiving the Symbolists. Likewise, the expression "*winged* chastisement" in the final stanza—first and foremost evoking the Russian for aphorism, "winged words" (*krylatye slova*)—also, in the context of the first stanza, recalls the mythological image of the half-bird, half-woman, who lures sailors to their deaths with her beautiful singing. "Sirens" (on a wharf, of a ship, the horn of a car) appear several times in Blok's poetry with a similar double-voicedness.

The figure of the drunken hero specifically echoes imagery from Blok, who is, as we will recall, in his most famous lyric, "The Stranger" (Neznakomka, 1906), a drunken philosophizer: "You're right, drunken monster! / I know: the truth is in wine" [Ty pravo, p'ianoe chudovishche! / Ia znaiu: istina v vine] (II, 213).[10] In addition, one common mask of Blok's lyric hero in the First Book is the "old man" (*starik*). One final textual echo ultimately confirms the powerful, subterranean presence of Blok. The reference is to his play *The Stranger*:[11]

Старик, похожий на Верлэна	У одного окна, за столиком, сидит пьяный старик — вылитый Верлэн.
Он богохульствует, бормочет Несвязные слова	Верлэн (бормочет громко, сам с собою) Верлэн (бормочет) И все проходит. И каждому — своя забота. Верлэн (бормочет) И всем свой черед… *И всем пора идти домой…* (Blok, *SS6*, III, 67, 68, 70, 74, my emphasis)
Old man, who looks like Verlaine	Near one window, at a table, sits a drunk old man—a dead ringer for Verlaine

He blasphemes, mutters	Verlaine (mutters loudly to himself)
Disconnected words	Verlaine (mutters) And everything passes.
	And to each his own cares.
	Verlaine (mutters) And to each in his turn . . .
	And it's time for everyone to go home . . .

Mandelstam follows Blok's "Verlaine" home to his wife, and the images of this character and Blok's lyric hero (conflated by many contemporaries with the poet himself) blend together, peeking out from behind Mandelstam's satirical street portrait.

Mandelstam's portrait functions perfectly well in the absence of the reader's recognition of this second layer, losing none of its playful stylishness and sharp characterization. Subconsciously or consciously, however, contemporaries were sure to sense the superficial reappropriation of Symbolist lexicon, which contributes in a crucial way to the stylistic play. Tynianov wrote about parody, "If the backdrop dissolves into a general understanding of 'style,' the parody becomes one element of the dialectical change of schools, borders upon stylization."[12] In "Old Man," this is not the case. The secondary Blokian plane of the poem, when recognized, retains a structural role, accentuating the poem's comedic effect through an unexpected elevation of the thematic material that is parodied. And, in this sense, the Blokian layer clearly expands the poem's scope and resonance.

MODERNIST TIME POETICS

The influence of Blok on Mandelstam's poetics was first noted by Zhirmunsky in 1921, the year of Blok's death:

> Blok's lyrics unusually boldly and consequentially develop the devices of the metaphorical style. The Romantic poet not only frees himself for good from a dependence on the logical norms of speech development, from the timid glance over the shoulder at logical clarity, consequentiality, he renounces even the possibility of actualizing the verbal construction in a non-contradictory image (visual conception [nagliadnoe predstavlenie]), i.e. he steps onto the path of logical contradiction, dissonance, as an artistic *device,* motivated by the irrationality of the poet's overarching conception. In this sense, Blok is completely original and has among the Russian Romantic poets and first Symbolists only timid precursors. As far as the

newest poets go, several of them, like Mandelstam, or Mayakovsky, or the Imaginists, went even further than Blok in freeing the metaphoric construction from the norms of logically understandable and consequential practical speech, but nonetheless, in the main, they are wholly his pupils.[13]

Analysis of Blok's influence on Mandelstam's poetics has been carried forward in more recent years by Pavel Gromov (with somewhat exaggerated conclusions, however), Mikhail Gasparov (who, unfortunately, deals with the topic only briefly), and, particularly, S. N. Broitman.[14]

One element of Blok's metaphorical poetics appears to have had a particularly meaningful—and traceable—influence on Mandelstam: Blok's poetic embodiment of Modernist time structures. The older poet's boldness and especially his consummate skill in generating convincing poetic embodiments of the "inseparability and unfusedness" [nerazdel'nost' i nesliiannost'][15] of disparate time frames, both mythical and historical ("Steps of the Knight Commander," "On Kulikovo Field"), clearly played a decisive role in Mandelstam's development.

Only gradually did Mandelstam acquire the technical and philosophical markers of that conception of time aphoristically embodied in his idiosyncratic reading of Henri Bergson in "On the Nature of the Word" (1922):[16]

> Bergson does not consider phenomena according to the way they submit to the law of temporal succession, but rather according to their spatial extension [. . .] Phenomena thus connected to one another form, as it were, a kind of fan whose folds can be opened up in time; however, this fan may also be closed up in a way intelligible to the human mind. (II, 242)[17]

A poetic analogue for this temporal syncretism is entirely absent in Mandelstam's earliest verse, in which the categories of eternity and atemporality are central, while the historical has yet to enter the picture.[18] As early as "Hagia-Sophia" (1912), disparate historical time frames are juxtaposed. However, the connection is justified by the history of the church itself, which is the living composite of several eras' temples. In other words, the compacting of time within space (under the aegis of eternity) is still linked to an external logic tied to a definable and specific historical "reality."

Panova notes of the next poem in *Stone*, "Notre Dame," that "a new technique gets our attention—through repetition, for the first time in Mandelstam's poetry, the idea of eternal return is introduced: "As once did Adam, splaying its nerves, / The light groined arch flexes its muscles" [Kak nekogda

Adam, rasplastyvaia nervy, / Igraet myshtsami krestovyi legkii svod]."¹⁹ Still, while Panova refers to eternal return in a cultural rather than existential or historical sense (itself a crucial development in Mandelstam's poetics), and despite the pointedly time-oriented "nekogda" [once], differences in quality and scale dictate that conceptual analogy, rather than temporal repetition, remains the primary mechanism underlying the association of Adam, cathedral, and poem as fruits of creation. Importantly for our own discussion, here we still do not see that dissolving of boundaries between past and present and the radical anachronism that will be characteristic of many of Mandelstam's mature poems and that clearly bears Blok's stamp.

In 1912, Mandelstam almost certainly became acquainted with Blok's "Steps of the Knight Commander."²⁰ Years later he would write:

> But the acme of Blok's historical poetics, the triumph of European myth, which moves freely in traditional forms and *does not fear anachronism and contemporaneity* is "Steps of the Knight Commander." Here the layers of time fell one upon another in a poetic consciousness plowed anew [Zdes' plasty vremeni legli drug na druga v zanovo vspakhannom poeticheskom soznanii]." (II, 273, my emphasis)

This may be seen as a confession, with pinpoint precision, of the sense in which Blok's poem had an impact on the younger poet. The next stage—after "Hagia-Sophia," "Notre Dame," and "Old Man"—in the simultaneous embodiment of disparate time frames in Mandelstam's poetry is specifically a confrontation with the Petersburg myth, seen through the prism of blatant, unapologetic "anachronism and contemporaneity." In "Petersburg Strophes" (1913), following references to Gogol's "Overcoat" (Shinel', 1842) and *Eugene Onegin,* Mandelstam evokes Blok's cuttingly anachronistic motorcar (*motor*) from "Steps of the Knight Commander" and transplants the Evgeny of *The Bronze Horseman* (Mednyi vsadnik, 1833) to the early years of the twentieth century:²¹

> Пролетает, брызнув в ночь огнями,
>   Черный, тихий, как сова, мотор.

> Having sprayed [its] lights into the night, flies by
>   A black motorcar, silent as an owl. (Blok, III, 94)

> Летит в туман моторов вереница:
> Самолюбивый, скромный пешеход —

Чудак Евгений — бедности стыдится,
Бензин вдыхает и судьбу клянет!

A string of motorcars flies into the fog:
The proud, unassuming pedestrian—
That eccentric Evgeny—is ashamed of his poverty,
Breathes gas fumes and curses his fate.

An excised strophe from "The Admiralty" (Admiralteistvo), written in the same year, similarly connects Blok, through subtext (this time his "Venice" [Venetsiia, 1909]), to a freeing from the bonds of temporal progression:[22]

Живая линия меняется, как лебедь.
Я с Музой зодчего беседую опять.
Взор омывается, стихает жизни трепет:
Мне все равно, когда и где существовать!

The living line meanders, like a swan.
I chat with the Muse of an architect once more.
The waters lap [my] gaze, life's tremor grows still:
I don't care when and where I might exist![23]

Quite possibly the apex of this Blokian Modernist time poetics in Mandelstam is reached in the poem "On a straw-covered sledge" (Na rozval'niakh, ulozhennykh solomoi, 1916). Broitman compares Blok's "Venice" with Mandelstam's poem:

[Gromov] saw that a definitively important role for the younger poet was played by the relation of inseparability and unfusedness [nerazdel'nost' i nesliianost'] of the "I" and the historical personage in [Blok's] "On Kulikovo Field" and the "Italian poems" [. . .] In both cases, we observe the inhabitation of a historical or mythological personage (John the Baptist—Tsarevich Dmitry) and first-person speech [. . .] But in both instances, the ultimate transformation of the speaker into the historic personage does not occur (as it would in mask lyric [rolevaia lirika]), nor the complete confluence of the hero with the "I." In the finale of the poems, a "sliding" transition arises to another point of view, which presents a vision of the "I" from outside: "But a head on a black platter . . ." [Lish' golova na chernom bliude . . .]—"The tsarevich is being taken . . ." [Tsarevicha vezut . . .]."[24]

Mandelstam's poetic stance in "On a straw-covered sledge" is as close as he will come, certainly through the end of *Tristia*, to the reviving of a Symbolist and more specifically Blokian hero in his poetry. The inseparability and unfusedness of epochs that triumphs in the poetry of *Tristia*, and that does bear the stamp of Blok's influence, is almost always accomplished without recourse to an "I" conflated with or playing the role of tragic hero in the historical drama.[25]

THE MYTHOPOETICS OF *TRISTIA*

In the Introduction, I wrote about the gravitation of mythopoetic (or myth-creating) Symbolism to the construction of overarching poetic plots defining whole periods of an artist's creative production, or even a whole lifetime of poetry, as in the case of Blok's lyric trilogy. Not only did this tendency consciously or unconsciously to mold overarching narratives and new myths have an impact upon the structure of Mandelstam's second book, *Tristia*, but it was in fact Friedrich Nietzsche, beloved of the Symbolists, and Viacheslav Ivanov, the Symbolist maître and theoretician, who helped Mandelstam to frame that new myth which, more than any other, animates his second book—the myth of forgotten Christianity.

Both Ivanov, implicitly, and Nietzsche, explicitly, wanted to turn back the clock of cultural evolution, awakening more ancient impulses that could heal the present maladies of aesthetically and spiritually moribund nineteenth-century civilization. In *Tristia*, Mandelstam reverses this retrograde trend, setting aright the course of time. Emerging out of the darkness and into memory, he traces that history of the ages of culture that Nietzsche and Ivanov define and lament.

Nietzsche, in his seminal work, *The Birth of Tragedy*, describes both the generation of ancient Greek tragedy out of Dionysian music and Apollonian dreams and the degeneration of this art form, which represents for him the finest achievements of western culture, into lesser, overly rational and slavishly realistic forms of art. In the second half of his book, he predicts and calls for the birth of a new tragic age:

> The Hellenic prototype retains this immeasurable value, that all these transitions and struggles are imprinted upon it in a classically instructive form; except that we, as it were, pass through the chief epochs of the Hellenic genius analogically, in *reverse* order, and seem now, for instance, to be passing backward from the Alexandrian age to the period of tragedy.[26]

The Alexandrian age—those centuries of late antiquity abutting the birth of Christianity—often evokes associations with musty libraries, scholarly compilations, and imitative art. Nietzsche criticizes this age, seeing in it an ethos similar to the rationalism and materialism of the nineteenth century.[27] The age of tragedy, in contrast, is, according to Nietzsche, characterized by a courageous pessimism that dares to stare into the terrors of existence, even as the Apollonian calm of the realized art work heals from the vertigo experienced at the edge of this abyss.[28]

Ivanov accepts wholeheartedly Nietzsche's call for a new tragic age. "The chorus ought to be freed and reinstated completely in the fullness of its ancient rights," he states in one essay.[29] In another, he intones, "We ought to cast ourselves aside and become ancient in spirit." "Nietzsche, the corybant" he continues, "first proclaimed the necessity of a return."[30] However, according to Ivanov, the seed from which Nietzsche's prophecy emerged fell on "the barren soil of contemporary ignorance of God."[31] If the Dionysian is, for Nietzsche, an eternal pole in art, for Ivanov it is tied to a historical religion.[32] Moreover, while Nietzsche rejects Christianity as false and enslaving, Ivanov sees a kinship, and even a genealogical continuity, between Christianity and the religion of Dionysus.[33] The ecstatic religion of the suffering god Dionysus is, according to Ivanov, at the roots of Christianity, with its own suffering, dying, and resurrected god.[34] Moreover, contemporary Christianity requires for its renewal a new influx of the Dionysian essence.[35]

In Mandelstam's understanding, Ivanov's religious experimentation and religious syncretism amount to participation in his generations' gravest sin.[36] "Time can flow backwards: the entire course of recent history, which with frightful strength turned from Christianity to Buddhism and Theosophy, bears witness to this . . . [. . .] What is this," wrote Mandelstam, "ravings or the end of Christianity?" (II, 314). And yet this gravest sin, a generation's amnesia, is turned by Mandelstam to good, as it provides the myth that will structure his second book.[37]

This structuring is implicit, loose, a chaotically unfolding internal imperative, and yet a palpable overarching presence.[38] In any case, it is only such a narrative that we can seek, for no authoritative edition exists of Mandelstam's second book. Mandelstam had little or no control over the shamefully poor 1922 Berlin edition of *Tristia*,[39] and he clearly set out actively to distinguish *Second Book* (Vtoraia kniga, 1923) from the earlier edition.[40] The largely restorative *Tristia* segment of *Poems* (1928), though the closest we have to representing the poet's final will, was distorted by censorship. The replacement of the original final poem cardinally changed the book's trajectory,[41] as did the absence of the Christian-themed poems, whether or not this may have better fit Mandelstam's mood in 1927. Thus we are forced to triangulate. It seems most logical to conclude that an "ideal" *Tristia*, undistorted and reflective of the original generative impulse, should include the Christian poems, adopt the more chronological structure and strict chronological boundaries of the later edition, and retain the quite meaningful original beginning and end points. It is roughly such a "hypothetical" *Tristia* (similar to that proposed by Freidin) to which I will appeal here. For reasons of space, I will present this mythopoetic narrative only at its most representative points. These are, however, characteristic of broader thematic and tonal vectors within the book.

Setting out on the path of anamnesis, Mandelstam's lyric "I" must first re-experience earlier stages of culture in order to arrive in memory at the pre-existing Christian truth. In order to initiate his book and spark this process, however, it is necessary for the poet first to achieve a powerful shift, a forgetting of self accomplished through an exertion of memory aimed at the deepest past (Ivanov's "We ought to cast ourselves aside and become ancient in spirit"). This shift occurs in Mandelstam's "How these coverings" (Kak etikh pokryval i etogo ubora, 1916).

If, in "I will not see the celebrated *Phèdre*," Mandelstam turns up the soil of several centuries with his poetic plow, in "How these coverings," the poet digs a good deal further. Pulling up the floorboards of a French seventeenth-century theater, he discovers the orchestra of the ancient Athenian theater of Dionysus and finds there not a stone horseshoe, but a living chorus and the ancient cultic roots of tragedy. That we may speak here not simply of the roots of tragedy in the chorus, but of a chorus emerging from its roots in Dionysian religion, is implied in the chorus's function—the "theurgic" appeasement, through a funeral dirge, of that dire force that is personified in the black sun:

— Мы боимся, мы не смеем
Горю царскому помочь.
Уязвленная Тезеем,
На него напала ночь.
Мы же, песнью похоронной
Провожая мертвых в дом,
Страсти дикой и бессонной
Солнце черное уймем.

—We fear to, we dare not
Help the royal grief.
Stung by Theseus,
Night fell upon him.
We, with funeral dirge,
Seeing the dead to the house,
Will the black sun
Of wild and sleepless passion appease.

For comparison, in Aeschylus's *Seven Against Thebes,* a "strange, archaic" play (David Grene) by the earliest author of full-fledged Greek tragedy, the chorus does not expressly mourn for the dead. Instead it sings "the ill-sounding Furies' dirge, / and the hateful Hades paean," mollifying those chthonic forces that have exacted the tragedy's tribute of blood.[42] Mandelstam rejects Ivanov's artistic intuition and does not echo stylistically the older poet's "dithyrambs" and tragedies in shaping his chorus. However, he draws his chorus in accordance with Ivanov's understanding of the roots of tragedy: heroic funeral rites serve as appeasement of an awe-provoking, threatening god.

Most of the first half of *Tristia* is dominated by the Dionysian impulse, by retrograde time and a thirst for the chaotic roots of culture, which is to say the chthonic underbelly of that social and architectural order, which forms the pathos of the second half of *Stone.* The first intimations of this approaching shift come in the deeply Ivanov-influenced "Ode to Beethoven" (Oda Betkhovenu, 1914).[43] However, within *Stone,* this poem, which presents a synchronic version of the myth of the emergence of Christian revelation from the Dionysian impulse, serves not as a declaration of a new approach to art, but rather as a Dionysian counterweight to the logical exultation of Bach ("Bach" [Bakh, 1913]), thus in fact establishing Acmeist balance.[44]

The diptych "I am cold. Transparent spring" (1916) illustrates well the retrograde pull that dominates the first half of *Tristia:*

I

Мне холодно. Прозрачная весна
В зеленый пух Петрополь одевает,
Но, как медуза, невская волна
Мне отвращенье легкое внушает.
По набережной северной реки
Автомобилей мчатся светляки,

Летят стрекозы и жуки стальные,
Мерцают звезд булавки золотые,
Но никакие звезды не убьют
Морской воды тяжелый изумруд.

II

В Петрополе прозрачном мы умрем,
Где властвует над нами Прозерпина.
Мы в каждом вздохе смертный воздух пьем,
И каждый час нам смертная година.
Богиня моря, грозная Афина,
Сними могучий каменный шелом.
В Петрополе прозрачном мы умрем, —
Здесь царствуешь не ты, а Прозерпина.

I

I am cold. Transparent spring
Dresses Petropolis in green down,
But, like a jellyfish [medusa], the Neva's waves
Fill me with mild disgust.
Along the embankment of the northern river
The fireflies of automobiles race,
Dragonflies and steel beetles fly,
The golden hairpins of stars shimmer,
But no stars will kill
The heavy emerald of the seawater.

II

In transparent Petropolis we shall die,
Where Proserpina reigns over us,
With every breath we drink deathly air,
And every hour is our mortal term.
Goddess of the sea, dread Athena,
Remove [your] mighty, stone helm.
In transparent Petropolis we shall die—
Here reigns not you but Proserpina.[45]

Ivanov's exquisite remark, "Spring was transparent to the gaze of the ancients: It was blossoming death [Vesna byla prozrachna dlia vzora drevnikh: Ona byla tsvetushchaia smert']," is the clear subtext of the poem.[46] First quoted in relation to *Tristia* by Kiril Taranovsky, this passage explains the poem's bipartite structure.[47] The spring of the first poem is the death of the second, and through the stateliness and supposed eunomia (good public order) of Petersburg emerges, for seeing eyes, Proserpina's kingdom in Hades. The translucent jellyfish, or *meduza*, is the conduit between the two stanzas.

This Medusa has larger implications, however, both for reading Mandelstam's poem and for understanding *Tristia* in general. The surfacing of the Medusa is really a roundabout way of hinting that the real culprits of the book's retrograde motion, the Furies, have come to the fore. As Richmond Lattimore states,

> The Furies are older than Apollo and Athene, and, being older, they are childish and barbarous [. . .] in a Greek world they stand for the childhood of the race before it won Hellenic culture, the barbarian phase of pre-Hellenism [. . .] they have archaic uprightness and strictest in action, with its attendant cruelty [. . .] Apollo stands for everything which the Furies are not: Hellenism, civilization, intellect, and enlightenment.[48]

Mandelstam, in his essay "The Nineteenth Century," written some years after this poem, directly connects the Furies with Medusa, a natural association based on their appearance: "they come like gorgons, they / wear robes of black, and they are wreathed in a tangle / of snakes" (Aeschylus, *The Libation Bearers*, 1048–50).[49] In his essay, the poet writes that the failing ancient Furies of the French Revolution washed "onto the shore of the nineteenth century already incomprehensible—not the head of the Gorgon, but a bundle of seaweed" (II, 280). That is, the washed-up Furies are something quite like this poem's jellyfish.

What implications, then, does this connection have for the second half of the diptych?

> Goddess of the sea, dread Athena,
> Remove [your] mighty, stone helm.
> In transparent Petropolis we shall die—
> Here reigns not you but Proserpina.

On the deepest level, the poem describes a ceding of power by the Olympian Athena, patron not only of Athens but also of seafaring Petersburg, to the chthonic and archaic power of the Furies.[50] Mandelstam thus reverses the historical process depicted in Aeschylus's *The Eumenides*. There, Athena establishes civic order in Athens and pacifies the Furies, incorporating them into the Olympian hierarchy by offering them a seat of honor in the underworld. Here, Athena relinquishes to the Furies power in the world above.[51] The Furies are represented in first poem of the diptych through their visual likeness to Medusa, and in the second through their physical proximity to Proserpina, queen of the underworld. Never mentioned in the collection, they nonetheless represent that archaic force that, allied with the Dionysian, must be overcome to reach the poet's goal of memory.

Characteristically, in its initial publication, this poem was constructed not as a diptych, but as a triptych, and the eliminated central poem, connecting the present-day Petrograd of the first stanza and the archaic mythological reality of the second, speaks of the city's "Alexandrian poplars" [Aleksandriiskie topolia]. Before he can move forward in his wanderings to the Alexandrian age, however, Mandelstam must neutralize the power of the Dionysian chaos. This finally occurs in a poem from 1918, in which a concert of Schubert *Lieder* produces, through a series of associations, what initially seems to be a triumph of the Dionysian impulse: "And the horrible force of nocturnal return / That song, wild as black wine" [I sila strashnaia nochnogo vozvrashcheniia / Ta pesnia dikaia, kak chernoe vino].[52] Instead, however, this Dionysian return is unexpectedly equated with a Doppelganger: "This is a double—an empty apparition— / Senselessly stares into the cold window" [Eto dvoinik—pustoe prividen'e— / Bessmyslenno gliadit v kholodnoe okno]. The Dionysian is reduced to a nightmare, false and without consequence, ecstatic disintegration to a Romantic perception of the divided and contradictory nature of man.

If Mandelstam's history of culture in *Tristia* is truly a reversal of the cultural trajectory envisioned by Nietzsche, then the tragic and Alexandrian ages should abut within the book at a turning point recognizable as the "present." Despite the fundamental non-linearity of Mandelstam's book, arising from its organic structure—and why should, after all, the "footpaths of mystery" ("Pushkin and Skriabin") not twist and turn on their way to the goal?—there are several poems at the center of *Tristia* that starkly represent this moment of the present. These are, most prominently, the prophecies of "To Cassandra" (Kassandre, 1917), the portents of "Among the priests a young Levite" ("Sredi sviashchennikov levitom molodym," 1917—though here the moment of reckoning occurs in the context of retrograde time), and finally, "The Twilight of Freedom" (Sumerki svobody, 1918), with its "huge, awkward, / Creaking turn of the wheel" [ogromnyi, neukliuzhii, / Skripuchii povorot rulia].[53]

The last large portion of *Tristia* is best understood as Mandelstam's tribute to Alexandrian culture. In any case, the psychology of his poems on the whole shifts rather dramatically.[54] Rather than stare into the abyss, courting chaos, as did Nietzsche's tragic man, Mandelstam's lyric "I" strives to build an idyllic cultural edifice over the danger that surrounds him. In the face of years of war and devastation, he seeks to quiet in his poetry the Furies that have been so devastatingly released.

Mandelstam adopts two key elements from Nietzsche's taxonomy of the Alexandrian in *The Birth of Tragedy*. These are the "yearning for the idyllic" and the culture of the opera, which answers this idyllic impulse. The thirst for the idyllic, which pervades many of the poems in the latter part of *Tristia*, is expressed most fully in a poem of 1919, "On the rocky spurs of Pieria" [Na kamennykh otrogakh Pierii].[55]

На каменных отрогах Пиэрии
Водили музы первый хоровод,
Чтобы, как пчелы, лирники слепые
Нам подарили ионийский мед.
И холодком повеяло высоким
От выпукло-девического лба,
Чтобы раскрылись правнукам далеким
Архипелага нежные гроба.

Бежит весна топтать луга Эллады,
Обула Сафо пестрый сапожок,
И молоточками куют цикады,
Как в песенке поется, перстенек.
Высокий дом построил плотник дюжий,
На свадьбу всех передушили кур,
И растянул сапожник неуклюжий
На башмаки все пять воловьих шкур.

Нерасторопна черепаха-лира,
Едва-едва беспалая ползет,
Лежит себе на солнышке Эпира,
Тихонько грея золотой живот.
Ну, кто ее такую приласкает,
Кто спящую ее перевернет?
Она во сне Терпандра ожидает,
Сухих перстов предчувствуя налет.

Поит дубы холодная криница,
Простоволосая шумит трава,
На радость осам пахнет медуница.
О, где же вы, святые острова,
Где не едят надломленного хлеба,
Где только мед, вино и молоко,
Скрипучий труд не омрачает неба
И колесо вращается легко?

On the rocky spurs of Pieria
The muses led the first circle dance
In order that, like bees, blind rhapsodists
Would give us Ionian honey.
And a lofty cold drafted
From a convex, maiden forehead
In order that the tender graves of the archipelago
Would open up to distant descendants.

Spring runs to trample the meadows of Hellas,
Sappho dons a dappled little boot,
And the cicadas forge with tiny hammers—
As in the song—a little ring.
A stout carpenter built a high house,
All the chickens were strangled for the wedding,
And an awkward cobbler stretched
All five ox-hides for shoes.

A turtle-lyre unhurriedly
Barely, barely crawls, toeless,
Lies, all to itself, in the sun of Epirus,
Quietly warming its golden belly.
Well, who will fondle her, such as she is,
Who will turn her over as she sleeps?
She, in dreams, awaits Terpander,
Anticipating the onslaught of dry fingers.

A cold spring waters the oaks,
Bare-headed grass rustles,
Lungwort wafts to the delight of wasps.

> O, where are you, sacred isles,
> Where broken bread is not eaten,
> Where there is only honey, wine and milk,
> Creaking labor does not darken the sky
> And the wheel turns lightly?

In Mandelstam's essay "Pushkin and Skriabin," the artist's death is viewed as the final creative act that sheds light on all of his or her preceding work, an act that, in fact, causes the artist's life and work to sound with its full resonance. In "On the rocky spurs," Mandelstam faces the implications of this artistic credo, at the time of his "wedding" to Nadezhda Khazina in Kiev in 1919, during bloody months of the Russian civil war.[56]

The "lofty, cold draft," which wafts from the "convex-maiden forehead" in line 6, is the breath that emerges from the empty skull of the sixth-century Greek lyric poetess Sappho, who will appear in the second stanza.[57] In the logic of Mandelstam's poem, Sappho must die "*in order that*" the "tender graves of the archipelago" should open up to "distant descendants." These graves, it seems likely, are tender because they house Sappho's ward-lovers, whose names and fates populate her fragments.[58] The last tender grave is Sappho's own, but Sappho's poetry unlocks these graves, overcoming the effacing force of death and time:[59] Life gushes forth in the second stanza's montage of Sappho's "wedding songs," in Ivanov's translation.[60] However, as spring is the underside of death, so, according to Ivanov, is the wedding an inversion of the funeral feast.

The third stanza of Mandelstam's poem is devoted to the turtle, the poem's central image, which also gave the poem its name in all its publications before *Second Book*. The turtle-lyre, *cherepakha-lira*, which transparently hides the word "skull" (*cherep*), is a correlate for the poet, who sounds not only in, but through, death.[61] The convex forehead from line 6 mirrors the turtle shell physically and functionally, and each of these in turn stands in for the poet's own skull.[62] A poet is also a turtle that must die in order to sing.

Sappho herself sings to her lyre in one fragment, "*Come to life*, O sacred one, / Sing me a song, turtle!"[63] The irony was clearly not lost on Mandelstam. The story of the creation of the first lyre is related in the Homeric Hymn to Hermes. In contrast to Sappho, Hermes says to the turtle about to become his lyre, but only after a gruesomely violent death, "*if you die*, you shall make sweetest song."[64] Mandelstam's turtle is pictured alive, i.e., awaiting the death that will turn her into the *instrument* of the archetypal lyric poet Terpander, as much as the animation that will come only afterwards from his fingers.

The turtle dreams of an erotic union with Terpander, who is himself *human* and a poet, hence "turtlish," in the idiom of Mandelstam's poem, which is to say—a potential soundbox.[65] (TerPANDR sounds like the Russian *pantsyr'*, or turtle shell.) The consequences of the poet's union with inspiration, which can turn him from a turtle into a seven-stringed lyre, lie immediately below the surface of the text. And those consequences are lasting poetry but the death of the poet. Note also that the turtle warms itself in the sun of Epirus. While it is quite possible that "the image of the Epirian sunshine [. . .] arose from the sonorous rhyme: *lira—Epira*," "Epirus" is not necessarily "simply" a "'signal-word'" for ancient Greece.[66] In any case, we cannot ignore the one concrete association of which Mandelstam was undoubtedly aware: Epirus was a gate to the underworld (Racine, Introduction to *Phèdre*).

Like the archetypal poets Terpander and Sappho, Mandelstam is both performer of, and sounding box for, his poetry. In an early programmatic poem, which nearly provided the title for his first collection, the poet is a "seashell" (*rakovina*), who will be animated with the in(spir)ation of a foreign night ("with whispers of foam, / Fog, wind, and rain . . ." [*shepotami peny, / Tumanom, vetrom i dozhdem* . . .]).[67] In the 1930s, he will return to the image of the human skull as the "soundbox" of poetry:

Размотавший на два завещанья
Слабовольных имуществ клубок
И в прощанье отдав, в верещанье
Мир, который как череп глубок

Having wound out into two testaments
A yarn of weak-willed possessions
And in parting given, in chirping
A world as deep as a skull
—"So that, friend of wind and drops" (*Chtob, priiatel' i vetra i kapel'*, 1937)

Для того ль должен череп развиться
Во весь лоб — от виска до виска, —
Чтоб в его дорогие глазницы
Не могли не вливаться войска?
Развивается череп от жизни
Во весь лоб — от виска до виска, —
Чистотой своих швов он дразнит себя,
Понимающим куполом яснится,
Мыслью пенится, сам себе снится, —

> Чаша чаш и отчизна отчизне,
> Звездным рубчиком шитый чепец,
> Чепчик счастья — Шекспира отец…

> For that ought a skull develop
> In full brow—from temple to temple
> That into its dear eye sockets
> Troops could not but pour?
> The skull develops from life
> In full brow—from temple to temple,—
> Teases itself with the purity of its seams,
> Shines with clarity, an understanding cupola,
> Foams with thought, sees itself in dreams,—
> Bowl of bowls and homeland to homeland,
> Bonnet sown with a starry scar,
> Fortune's bonnet—the father of Shakespeare…
> —"Verses on the unknown soldier" (Stikhi o neizvestnom soldate, 1937)

Salience (*vypuklost'*), particularly in Mandelstam's later writings, is cognate with semantic and creative fullness: the salience of the word-sheath, from which associations radiate ("Conversation about Dante"), and the salience of the skull-cupola.[68]

Mandelstam's idyll, in the final stanza of "On the rocky spurs," is not an imagining of the golden age of Sappho or the archipelago. Instead it expresses, from a setting within the world, a desire for a life on the Blessed Isles, which represent escape from the circle of life and death.[69] Friedrich Schiller, in his "Elysium," wrote:

> Ihre Krone findet hier die Liebe,
> Sicher vor des Todes strengem Hiebe
>   Feyert sie ein ewig Hochzeitfest.

> Here love is crowned;
> Safe from the harsh stroke of death,
>   It celebrates an eternal wedding feast.[70]

What better sentiment could there be for a "wedding song"—and especially at a time of civil war—than a desire to escape from Mandelstam's own pronouncement that "to die means to remember" and that death is the ultimate creative act of the poet?

These same lines betray an allusion to Schiller's "Die Götter Griechenlands" (The Gods of Greece, 1788, 1793?), like "Elysium," set to music by Franz Schubert. Schiller's poem describes humanity's loss of a pantheistic sense of the meaningfulness of nature, which has become dead and rationally mechanistic.[71] The main intertextual link to Mandelstam's poem comes in the twelfth stanza of the poem's later version, the single stanza, which Schubert took for his *Lieder*:

Schöne Welt, wo bist du? Kehre wieder,
Holdes Blüthenalter der Natur!
Ach nur in dem Feenland der Lieder
Lebt noch deine fabelhafte Spur.
Ausgestorben trauert das Gefilde,
Keine Gottheit zeigt sich meinem Blick,
Ach von jenem lebenwarmen Bilde
Blieb der Schatten nur zurück.

Beauteous world, where art thou? Return again,
Fair springtime of nature.
But, ah, your fabled dream lives on
Only in the enchanted realm of song.
The fields, deserted, mourn;
No god appears before my eyes.
Of all that vivid image of life
Only the shadows have survived.[72]

In addition to the direct address to comparable—though not equivalent—idyllic realms with the identical complaint, "Where are you?", the poems share a characterization of Greece as springtime and a fascination with the poetry that preserves the departed world. Moreover, the interlocking of Mandelstam's poem—as we have read it here—and the Schiller context is powerfully reinforced in the final lines of "Die Götter Griechenlands": "Was unsterblich im Gesang soll leben, / Muss im Leben untergehn" [Whatever shall live on forever in the poet's song is destined to perish in life].[73] In addition, the image through which Schiller characterizes the present—"Ausgestorben trauert das Gefilde" [Deserted, the field mourns]—is quite similar to Mandelstam's "Prostovolosaia shumit trava" [The bare-headed grass rustles]. In the Slavic world, as in antiquity, women bared their unbraided or disheveled hair in mourning, and, in any case, the phrase evokes the opening of Mandelstam's sister poem to "On the rocky spurs,"

"Tristia" (as the title of Ovid's work, usually translated into Russian as *Skorbnye elegii,* with its connection to *skorb'*—mourning). In Mandelstam's poem, a lovers' parting is mapped onto Ovid's departure into exile—itself represented by Ovid as a death, which is mourned.[74] Mandelstam's mournful grass, like Schiller's field, is orphaned, left behind, in our late-born world.

Schiller himself forcefully rejected the idea that his poem should be read as anti-Christian. However, this is just how his contemporaries interpreted it in its first publication, and the scandal and vitriol that surrounded the poem were enough to force Schiller to revise it, cutting it back from 25 to 16 stanzas. Even in the later version, the temptation remains to read it as a rejection of the Judeo-Christian God, all the more so if we take Fet's translation. There, the lines "Einen zu bereichern unter allen, / Mußte diese Götterwelt vergehn" [So as to enrich one at the cost of all others / This cosmos of gods had to vanish] read "Chtob odin vozvysilsia vladykoi, / Mir bogov na gibel' osuzhden" [In order that one be raised up as potentate, / The world of gods is sentenced to perish].[75]

Mandelstam's poem reinforces this sense that Schiller's work expresses a nostalgia for a time before Christianity. The "broken" (*nadlomlennyi,* cracked, but not sheared in half) bread of the final lines may be read as an allusion to the Eucharist, the adjective hinting at this through recalling the broken body of Christ.[76] Moreover, the appropriateness of such an interpretation is confirmed in the next line, which contrasts the Eucharistic (or hard-earned) bread, not only to idyllic shepherds' fare but also to the components of an ancient Greek libation for the dead.[77] In this final stanza, we see a powerful nostalgia for a simpler, ideal time and space, free of "creaking labor" and need, a time when history's wheel—taking one potential set of associations—turned easily and smoothly, without the blood-soaked pivots of revolution and civil war. However, we also see a nostalgia for a morally uncomplicated, pre-Christian world, a world of still as-yet-forgotten Christianity. The pull of retrograde time is thus not yet overcome, though the Eucharist is already on the tip of the poet's tongue.[78]

As we have noted, for Nietzsche, the idyllic impulse of Alexandrian culture finds its ultimate expression in the art of opera. Several scholars have noted the repeated references to Meyerhold, Golovin, and Fokin's contemporary production of Gluck's opera *Orpheus and Eurydice* in the latter half of Mandelstam's collection.[79] *Orpheus and Eurydice* is an opera particularly well suited to supplant the tragic theater that colors the collection's opening. First, there is, in this particular work, a highly unusual emphasis on the chorus.

Second, the same Furies that ascend anew to power in Mandelstam's diptych are appeased in the opera by Orpheus' singing. Finally, the plot of *Orpheus and Eurydice* provides a mythopoetic correlate for the drama of anamnesis, which is central both to the latter portion of *Tristia* and to the structuring of the book as a whole: Orpheus' leading of Eurydice from Hades is akin to the poet's attempt to regain the forgotten word.[80]

For the larger context of *Tristia*, it is important to recall also that Christianity came into being during the Alexandrian age. To quote Blok, the Alexandrian was that epoch "in which the Word was destined to be born" [v kotoroi nadlezhalo rodit'sia Slovu].[81] *Tristia* ends with a poem that may be understood as an apotheosis of remembered Christianity, "St. Isaac's under a veil of milky white" (Isakii pod fatoi molochnoi belizny, 1921).[82] Taken together with "O, this air, drunk with trouble," it enacts a Eucharist of Christian culture through representation of the physical church-"vessels" that carry the essence of the Christian revelation and Christian belief into the world in both the present and the implied future.

The rite of the Eucharist was clearly of symbolic importance to Mandelstam (as indeed it was for Ivanov). In 1915, the last year before the first poems of *Tristia* were written, Mandelstam wrote "Behold the pyx" (Vot daronositsa), entitled in an early version "Eucharist" (Evkharistiia). It is ecstatic in tone and describes a moment of timeless and unmitigated joy as the Tabernacle, the ornate chest that holds the Host (in Russian, the Gifts [*Dary*]), is held aloft before the congregation.

Importantly, in this poem Mandelstam uses the wrong word to refer to the Tabernacle. By using the word "daronositsa," which technically refers to a small Tabernacle used for transporting the Gifts outside the church to the ill and dying, rather than the more correct "darokhranitel'nitsa," Mandelstam wittingly or unwittingly emphasizes the fact that the Eucharist, and the gifts it holds, may be kept safe and transported through space and time. That Russian Tabernacles are often made in the shape of a church also has important implications in this regard. In both "O, this air" and "St. Isaac's," Russian cathedrals function as the Tabernacles that transport the Christian revelation through troubled and threatening times.

О, этот воздух, смутой пьяный
На черной площади Кремля.
. . .
А в запечатанных соборах,
Где и прохладно и темно,

Как в нежных глиняных амфорах,
Играет русское вино.

Успенский, дивно округленный,
Весь удивленье райских дуг,
И Благовещенский, зеленый,
И, мнится, заворкует вдруг.

Архангельский и Воскресенья
Просвечивают, как ладонь, —
Повсюду скрытое горенье,
В кувшинах спрятанный огонь...

O, this air, drunk with trouble,
In the black square of the Kremlin!
. . .
But in the sealed cathedrals,
Where it is both cool and dark,
As in tender, clay amphoras,
Plays Russian wine.

The [cathedral of the] Dormition, wondrously rounded,
All an amazement of heavenly arches,
And the Annunciation, green,
And it seems it will suddenly coo.

The [cathedrals of the] Archangel and the Resurrection
Are translucent like the palm of your hand
—Concealed burning is everywhere,
Fire hidden in jugs . . .[83]

In one stanza, the church-vessels carry wine. In another, they are filled with the Holy Spirit (it seems that the Cathedral of the Annunciation will suddenly coo like a dove). In the final stanza, they are infused with fire. All three of these elements are associated with the Eucharist.[84] However, these are also elements that potentially echo the Dionysian roots of Christianity pointed out by Ivanov, for whom fire is as much connected to Dionysus as wine.[85] And Dionysus, like Christ, comes bringing a spiritual message about the immortality of the soul.[86] Moreover, the spiritual fire within the churches betrays a disquieting kinship with the *smuta* (troubles) outside, distantly recalling the "Russian schismatics, who immolated themselves in coffins" (II, 314), that Christian and Russian side of the Dionysiac Skriabin. This cleansing danger is present in the ritual of the Eucharist itself. The "flaming tongue of a new Pentecost [descent of the Holy Spirit, S.G.], which would burn away the old [vetkhii] person" in Skriabin's Mysterium, can instead devour the unprepared.[87] The Christian Revelation is preserved in the Church vessels, but it threatens to burst forth, scorching the world. In hindsight, it is possible to see in this final stanza a hint of the coming revolution, intuited as an inherently Russian and spiritual retribution.[88]

Both "Behold the pyx" and "O, this air" were among four poems that Mandelstam labeled "Nonsense" (Erunda) and crossed out in the copy of *Tristia* he gave for posterity to the State Literary Museum in Moscow. By 1923, he may have rejected or, at the least, found too straightforward the exultant Eucharistic imagery of the former, while the latter poem was perhaps *too forgetful*, too easily lending itself to interpretation along the lines of Ivanov's equation of Christianity and the Dionysian. Still, one cannot deny that "O, this air" profoundly anticipated "St. Isaac's." For, in "St. Isaac's," written five years later, the Russian wine is finally complemented with the bread that makes the experience of anamnesis complete. The cathedral itself serves in symbolic terms as the paten (in Russian, *diskos*) on which the Eucharistic bread is carried. The paten in the liturgy symbolizes the grave of Christ, and Mandelstam, elsewhere, calls St. Isaac's Cathedral a "magnificent sarcophagus" (II, 313) and even a sarcophagus that is "part of an architectural ensemble, whole as a Tabernacle [darokhranitel'nitsa]" (III, 131–32). Moreover, the paten, in a Russian Orthodox service, is covered with veils, as is the cathedral in the poem. The dovecot, of course, refers us to the presence of the Holy Spirit.[89]

Исакий под фатой молочной белизны
Стоит седою голубятней,
И посох бередит седыя тишины
И чин воздушный сердцу внятный.

Столетних панихид блуждающий призра́к
Широкий вынос плащаницы
И в ветхом неводе генисаретский мрак
Великопостныя седмицы.[90]

St. Isaac's under a veil of milky white
Stands, a hoary dovecote,

And the staff chafes the gray silences
And the airy rite is audible to the heart.

The wandering phantom of century-old funeral masses,
The broad bearing-out of the winding-sheet,
And in an ancient fishing net the Gennesaretic darkness
Of the Lenten week.

The service depicted in the poem appears to be a composite of the Good Friday service and a memorial service for Pushkin, which Mandelstam had initiated in February 1921.[91] This belated *panikhida* can only have been intended to return the night sun to its radiant aspect after almost 100 years of dormancy. As Mandelstam wrote in "Pushkin and Skriabin," "Pushkin was buried at night [. . .] Marble St. Isaac's—a magnificent sarcophagus—never did receive the poet's solar body. In the night the sun was laid into a coffin" (II, 313). Moreover, in terms of the volume's mythopoetic emplotment, Mandelstam's real-life *panikhida* for Pushkin, when transfigured in its poetic re-embodiment in "St. Isaac's," recasts the archaic chorus's theurgic appeasement of the black sun, from which the book began, in the mode of cathartically remembered Christianity.

After the opening, the poet turns in thought to St. Peter's Cathedral in Rome and Hagia Sophia in Constantinople:

Соборы вечные Софии и Петра,
Амбары воздуха и света,
Зернохранилища вселенского добра
И риги Нового Завета.

Не к вам влечется дух в годины тяжких бед,
Сюда влачится по ступеням
Широкопасмурным несчастья волчий след,
Ему ж вовеки не изменим.

Зане свободен раб, преодолевший страх,
И сохранилось свыше меры
В прохладных житницах, в глубоких закромах
Зерно глубокой, полной веры.

Eternal cathedrals of Sophia and Peter,
Storehouses of air and light,

Granaries of universal good
And threshing barns of the New Testament.

Not to you is the spirit drawn in times of calamity,
The lupine tread of misfortune drags itself
Here up broadly sullen steps,
We will not betray it for all eternity.

For the slave is free, having overcome fear,
And above measure has been preserved,
In the cool granaries, in the deep bins,
The grain of profound, complete faith.

The path to the eternal cathedrals of Peter and Sophia lies through St. Isaac's, which exists in time. Misfortune crawls up the steps to the very doors of St. Isaac's, and, inside, a Russian Orthodox ceremony is being performed by a real congregation. At the moment of Eucharistic transfiguration, this worldly congregation can become united grains of that timeless bread that is the Church and the body of Christ.[92] However, it is not enough simply to desire this communion. To be free, one must confront the world outside the Church, with all the fear this entails in times of war and famine: "For the slave is free, having *overcome* fear." A Christian can confront this fear knowing that regardless of one's personal fate, the grain of faith has been preserved. And in the same way, Mandelstam, in *Tristia*, can confront the Dionysian abyss, held strong by his "forgotten" faith in a pre-existing salvation.

It is the Christian artist's firm belief that allows him to flirt with the Dionysian siren of pianism, to part in music with the voice, the anchor of personhood ("Pushkin and Skriabin"). And it is for this reason that the Christian artist Beethoven can create in his Dionysian hypostasis, without fear of the outcome.[93] According to Mandelstam's essay "Pushkin and Skriabin," which was both deeply influenced by and argues with Ivanov's writings, this pre-existing state of redemption is the source of the all-encompassing freedom of Christian art, which does not have to serve salvation—as the Symbolists would have had it—since the world along with the artist is already saved.[94]

> ... Christian art is always action [...] It is "imitation of Christ," infinitely varied in its manifestations, eternal return to that single creative act which laid the beginning of our historical era [...] Art cannot be a sacrifice, because it [the sacrifice] has already come to pass; it cannot be redemption,

> because the world, together with the artist, is already redeemed—what remains? Joyful communion with God [. . .] hide-and-seek of the spirit! The divine illusion of redemption contained in Christian art is explained specifically by this play with us of the Deity, who allows us to wander along the footpaths of mystery [misteriia] in order that we, as if of our own accord, should happen upon redemption, having experienced catharsis, redemption in art. (II, 314–15)[95]

And so Christian art is free—but for what? It is free, it turns out, to forget, to tempt the abyss—so that artist and audience can experience redemption anew.

The theories of anthropologist Clifford Geertz are helpful in parsing the powerful emotional impact and real meaning that may be attached to this poetry as play, despite its separation from the drama of history. Play and world exist on symbolically connected, but distinct, planes. To help understand their connection, Geertz develops a notion of deep play. Play is deep (meaningful, aesthetically and emotionally charged) in that it compacts multiple layers of meaning and that the "marginal disutility of loss" is great.[96] That is, the potential losses engendered by entering into the game far outweigh the potential gains. In the Balinese cock-fighting described by Geertz, excessively large sums of money are risked. In poetry, as per Mandelstam, the artist's *real* death is cast into play.[97] Geertz, who borrows the term "marginal disutility of loss" from the theoretical language of the Utilitarianist Benthamites, points out their error in attributing irrationality to play under these circumstances. It is, after all, not really money—or the individual life—which is at issue, but rather meaning. The poet's play, while re-enacting in art the drama of redemption rather than redeeming the world, nonetheless creates meaning that exists beyond the text, within the world.

Ivanov's greatest gift to Mandelstam was to present the younger poet with a far-reaching, almost all-encompassing conceptual framework, embracing huge swaths of Western culture, from which the younger poet could borrow, which he could transform or refute, but which would never run dry of material.[98] In this sense, Ivanov is the author of a great "prayerbook" [trebnik], if in a slightly different meaning than his Futurist continuer, Khlebnikov, from whose "vast, all-Russian prayer book-image book" [ogromnyi vserossiiskii trebnik-obraznik] Russian poets "will draw for centuries and centuries" (II, 349).[99] As Mandelstam wrote, conveying the relationship between the poetic innovator and the Pushkinesque synthesizer, "When the prayer books are written, then it is time to serve mass" [Kogda trebniki napisany, togda-to i sluzhit' obedniu] (II, 350).

Ivanov's "barbarism" and Dionysiasm may fall closer to the negative end of Mandelstam's "unshakeable scale of values,"[100] but they have a positive value as elements in his poetic and cultural metabolism. The Dionysian, the feminine, the barbaric "new life" that must ever be conquered by the illuminating Hellenic "Death" of Christianity, renewing the fabric of the world ("Pushkin and Skriabin")—these chthonic, chaotic elements are as essential as Apollonian form and culture to the Acmeist lyric poet and his whole and balanced art.

CHAPTER 8

BLOK'S THEATER POEMS

Mandelstam's ongoing interest in theater has been well noted.[1] Clearly, not in every instance in which the theater appears in Mandelstam's poetry is there a link to Blok. However, in the final portion of *Tristia*, it seems that almost everywhere that the poet openly appeals to Blok, it is in the context of theater and the theatrical. This connection is well founded. The great avant-garde director Vsevolod Meyerhold, himself an outspoken advocate of theatricality and conventionality (*uslovnost'*) in theater, called Blok "a true magus of theatricality" [istinnyi mag teatral'nosti].[2]

As a prelude to analyzing the role of Blok in Mandelstam's theater poems—I will also examine one poem engaging the semiotics of masquerade—it is worth examining Blok's model, particularly since both poets embody theatrical space in their poems with great originality. The cliché that a great actress "embodies the stage" turns out to be quite judicious when applied to Blok's poetry. In fact, the Heroine's embodiment, in the most literal sense, of the stage essence is one of Blok's central metaphors, the foundation for the modeling of theatrical space in his later poems. In light of

Blok's intimate knowledge of and feel for the theater, it is unsurprising that his spatial modeling reveals a sophisticated approach to the semiotics of theater.[3]

Theater is a laboratory of the pragmatics of the text, where text and audience, art and extratextual reality come face to face. Theater *poems* may mute or, alternatively, lay bare this semiotically charged confrontation. Yuri Lotman presents three fundamental models for the pragmatics of the theatrical "text," corresponding to three major movements in art. In the theater of Classicism, stage and hall are separate, mutually exclusive realms. Art and world remain distinct. In Romanticism, life imitates art (i.e., art serves as a model for life), while, in Realism, art imitates life.[4] Symbolism, with its focus on life-creation (*zhiznetvorchestvo*), the structuring of artistic myths through real-life, extratextual relations and actions, can be seen, with some degree of generalization, as a variation on the Romantic model.[5]

In addition, Symbolism, particularly that of the younger generation of Russian Symbolists, always strove toward the transcendence of boundaries, toward the resolution of those dualities characteristic of the Romantic worldview: this and other world, flesh and spirit, art and life. As the movement aged, the inevitable result of this constant and collective striving to unite the this-worldly "here" and the otherworldly "there" was the appearance of armies of epigones, "armchair mystics," who "cake-walk" over the "abyss" without ever going anywhere.[6] As Mandelstam put it (not limiting himself to the epigones), "Other Symbolists were more careful [than Bely], but, in general, Russian Symbolism shouted so much and so loudly about the 'ineffable' [neskazannoe] that this 'ineffable' passed hands like paper money" (II, 423). In order to shore up this devalued currency, it became necessary to re-establish boundaries. However, it should be kept in mind that reinforcing of boundaries safeguards the value of transcendence. The *rampa*, or footlights, physically embodying the dividing wall between life and art, is one such boundary that may be effectively re-established in order to be more meaningfully breached.

Theatricality, which I will roughly define as "self- or collective transformation through play," can be usefully divided into two diametrically opposed realms—theater and masquerade. Masquerade is transformation in which a consciousness of the transformation, and hence of the duality of the situation, is maintained, at the same time that the worlds of actors and spectators are conflated. No division is present into actors and spectators, nor is there any spatial division between stage and hall; masquerade is demarcated in time only.⁷

In masquerade, theater becomes carnival and cedes its power to signify. No thing is itself, and no thing is only itself. A is not equal to A.⁸ Clearly, masquerade, aside from the major role it plays in Symbolist aesthetics, presents a powerful model for the representation of the Symbolist worldview. Masquerade is the ethical antipode of the semiotically analogous transformation of theater back into a religious *mysterium,* a devout goal of an influential subset of Russian Symbolists. (The *mysterium,* in the understanding of the Symbolists, was to be a neo-archaic, religio-theatrical fusing of performers and audience.) It is no accident that, in Blok's *The Fair Booth,* the *mysterium* is travestied through masquerade.

In both masquerade and *mysterium,* audience and actors become a united throng—in the latter case, welded through spiritual communion and catharsis, in the former, integrated in the same individuals.⁹ The footlights cease to be a meaningful boundary. In the *mysterium,* however, duality is transcended; in masquerade, it is celebrated. Symbolist life creation, understood (or undertaken) without a belief in the reality of complete transformation, is masquerade. Hence, the "antithesis" of the younger Symbolists (like the "demonic" Symbolism of the older generation) is masquerade,¹⁰ and the Symbolism of the younger generation, more generally, when approached skeptically, from without, may also appear to be masquerade. "Lzhe-simvolizm" (pseudo-Symbolism, Mandelstam's term for Symbolism as it existed on Russian soil [II, 342]) is decadence, is masquerade.

Theater is built upon an entirely different semiotic foundation. Stage and hall are separated by a physical boundary: in the modern theater, the footlights (*rampa*). Participants are divided into actors and audience, and, with some notable exceptions (for instance, the "star-vehicle"), dualities are expressed not within the person of the actor, whose non-stage aspect is semiotically mute, but in the potential correspondence between stage and non-stage. These correspondences and the permeability of the *rampa* allow for play with the embodied boundary between art and life (rather than, as in masquerade, for the living of life as art).¹¹

Among Blok's theatrical poems, the masquerade aesthetic is most visible in the arch-Symbolist cycle "The Snow Mask" (Snezhnaia maska, 1907). Lydia Ginzburg writes:

> "The Snow Mask" is full of *realia*—from the unusually snowy winter of 1906–1907 to the details of the masquerade costumes for the ball of "paper ladies," organized in December 1906 by the young actresses of Komissar-

zhevskaya's theater [. . .] Before us is not the entry of the world of objects into the metaphorical element, but rather the opposite process—*the projection of poetic symbolism into life, "theater for oneself [or itself],"*[12] that *mixing of life with art* which Blok feared and which he himself considered the most characteristic feature of decadence.[13]

The participants in the events that became the basis for "The Snow Mask" also recognized that they were living life as art. Natalya Nikolaevna Volokhova, the actress who inspired the heroines of this and the following cycle, "Faina," notes:

> We did not content ourselves with loving and reading verse, we lived in it. . . . Poetry was almost our everyday language. It was only natural that sometimes I yielded to the persuasive power of Blok's poetry and felt myself to be now Faina, now the Stranger.[14]

In the cycles "Faina" (including poems written Dec. 1906–8) and "Carmen" [Karmen, 1914], however, masquerade gives way to theater, and theater provides the framework for the spatial and conceptual structuring of the world of Blok's poems.[15] The single most fundamental characteristic of theatrical space in the modern theater is not the dissolving of boundaries, but the erecting of one—the *rampa*. The aesthetic potential of theater is realized in the penetration of this boundary, either through active subversion and play or simply through the passage of word and image from stage to hall.

In "Letter on the Theater" (Pis'mo o teatre, 1918), Blok wrote:

> Theater is that sphere of art, about which, above [all] others, one can say: here art comes into contact [soprikasaetsia] with life, here they meet face-to-face [. . .] here these eternal enemies, who one day ought to become friends, tear from one another the most invaluable trophies; the footlights [rampa] are the front line [or line of *fire, liniia ognia*]; an empathetic and strong viewer is tempered in the testing by fire. A weak one is corrupted and perishes.[16]

Two separate and distinct—even warring—spheres abut at a spatially defined boundary (*rampa*). For the mature Blok, it appears that the *rampa* is the quintessential structural unit of theater taken in a positive sense; it conjoins life and art and allows them to pass their mutual gifts.[17] The mask is the correlate for the negative theatricality that *conflates* life and art.[18]

As early as "At the hour when the daffodils become intoxicated" (V chas, kogda p'ianeiut nartsissy, 1904), the theater in Blok's poetry is characterized by the presence of a *rampa*. In this early poem, the footlights of an enclosed, physical theater coexist, paradoxically, with a sunset, presumably across an open field. On the one hand, the hero intones, "I, a clown, near the shining footlights / Appear through the open trap. / An abyss watches through the lights— / An insatiably hungry spider" [Ia, paiats, u blestiashchei rampy / Voznikaiu v otkrytyi liuk. / Eto—bezdna smotrit skvoz' lampy— / Nenasytno-zhadnyi pauk], while, on the other, "the theater is in sunset flames" [teatr v zakatnom ogne] and a sigh from the back curtains may be a breeze from the field (I, 339).[19] Life is mapped onto and roughly conflated with theatrical reality, but theatrical space, rather than masquerade, provides the conceptual framework for the poem. Space is demarcated by the footlights, with a backstage in the half-shadows behind the speaker (cf. "into the half shadow of the final coulisse" [v poluten' poslednei kulisy]) and the invisible and threatening implied darkness of the "audience" ahead ("an abyss ... An insatiably hungry spider"). In the poem "The Fair Booth" (Balaganchik), written the next year, the disintegration of theatrical illusion is signaled through a crossing of the *rampa*: "Suddenly the clown bent over the footlights" [Vdrug paiats peregnulsia za rampu] (II, 83).

In the cycle "Faina," which, in the author's final version of the lyric trilogy, immediately follows the masquerade poems of "The Snow Mask," Blok reintroduces a physical *rampa* after the equally boundless snowy planes and masquerade of the latter cycle. However, the division between audience and "stage" in "Faina" does not always correspond to this physical boundary. The true *rampa* is often present in the form of other related spatial and conceptual boundaries.

As is well known, the first deep emotional connection between Blok and his future wife, the muse of his first book of poetry, Lyubov Mendeleeva, came on the night of their performance of Hamlet and Ophelia in an amateur production. In contrast, Natalya Volokhova, who inspired both "The Snow Mask" and "Faina," was a professional actress in Vera Kommissarzhevskaya's theater, with which Blok collaborated as author. In this new situation, the biographical connection between heroine and stage is intensified and Blok finds himself either backstage or in the audience. "Faina" contains the first set of "theatrical" poems in which Blok's hero is located not on "stage" (as clown, Hamlet, etc.), but in the audience, and thus his first poems in which the stage can function as an analogue for or conduit to the "other" world.

In the first poem of "Faina," "She appeared. She overshadowed" (Vot iavilas'. Zaslonila, 1906), which functions as a transition from the poems of "The

Snow Mask," the masquerade aesthetics is still in effect. The poem's "stage" is physically boundless ("And under the sultry snow wail / Your features blossomed. / Only a troika rushes with a ring / In the snow-white oblivion" [I pod znoinym snezhnym stonom / Rastsveli cherty tvoi. / Tol'ko troika mchit so zvonom / V snezhno-belom zabyt'i] [II, 287]). Most importantly, the poem's pathos is in the hero's desire to penetrate the heroine's *mask,* her veil:[20] "How beyond the dark veil / For an instant the distance opened up to me . . ." [Kak za temnoiu vual'iu / Mne na mig otkrylas' dal' . . .] (II, 288). At the end of the poem, this mask appears to fall away entirely, promising an interpenetration of the hero's and heroine's worlds: "How above the white, snowy distance / Fell the dark veil . . ." [Kak nad beloi, snezhnoi dal'iu / Pala temnaia vual' . . .] (ibid.).

The next poem depicts, however, in the purest form, the function of the *rampa,* which serves, first and foremost, to separate hero and heroine:

Я был смущенный и веселый.
Меня дразнил твой темный шелк,
Когда твой занавес тяжелый
Раздвинулся — театр умолк.

Живым огнем разъединило
Нас рампы светлое кольцо,
И музыка преобразила
И обожгла твое лицо.

И вот, опять сияют свечи,
Душа одна, душа слепа…
Твои блистательные плечи
Тобою пьяная толпа…

Звезда, ушедшая от мира,
Ты над равниной — вдалеке…
Дрожит серебряная лира
В твоей протянутой руке… (II, 289)

I was embarrassed and joyous,
Your dark silk teased me;
When your heavy curtain
Parted, the theater fell silent.

With living fire the footlights'
Bright ring divided us,
And music transfigured
And burnt your face.

And here again candles shine,
The soul is alone, the soul is blind . . .
Your magnificent shoulders,
The crowd drunk with you . . .

Star which has left the world,
You are above the plain in the distance . . .
A silver lyre quivers
In your outstretched hand . . .

The light, semi-transparent veil of "She appeared" is replaced by the heavy, dividing curtain of the heroine's theater. The parting of this curtain (mimicking the dropping of the veil above) does not bring a conflation of the two worlds. The heroine remains separated from the poet by the "living fire" of the footlights. Some vague communion of the worlds is, it seems, possible, however. The heroine, transfigured—even burnt—by her participation in the world of the stage, is able to pass on an extraction of its essence directly to the crowd ("The crowd drunk with you . . ."). Still, she remains unreachable: "Star which has left the world, / You are above the plain in the distance . . . ."[21] Note also the vertical hierarchy of space ("You are *above* the plain"), which felicitously corresponds to the physical elevation of the stage over the orchestra seats.

It is in the third poem, "I entered the lower world as a theater box" (Ia v dol'nii mir voshla, kak v lozhu, 1907), that Blok, having established the concept and imagery of the *rampa,* can begin to manipulate it: the Heroine (here, a capital letter is appropriate given her higher-worldly provenance) appears not on stage, but in the box seats of the theater-world.[22] She is, presumably, observed at an untouchable distance by a hero located far below.[23] His presence, however, is not signaled by anything in the poem other than his ability to hear her words.

Н. Н. В.

Я в дольний мир вошла, как в ложу.
Театр взволнованный погас.

И я одна лишь мрак тревожу
Живым огнем крылатых глаз.

Они поют из темной ложи:
«Найди. Люби. Возьми. Умчи».
И все, кто властен и ничтожен,
Опустят предо мной мечи.

И все придут, как волны в море,
Как за грозой идет гроза.
Пылайте, траурные зори,
Мои крылатые глаза!

Взор мой — факел, к высям кинут,
Словно в небо опрокинут
    Кубок темного вина!
Тонкий стан мой шелком схвачен.
Темный жребий вам назначен,
    Люди! Я стройна!

Я — звезда мечтаний нежных,
И в венце метелей снежных
    Я плыву, скользя...
В серебре метелей кроясь,
Ты горишь, мой узкий пояс —
    Млечная стезя! (II, 290–91)

N[atalya] N[ikolaevna] V[olokhova]

I entered the lower world as theater box.
The agitated house went dark.
And I alone disturb the gloom
With the living fire of wingèd eyes.

They sing from out the darkened box
"Find me. Love me. Take me. Whisk me away."
And all who are powerful and lowly
Will their swords before me stay.

And all will come, like ocean waves,

> As storm treads on the heels of storm.
> Burn bright, you mournful sunsets,
> My wingèd eyes!
>
> My gaze is a torch cast up the heights,
> As if were spilt into the sky
>   A chalice of dark wine!
> My slender frame is grasped by silk.
> How dark a lot is cast your ilk,
>   People! I am lithe!
>
> I am the star of tender yearnings,
> And in a crown of snowy churnings
>   Smoothly gliding, pass . . .
> In the blizzards' silver lurking,
> You burn, my slender belt—
>   The Milky Path!

In this "theater" poem, the stage plays no role. The Heroine is instead framed by her box. However, the box is also a false *rampa*. The real *rampa* is the physical "shell" of Faina, encased in which she is able to enter the "lower world."

Faina's silk dress (black throughout the other poems of the cycle) resembles the theater curtain of "I was embarrassed and joyous":

Тонкий стан мой *шелком* схвачен.	Меня дразнил *твой темный шелк*,
	Когда *твой занавес* тяжелый
	Раздвинулся — театр умолк.
My thin frame is wrapped in *silk*.	*Your dark silk* teased me;
	When *your* heavy *curtain*
	Parted, the theater fell silent.

Her brilliantly shining eyes and her radiant belt mimic the *rampa* itself:

И я одна лишь мрак тревожу	*Живым огнем* разъединило
Живым огнем крылатых глаз.	Нас рампы светлое кольцо
Ты *горишь*, мой узкий пояс —	
Млечная стезя!	

And I alone disturb the gloom
With the *living fire* of wingèd eyes.

With *living fire* the footlights'
Bright ring divided us

You *burn*, my slender belt—
   The Milky Path!

The Milky Way is a curved band of light. Moreover, it is *concave*, like the *rampa* from the point of view of a performer, rather than convex, like the belt of an interlocutor. This spatial aporia is suggestive of the poem's ambivalence regarding the side of the *rampa* on which the hero/"hearer" finds himself.

The Heroine remains "center-stage" within this theater-world. All eyes are, after all, riveted on her. However, the theatrical space of "I was embarrassed" is paradoxically inverted, hero and Heroine having exchanged places. Faina's eyes and belt become footlights turned on the world and the hero. It is the world that is the theater, and the unexpected implication is that the hero stares out from an "orchestra seat"-stage past the "footlights" and into the darkness of an ineffable "audience," as did the clown of "At the hour when the daffodils become intoxicated." Like the hall of the earlier poem, the box itself is dark behind the Heroine's fiery eyes ("They sing from the *dark* box" [Oni poiut iz *temnoi* lozhi]). In "At the hour when the daffodils become intoxicated," the dissonance between this wholly theatrical image (blinding lights and darkness beyond) and the sunset image that dominates in the first stanza remains unresolved. In "I entered the lower world as a theater box," the Heroine's eyes are also "traurnye *zori*" [mournful *sunsets*]. The conflation of footlights and sunset thus remains, with both images displaced to the Heroine's eyes.

Given Blok's metaphysical bent and the focus in his poetry on glimpses of the Divine Feminine (and its transformations), one might have expected that the hero's new position among the audience would have engendered a neat reversal of the time-tested metaphor: The world is a stage; we—and with us the lyric hero—are puppets or actors *viewed* by divine or demiurgic director (Omar Khayyam, Jan Kochanowski, Shakespeare, etc.).[24] This is not the case, however. The opening line of "I entered the lower world as a theater box" means just what it says. The Lady in the theater box is not only, or even so much, the object of observation that both her own words and the culture of the theater seem to imply.[25] She is also the viewer of the "performance" that proceeds in the lower world. Thus, in "I entered the lower world," the classic *topos* of the "world-stage," with its implicitly unsympathetic divine viewer, is faithfully re-embodied, but in counterpoint to the outward correlates of theatrical space, the presumed position of the hero in the orchestra seats.[26]

The next major exploration of theatrical *topoi* in the lyric poems comes in Blok's cycle "Carmen" (1914). Ginzburg has noted that "Carmen" returns us (though with a difference) to the stylistics of "The Snow Mask."[27] However, the *rampa* plays a role here that it cannot play, in the earlier cycle with its masquerade atmosphere. This role extends beyond the cycle's strictly "theatrical" poems. In the "prologue," which parallels the opera's overture and similarly gives an "emotional concentrate, abstracted from imagery, of the upcoming work,"[28] the spatial coordinates of ocean (the poet's heart) and the storm clouds from which Carmencita will emerge (the music of the overture) mimic the vertical hierarchy of stage and orchestra seats. In addition, the Aurora-like quality of Carmencita implies her distance, although she can cast her light on the hero's dark soul and effect a change in his "aspect."

As Mints has noted, the artistic force of the cycle depends to a large extent on the overlaying of the Jose and Carmen of the opera with Blok and Lyubov' Del'mas, who sings Carmen's role and is the object of Blok's infatuation.[29] Still, the boundaries between the stage world and life are continually reinforced in the cycle. Every potential contact between "Blok" and "Carmen" *must* be a trophy in a hard-fought war between their two contiguous but distinct worlds. One way in which this separation is maintained is through the marking of all lines sung in the opera with cursive. These lines are additionally delineated with the phrases "But the voice sang:" (III, 264), "But there:" (III, 267), and "*O, yes*" (III, 270), rather than being integrated into the texture of Blok's verse.

The most literally theatrical poem of the cycle, which also falls at the center of the cycle's composition,[30] is typical of Blok's play with a false and "shifted" *rampa*. "The angry gaze of colorless eyes" (Serdityi vzor bestsvetnykh glaz, 1914) is constructed upon an expected contrast between stage and hall and the unexpected appearance of the heroine on the wrong side of the boundary. As Etkind writes, the poem is the "story of a meeting with the heroine in the orchestra seats, where the author unexpectedly turns out to be her neighbor, while the role of Carmen is performed by a different singer."[31] A description of just such a situation appears in Blok's notebooks three weeks before the writing of the poem.[32]

Сердитый взор бесцветных глаз.
Их гордый вызов, их презренье.
Всех линий — таянье и пенье.
Так я Вас встретил в первый раз.
В партере — ночь. Нельзя дышать.
Нагрудник черный близко, близко...

И бледное лицо... и прядь
Волос, спадающая низко...
О, не впервые странных встреч
Я испытал немую жуткость!
Но этих нервных рук и плеч
Почти пугающая чуткость...
В движеньях гордой головы
Прямые признаки досады...
(Так на людей из-за ограды
Угрюмо взглядывают львы).
А там, под круглой лампой, там
Уже замолкла сегидилья,
И злость, и ревность, что не к Вам
Идет влюбленный Эскамильо,
Не Вы возьметесь за тесьму,
Чтобы убавить свет ненужный,
И не блеснет уж ряд жемчужный
Зубов — несчастному тому...
О, не глядеть, молчать — нет мочи,
Сказать — не надо и нельзя...
И Вы уже (звездой средь ночи),
Скользящей поступью скользя,
Идете — в поступи истома,
И песня Ваших нежных плеч
Уже до ужаса знакома,
И сердцу суждено беречь,
Как память об иной отчизне, —
Ваш образ, дорогой навек...

А там: *Уйдем, уйдем от жизни,*
Уйдем от этой грустной жизни!
Кричит погибший человек...

И март наносит мокрый снег. (III, 266–67)

The angry gaze of colorless eyes.
Their haughty challenge, their disdain.
The melting and singing of all lines.
So I met you for the first time.
In the orchestra seats it is night. One cannot breathe.

The black bodice is close, close . . .
And the pale face . . . and the tress
Of hair falling low . . .
O, this is not the first time I have felt
The dumb horror of strange meetings!
But these nervous hands and shoulders'
Almost frightening sensitivity . . .
In the motions of the proud head
Direct signs of irritation . . .
(So lions grumpily glance up
At people from behind their bars.)
But there, under the round lamp, there,
The seguidilla has already fallen silent,
And anger and envy that not to you
Comes the enamoured Escamillo,
Not you take in hand the cord
To dim the unneeded light,
And [your] pearl row of teeth
Will not flash for that unfortunate . . .
O, not to look, to keep silent, there is not the strength,
To say, unnecessary and impossible . . .
And you already (a star in the night),
Gliding with slippery stride,
Go, langour in your step,
And the song of your tender shoulders
Is already familiar to the point of horror,
And the heart is destined to keep safe,
Like the memory of another homeland,
Your image, dear forever . . .

But there: *Let's leave, let's leave life,*
Let's leave this sad life!
Screams a lost man . . .

And March dumps wet snow.

On the one hand, space within the poem is unambiguously delineated into stage and orchestra: "In the orchestra seats it is night. One cannot breathe . . . *But there, under the round lamp, there*" [V partere noch'. Nel'zia dyshat' . . . *A tam, pod krugloi lampoi, tam*]. Perhaps we might even see the form of the *rampa* in the shaping of this line. Two flat, even sides, mirroring one another ("A tam . . . tam"), are divided by the rounded central phrase, set off by the commas, which seems to bulge with the word "krugloi" [round]. On the other hand, the theatrical action that takes place on the physical stage is only a counterfeit of the real artistic spirit that abides within the heroine. As Blok wrote in his notebook, describing his impression of the prototype performance, "Out comes some short-legged and slavish imitator of Andreeva-Del'mas. There is no Carmen [Net Karmen]."[33] The real stage can only be in the seats, with Del'mas.

Without a knowledge of the real-life situation that was the catalyst for the poem, the reader may experience, at least initially, spatial confusion. While the poem's Del'mas is located in the audience, the hero and heroine are initially situated face-to-face. In fact, the opening lines of the poem can initially be read *as if* Del'mas were on stage, with the hero in the front rows of the audience:[34]

> В партере — ночь. Нельзя дышать.
> Нагрудник черный близко, близко...
> И бледное лицо...и прядь
> Волос, спадающая низко...

> In the orchestra seats it is night. One cannot breathe.
> The black bodice is close, close . . .
> And the pale face . . . and the tress
> Of hair falling low . . .

It is as if the heroine stands at the edge of the stage, even leaning forward and downward toward the hero. Her bodice is so close it can almost be felt, but it is still untouchable. Her "Rapunzel" hair (which actually only falls low upon her face) seems to hang down, *almost* touching the hero, *almost* breaching the gap between the world of "Carmen" and the world of the "poet" in the audience. However, even here, the poet emphasizes the boundary between hero and heroine: "The *angry gaze* of colorless eyes [. . .] (So lions grumpily glance up / At people *from behind their bars*)." These latter lines, however, give the heroine's eyes a slight upward tilt, betraying the real spatial layout of the poem. (Blok, in his diary entry, is seated behind and, hence, slightly above Del'mas; she keeps turning round to look at him.)

Mints sees in this poem (and the two that precede it) a purely horizontal delineation of space, in contrast to a vertical spatial hierarchy in the first three poems of the cycle and a reconciliation of all antithetical elements in the final four.³⁵ However, though subtly presented, it is the vestiges of a vertical hierarchy (along with the poet's play with the *rampa*) that organize space in "The angry gaze," *even after we become aware of the true spatial layout.* The heroine's prior descent to the hero's level is hinted at in the metaphor "a star in the night." Blok distances these words with parentheses, emphasizing the wornness of the trope, but they still evoke the image of the heroine as fallen star, a repeated image within Blok's works of the antithesis period. Moreover, a vertical hierarchy is embedded in the rhyme *blizko / nizko* [near / low]. It is ultimately descent (from stage and sky), which has brought her briefly near (even if the immediate referent of *nizko* is the heroine's hair).

As an unattainable star, the heroine also betrays her link to the Heroine of "I entered the lower world." Now she glides not through a blizzard, though, but through the "night" of the orchestra seats on her way out of the theater. Even as spectator, however, she retains the inner musicality of her role ("the song of your tender shoulders"). The heroine holds this role within herself and needs neither makeup nor elaborate costumes, the accoutrements of the physical stage, in order to convey its essence. Her black bodice is, for Blok, the attribute of Del'mas *as artist,* as Carmen:

> I beg you, have your pictures taken, finally, in the role of Carmen and without stage makeup [. . .] You should have your pictures taken *without makeup and in the work-a-day rehearsal dress with the black bodice* [*rabochee, repetitsionnoe plat'e s chernym nagrudnikom*]. [. . .] Fourth Act [Blok has been listing the moments from the play which he would like photographed] . . . some pose from the conversation with Jose—for the last time, Carmen in all her grandeur, so that one *feels the tangle of lace, the gold of the dress, the fan and heels.* (Letter to L. A. Del'mas [11 March 1914], *SS8*, VIII, 435, my emphasis)

The heroine of "Carmen" simultaneously, distinctly, and inseparably embodies both art and life. In the relatively "realistic" "The angry gaze," her "duality in unity" (*dvuedinstvo*) is conveyed in the phrases "the song of your tender shoulders," which implies a unity of inner musicality and outer physical manifestation, and "Like the *memory* of another homeland, / Your *image,* dear forever . . ." [Kak *pamiat'* ob inoi otchizne,— / Vash *obraz*, dorogoi navek . . .], in which memory (of the other realm) and image (related to the heroine's physical embodiment) are cautiously equated.³⁶

Across the boundary between them, which is the real *rampa* within the poem, the heroine passes to the hero her image, "dear forever," which is like the memory of another homeland.³⁷ That "other" homeland is the South of

Carmen's Spain, which contrasts to the wet spring snow of Petersburg in the final line. It is also the world of art, the stage, and especially music that contrasts to the hero's "life."[38] Thus, the hero's communion with the world of music through the "intercession" of "Del'mas" is understood as an act of anamnesis (an intuitive remembering of this other realm).[39]

Out among the theater seats, the function of the footlights, to both divide and link life and art, is fully realized. In contrast, the scene of histrionic pathos that plays out on the physical stage, after the real Carmen's exit from the theater, can only appear false and overdone ("a lost man *screams*" [*krichit* pogibshii chelovek]"). The hero of this poem *does not* find a double in the Jose on stage. Instead, the stage itself is doubled, as is his experience as viewer—of real and false theater.[40]

All of the key, semioticized elements of *rampa* and stage are reproduced in the heroine of "The angry gaze." Her body—and note the continuing focus on dress and eyes—is the poet's living, moving, shifting *rampa*. Her outer, physical form separates the hero from the inner, musical/artistic essence toward which his mature poetry strives. Across this divide is conveyed an "image" and also a draught of that essence. The antagonistic relations between hero and actress-heroine (which are particularly apparent in "Faina" but extend to "Carmen," as well) correlate to that ongoing battle between stage and life that allows art to pass the world its gifts.

Blok's theater poems demonstrate a constant play with the *rampa*, which lies at the heart of what is theater. Poetry provides his metatheatrical genius space for play with the concept of theater on a grand level of abstraction and inventiveness. Moreover, he is able to raise the inherent semiotics of the stage to a high "power" of emotional resonance through the organic integration of the stage heroine into his lyric trilogy. Faina and Carmen take their place within the tension-laden nexus of hero-heroine-*Ty* (Thou), which accrues new layers of sophistication and meaning with each appearance. In "I entered the lower world," the heroine is clearly still the Heroine of the second book (as multiple allusions to "The Stranger" imply), though her theatrical framing provides a transition to the poetics of "Carmen." At the same time, on the backdrop of the earlier poetry, the artistic/musical essence of Blok's actress-heroine in "Carmen" acquires a "mystical" depth of truly cosmic proportions—fully realized in the final poem of the cycle, "No, never mine, nor anyone's will you be" (Net, nikogda moei, i ty nichei ne budesh'). The result is a powerful integration of the sense of boundaries, which the semiotics of the stage facilitate, with the Symbolist active thirst for these boundaries' permeability.

In this, Blok's play with the theatrical footlights, we can see a synthetic revision of Symbolist poetics. The sacral retains its functional place in Blok's poetic system but, as so often in the poetics of modernism, is replaced by an artistic "absolute." "Del'mas," as heroine, is carrier and transmitter of this otherworldly essence, but it is an essence encased in her physical form, accessible to the hero only indirectly and incompletely.[41] Rather than the catastrophic absence of an inherently all-fulfilling meeting with the divine that we witness in the first two books of Blok's trilogy, here we view the hero's rewarding confrontation with the artistic essence in time. Art and life, passing their mutual gifts, are enemies who "should one day become friends"— one day, but not now. For now, the poet's fulfilling meeting with art through "Del'mas" is modeled on the delicate passage of word and emotion across the footlights.

Such was Blok's own development. The next chapter explores Mandelstam's poetic modeling of the semiotics first of masquerade and then of theater, in poems that bear the distinct trace of Blok.

CHAPTER 9

BOUNDARIES ERECTED, BOUNDARIES EFFACED

> Poetry and life in the 15th century are two independent, antagonistic dimensions. It is hard to believe that Maistre Alain Chartier suffered real persecution and life troubles, having stirred up contemporary public opinion through his too severe sentencing of the Cruel Lady, whom he drowned in a well of tears after a spectacular trial honoring every nuance of medieval judicial process. [. . .] Let us recall the Court of Love of Charles VI: varied positions are occupied by 700 people, starting with the signory, ending with petit bourgeois and impoverished clerks. The surpassingly literary character of this institution explains the disregard for class divisions. The hypnosis of literature was so strong that members of such associations paraded through the streets adorned with green wreaths—the symbol of enamourment, desiring to continue the literary dream in reality.
>
> —Mandelstam, "François Villon"

Poetry as autonomous, sovereign realm or poetry as servant of a higher cause, and, hence, of life? Such, to simplify, were the antagonistic viewpoints that splintered Russian Symbolism during the crisis of 1909–10. Gumilev, in "The Life of Verse" (Zhizn' stikha, 1910 [*Apollon*]), hoped to transcend this dichotomy, to show its falsehood. "So art, born of life," he wrote, "comes back to it again, but not as a two-bit day worker, not as a cantankerous grouch,—as an equal to an equal."[1]

Mandelstam seems more interested in exploring those moments in the history of culture when art and life bare the full, paradoxical complexity of their interconnectedness. Thus, in the epigraph to this chapter, he considers the fifteenth-century Court of Love of

Charles VI, in which art is lived but is distant from reality. Poetry is supposedly "autonomous"—but court life is modeled on literature, and a poet suffers real life hardships at the literary whims of the court. In his essay "The Nineteenth Century," Mandelstam describes that moment when the real furies of the French Revolution (i.e., life) burst into the hermetic world of the French court with its "pseudoclassical theatricalization of life and politics" (II, 279). In relation to his own time and to Russian Symbolism, the interrelation of life and art is considered in "In a Fur Coat above His Station," which was analyzed in this regard in the Introduction.

The two poems that will be discussed below, each bearing the distinct trace of Blok's poetry and of Symbolism more broadly, present competing and, in fact, complementary visions of the relation between life and art. The first draws upon and complicates the semiotics of masquerade, the second the semiotics of theater.

MASQUERADE BOUNDED

> Да маски глупой нет:
> Молчит... таинственна, заговорит... так мило.
> Вы можете придать ее словам
> Улыбку, взор, какие вам угодно...
>
> There's no such thing as a silly mask:
> Silent . . . it's mysterious, if it speaks . . . so charming.
> You can impart to its words
> Whatever smile or gaze you wish . . .
>
> —Mikhail Lermontov, *Masquerade*

In the previous chapter, I noted the analogies between masquerade and Symbolist aesthetics. From Pavel Muratov's book *Images of Italy* (Obrazy Italii), long recognized as a primary source for Mandelstam's "Venetian Life," the poet would have learned to what a remarkable degree masquerade permeated eighteenth-century Venetian existence.[2] Half the calendar, it seems, was devoted to carnival, and the iconic images of mirror, candle and mask dapple the canvases of eighteenth-century Venetian genre painter Pietro Longhi. Two of these emblems are depicted in Mandelstam's poem, while the theatricalization of life and death runs through the poem and appears to be the very essence of Venetian life.

> Веницейской жизни, мрачной и бесплодной,

Для меня значение светло:
Вот она глядит с улыбкою холодной
В голубое дряхлое стекло.

. . .

И горят, горят в корзинах свечи,
Словно голубь залетел в ковчег.
На театре и на праздном вече
Умирает человек.

Ибо нет спасенья от любви и страха:
Тяжелее платины Сатурново кольцо!
Черным бархатом завешенная плаха
И прекрасное лицо.

. . .

Только в пальцах роза или склянка —
Адриатика зеленая, прости!
Что же ты молчишь, скажи, венецианка,
Как от этой смерти праздничной уйти?

Черный Веспер в зеркале мерцает.
Все проходит. Истина темна.
Человек родится. Жемчуг умирает.
И Сусанна старцев ждать должна.

Venetian life, morbid and infertile,
Possesses, for me, a bright meaning.
There she looks with a cold smile
Into the pale blue, decrepit glass

. . .

In the baskets candles burn and burn,
As if a dove has flown into the ark.
In the theater and at the idle council
A person dies.

For there is no salvation from love and fear:
Heavier than platinum is Saturn's ring!
An executioner's block draped in black velvet
And an exquisite face.

. . .

In the fingers but a rose or phial—

> Green Adriatic, farewell!
> Why are you silent, do tell, veneziana,
> How can one escape this festive death?
>
> A black Vesper sparkles in the mirror.
> Everything passes. Truth is dark.
> A person is born. A pearl dies.
> And Susanna must await the elders.

On the surface, "Venetian life" is all about the sublation of dichotomies, the effacing of habituary boundaries—between life and art, beauty and horror, the decrepit and the enticing, festivity and death.[3] Thus, an antinomy between theater and council, with their presumably competing images of death, initially appears to divide the city: "In the theater and at the idle council / A person dies" [Na teatre i na prazdnom veche / Umiraet chelovek]. However, the distinction is dissolved through the paronomastic and etymological affinity between the epithets *prazdnyi* (idle—prazdnoe veche [idle council]) and *prazdnichnyi* (festive—prazdnichnaia smert' [festive death]). Similarly, the contrast between "love" and "fear," counterweights on Saturn's ring, is resolved in the composite image of "An executioner's block draped in black velvet / And an exquisite face" [Chernym barkhatom zaveshennaia plakha / I prekrasnoe litso].

These lines, taken in conjunction with the poem's other echoes of Blok's "Venice" (Venetsiia, 1909), hint at the image of Salome carrying the head of the poet as John the Baptist ("Salome creeps past / With my bloody head [. . .] Just a head *on a black platter* / Looks with melancholy into the surrounding darkness" [Taias', prokhodit Salomeia / S moei krovavoi golovoi [. . .] Lish' golova *na chernom bliude* / Gliadit s toskoi v okrestnyi mrak] [III, 120, emphasis mine]).[4] Blok reproduces this image in immediate proximity to a *poet's* beheading on a black scaffold in the Prologue to his long poem "Retribution" (publ., 1917):[5]

> В толпе всё кто-нибудь поет.
> Вот — голову его на блюде
> Царю плясунья подает;
> Там — он на эшафоте черном
> Слагает голову свою [. . .]
>
> In the crowd ever someone is singing.
> Look—a dancing girl is handing

A potentate his head on a platter;
There—on a black scaffold
He lays down his head [...]⁶

In Mandelstam's re-creation, a specifically theatrical context comes to the fore. Olga Matich relates that Nikolai Evreinov, who staged Oscar Wilde's *Salome* for Kommissarzhevskaya's theater in a legendary production canceled by authorities after the dress rehearsal, gave a series of lectures exploring the kinship between theater and scaffold in the period from 1918 to 1924, while Dimitrii Segal notes set designer Gordon Craig's use of black velvet in stage experiments at the Moscow Art Theater.⁷ If we understand Mandelstam's *plakha* (execution block/place) in the sense of scaffold—*échafaud*—the *place of execution* forms a velvet-draped *stage* that frames the face of the Baptist-victim or Salome, his beautiful and horrible "executioner."

Mandelstam would later link the disintegration of the boundaries between stage and life to Venice and its theatrical deaths in his 1930s radio program "Goethe's Youth" (Iunost' Gete, 1935):⁸

> And a few days later, *in a small Venetian theater* a rather absurd play was running: the actors in the course of the action almost all stabbed themselves with daggers. The frenzied Venetian public, calling for *the actors*, cried out: 'Bravo, *corpses!*'
>
> What made Goethe so constantly, so generously, so spark-shootingly joyous in Italy? The popularity and *infectiousness* of art, the *intimacy of the actors and the crowd* [blizost' artistov k tolpe], the liveliness of [the crowd's] responses, its giftedness, receptiveness. *Nothing bothered him more than the fencing off of art from life*" (III, 79, emphasis mine).

Theatrical death occurs both inside and outside of the theater in Mandelstam's Venice. The *veche*, the seat of civic life, is also like a theater, and love takes on the traits of an opera or melodrama:⁹ "In the fingers but a rose or phial— / Green Adriatic, farewell!" [Tol'ko v pal'tsakh roza ili sklianka— / Adriatika zelenaia, prosti!].¹⁰

This apotheosis of theatrical death is evocatively linked to Blok, who ends the first poem of his "Venice" cycle with not uncharacteristic pathos:

Адриатической любови —
Моей последней —
Прости, прости!

> To my last—
> My Adriatic love—
> Farewell, farewell! [or: Forgive, forgive!] (III, 119)[11]

Blok uses the archaic/poetic dative form "liubovi," rather than "liubvi," both increasing the rhetorical pathos and possibly hinting at the *name* Liubov', for which this form is standard. Liubov' Dmitrievna Mendeleeva was Blok's wife and the object of his youthful veneration.

Mandelstam recasts this, the poet's farewell verses to the maiden Venice—who is for Blok also the Adriatic, bride of the Doge, and even a (purportedly) last hypostasis of his heroine, distinctly in the key of melodrama. However, melodrama is not necessarily a negative attribute in Mandelstam's poem.[12] The lyric persona is simultaneously drawn and repelled by the decadence and morbid theatricality of Venetian life, which has a "bright meaning," as the poem's opening states. This is why his desire "to escape from this festive death" sounds so indecisive.

Mandelstam's poem harmonized sufficiently with Blok's own tastes to finally win for him the older poet's recognition. Blok's diary entry from 22 October 1920, reads:

> The highlight of the evening—I[osif] Mandelstam, who arrived having spent time in one of Wrangel's prisons. He has grown greatly. At first it's unbearable to listen to the Gumilevian singsong. Gradually you adjust, the "little yid" hides, the artist is visible ["zhidochek" priachetsia, viden artist]. His poetry arises from highly original dreams, lying in the sphere of art alone. Gumilev defines his path: from the irrational to the rational (the opposite of mine). His "Venice." (*SS8*, VII, 371)[13]

Dimitrii Segal has called this passage a "reluctantly admiring and jealous account."[14] But, jealous or not, these words remain a powerful affirmation of Mandelstam's achievement, if anything the more resounding for their sheen of underlying anti-Semitism.[15]

More importantly, Blok's description of the poem is essentially accurate: "His poetry arises from highly original dreams, lying in the sphere of art alone."[16] Paradoxically, in "Venetian life," art and life mix literally within the *frame* of art.[17] This bounding is emphasized in the poem's images of mirrors and paintings. The last lines of the opening stanza are easily recognizable as a painting, so familiar is the theme—the "Lady (or Venus) at her Toilet": "There she is looking with a cold smile / Into the pale blue, decrepit glass" [Vot ona gliadit s ulybkoiu kholodnoi / V goluboe, driakhloe steklo].[18] Drawing his composition from a tradition initiated by and deeply bound up with the painters of the Venetian school, the poet, as artist, observes "Venetian life," in the form of a woman, looking at herself in a mirror.[19] Venetian life is thus bared by the imagination of the poet-artist and observed at least partially bounded by a mirror's frame, which itself is set within the frame of an implied painting. Moreover, his gaze, as artist within this tradition, establishes his distance, his implicit voyeurism.[20]

The poem's last stanza again evokes a painting—this time, specifically Tintoretto's "Susanna and the Elders" (1555–56), in which the naked Susanna, the object of the elders', the artist's, and our own gaze, looks intently into the *black* glass of a *mirror*.[21] In general, the masquerade aesthetics of Venetian life are viewed from within multiple mirrors ("The mirrors are in cypress frames"). These reside in easily conjured paintings, framed by the poem as work of art.

Through this elaborate framing, the poet generates multiple layers of remove between himself and the object of his contemplation. And he contemplates—not without some longing—one of the key elements of the aesthetics of Symbolism—the confluence of art and life.

THEATRICAL WONDER BREAKS FREE

> [. . .] In my lexicon, there are no words which could convey the enchantment of these marvelous decorations. I watched and thought: "How can it be that carpenters will come, pull on the ropes, and this amazing dream, this beauty and this tenderness will disappear?" And I prayed to the gods: "Let these decorations remain forever—this dream of the artist of the 18th-century, possessing the technical skills and means of the 20th century, and in love with the ideal Greece of our ancestors. Let it turn into a picture, and may the Mariinsky Theater be its museum."
>
> But the side curtains came together, the tulle front curtain descended, and the [main] curtain of the Mariinsky Theater rolled heavily down.
>
> The beautiful dream has ended. We are in Petersburg. Snow is falling. Automobiles honk. A tram rings.
>
> If we did not sometimes in fantasy pierce through the lifeless gray vault which hangs over us . . . how would we live?
>
> —Vladimir Azov, Review of the dress rehearsal of Meyerhold's
>   *Orpheus and Eurydice* (1911)[22]

In "The spectral stage barely glimmers," Mandelstam explores the limits of theater's potential to transgress the spatial and temporal limits of the artistic realm:

Чуть мерцает призрачная сцена,
Хоры слабые теней,
Захлестнула шелком Мельпомена
Окна храмины своей.
Черным табором стоят кареты,
На дворе мороз трещит,
Все косматo: люди и предметы,
И горячий снег хрустит.

Понемногу челядь разбирает
Шуб медвежьих вороха.
В суматохе бабочка летает,
Розу кутают в меха.
Модной пестряди кружки и мошки,[23]
Театральный легкий жар,
А на улице мигают плошки
И тяжелый валит пар.

Кучера измаялись от крика,
И храпит и дышит тьма.
Ничего, голубка Эвридика,
Что у нас студеная зима.
Слаще пенья итальянской речи
Для меня родной язык,
Ибо в нем таинственно лепечет
Чужеземных арф родник.

Пахнет дымом бедная овчина,
От сугроба улица черна.
Из блаженного, певучего притина
К нам летит бессмертная весна;
Чтобы вечно ария звучала:
«Ты вернешься на зеленые луга», —
И живая ласточка упала
На горячие снега.

The spectral stage barely glimmers,
The frail choruses of shades;
Melpomene has whipped shut with silk

The windows of her abode.
The carriages stand, a black encampment,
In the courtyard the frost crackles,
Everything is woolly: people and objects,
And the hot snow crunches.

Little by little, the houseboys sort
The mounds of bearskin coats.
A butterfly flits in the commotion,
A rose is wrapped in fur.
The circles and midges of fashionable motley,
A light theatrical fever,
And outside the saucers blink
And a heavy steam rolls.

The coachmen are run ragged from shouting,
And the darkness snorts and breathes.
It's nothing, Eurydice my dove,
That we have a frigid winter.
Sweeter than the singing of Italian speech
Is, for me, my native tongue,
For in it mysteriously babbles
A spring of foreign harps.

The simple sheepskin smells of smoke,
The street is black from a snow drift.
From the blessed, singing zenith
Immortal spring is flying toward us;
So that the aria will sound forever:
"You will return to the green meadows"—
And a living swallow fell
Onto the hot snows.

As a number of studies have shown, "The spectral stage" is built upon the forceful juxtaposition of opposites, culminating in the final oxymoron, "hot snows" [goriachie snega].[24] Drawing upon these works, we can say that the fundamental contrasts upon which the poem is based are those between light and darkness, warmth and cold, tenderness and coarseness, spring and winter, south (Italy) and north (Russia), the cosmos of culture and the "chaos of disorganized life."²⁵ In short, we are faced with the contrast between the inner space of the theater and the snorting, breathing (and in one version, infernal) darkness of the Petersburg/Petrograd winter outside.²⁶

This powerful and thorough contrast dwarfs, if it does not in fact nullify altogether, the latent opposition in this theatrical poem between stage and non-stage. The viewers appear only in lines 9–14, while, in the opening lines, Melpomene has already thrown her curtain closed. Even at this point, it seems that art has begun to slip its confines: a light aura of wonderment remains on stage, a faint shimmering, and "frail choruses of shades." Still, we are inclined to ascribe this to the play of an imagination excited by the performance or to a figurative description of the glimmering curtain and real members of the chorus, who remain on stage.

This "spectral stage" alludes, as is well known, to Vsevolod Meyerhold's storied 1911 production of Gluck's *Orpheus and Eurydice* (1774 Paris version; Meyerhold's production renewed in 1919 and 1920).²⁷ The sets, including a pale blue transparent Elysium, were created by stage artist Alexander Golovin. Meyerhold had made his name with a theater of bared conventions, and Golovin interpreted *Orpheus* in the spirit of the conventionalized antiquity of the eighteenth century.²⁸ The excesses of the staging were remarkable. (The main curtain was sewn over the course of many months by a crew of almost 80 seamstresses.)²⁹ Mandelstam, in the draft of the poem, calls Gluck "mild" (miagkii) and tests the epithet "Greek" (grecheskii). Taking the liberty to combine these two variants, we end up with *"Mild Gluck calls forth the sweet shades from Greek captivity" [Miagkii Gliuk iz grecheskogo plena / Vyzyvaet sladostnykh tenei].³⁰ It thus becomes clear why the muse of tragedy, Melpomene, has shut tight the windows of her abode. Gluck's "soft," optimistic creation has little in common with Ancient Greek tragedy. Quite the contrary—it could serve as a wonderful example in Nietzsche's *The Birth of Tragedy* of degraded pre-Wagnerian opera (see chapter 7). However, out of the opera's hothouse atmosphere of theatrical convention and unwarranted optimism is born *theatrical wonder*.

Mandelstam himself uses this phrase in relation to Kommissarzhevskaya's theater, where Meyerhold had earlier been director: "Here they breathed the false and impossible oxygen of theatrical wonder [teatral'noe chudo]" (II, 101). Kommissarzhevskaya, according to Mandelstam, is drawn to the European tradition but sees no further than Ibsen. And, therefore, her "incorporeal, tiny world" will remain a miracle locked in itself. But Gluck is that very European culture that is needed now: Meyerhold stages him in Russian, with tremendous originality and talent, and thus arises theatrical wonder capable of breaching the unbreachable boundary between art and life.³¹

Both Gluck's opera and Mandelstam's poem describe a miracle of embodiment. In *Orpheus,* contrary to the structure of the myth, Amor takes pity on the hero and returns Eurydice to him *for a second time.* The opera ends with an "apotheosis," a trio sung before the "Temple of Love" (and, in Meyerhold's production, in front of the main curtain).[32] In Mandelstam's poem, Eurydice is embodied in the swallow that falls, "living," i.e. successfully returned from the underworld, upon the "hot snows" of the square outside the theater. (Associations with the broader symbolism of the swallow, which returns from the underworld in spring, are intensified through the obvious contrast with Mandelstam's poem "I've forgotten the word." There, the not-quite-remembered word flings itself to the poet's feet in the form of a swallow flown from the underworld, dead, but carrying a green bough.)[33] Gluck's "happy ending," however, evokes both hope and doubt in the "poet"—particularly in the final stanza.

Кучера измаялись от крика,
И храпит и дышит тьма.
Ничего, голубка Эвридика,
Что у нас студеная зима.
. . .
Пахнет дымом бедная овчина.
От сугроба улица черна.
Из блаженного, певучего притина
К нам летит бессмертная весна;
Чтобы вечно ария звучала:
«Ты вернешься на зеленые луга», —
И живая ласточка упала
На горячие снега.

The coachmen are run ragged from shouting,
And the darkness snorts and breathes.
It's nothing, Eurydice my dove,
That we have a frigid winter.
. . .
The simple sheepskin smells of smoke,
The street is black from a snow drift.
From the blessed, singing zenith
Immortal spring is flying toward us;
So that the aria will sound forever:
"You will return to the green meadows"—

> And a living swallow fell
> Onto the hot snows.

It is precisely the balance between faith and doubt, pessimism and optimism that is most striking here.[34] The blackness of the street is juxtaposed with the "blessed, singing zenith." Embodied, immortal spring is flying toward us (present tense, continuous). Will it arrive? Will it reach its goal? And, even then, it is flying toward us, "so that the aria will sound forever." Will it? And if it will, it only promises: "You will return to the green meadows!" (in the future). Who exactly will return? When? And do we really believe this promise? Then why does the poet mention Melpomene—the muse of tragedy—in the opening lines? What about the underlying tragic structure of the myth? Finally, what is the significance of the "hot snows"?

Much has been written about this image, but it seems to me that the whole sense of its appearance here—at the end of the poem—is that it cannot be rationally explained. It underscores the fact that the swallow has done the impossible, united the un-unitable. Toddes notes a parallel from Tiutchev through which the incongruity is emphasized:

> Впросонках слышу я и не могу
> Вообразить такое сочетанье,
> А слышу свист полозьев на снегу
> И ласточки весенней щебетанье
>
> Through sleep I hear and can't
> Imagine such a combination,
> But I hear the whistle of sled runners on the snow
> And the chirping of a spring swallow.[35]

One thing is certain: the swallow from another world has arrived. The theater is that other world, simultaneously Hades and Elysium (scenes of the opera's action), heaven and hell. It is the Hades from which ascends the swallow-Eurydice (*lastochka*) bringing art as word into the world, and the heaven from which descends the dove-Eurydice ("golubka Evridika"), bringing art as spirit. The theatrical experience is like a communion, which calls forth Eurydice-Spring, an analogue of the Holy Spirit, to descend upon the participants, allowing them to experience a bit of eternity ("From the blessed, singing *zenith* / Immortal spring is flying *toward us*").[36]

Averintsev has commented on the debt to the Symbolists in the final stanza of "The spectral stage," specifically to Ivanov's highly characteristic usage of the word "pritin" (zenith) (and possibly an Ivanovan rhyme in the final quatrain as well), and to Blok's "Steps of the Knight Commander," both subtextually ("Iz strany blazhennoi, neznakomoi, dal'nei" [From a blessed, unfamiliar, distant country]) and metrically.[37] His remarks should be expanded upon. Mandelstam's "blessed, singing zenith" [blazhennyi, pevuchii pritin] also evokes the image of the blessed, singing eternal noontime of the heroine's native south in Blok's "You are like the echo of a forgotten hymn" (Ty, kak otzvuk zabytogo gimna, 1914) from "Carmen":

> Видишь день беззакатный и жгучий
> И любимый, родимый свой край,
> Синий, синий, певучий, певучий,
> Неподвижно-блаженный, как рай.

> You see a burning day without sunset
> And your beloved native land,
> Blue, blue, singing, singing,
> Motionlessly blessed like paradise. (III, 269)

More importantly, the very concept of "immortal spring" draws heavily upon the Symbolists' usage, and particularly on Blok's elegy "On the Death of Kommissarzhevskaya" (Na smert' Kommissarzhevskoi, 1910). Blok's poem is built upon several of the same dichotomies as Mandelstam's: spring and winter, warmth and cold, south (implicit) and north, "dream" [mechta] and life—manipulated as spatial metaphors. Kommissarzhevskaya, through her musical and "vernal" voice, which is the voice of an *actress*, brings both Belief (*Vera*, her name) and spring into the frozen crypt of a Russian spiritual winter:

> Пришла порою полуночной
> На крайний полюс, в мертвый край.
> Не верили. Не ждали. Точно
> Не таял снег, не веял май.

> Не верили. А голос юный
> Нам пел и плакал о весне,
> Как будто ветер тронул струны
> Там, в незнакомой вышине.

. . .
Пускай хоть в небе — Вера с нами.
Смотри сквозь тучи: там она —
Развернутое ветром знамя,
Обетованная весна. (III, 221–22)

She came amid the night
To the furthest pole, to a deadened land,
No one believed. No one was waiting.
The snow wasn't melting. No scent of May.

No one believed. But a youthful voice
Sang and lamented of the spring,
As if a wind had touched the strings
There, up in the unfamiliar heights.
. . .
At least in heaven—Vera's with us.
Look through the clouds: there she is—
A standard unfurled by the wind,
The promised spring.

Nadezhda Mandelstam epitomizes what she feels is the weakness of Kiril Taranovsky's subtextual reading of "On the rocky spurs of Pieria," through the claim that, in her words, some "American-Russian professors" think that "even the word 'spring' Mandelstam borrowed from Viacheslav Ivanov."[38] In fact, in that particular poem, "vesna" (spring), despite Mandelstam's borrowings from Ivanov's translations of Sappho, bears no relation to broader Symbolist usage.[39] That "spring" is even contrasted to the implied "eternal spring" of the Sacred Isles in the final stanza (itself a traditional, rather than particularly Symbolist *topos*). In "The spectral stage," however, Mandelstam's usage reactivates the connection of the word "vesna" to a set of specifically Symbolist connotations and contexts.

The connection to a Symbolist "spring" is even stronger in Mandelstam's "I into the circle dance of shades," written in the same year. There, "spring" is clearly personified as a maiden-shade, and consummation is couched, through an allusion to Pushkin's "Gabrieliade" (Gavriiliada, 1821),[40] in terms of an erotic union with the sacred:

А счастье катится, как обруч золотой,
Чужую волю исполняя,

И ты гоняешься за легкою весной,
Ладонью воздух рассекая.

И так устроено, что не выходим мы
Из заколдованного круга;
Земли девической упругие холмы
Лежат спеленатые туго.

But happiness rolls, like a golden hoop,
Fulfilling someone else's will,
And you chase after light[-footed] spring,
Slicing the air with a palm.

And it's so arranged that we do not escape
The enchanted [i.e. vicious] circle;
The supple hills of virgin Earth
Lie tightly swaddled.

Drawing upon Pushkin's burlesque, Mandelstam ironically deflates the tone of this unconsummated union with spring. However, he retains its underlying Romantic/Symbolist sense: spring as fulfillment, spring as "new Earth."

In "The spectral stage," the swallow emerges from the theatrical reality of the underworld into the cold Russian night. In doing so, however, it passes not from the poem into life, but *within* the poem—from a represented theater to a represented "world." A Pushkinian subtext underscores that, like the semioticized space of the poem itself, all of the internal space of the theater is an area of cultural cosmos, uniformly conventional, encoded. Moreover, this semioticization of space extends not only to the vestibule, but to the "woolly" street beyond.

Еще амуры, черти, змеи
На сцене скачут и шумят;
Еще усталые лакеи
На шубах у подъезда спят;
Еще не перестали топать,
Сморкаться, кашлять, шикать, хлопать;
Еще снаружи и внутри

Везде блистают фонари;
Еще, прозябнув, бьются кони,
Наскуча упряжью своей,
И кучера, вокруг огней,
Бранят господ и бьют в ладони, —
А уж Онегин вышел вон;
Домой одеться едет он.[41]

Still the cupids, devils, serpents
Cavort and clamor on the stage;
Still the worn out lackeys sleep
On the fur coats by the doors;
Still [the public] goes on stamping
Blows noses, coughs, they hiss and clap;
And on the outside and within
Everywhere the lamps still shine;
Still, from chill, the horses stamp,
Grown tired of their harnesses,
And the drivers, round the fires,
Abuse their lords and beat their palms—
But [my hero's] up and left;
Onegin now rides home to dress.

Mandelstam retrospectively affirms this vision of the expanded semiotic space of theater in his note on the one-man shows of Vladimir Nikolaevich Yakhontov ("Iakhontov," 1927): "In the text, the gallery [raek] is still applauding, but Yakhontov is already showing the footmen with fur coats and the freezing coachmen, broadening the picture to encompass a *whole* theater, complete with square and frosty night" [*tsel'nyi* teatr, s ploshchad'iu i moroznoi noch'iu] (III, 113, author's emphasis).[42] Thus it may seem that no miracle has occurred.

Note, however, the transformation that occurs in the repeated image "hot snow" [goriachii sneg]—"hot snows" [goriachie snega]. The first time that this forceful oxymoron appears, we are liable to let it slip past, to process it within the general context of Mandelstam's "metaphorical poetics" (Zhirmunsky). In the final line, it is exceptional.[43] Why? In the first stanza "snow" is in the singular. "Snow crunches," save the epithet, is an entirely realistic and tangible image. Not so with a "swallow fell / Onto the [. . .] snows," which presents an expanded picture in which hyperbole and metonym mix with the physical.[44] Furthermore, "hot snow" falls discreetly mid-line, and the tetrameter line in which it appears rounds out a regular alternation of trochaic pentameter and tetrameter throughout the first strophe (5-4-5-4-5-4-5-4). "Hot snows" are the last words of the line and of the poem, and their tetrameter line feels pointedly abrupt, coming after a full strophe of longer pentameters and hexameters (5-5-6-5-5-6-5-4). Yet more important is the shift in perspective. The first two stanzas are descriptive: subtext and lexicon set them firmly in the past, even if we sense that the lyric persona is a direct witness. Poliakova sees the snow in this early line as "warmed with the atmosphere of theatrical excitement, which has flowed from the hall to the cloakroom, and from there into the street," that is, as part and parcel of the scene depicted.[45] The final lines, instead, come as the culmination of the "poet's" personal drama of uplift and doubt, occurring, thus, in a Petersburg of the present (or at least in one that is not so firmly located within the space of culture). In this sense, the swallow's arrival is palpably transformative, transfiguring a reality in which the "poet," with whom we identify, seems to stand with both legs.

This also, of course, occurs not in life, but in a poem. However, the wall separating the theater from the Petersburg night within the poem is analogous not only to the boundaries between stage and non-stage (already undermined in the opening lines), but also to the more formidable barrier that divides Mandelstam's poem from our world. In depicting a swallow that has fallen living onto the snows in the frigid Russian night, the poem hints at the possibility that a miracle will happen and Mandelstam's word too will reach its goal.

So, while Mandelstam unquestionably believed in the possibility of "theatrical wonder" within the theater, "The spectral stage" ultimately asks questions about the ontology of art not within the theatrical hothouse, but in its relation to life. Can art cross the boundary into life? Can theatrical wonder be embodied, even for an instant? A tremendous performance of *Orpheus* seems to accomplish this feat. The penetration of life by art, while ephemeral, would appear to be real. Steven Broyde concludes that the poem demonstrates that art cannot survive outside of the theater.[46] This is ultimately the case. The swallow fallen onto the snows will inevitably perish. However, Broyde underestimates the tremendous gravity that has been overcome in Mandelstam's poem. A wall must be broken through in the colossal effort of art, this one time, to bring its essence into the temporal world, even if only for a moment. "The spectral stage" is a triumph of belief in "theatrical wonder"—in spite of the innate skepticism that makes this breakthrough a truly grand and unusual landmark in Mandelstam's poetry.

"The spectral stage" is a prime example of Mandelstam's play with the translucent curtain. Symbolist problematics (including a desire for the "messianic" arrival of immortal spring) lie at the heart of the poem, depicted at an ambiguous state of remove. This distance, allowing for ironic doubt, also allows for a simultaneously forceful and tentative, circumscribed but ever-so-real transcendence of the boundary between life and art. On the level of pragmatics, we have a precise inversion of the dynamics of "Venetian life."

PART IV

CHAPTER 10

"TO ANAXAGORAS" IN THE VELVET NIGHT

> Немотствует дневная ночь
> [The daytime night is voiceless.]
> —Alexander Blok

Having banished the Symbolist lyric hero from his poetry during the earliest wave of Acmeism, Mandelstam, as we have seen, found himself in an enviable state of freedom in relation to the Symbolist heritage and to Blok in particular. However, three poems, all raising questions of theater and theatricality, bearing deep traces of Blok's influence, and borrowing the characteristic meter of "Steps of the Knight Commander," attest to the intensity of Mandelstam's re-evaluation of Blok in 1920.[1] Moreover, if, in the first two—"Venetian life, morbid and barren" and "The spectral stage barely glimmers"—Blok's works and poetic persona serve primarily as a touchstone allowing Mandelstam to flesh out questions of theater and theatricality (see chapter 9), in the third, "We shall gather anew in Petersburg" (V Peterburge my soidemsia snova), the older poet's role is more central. It is that role which I will interrogate here.

It is an understatement to say that Blok's "Steps of the Knight Commander" was poetically compelling for Mandelstam. In "Badger Hole," written after Blok's death in 1922, Mandelstam calls this poem "the summit of Blok's historical poetics" and praises the older poet's rejuvenation of myth, his conflation of layers of time and history, in words reminiscent of his own poetic credo (II, 273). As perceptive a scholar as S. N. Broitman apparently felt no friction between the visions of Blok in "Steps of the Knight Commander" and of Mandelstam in "We shall gather anew in Petersburg." He sees Blok as the entry point and prism through which Mandelstam engages a whole range of historically diverse strata of poetic culture (a position resonant with the most positive of Mandelstam's subsequent statements about Blok).[2] In truth, however, Mandelstam's powerful engagement of Blok in "We shall gather anew in Petersburg," rather than integrating Blok into the curative cultural tradition represented by the hidden night sun of the poem, underscores most saliently the irreconcilable differences that distinguish their poetics and personalities.

In addition, the dominant subtexts of "We shall gather anew in Petersburg"—Blok's "Steps of the Knight Commander" and Pushkin's "To Krivtsov" (Krivtsovu, 1817)—interact in a far more potent way than previously understood.[3] Indeed, "To Krivtsov"—or "To Anaxagoras" (K Anaksagoru), as it was initially called—provides the discursive framework for a very personal challenge to Blok.

In exploring this intertextual and interpersonal nexus, I seek to reconstruct Mandelstam's positioning of himself in relation to Blok at one precise moment, on the day in late fall 1920—24 November to be exact—when he made those changes that brought "We shall gather anew in Petersburg" to completion in the version published in *Tristia*. The document illustrating this moment is the signed and dated manuscript of the poem held in the Ivich collection.[4] On this sheet, Mandelstam had written out a clean copy of the earliest extant version of the poem. He then made a significant and coherent set of revisions, bringing into focus (and in fact constituting anew) his relation to Blok in the poem.

The reading presented here of course does not pretend to any sort of exclusivity. That could only be a distortion of Mandelstam's poetics, in which, as the poet wrote in "Conversation about Dante" (Razgovor o Dante, 1933), "Semantic wave-signals disappear, having performed their work: the stronger they are, the more yielding, the less inclined to tarry" (II, 364). Still, a rich and integral layer in the poem's semantics and function stands to be recovered, and excavation of this layer is crucial to an adequate understanding of Mandelstam's relation to Blok during his fantastically productive poetic fall of 1920.

If others saw in the Petersburg of 1920 a universal masquerade or a vast stage for monumental re-enactments of the revolution, Mandelstam appears to have seen in it, in "We shall gather anew in Petersburg," the potential for that inversion of masquerade that was the *telos* of the mythopoetic Symbolists: the *mysterium*.[5] In Mandelstam's 1922 essay "The Bloody Mystery Play of the 9th of January" (Krovavaia misteriia 9-go ianvaria), Petersburg will be envisioned as an amphitheater where the mystery of the revolution of 1905 is played out. In "We shall gather anew in Petersburg," the city is an open-air temple ("I will pray in the Soviet night"), carrying forward into the threatening present and uncertain future the buried revelation of art, visible to those who would see.[6] The speaker's esoteric vision of the buried Orphic sun, which is most likely the same "blessed, senseless word" for which the lyric persona prays in stanza two, identifies the poem's "we" as members of a mystery religion. Their esoteric insight, however, is lost on the poem's uninitiated, or imperceptive, *ty* (you, sing.):

В Петербурге мы сойдемся снова,
Словно солнце мы похоронили в нем,
И блаженное, бессмысленное слово
В первый раз произнесем.
В черном бархате советской ночи,
В бархате всемирной пустоты,
Всё поют блаженных жен родные очи,
Всё цветут бессмертные цветы.

Дикой кошкой горбится столица,
На мосту патруль стоит,
Только злой мотор во мгле промчится
И кукушкой прокричит.
Мне не надо пропуска ночного,
Часовых я не боюсь:
За блаженное, бессмысленное слово
Я в ночи советской помолюсь.

Слышу легкий театральный шорох
И девическое "ах" —
И бессмертных роз огромный ворох
У Киприды на руках.
У костра мы греемся от скуки,
Может быть, века пройдут,
И блаженных жен родные руки
Легкий пепел соберут.

Где-то грядки красные партера,
Пышно взбиты шифоньерки лож;
Заводная кукла офицера;
Не для черных душ и низменных святош...
Что ж, гаси, пожалуй, наши свечи,
В черном бархате всемирной пустоты
Всё поют блаженных жен крутые плечи,
А ночного солнца не заметишь ты.[7]

In Petersburg we will gather anew,
As if we had there buried the sun,
And for the first time we will pronounce
The blessed, senseless word.
In the black velvet of the Soviet night,
In the velvet of universal emptiness,
The dear eyes of the blessed women sing on,
Immortal flowers ever bloom.

The capital arches like a wild cat,
A patrol stands on a bridge,
Only a wicked motorcar will rush through the darkness
And cry out like a cuckoo.
I don't need a night pass,
I do not fear the watchmen:
I will pray in the Soviet night
For the blessed, senseless word.

I hear the light theatrical rustling
And a young woman's "ah"—
And a huge bundle of immortal roses
Is in Cypris's hands.
We warm ourselves from boredom at the bonfire,
Maybe centuries will pass,
And the dear hands of the blessed women
Will gather our light ash.

Somewhere are the red garden rows of the orchestra seats,
The chiffoniers of the boxes are sumptuously fluffed;
An officer's wind-up doll;
Not for black souls and base hypocrites ...

Go on, if you will, extinguish our candles,
In the black velvet of universal emptiness,
The high shoulders of the blessed women sing on,
But you will not notice the night sun.

Several factors contribute to a distinctly Symbolist tonality in this masterpiece of Acmeist poetics. Among them are the legacy of Viacheslav Ivanov's "teachings," that Orphic heritage clearly implicated in the image of the night sun, and an expansive debt to Blok.[8] Mandelstam's multi-layered allusion to Blok is well documented and, besides "Steps of the Knight Commander," includes reminiscences of "On the Snow Pyre" (Na snezhnom kostre, 1907), "Venice" (Venetsiia, 1909), "Three Missives" (Tri poslaniia, 1908–10), "The angry gaze of colorless eyes" (Serdityi vzor bestsvetnykh glaz, 1914) and "Voice from the Chorus" (Golos iz khora, 1910–14), as well as elements of Blok's poetics taken in a broader sense.[9]

In addition, Mandelstam's prayer for the "blessed, senseless word" calls out for comparison with the Symbolists' valorization of music, though this sense is transcended through a paradoxically conflicting association with the Logos—God as word (and, in its modernist inversion, the Word as god). Moreover, while not devoid of the connotations of romantic love more prominent in the draft version, this "blessed, senseless word" clearly has a transcendent quality, conveyed through its *singularity* and the fact that it will be pronounced, at least by this "we," in the future for the first time.[10] In this sense, as has often been noted, it resonates with Nikolai Gumilev's theory of the word.[11] According to an abstract in Blok's diary, Gumilev proclaimed: "In the beginning was the *Word*, from the Word arose thoughts, *words*, no longer resembling the Word, but having, however, It as their source; and *all will end with the Word*—all will disappear, and It alone will remain."[12]

Equally important, the lyric "I" of "We shall gather anew in Petersburg" finds himself part of a collective hero of a historically engaged cosmic narrative. It is the evidently *theurgic* nature of the lyric "we's" relation to history, the world, and divinity, the focus on transfiguring reality through healing the now-nocturnal Sun of culture to allow for its ascendance in its diurnal aspect, which makes this poem the Acmeist heir apparent to the younger Symbolists' works. A similar example of (literally) choral theurgy occurs at the end of Mandelstam's second Phaedra poem, "How these coverings" (Kak etikh pokryval, 1916).[13] There, however, the song of the chorus is destined to appease the dread Black Sun of incestuous guilt and history turned backward, the precise inverse of this poem's night sun.[14]

VISIONS APART

It is instructive to dwell in some detail on the ways in which the broader tensions between Mandelstam and Blok play out specifically in these two poems and in this period, before moving on to discuss the precise role of Blok in "We shall gather anew in Petersburg." Despite Mandelstam's effusive later praise of Blok's poem, "We shall gather" represents a powerful swerve, in the Bloomian sense, in relation to Blok's vision in "Steps of the Knight Commander." The poets' differences concern the nature and shape of history and time, the role of the individual in history, the character of the ideal, ethics, and the relation of the world to esoteric truth. (The full text of Blok's poem may be found in the appendix.)

If "Steps of the Knight Commander" powerfully inspired Mandelstam, it also, one suspects, evoked deep ambivalence, not least due to the relation of the poet to history implied in the crucial concluding lines: *"Donna Anna will rise at your mortal hour / Anna will rise at the mortal hour"* [*Donna Anna v smertnyi chas tvoi vstanet / Anna vstanet v smertnyi chas*]. The presumably world-transforming awakening of Donna Anna, Maiden of Light [Deva Sveta], who has been courted by the unworthy, philandering Don Juan (with his worldly/demonic mistresses), is brought into a complex and subtly causal relationship with the hero's death, which itself is implicitly necessary to the world's redemption.[15] The syntactic equation of universal and personal "mortal hours" in these final lines makes it clear that the moment of universal judgment and universal renewal is to coincide with the imminent hour of Don Juan's own death. (And one cannot help overlaying this Don Juan onto the "poet," given pervasive connections to Blok's poetic mythology.)

Mandelstam was to write approvingly in *The Noise of Time* of how his boyhood friend, Boris Sinani, who grew up among the elite of the Socialist Revolutionary movement, very early put his finger on a fundamental inadequacy of a certain type of revolutionary. Sinani, with "scathing irony," called "the carriers of 'the idea of the individual in history'" Christlings (*khristosiki*) (II, 96). In this light, one may easily envision how Blok's own Romantic individualism must have struck Mandelstam. Blok was author, for instance, of the famous (if inevitably misconstrued) lines "O, my Rus! My wife! The long path / Is painfully clear to us!" [O, Rus' moia! Zhena moia! Do boli / Nam iasen dolgii put'!] (III, 286).[16] True, he is monumentally self-critical, seeing himself, his generation, and his own social sphere as deeply flawed, as is readily apparent from his essays. This, however, did not prevent him from imagining how the child, who "maybe, finally, with his little human hand, will grab hold of the wheel moving human history," will be born from the seed of someone strikingly similar to Blok himself.[17]

In contrast to Blok's hero in "Steps of the Knight Commander," Mandelstam's hero in "We shall gather anew in Petersburg" is collective, and with this collectivity comes an undeniable, if perhaps qualified, humility. In death, the heroes' gathered ashes will become, at best, a physical locus and artifact of the cultural memory. *Their* death does not in itself herald the sun's disinterment (as Don Juan's death coincides with Donna Anna's awakening), nor is it apparent in what world or life they will eventually come together to pronounce the transformative "blessed, senseless word."[18]

Mandelstam also envisions a different structure of history from Blok. Despite that anachronism and contemporaneity, that renewal of myth through collapsing of disparate time frames which Mandelstam so valued in Blok's poem (II, 273), Blok's historical myth in "Steps of the Knight Commander" essentially harmonizes with the Christian/apocalyptic model: it describes a nodal, transformative moment in the path to paradise regained, in contrast to those long stretches of "eventless" time, which Blok himself called *bezvremen'e*.[19] This Romantic model of history underlies the younger Symbolists' service to the Eternal Feminine and thus implicitly informs large swaths of Blok's poetry, serving as the desired escape from the tragedy of Nietzschean eternal return that is the poet's lot in our frightening world (*strashnyi mir*).

In "We shall gather anew in Petersburg," the words "We will pronounce for the first time" [V pervyi raz proiznesem] likewise can hint at a Christian/apocalyptic sense of time, in which this long-awaited act of pronunciation, *prefigured* by prior gathering, would become a nodal moment, transforming the world and bringing about a categorically new state. However, even if we assume the transformative character of the blessed, senseless word, the overwhelmingly cyclical associations connected to the image of the night *sun* return us to an archaic, mythological viewpoint, in which the current darkness is only one phase in the ongoing drama of culture.

In addition, the poets find themselves at different points on the continuum. Blok's Christian/apocalyptic pathos in "Steps of the Knight Commander" is founded on a sense that the moment of transfiguration is near. Moreover, his immediate post-revolutionary works, including "Intelligentsia and Revolution" (Intelligentsiia i revoliutsiia, 1918) and "The Twelve" (Dvenadtsat', 1918), would have given Mandelstam the impression that Blok believed he had been correct. In Mandelstam's vision, "maybe centuries will pass." The Soviet Revolution ushers in, or maybe simply continues, a period of outwardly bleak, contentless time (hence the boredom in line 21). This time will be spent awaiting the next nodal moment, participating vicariously in the inner, secret present, and embodying the still living, but now marginalized, past.[20]

A shifting of spatial relations also distinguishes "We shall gather anew in Petersburg" from "Steps of the Knight Commander." While both poems are characterized by a perceptual penetration of the boundaries between disparate spatial realms, the relation between, and valorization of, these realms in the two poems are precisely reversed. Blok's Don Juan/poet is located "within," in a room that is characterized by its physical and spiritual emptiness: "It is cold and empty in the luxurious bedroom . . . the night is desolate" [Kholodno i pusto v pyshnoi spal'ne . . . noch' glukha]. This same state is characteristic of life in general, which is symbolized by the room (a variation on the Symbolists' world-prison): "Life is empty, crazy and unfathomable" [Zhizn' pusta, bezumna i bezdonna]. The word *bezdonna* (lit. bottomless, but also a neologism that sounds as if it might mean "Donna-less") reveals the absence of the Eternal Feminine from the hero's world.[21]

Retribution/fate (the *motor* [automobile] and the Knight Commander) is located just beyond the boundaries of this room. The forceful entrance of the Knight Commander ("the door flung wide" [nastezh' dver']) breaks down the boundaries between the room and the near-beyond, supplanting the heavy curtain and fog that enclose and isolate the inner space of the poem until this moment. Beyond the intermediary space of the street is the outermost "blessed realm" ("Iz strany blazhennoi, neznakomoi, dal'nei"). However, the hero is able to hear, through the walls, the *motor* with its horn, located in the near beyond, and perceive or intuit the song of the rooster, sounding in the distant, blessed realm—spatially overcoming his isolation. The whole poem serves as a record of the poet's intuition of the distant presence of the blessed realm and of the mechanisms of historical retribution already set in motion to wake the World Soul/Maiden of Light/Donna Anna, returning her to his empty, aspiritual world.

In Mandelstam's poem, in contrast, the poet is located *without*, perceiving or intuiting that which is *within*. The poem's "we" gather, like the coachmen of *Eugene Onegin* (and Mandelstam's own Pushkin-influenced "The spectral stage barely glimmers" and "Valkyries fly, bows sing" [Letaiut val'kirii, poiut smychki, 1914]), at a bonfire outside the theater (read: temple of culture) in the dark of the cold and formidable Soviet night.[22] In a sense, they gather in the near beyond of Blok's poem, complete with its *motor*.[23] Night, however, is warmed for the poet by the presence, which he senses, of the theater (in the final 1920 version), love/Aphrodite (in the draft version of the poem), or the memory of a theatrical past, subtly underscored by the lexicon (in the 1928 version).[24] The poet perceives, or intuits, what is happening within the inner, theatrical sanctum. ("I hear the light theatrical rustling" [Slyshu legkii teatral'nyi shorokh]; "Somewhere are the red garden rows of the orchestra seats" [Gde-to griadki krasnye partera]). Moreover, just as in Blok's poem there are concentric outer realms, one more distant than the other, in Mandelstam's poem there is an inner and even more "inner" realm. This is the esoteric realm of the night sun. As has been much noted, this night sun can also be seen as Pushkin, whose "solar body" is buried in the night in "Pushkin and Skriabin."[25]

One fundamental underlying disagreement between Mandelstam and Blok therefore concerns the *location* of the ideal and its presence within or absence from our world. While the two poems are united by the heroes' perception or intuition of the ideal realm and share that night space, which is traversed by the *motor*, for the younger poet an Orphic/Kabalistic sense of the divine presence within the world leads to an overarching optimism in the face of "darkness." For the older, an expectation of salvation from beyond (compare the *topoi* of distance [*dal'*], sunsets/sunrises [*zori*], the fallen star [*padshaia zvezda*], the other shore [*tot bereg*], etc., in Blok's poetry) leads ultimately to a dualistic/Gnostic view of the spiritual emptiness of the given world ("strashnyi mir") and, in its most pessimistic form, a "courageously sober" [muzhestvenno-tverdyi] gaze into the heart of the unbroken "Darkness and cold of the coming days" [Kholod i mrak griadushchikh dnei].[26]

For the Blok of "Intelligentsia and Revolution," published in 1918 and republished in 1919 and 1920, the revolutionary destruction and bloodshed to which the intelligentsia is destined is the inevitable and just retribution for the collective prior sins of the upper classes and will lead to collective good. The honest intellectual must recognize this and accept the pain that comes with the death and destruction of that which is personally cherished. Note, however, that, in Blok's vision, if our love is not misplaced—in physical kremlins,[27] palaces, paintings, or books, rather than "eternal forms"—that which we love will endure.[28] For Blok, "love" is a form of spiritual vision ("perfect love drives out fear," 1 John 4:18). In contrast, Mandelstam's ethics centers on *romantic* love and beauty (poetry), camaraderie and tradition, as counterpoints to the bleakness of the surrounding night.[29]

"TO ANAXAGORAS" IN THE VELVET NIGHT

It is these powerful discrepancies between the two poets' worldviews that make it possible to set forth here a rather radical hypothesis about "We shall gather anew in Petersburg." Given that what I am about to say is in some ways fairly obvious (as the metrical and other ties to Blok's poetry were established long ago), I believe that the reason no one—to the best of my knowledge—has ever made the claim before is that the equation I will make appears, if taken out of context, vulgar and reductionist. However, through an analysis of the changes to the draft version, appropriate contextualization of the nature of Mandelstam's challenge to Blok, and analysis of the structure of the Pushkinian layer of citation in the poem, I will demonstrate, I think convincingly, that, while not excluding other associations, the unseeing and apparently adversarial "ty" of Mandelstam's poem is, in its published version, primarily Blok.

Gasparov and Ronen have noted that

> in "We shall gather anew in Petersburg," the association of pronouns was undermined, inhibiting understanding: "we," in line 1, by force of poetic tradition, is understood as "the poet and his beloved," "we" in line 21 as "the poet and his comrades in art," while the "you" in line 29–32 (as a result of the disappearance of the image of "fear, detester of the sun," alluding to the distant beginning of the poem, to the "Soviet night" and emptiness) can be falsely understood as "the beloved," as if the addressee of the poem does not believe in the rebirth of art in which the hero believes.[30]

I would argue, however, that no such confusion exists—beyond the deep and clearly intentional traces of Olga Arbenina's initial presence, which are retained in the final version from the draft version. In fact, the changes recorded on the autograph of Mandelstam's poem illustrate the way in which the poet reconfigured the "ty" of his poem in the final stages of his writing to allow for equation with a single contemporary. In the draft version, the "ty" of the poem relates to two completely distinct and irreconcilable entities— one potential motivation for Mandelstam's revisions. The first of these entities, made explicit, is "Fear, detester of the sun" [Nenavistnik solntsa, strakh], a cosmic and unambiguously negative force.[31] The second likely relates to his current love interest, Arbenina, an actress of the Aleksandrinsky Theater. In lines 25–28 of the draft version, she assumes a role fashioned upon that of Blok's most recent theatrical heroine. Like Karmen-Del'mas, who retains her musical essence as she glides out of the theater through the orchestra seats in

"The angry gaze," Mandelstam's "ty" becomes a focal point for the theatrical essence as she similarly slips through the audience:

Через грядки красные партера
Узкою дорожкой ты идешь
И старинная клубится голубая сфера
Не для черных душ и низменных святош:

Through the red garden rows of the orchestra seats
You walk a narrow path
And the pale-blue, antique sphere billows
Not for black souls and base hypocrites:

The heroine, and the venerable, theatrical essence to which she is linked, exist not for the profane.[32] This positively valenced "you," which the poet must defend from "black souls and base hypocrites," allows for no equation with the "you" of the final line, which, given the cosmic scale of its (vain) threat to the night sun, appears to be "Fear, detester of the sun": "But you will not destroy the night sun" [A nochnogo solntsa ne pogubish' ty].[33] The overall sense of this early version is that the greatest threat to the night sun of culture is our own fear, while Aphrodite's "unwilting roses" (love) are the even more powerful antidote.[34]

Mandelstam resolves the confusion of pronouns by removing both "fear, detester of the sun" and the above image of Arbenina (i.e., both earlier incidences of the second person) from the poem, leaving the second person only in the final quatrain. This, combined with the simple, but profound, change from cosmic "you will not destroy" [ne pogubish'] to personal "you will not notice" [ne zametish'], opens the door for the poem in its negative aspect to be addressed to an individual.

In doing so, Mandelstam recreates precisely the discursive situation of "To Krivtsov," the main contrastive subtext through which he challenges Blok's ethos:

Не пугай нас, милый друг,
Гроба близким новосельем:
Право, нам таким бездельем
Заниматься недосуг.
Пусть остылой жизни чашу
Тянет медленно другой;
Мы ж утратим юность нашу

Вместе с жизнью дорогой;
Каждый у своей гробницы
Мы присядем на порог;
У пафосския царицы
Свежий выпросим венок,
Лишний миг у верной лени,
Круговой нальем сосуд —
И толпою наши тени
К тихой Лете убегут.
Смертный миг наш будет светел;
И подруги шалунов
Соберут их легкий пепел
В урны праздные пиров.

Don't frighten us, kind friend,
With the grave's near housewarming:
Really, we have no time
To spend on such idleness.
Let someone else slowly sip
From the cup of cooled-off life;
We will lose our youth
Together with dear life;
Each of us will perch
On the doorstep of his tomb;
From the Paphian queen [Aphrodite]
We'll coax a fresh garland,
An extra moment by faithful indolence
We'll pour a vessel to pass—
And our shades in a cluster
Will run off to quiet Lethe.
Our mortal moment will be bright;
And the playful pranksters' girls
Will gather their light ashes
Into the feasts' now-idle urns.[35]

Pushkinian fearlessness in "To Krivtsov" contrasts with Blokian fear ("It is frightening in the luxurious bedroom at the hour of dawn" [V pyshnoi spal'ne strashno v chas rassveta]); Pushkinian "'lightness' in relation to 'the accursed questions of existence,' among them fate and death" (Broitman) to Blokian self-importance and seriousness; Pushkinian comradeship with Blokian individualism; Pushkinian gathering of memory ("[They] will gather their light ashes" [Soberut ikh legkii pepel]) with Blokian dispersion ("I will scatter your light ashes" [Razmetu tvoi legkii pepel]).³⁶ Moreover, in all of these instances, Mandelstam stands firmly with Pushkin, who, like Mandelstam in the draft version, finds his intercessor in the Paphian queen, Aphrodite, and her this-worldly love and beauty.

In fact, "We shall gather anew in Petersburg," as a speech act, functions as a repetition of "To Krivtsov," but with the revelers of the earlier poem exiled to the dark night of Soviet Russia. As Evgenii Toddes notes, Mandelstam's poem was written almost exactly 100 years after "To Krivtsov," i.e., one "cycle" (compare Boris Gasparov on motifs of "hundred-year return" in Mandelstam) after the "golden" moment in Russian poetry before Pushkin's exile.³⁷ It is surely through the discursive isomorphism between "We shall gather anew in Petersburg" and "To Krivtsov"—through the poem's profound *imitatio Pushkin*—that the former is meant to achieve its fullest power as an act of theurgy, a healing of the Pushkinian sun.³⁸

"To Krivtsov," initially entitled "To Anaxagoras" in reference to the fifth-century B.C.E. Greek philosopher accused of atheism, is addressed, like "We shall gather anew in Petersburg," on the part of a "we" to a "ty"—an older friend, Nikolai Ivanovich Krivtsov, who is both part of and not quite part of the poet's "circle." Moreover, in addressing the poem to Krivtsov, Pushkin had addressed it to a pessimist (such at least is apparent from the poem itself) and materialist, who tried to sway the opinion of the young poet but whose ethos will always remain foreign.³⁹ "Don't frighten us, kind friend, / With the grave's near housewarming" [Ne pugai nas, milyi drug, / Groba blizkim novosel'em], Pushkin's poem begins.⁴⁰ Could not virtually the same sentiment ("Don't frighten us!") be addressed to the author of "Voice from the Chorus"? Don't try to frighten us with your dire, historiosophic prophecies!⁴¹

Blok wasn't exactly an atheist materialist like Krivtsov.⁴² However, in Mandelstam's poem, the "you" of the final line is accused not of atheism, but of something far narrower and more specific: "But you will not notice the night sun" [A nochnogo solntsa ne zametish' ty]. Why Mandelstam should have directed precisely this accusation precisely at Blok is in fact quite obvious: in a poetic debate that was surely closely followed by Mandelstam, Blok had publicly declared himself incapable of recognizing the "light" streaming through our everyday darkness. This was the exchange, published in no. 2 of *The Hyperborean* in 1912, between Blok and Vladimir Gippius, Symbolist poet and Mandelstam's former teacher of literature from the Tenishev School.

Notably, the draft version of "We shall gather anew in Petersburg" seems, in part, to follow the outlines of what must have been some of Gippius's most beloved lines, at least to judge by the inscription on one copy of his book, *Starry Night* (Noch' v zvezdakh, 1915), held by the Russian National Library in St. Petersburg. Gippius quotes from the following stanza of his poem, "I was overtaken by ecstasy in the steppe" (Menia vostorg v stepi nastig):

И я не верю в гулкий страх
Людского трепетного стада:
Мне солнца в небесах не надо —
Я вижу розы в вещих снах!

And I believe not in the resonant fear
Of the trembling human herd:
I need no sun in the heavens—
I see roses in prophetic dreams![43]

Here we have the same constellation of fear, darkness, roses, and (prophetic) art as in Mandelstam's poem—the same claim to weather the outer darkness through connection to an inner artistic impulse.

But let us return to the dispute between Gippius and Blok. In his poem "All on Earth will die—both mother and youth" (Vse na zemle umret—i mat', i mladost', 1909), Blok had set forth an extreme program of asceticism and disavowal of life, calling upon his addressee (himself?) to sail for the North Pole and accustom his "tired soul" to the "shudderings of sluggish cold," "So it would need nothing *here*, / When the rays rush *from there*" [Chto b bylo zdes' ei nichego ne nado, / Kogda *ottuda* rinutsia luchi] (III, 220). It was the "*from there*" with which Gippius took issue. In his understanding, the divine light was already streaming invisibly through our world:

Ты думаешь — они оттуда ринутся?
  Мне кажется, что — нет:
Но в час назначенный все опрокинутся —
  Все зримые в незримый свет —

Незримый свет, который в зримом стелется [...]

You think—they'll rush from there?
  It seems to me, they won't:

But in the appointed hour everyone will be toppled—
  All the visible into the invisible light—

The invisible light, which spreads throughout the visible [. . .]⁴⁴

Blok answered, in the meter and strophe chosen by Gippius:

> Да, знаю я: пронзили ночь отвека
> Незримые лучи.
> Но меры нет страданью человека,
> Ослепшего в ночи!
> . . .
> Ты ведаешь, что некий свет струится,
> Объемля всё до дна,
> Что ищет нас, что в свисте ветра длится,
> Иная тишина...
>
> Но страннику, кто снежной ночью полон,
> Кто заглоделся в тьму,
> Приснится, что не в вечный свет вошел он,
> А луч сошел к нему.

> Yes, I know: from of old invisible rays
> Have pierced the night.
> But there is no measure to the suffering of a person
> Gone blind in the night!
> . . .
> You know some such light flows,
> Encompassing all to the core,
> That in the whistle of the wind another quiet
> Seeks us, persists . . .
>
> But the pilgrim, who is full of snowy night,
> Who has stared out his eyes gazing into the dark,
> Will dream not that he has entered the eternal light,
> But that a ray has descended to him.⁴⁵

Gippius' bloated, 64-line rebuttal to Blok's inspired reply was weak and didactic.⁴⁶ Mandelstam answers Blok far more forcefully. Salvation is to be sought not without ("from the blessed, unfamiliar, distant realm"), but within—and you, among us, will not notice it.

Some additional evidence suggesting that Blok is intended here is to be found in Mandelstam's "Humanism and Modernity" (Gumanizm i sovremennost', 1922): "*The future [griadushchee] is cold and frightening for those who do not understand this,* but the *inner warmth* of the future [. . .] is as obvious to the contemporary humanist as the heat of a piping stove today" (II, 354, emphasis mine). Through an allusion to Blok's "Voice from the Chorus" ("O, if only you knew, you children, / The cold and darkness of coming days" [O, esli by znali, deti, vy, / Kholod i mrak griadushchikh dnei]), Mandelstam makes it clear that Blok is one of those "who do not understand *this*" [kto *etogo* ne ponimaet], one of those who is blind to the inner warmth of the future, which is so obvious to the poet.[47] The similarity to the "you will not notice . . . the sun" of "We shall gather anew in Petersburg" is apparent.

One cannot help feeling some modicum of unfairness in the singling out of Blok, if indeed that is what is happening in "We shall gather anew in Petersburg." Not that it should matter: Anna Akhmatova wrote that Mandelstam spoke about poetry "dazzlingly [. . .] and sometimes was monstrously unfair, for instance, to Blok."[48] Moreover, we should not forget that, if the poem mirrors "To Krivtsov," as it appears to, then Blok is being accorded the role not of the *chern'*, the *profani*, despised and rejected out-of-hand, but of the "dear friend" (milyi drug), who, however, remains foreign to the ethos of the poet's inner circle.

Why is it, though, that the accusation "But you will not notice the night sun" seems so unfair? First of all, it is difficult to rid ourselves of our knowledge, in hindsight, of Blok's quickly approaching early death and his soon-to-be-pronounced Pushkin speech, through which the older poet will write himself indelibly into the Pushkinian cultural tradition—which is *the* cultural tradition in Russia and which lies at the heart of "We shall gather anew in Petersburg" and its project. Second, there is a natural desire, in evaluating any such accusation, to cast the broadest possible gaze at Blok's writings (though no law required Mandelstam, of course, to react to all of Blok, rather than to specific poems). Blok's poetry, particularly the poetry of the third book, is characterized by a rich, subtle, and pervasive counterpoint, which becomes one of the underlying organizational principles of his book and its cycles.

A third factor is the line "Go on, perhaps, extinguish our candles" [Chto zh, gasi, pozhalui nashi svechi]. There is a natural desire to read this trope as a maximally threatening metonymy, and, undoubtedly, this is one important sense of the poem.[49] However, the sense of "we fear not death" (spiritual or physical) is, given the imagistic structure of the poem in its final version, complementary to the sense of "we fear not the dark." Note also that Mandelstam had already used an absence of candles to refer specifically to metaphorical, spiritual darkness in "Who knows, maybe, my candle will burn out" (Kto znaet, mozhet byt', ne khvatit mne svechi, 1917). And, while Blok had not threatened the physical and spiritual existence of the artistic community, he had forcefully warned of the oncoming blackness, which one ought to fear, in no less prominent a place than the opening poem of his freshly published collection *Gray Morning* (Sedoe utro [Petersburg: Alkonost, 1920]):[50]

Все будет чернее страшный свет [. . .]
    Еще века, века!

И век последний, ужасней всех,
    Увидим и вы и я [. . .]

Весны, дитя, ты будешь ждать —
    Весна обманет.
Ты будешь солнце на небо звать —
    Солнце не встанет.
И крик, когда начнешь кричать,
    Как камень, канет...

The horrible light will be ever blacker [. . .]
    For centuries, centuries on!

And the final age, most terrible of all,
    You and I will see [. . .]

You, child, will await the spring—
    Spring will deceive you.
You will call the sun into the sky—
    The sun will not rise.
And [your] cry, when you begin to scream,
    Will sink like a stone . . . (III, 71–72)[51]

The final quatrain of Mandelstam's poem can be read as a moment of revelation when all Petersburg bares itself as a vast theater.[52] The extinguishing of the candles, rather than signaling an ending, removes the last barrier to true vision.[53] It is in their absence that the blessed women's bare shoulders are fully visible, phosphorescent in the darkness on a universal stage, illuminated by the ever-present, but invisible, rays of the buried night sun. Two readings remain equally relevant: we fear not our death, in the knowledge that the performance will go on, and we fear not the historiosophic dark, knowing that it is illuminated from within.

The fundamental paradox of Mandelstam's poem, in its relation to Blok, is that Mandelstam simultaneously singles out the older poet to polemicize with his vision and draws upon that vision to immense creative effect. Meter, imagery, phraseology, and particularly a pervasive sense of theater and theatricality are borrowed from Blok and re-embodied with undeniable enthusiasm. Blok's art is thus accepted as theater and as part of that poetic-theatrical heritage which lives on in the heart of the Petersburg night. However, Blok's worldview is rejected as a pessimistic vision blind to that very presence of which his art is an essential element.

So, fair or unfair, in late fall 1920, Blok found himself, in Mandelstam's eyes, marginal to the circle of continuers and worshippers of Pushkinian culture, worshippers of the Word.[54] This was a fate he would not have to suffer for long, however, for on 11 February 1921, Petersburg would celebrate the eighty-fourth anniversary of Pushkin's death and Blok would read his famous memorial speech, "On the Calling of the Poet" (O naznachenii poeta), linking his own impending, but still hidden, tragic death to Pushkin's for all time.

CHAPTER 11

FROM THEATRICALITY TO TRAGEDY

> Two things are most foreign to the poetry of Sologub, as much as I have come to study it. First of all, immediacy [neposredstvennost'] (though where [is it] in general among us [. . .] Not the crafty Blok, surely? [Uzh ne lukavyi li Blok?])
> —Innokenty Annensky, "On Contemporary Lyricism"

> The footlights are shattered. Hamlet-Blok really perished.
> —Boris Eikhenbaum, "Blok's Fate"

Mandelstam's struggle, not with Blok's ideas or with Blok as a person, but with Blok as a poet, is most fundamentally an attempt to evaluate him on the axis that stretches from theatricality to tragedy. Put another way, Mandelstam's poems seem, on one level, to problematize and wrestle with the ontological status of the tragic drama represented in Blok's poetry. Do we believe in Blok as the figure represented in his art, in its totality (irony included)? Is Blok's mask simply a mask, or is his mask an illusion that distracts us from the real face of his tragedy as a poet? Can there be a real confluence of life and art—can there be tragedy—in the present?

Mandelstam was skeptical of tragedy in contemporary, and especially Symbolist, art. As early as 1914, he cast the nineteenth and twentieth centuries as an age no longer capable of producing tragedies:

Что делать вам в театре полуслова
И полумаск, герои и цари?
И для меня явленье Озерова —
Последний луч трагической зари.

What are you to do in the theater of innuendo
And half masks, you heroes and kings?
And for me the appearance of [eighteenth-century
                                        Russian tragedian] Ozerov
Is the final ray of the tragic sunset.[1]

At the other extreme of his creative life, in "Where is the bound and crucified moan?" (Gde sviazannyi i prigvozhdennyi ston?, 1937), the poet would assert: "It's not to be—one cannot bring back tragedies" [Tomu ne byt'— tragedii ne vernut']. While this poem's "Airy-stone theater of expanding times" [Vozdushno-kamennyi teatr vremen rastushchikh] would seem to be a new amphitheater, in which spectators and participants are fused (a key element of Ivanov's project), collectivity here exists in opposition to the traditional, individual face of tragedy: "[. . .] everyone wants to see *everyone*— / Born, mortal and defying [not taking] death" [vse khotiat uvidet' *vsekh*— / Rozhdennykh, gibel'nykh i smerti ne imushchikh, emphasis mine]. The *individual* tragic hero, heir to Prometheus's legacy, is no more. "Where is Prometheus—support and succor of the cliff?" [Gde Prometei—skaly podspor'e i posob'e?], he intones.

Mandelstam was not alone in his doubt. Annensky, an important arbiter of taste for the Acmeists, had also remarked on the emptiness of pretensions to tragedy among his contemporaries:

> Those previous romantics could only believe and perish; they sacrificed to their God even the last flowers of youth—the beauty of [their] dream. But contemporary poets are not at all that way [. . .] Their justification is in art, and not in anything more [. . .] And so legends, perhaps, do form around poets, but not one legend will arise surrounding the contemporary poetic names.[2] [. . .] Cyrano de Bergerac or even just Gérard de Nerval? Pushkin? Shevchenko?
>
>   Forget it, please. [. . .] Those non-aesthetic romantics in contrast don't depict any legends, but they themselves are legends. [. . .] All these aesthetes from time to time imagine themselves tragic, as if it's the same thing as writing tragedies.[3]

Tragedy demands a real, larger-than-life, but still individual, catastrophe, and it demands a hero large enough to fall hard. But what if we doubt the authenticity of the catastrophe at the core of the drama? In *The Egyptian Stamp* (Egipetskaia marka, 1927–28), Mandelstam wrote:

> A scandal is what we call that demon discovered by Russian prose or Russian life itself in the [eighteen-]forties or there about. It's not a catastrophe, but its impersonator, its base transformation [. . .] Scandal lives on the grease-stained, out-of-date passport issued by literature. (II, 27)

In regard to the Andrei Bely of 1923, Mandelstam noted, "If a person experiences colossal spiritual catastrophes three times a day, we cease to believe him" (II, 423).[4] Is Blok's tragedy a real catastrophe, or does it simply ape a catastrophe, while living on a "passport issued by literature"?

Mandelstam clearly deems Symbolist art as it existed for the most part in Russia "theatrical" in a negative sense. The bulk of Symbolist poetry is lacking that which can anchor it within the world, give it longevity, make it "real," as art: "That which is objectively valuable hides under a heap of *stage-prop*, pseudo-Symbolist trash [pod kuchei *butaforskogo*, lzhe-simvolistskogo khlama]" (II, 342, my emphasis). The "grandiose constructions of Russian Symbolism," which remind the poet of installations at a world's fair, are whisked away like stage decorations ("the exhibition ended, and they hauled away the wooden planks on carts" (*SP,* 525).

Mandelstam's distrust in the authenticity of Symbolist art is also linked to the Symbolists' histrionics. As he wrote in "A Letter about Russian Poetry," "they struck the highest, most tensile note right away, deafened themselves and did not use the voice [in its] organic capacity for development." Notably, their histrionics is also a dissolution of boundaries, "[. . .] hypertrophy of the creative 'I,' which has conflated its own boundaries with the boundaries of a newly discovered, exciting world, has been left without firm contours, and no longer feels a single cell its own, stricken with the morbid dropsy of universal themes" (*SP,* 526). In this article, written after Blok's death, Mandelstam is at his most charitable (or fair) regarding the older poet. Here, Mandelstam contrasts the unnatural, false voice of the Symbolists with the natural voice of Blok: "It is most convenient to measure our Symbolism on the scale of Blok's poetry. That is living mercury. He has it both warm and cold, while there it is always hot" (ibid.). Similarly, in the essay "Komissarzhevskaya," written in 1923, the unnatural and demonic metatheatricality of Meyerhold besets the great actress, who is nonetheless gifted with a tragic voice:[5] "*Amidst grunting and bellowing, whining and declamation,* her voice, akin to the voice of Blok, grew mature and firm" [*Sredi khriukan'ia i reva, nyt'ia i deklamatsii muzhal i krep ee golos, rodstvennyi golosu Bloka*] (*SP,* 308, emphasis mine).⁶

Mandelstam's recognition of the incomparably greater affective power and organicity of Blok's poetry—deemed "living mercury" [*zhivaia rtut'*]—did not exempt the latter poet, certainly in 1920, from questions of histrionics and disingenuousness. The theatricality that seemed naturally to attach to Blok was evident in his public persona, his connections to the theater and theatrical life, and his poetry itself (for instance in such images as those of Hamlet, the Snow Mask, Carmen, and Don Juan). Mandelstam underscores Blok's theatricality when he connects Blok's image of "black velvet" to the theater, when he rehearses the older poet's farewell to the Adriatic as melodrama, or when he so powerfully evokes "The Steps of the Knight Commander" ("A heavy, dense curtain at the entrance") in a poem as permeated with theatrical images as "We shall gather anew in Petersburg."

Shortly after Blok's death in 1921, Boris Eikhenbaum wrote that Blok's art presented to the viewer in the 1910s, "instead of the desired confluence of art, life, and politics—a contrast terrifying in its 'inseparability and unfusedness': Symbolism, maximalism, and . . . dandyism."⁷ Blok himself prepared the public for the outcome of his tragedy in his verse, asserts Eikhenbaum in his essay "Blok's Fate" (Sud'ba Bloka). The tragic dénouement that was his death seemed to arise not from external forces, but from within. First there had been a mixture of disbelief and unwitting belief regarding Blok's poetry. On the one hand, contemporaries "saw only a 'tragic game'"; Blok became a tragic actor playing himself, "instead of the authentic and impossible confluence of art and life [which Blok wished for]—a stage illusion." On the other hand, "When Blok appeared, it became terrifying [*zhutko*]: he looked so much like himself [*tak pokhozh byl na samogo sebia*]"; people "ceased to see the poet and person, they saw the mask of a tragic actor and gave themselves up to the hypnosis of his performance [*igra*]."

> And here came the sudden end of his tragedy: the stage death prepared by the entire course of [the tragedy] turned out to be a real death . . .
> And we are shaken, as the viewer is shaken, when before his eyes, in the fifth act of a tragedy, the actor pours out real blood [*istekaet nastoiashchei krov'iu*].
> The *rampa* is destroyed. Hamlet-Blok really perished.⁸

Eikhenbaum is of course inverting the classic motif of the destruction of stage illusion from Blok's own play and poem "The Fair Booth." In the central stanzas of the poem, written in 1905, a small boy and girl discuss the action of a fairground puppet show, mirroring in their argument the discourse questioning the signs of Sophia's approach in Blok's poetry. The boy misinterprets the light of torches at stage *left* (already a bad sign, perhaps) as a hint that the "queen" is approaching to save a tot from his demonic kidnapper. The girl retorts that he has mistaken the signs, and she exposes the "true" nature of the approaching "hellish retinue." Still, her words betray an engagement which demonstrates that she accords the stage action meaning. Then comes the truly "demonic" dénouement: "Suddenly a clown bent over the footlights / And screamed: 'Help! / I'm hemorrhaging cranberry juice!'" [Vdrug paiats peregnulsia za rampu / I krichit: 'Pomogite! / Istekaiu ia kliukvennym sokom!'] (II, 83). Theatrical illusion is destroyed, and it is this destruction of the illusion of meaning that is most painful for the boy and girl, as clearly it is for the poet too. In Eikhenbaum's revision, the *rampa* is again subverted. However, what appeared to be Blok's mocking of tragedy turns out to be its heretofore "impossible" realization. Blok's fate becomes proof that the most caustic romantic irony can be a hairsbreadth away from tragedy.

For Mandelstam, Eikhenbaum's article clearly had a deep resonance. In "A. Blok," he respectfully calls it and Zhirmunsky's "The Poetry of Alexander Blok" (Poeziia Aleksandra Bloka) "studies, precisely studies [raboty, imenno raboty]" and contrasts them to the "swamp vapors of Russian criticism" that have surrounded Blok since his death (II, 270).

Blok's convincing transformation from actor to protagonist in his own tragedy—or rather from actor and protagonist in a potentially only literary tragedy to actor and protagonist in a real one—was prepared not only by his poetry, but also by his celebrated Pushkin speech. Among the privations of the post–Civil War winter of 1921, the Petrograd art community decided to mark the eighty-fourth anniversary of the great poet's death.[9] Mandelstam himself, in keeping with his project to heal the Pushkinian sun of culture, instigated a memorial service for Pushkin at St. Isaac's Cathedral.[10] Three days earlier, on 11 February, had been the opening ceremonies, at which Kuzmin read his poem "Pushkin" and Blok gave his much anticipated address, "On the Calling of the Poet" (O naznachenii poeta).

We have seen the role that Pushkin played in Mandelstam's poetic mythology in the fall of 1920. The opening lines of "Pushkin and Skriabin," describing Pushkin's death, as well as Mandelstam's own construction of his life and poetry in the 1930s as an echo of Pushkin's fate and poetry in the 1830s, leave little room for doubt that Pushkin's death continued to represent the quintessential positive model of the death of the artist over a long swath of Mandelstam's creative life.[11]

How remarkable then, and replete with meaning, must it have been for Mandelstam to hear (almost certainly) or, in any case, read Blok's speech. In words that in retrospect seem to foreshadow his own tragic end, Blok not only stood firmly with the Pushkinian heritage of Russian culture, but defended it with evident civic courage from that contemporary "rabble," the enemies of culture, who remain powerfully present as the *other*—and no less primary—addressee of the final stanza of "We shall gather anew."[12] Moreover, the tropes Blok chose—secret freedom, asphyxiation—surely demonstrated for Mandelstam his uncommon *perspicacity*. Thus, Blok himself gave the lie to Mandelstam's misgivings and unequivocally aligned himself with the defenders of the Word. Six months later, he was dead from what seemed to contemporaries an entirely mysterious illness.[13]

Mandelstam wrote in "Pushkin and Skriabin":

> It seems to me that the death of an artist should not be excluded from the chain of his creative accomplishments, but should be considered the final, crowning link. From this entirely Christian point of view, the death of Skriabin is surprising. [. . .] If one is to tear the shroud of death from this creative life, it will flow freely from its source—death, arranging itself around [this death], as around its sun, and soaking up its light. (II, 313)

Skriabin's theosophical searchings are revealed to be a struggle for Christian memory when placed before the "blinding and unexpected light" (II, 318) of his Christ-like kenosis. Similarly, Blok's tragic wasting away, in combination with his self-reflexively prophetic words about the death of Pushkin, had the power to transfigure his tragic pose into the material of real tragedy. Death completes the greatest works of art by providing an outlet to life.[14]

Mandelstam's poetic response to Blok's death is to be sought in "Concert at the Railway Station" (Kontsert na vokzale, 1921?).[15] Here, Mandelstam elevates Blok through connecting him to Pushkin, and, more broadly, integrating him into the composite tragic face of the dying nineteenth century.[16] In that same August of 1921 in which Blok died, Mandelstam's brother in Acmeism, Nikolai Gumilev, was executed by the Bolsheviks for his alleged role in the Kronstadt uprising. The deaths of Blok and Gumilev were deeply bound up in the contemporary consciousness.[17] As Boris Gasparov has convincingly argued, in Mandelstam's poem, "the images of Pushkin, Blok and Gumilev combine in a single mythological paradigm of the 'death of the poet' as a symbol of the exit from the world of the 'spirit of music.'"[18]

Концерт на вокзале

Нельзя дышать, и твердь кишит червями,
И ни одна звезда не говорит,
Но, видит Бог, есть музыка над нами,
Дрожит вокзал от пенья Аонид
И снова, паровозными свистками
Разорванный, скрипичный воздух слит.

Огромный парк. Вокзала шар стеклянный.
Железный мир опять заворожен.
На звучный пир в элизиум туманный
Торжественно уносится вагон.
Павлиний крик и рокот фортепьянный —
Я опоздал. Мне страшно. Это сон.

И я вхожу в стеклянный лес вокзала,
Скрипичный строй в смятеньи и слезах.
Ночного хора дикое начало
И запах роз в гниющих парниках,
Где под стеклянным небом ночевала
Родная тень в кочующих толпах.

И мнится мне: весь в музыке и пене,
Железный мир так нищенски дрожит,
В стеклянные я упираюсь сени;
<Горячий пар зрачки смычков слепит.>
Куда же ты? На тризне милой тени
В последний раз нам музыка звучит.

1921

Concert at the Railway Station

One cannot breathe, and the firmament writhes with worms,
And not a single star doth speak,
But, as God is witness, there is music above us,
The station trembles with the singing of the Aonides,
And once again, the torn, violin-filled air

Is fused by the whistles of steam engines.[20]

A giant park. The glass sphere of the station.
The iron world is once again enthralled.
To a sonorous feast in foggy Elysium
The train car is solemnly whisked off.
The cry of a peacock and the piano's rumble—
I'm late. I'm frightened. This is a dream.

And I walk into the glass forest of the station,
The formation of violins is in disarray and tears.
The wild beginning of the night chorus,
The scent of roses in rotting hothouses,
Where under a glass heavens passed the night
A native shade among nomadic crowds.

And it seems to me: all in music and in foam,
The iron world so like a beggar trembles,
I stare into the glass canopy;
<Hot steam blinds the pupils of the violin bows.>
Where are you off to? At the funeral feast of a dear shade
Music plays for us for the last time.

1921

We can perhaps agree with Taranovsky that Blok's lyric voice is not *heard* in the poem in the same way that the voices of Lermontov or Tiutchev are.[21] However, Blok's presence is not only strongly signaled, but also of structural importance. The primary references have already been noted. First, there is the date—"1921." Ronen presents highly convincing evidence that the poem was completed no earlier than 1922. The implication, noted by Boris Gasparov, is that the marked date, evoking the Pushkin anniversary and Blok's and Gumilev's deaths, is not a source of biographical information, but an integral element of the poem's symbolic structure.[22] Second, Blok is evinced as a key voice in the debate on the nature of the "iron" nineteenth century and its music. Eminently musical and musicocentric, Blok had linked in his essays the catastrophic end of the "iron age" and the elementally destructive and renewing "spirit of music."[23] In this regard, Ronen and Freidin cite a number of deeply resonant passages from Blok's prose.[24]

Blok's words and experience are integrated directly into the "poet's" in the poem's first line. In "On the Calling of the Poet," Blok had said of Pushkin's death:

> And Pushkin also was not at all killed by the bullet of D'Anthès. He was killed by a lack of air . . . *Peace* [Pokoi] and *freedom* [volia]. They are necessary to the poet for the emancipation of harmony. But serenity and freedom are also taken away. Not outward peace, but creative peace. Not childish freedom, not a freedom for liberalism, but creative freedom—secret freedom [tainaia svoboda]. And the poet dies, because there is nothing left for him to breathe [dyshat' emu uzhe nechem]. (VI, 187).

Blok's words surely resonated with Mandelstam's own deep-rooted feelings about the connection between air, breathing, freedom, and poetry.[25] Mandelstam's "One cannot breathe" [Nel'zia dyshat'] simultaneously evokes all of the following: Pushkin's reported last words ("It's hard to breathe" [Tiazhelo dyshat', davit]); Blok's Pushkin speech; Blok's own "One cannot breathe. In the orchestra seats it is night" [Nel'zia dyshat'. V partere noch'] (at an opera);[26] Blok's outwardly mysterious physical deterioration and death[27] and Mandelstam's feeling of suffocation, both as an asthmatic child in the dense crowd at Pavlovsk[28] and as a poet in the Soviet night. One palpably senses the suffocation at the news of Blok's and Gumilev's deaths.

If the glass ceiling of the station is a firmament that writhes with worms, then, on some level, the station has become a grave or underworld.[29] The presence of the Aonides (Muses) as the personification of the poet's inspiration underscores this fact. Mandelstam's only other use of the word (the meaning of which was initially uncertain to him), is in "I have forgotten the word," where the wailing Aonides are unequivocally connected to Hades.[30] The 1890s, for the poet, are a time of "dying-out life" (II, 45). As his lyric persona returns to "Pavlovsk," he finds it not dying, but dead. His own words, beginning with the incantatory "vidit Bog" [God sees], are the requiem that animates it anew.[31]

The end of the nineteenth century resounds not with the harmonious music of Lermontov's stars (which echoes so indelibly in the mellifluous romance set by Elizaveta Shashina).[32] Its music is the dissonance of train whistles, Blok's screeching violins (from the cycles "Frightening World" and "Harps and Violins" [Arfy i skripki]),[33] and, quite possibly, the strange and frightening music of Skriabin's *Prometheus*:

> Какая нить протянута от этих первых убогих концертов к шелковому пожару Дворянского собрания и *тщедушному* Скрябину,

> который вот-вот сейчас будет раздавлен *обступившим его со всех сторон, еще немым полукружием певцов и скрипичным лесом* «Прометея», *над которым высится, как щит, звукоприемник — странный стеклянный прибор.*

> What a thread is stretched from these first paltry concerts to the silk fire of the Assembly of the Nobility and *frail* Skriabin, who is about to be crushed by the *still mute half circle of singers* and *Prometheus's forest of violins, surrounding him from all sides, above whom [which?] looms, like a shield, the sound receiver—a strange glass instrument.* (II, 70, emphasis mine)

In "Pushkin and Skriabin" as well, Mandelstam recalled the "wordless, strangely obmutescent chorus of *Prometheus*" (II, 317).[34]

It is of little import that Skriabin's *Prometheus* premiered at the Assembly of the Nobility and not in Pavlovsk. The station (*vokzal/vauxhall*) is a "perfect symbol" of the nineteenth century, with its music and iron,[35] and Skriabin was one of its most profound concluding voices. Nor in any case does the poem's spatiality—or ontology or temporality, for that matter—afford any simple logical resolution.[36] Like most poems by Mandelstam, it demands an appropriate mindset, ready to accept the artistic truths that arise among logical "inconsistencies," while not giving up on the quest to plumb the poem for the deeper levels of meaning embedded in its subtle architectonics.[37]

"Concert at the Railway Station" is particularly well studied. I will not attempt to present a comprehensive reading here. I will, however, highlight some of the subtle spatial aporia, which, not interfering with the poem's overall impression, collaborate with subtext to actively draw in a broad range of relevant fates, voices and contexts. For one, point of view is not entirely clear. A fundamental premise of the poem is that the poet has missed the train to the poets' Elysium. However, the "The *train car* [singular] is solemnly whisked off" logically implies a view from inside (unless the train were to be made up of a single car—in the early nineteenth century?—or were the tramcar of Gumilev's "Wayward Tram" [Zabludivshiisia tramvai, publ. 1921]). Neither of the latter possibilities can come close to encompassing the poem's entire broader context. However, the early history of the train line, founded in 1837, the year of Pushkin's death, and Gumilev's iconic and retrospectively prophetic poem, both relevant to the overall theme—death of the poet—are, through this logical "inconsistency," drawn deeper into the poem's fabric.[38]

Similarly contradictory—the imagery of the poem, in that the poet watches a train depart from a space reminiscent of the Pavlovsk station and its concerts, implies a departure *from* Pavlovsk to Elysium. However, the poet's gloss in *The Noise of Time*—"In the middle of the 1890s, to Pavlovsk, as to some Elysium, rushed all of Petersburg" (II, 45)—as well as extra-poetic biographical details implicating Gumilev and Annensky (see below), would imply departure from Petersburg toward Pavlovsk/Elysium instead. At the same time, the "poet," despite having missed the train, still finds himself at a sonorous feast in a misty underworld—though his, to be sure, is no joyous Elysium. Thus are introduced a number of richly complex parallels and inversions.

In this sense, as has been noted, the poem spatially compacts Pavlovsk, possibly Tsarskoe selo, on the same line—home at times to poets dear to Mandelstam, including Pushkin, Annensky, and Gumilev—and also, possibly, the Tsarskoe selo train station at the other end of the line in Petersburg.[39] On its steps Annensky died of a heart attack,[40] and to this same station Gumilev would have hurried to catch the last train from meetings in Petersburg of the first season of the Poets' Guild. Mets deduces such an exit from the meeting of 20 December 1911 at Lozinsky's flat—Mandelstam did not attend—on the basis of the following lines of an acrostic composed that evening by L. V. Lebedev. (The Gumilevs left before the later meeting of the playful literary circle Trankhops.)

Ахматова-пиит с искусным Гумилевым!
Далече вас умчал проворный паровоз.
Ей, роком вы от бед охранены суровым.

Мне стоил сей сонет потоков горьких слёз.

Akhmatova-oh poet and subtle Gumilev!
The speedy locomotive has whisked you far away.
Indeed, harsh fate has kept you from misfortune.

This sonnet cost me streams of bitter tears.[41]

But let us return to the figure of Blok and his role in the poem. Boris Gasparov has powerfully argued that the dominant association for the "dear shade" in the final line is Pushkin.[42] It is worth clarifying that we *cannot* see in this image Blok or Gumilev. One cannot speak, after all, of a funeral feast for the recently deceased as "trizna miloi *teni*" [the funeral feast of a dear *shade*]. These words imply precisely the distance between death and commemoration characteristic of Pushkin. While the poem draws in the poet's memories of 1890s Pavlovsk and evokes the launching of the first Russian railway line in 1837, the main action (once the music begins) takes place in an atemporal space compacting the memorial service and celebration for Pushkin in February 1921 and Gumilev's and Blok's untimely departures for the poets' Elysium in August. It is to a composite of these two leading poets of the day that the "poet" exclaims "Where are you off to?" [Kuda zhe ty?].

The poem's 1928 version, from which line 22 was removed, accentuates this image of parting. Billowing steam and the vertically projecting "pupils" of violin bows force us to imagine the poet staring up at the glass ceiling (*seni*). In the absence of these images, the contiguity of line 21 ("I stare into the glass *seni*") with the question "Where are you off to?" can inspire a different reading. The word "seni" was also used in the nineteenth century to designate the entrance compartment (*tambour*) of a train car. (Tolstoy, for instance, uses this expression, *seni vagona*, in describing a parting in *Anna Karenina*.) Thus, for an instant, flashes a picture of the lyric "I," staring through the closed doors, as the train with his comrades departs the station.[43]

Musatov argues that according to the interpretation of Gasparov (and one could add Ronen), Mandelstam would have to be seen as sorry that he has missed the train rushing off his perished contemporaries to Elysium, and that this implies a desire for death uncharacteristic of Mandelstam.[44] Rather, the poem implies an entirely natural and psychologically genuine ambivalence about being *the one left alive*, all the more so in a new world bereft of music.

It is only natural that Mandelstam's requiem for the nineteenth century and its music should contain overtones of Blok, that poet who "gathered its accomplishments" and was the final, resounding voice that carried them into the future.[45] However, Blok and Pushkin remain far from equals. While Blok leaves his "terrible world" in near complete poetic silence, Pushkin leaves the iron reality of Nikolai's Russia, as Mandelstam surely appreciated, with a final infusion of harmony in the form of the Stone Island cycle.[46] Mandelstam's own "feast in the time of plague" continues this Pushkinian harmony and also extends it—even as he ostensibly parts with it—into the iron century's more frightening successor, the twentieth. However, by associating Blok metonymically with Pushkin's "dear shade" (and reinforcing the real-life resonance of the Pushkin speech), by writing a requiem not only for Pushkin, but at least in some part for Blok as well, as the poet of the nineteenth century and its music, Mandelstam elevates Blok and recognizes in him a realized potential for tragedy.[47] Blok's real death has exorcised his theatricality, illuminating anew his poetic path.

CHAPTER 12

OF BADGERS AND *BARSTVENNOST'*[1]

И в этот зимний период русской истории литература в целом и в общем представляется мне как нечто барственное, смущающее меня.

And in this wintry period of Russian history, literature, taken at large, strikes me as something lordly, unsettling to me.

—Osip Mandelstam, *The Noise of Time* (1923)

Outwardly, Mandelstam's essay "A. Blok: 7 August 1921–7 August 1922"—renamed "Badger Hole" (Barsuch'ia nora) when republished in *On Poetry* (1928)—is a tribute to the recently deceased poet.[2] In the earlier version, it ends with recognition of his "service to Russian culture and revolution," the latter understood as "the highest musical tension and catastrophic essence of culture" (II, 275). In its shorter, later version, it ends with Mandelstam's praise for "Steps of the Knight Commander" as the "acme" [vershina] of Blok's "historical poetics." Blok's achievements in this poem are described in terms that represent the highest praise for Mandelstam. "Steps of the Knight Commander" is a triumph of European myth, which "moves freely in traditional forms" (II, 273). Similarly, André Chénier, one of Mandelstam's most beloved poetic precursors, realized "absolute fullness of poetic freedom within the boundaries of the narrowest canon" (II, 296). In addition, Blok does not fear "anachronism and contemporaneity . . . Here the layers of time fell one upon another in a poetic consciousness plowed anew" (II, 273). Mandelstam thus repeats his own "trademark" definition of poetry from "The Word and Culture": "Poetry is a plow, churning up time so that the deep layers of time, its black earth, end up on top" (II, 224). Clearly, Mandelstam sees a premonition of his own poetics in this, for him, greatest achievement of Blok's poetry.

The place of "Badger Hole" within the compositional structure of Mandelstam's book of essays *On Poetry* additionally underscores the fundamental importance of Blok as a historical figure.[3] The essay on Blok is the first within the historically arranged second half of the book and is followed, after an essay on the nineteenth century, by essays on Petr Chaadaev, André Chénier, and François Villon, key precursors from the early nineteenth, eighteenth, and sixteenth centuries, respectively. Blok is thus implicitly acknowledged as the most important figure in early twentieth-century poetry. Blok is also the only Russian poet to whom Mandelstam devotes an individual essay.

Mandelstam handily reconciles the revolutionary zeitgeist of the Blok of 1918 with the stance of defender of culture and cultural autonomy that emerges in the poet's final essays:

> The spiritual cast of the poet predisposes him to catastrophe [. . .] Poetic culture arises from a striving to avert catastrophe, to place it into dependence upon the central sun of the entire system, whether that be love, about which Dante spoke, or music, at which Blok finally arrived [. . .] One and the same need for cult, that is, for the teleological expense of poetic energy, governed his thematic creativity and found its highest satisfaction in the service of Russian culture and revolution. (II, 275)

A constant undertow of reservation, however, is to be observed in Mandelstam's references to Blok's conservatism.[4] This goes far beyond a playful challenge—in the mode of "literary malice"—to claims that Blok is the poet of the revolution or a revolutionary poet, although Mandelstam does directly comment on those claims.[5] Mandelstam's accusations of poetic conservatism gradually shade into thinly veiled accusations of a personal sort.

The formalistic approach to Blok's poetic genealogy that Mandelstam takes in "Badger Hole" is a fine tactical maneuver, as it removes from the picture that single element which most powerfully defines Blok's poetry and which cannot be openly challenged—the poet's charisma. Mandelstam states outright that "we ought to learn to *study* [poznavat'] Blok, to struggle with the optical illusion of perception, the inevitable coefficient of distortion" (II, 270). Moreover, by writing in abstract terms, for instance, of how the "need for a teleological expense of poetic energy governed his thematic creativity," Mandelstam draws the discussion away from Blok's "enchanting," "tragic" persona, at the same time that his underhanded jabs constantly draw attention to Blok's "aristocratic" person:

> In a literary sense, Blok was an *enlightened conservative*. In everything that touched upon questions of style, rhythm, imagery, he was surprisingly cautious: not a single open break with the past. Envisioning Blok as an innovator in literature, *one recalls an English lord, passing a bill through the parliament with great tact*. This was some kind of non-Russian, more English conservatism. *Literary revolution within the bounds of tradition and impeccable loyalty.* (II, 273–74, my emphasis)

For Mandelstam, who had no love for aristocracy or England, these remarks carry only slightly submerged innuendoes of aloofness, snobbery, and hypocritical liberalism.[6]

In another essay, Blok's conservatism is manifestly Russian, and Blok a Muscovite autocrat:

> Blok's acquisitive nature, his striving to *centralize verse and language*, are reminiscent of the *governmental instinct of the historical leaders of Muscovy*. His is an *authoritative, stern hand* in relation to all provincialisms: all is for Moscow. (II, 348, my emphasis)[7]

Finally, there is the most central portion of "Badger Hole," that from which it eventually took its name:

> Blok was a man of the nineteenth century and knew that the days of his century were numbered. He hungrily expanded and deepened his inner world in time, as a badger [barsuk] digs in the earth, organizing its home, laying two exits from it. The century is a badger hole [barsuch'ia nora], and a man of his century lives and moves in a stingily meted-out space, feverishly attempts to expand his dominions and more than anything values the exits from this subterranean burrow. And, impelled by this badger instinct [barsuch'im instinktom], Blok deepened his poetic knowledge of the nineteenth century. (II, 272)

The general thrust of these lines is a diminishing of the figure of Blok. He is compared to a badger, tunneling in the dark through his century. The Futurist poet Velimir Khlebnikov, who is presented in "Storm and Stress" as Blok's antipode, is also compared (in "On the Nature of the Word" [1922]) to a small mammal: "Khlebnikov putters about with words like a mole" (II,

247). However, Khlebnikov's activity is a constant, if undirected, labor with the word. In addition, not only does a mole have a substantially more pleasant demeanor than a badger, but it is also *blind,* an archetypal characteristic of great poets. And, whereas Blok is stuck digging in his own immediate surroundings, ever seeking a historical outlet, "Khlebnikov has dug passages into the future for an entire century" (II, 247):

> Blok is a contemporary to his very bones, his era will crumble and be forgotten, and still he will remain in the consciousness of [future] generations a contemporary of his time. Khlebnikov does not know what a contemporary is. He is a citizen of all history, the entire system of language and poetry, some kind of idiotic Einstein, unable to tell what is closer, a railroad bridge or the [twelfth-century] "Lay of Igor's Campaign." (II, 348)[8]

What appears to badger-Blok an entire universe is to those who are above ground "a stingily meted-out space."

> *The entire poetics of the nineteenth century*—there are the boundaries of Blok's power [mogushchestvo], that is where he is tsar, that is the ground on which his voice becomes firm [vot na chem ego golos krepnet], where his movements become imperious [vlastnye], [his] intonations commanding [povelitel'nye]. (II, 272–73, my emphasis)

Blok is an autocratic tsar, but his massive domain, we are aware, is only a tiny portion of the "blessed inheritance" to which Mandelstam is privy ("I did not hear the tales of Ossian"). Similarly, Mandelstam wrote of Kommissarzhevskaya, "In creating the theater of Ibsen and Maeterlinck, she was groping for the European drama, sincerely convinced that Europe could offer nothing better or greater" (II, 101).[9] Kommissarzhevskaya, who is akin to Blok, suffers the same illness in Mandelstam's eyes: a blindness to European culture beyond (which is to say before) the nineteenth century.

While Blok's broader interests are evidenced, for instance, in his translation of a twelfth-century mystery play and adoration of Shakespeare or his interest in classical philology and especially philosophy, there is a clear qualitative difference in comparison with Mandelstam.[10] Moreover, in Mandelstam's eyes, the nineteenth century was an age of relativism, one that cast its gaze upon many centuries, but only for a moment, and only in order to project its *self* upon them (II, 277).

In publishing "A. Blok: 7 August 1921–7 August 1922" for the second time, Mandelstam shortened the essay substantially, removed the open accusations of literary conservatism, and changed the title to "Badger Hole." All three of these changes intensify the impact of the above central paragraph ("Blok was a man of the nineteenth century . . ."). The leitmotif of the now very short essay becomes the lexical repetition: "*Barsuch'ia* nora," "*barsuk*," "*barsuch'ia* nora," "dvizhimyi *barsuch'im* instinktom." These repetitions echo with words like *barsuk*—badger; *barchuk*—lordlet; *bar-suchii, barin suchii*— that is, son-of-a-bitch lord; and finally *barin sushchii*—lord in essence. This is in fact the central and hidden accusation of Mandelstam's essay: above all, it is Blok's *barstvennost'*, his aristocratic demeanor, that is repellent to Mandelstam.[11]

One might be tempted to question the validity of deciphering such "anagrams" were it not that Blok's *barstvennost'* is variously and clandestinely alluded to throughout Mandelstam's writings.[12] It is abundantly clear that Mandelstam felt the connection of Blok to the nineteenth century, and especially the 1880s, in the deepest possible way.[13] David A. Sloane is, in my judgment, incorrect in his statement that "in essence Mandel'štam is saying that Blok's poetic legacy spans the gap between two centuries and epitomizes their interconnection."[14] Fairly or unfairly, Blok is always connected first and foremost by Mandelstam to the dying nineteenth century, and almost never to the incipient twentieth.[15] To my mind, there is only one true exception—Blok's "anachronism and contemporaneity" in "Steps of the Knight Commander" (II, 273). Even in "Letter on Russian Poetry" (1922), where Mandelstam presents Blok in a highly positive light, contrasting his normal development and range of voice with the Symbolists, who "immediately hit the highest, most tensile note" and suffered from a "hypertrophic expansion of the creative 'I'" (III, 33), and where, through Blok, Goethe and Pushkin, Baratynsky and Novalis are integrated into the undiminishing stream of Russian poetry (i.e., the poetic future), Blok is still ever so subtly diminished:

> With Blok we measured the past as a land surveyor parcels with a fine net the boundless fields. Through Blok we saw Pushkin and Goethe and Baratynsky and Novalis, but in a new order, for they all stood before us as tributaries of Russian poetry, flowing into the distance, unitary and undiminishing, in eternal motion.[16]

Mandelstam's praise here is combined with a hesitancy audible in the unexpected past-tense verbs (in what was most likely a republication in the same year, they are corrected to present tense) and particularly in the fact that the past that is seen through Blok goes no deeper than Goethe.[17] The next paragraph, about Blok's poetic genealogy, ends with "and—strange—he somehow returns us to the 1870s of [civic poet Nikolai] Nekrasov, when birthdays were celebrated in taverns, and in the theater sang Garcia."[18] In "Komissarzhevskaya," Blok "leans over the deathbed of Russian theater" (II, 101). In "Badger Hole," Blok's verse is a "final asylum" [poslednee ubezhishche] for the youngest European myth, the nineteenth century's own myth, Carmen (II, 273). In "Storm and Stress," the essay in which Mandelstam's treacherous (or playful) weaving of praise and insult most obviously inclines toward the latter, Mandelstam put things as follows, extending his barbs to Akhmatova as well:

> All of the misfortune [occurs] when in the place of the true past, with its deep roots, is set a "yesterday" [vcherashnii den']. This "yesterday" is easily assimilated poetry, a fenced off chicken coop, a comfortable sty, where domesticated fowl cluck and stamp. This is not work at the word, but rather rest from the word. The boundaries of such a world, comfortable rest from active poetry, are now defined approximately by Akhmatova and Blok, and not that Akhmatova and Blok, after a necessary selection of their works, turned out to be bad in and of themselves. After all, Akhmatova and Blok were never meant for people with a dying linguistic consciousness. If the linguistic consciousness of the epoch died within them, it died a glorious death. (II, 347).

The "domesticated fowl" are of course 1920s imitators, but it is no wonder that Akhmatova later recalled Mandelstam's "monstrous unfairness" in speaking about Blok.

The literature of the Russian nineteenth century as a whole is, in turn, characterized by its *barstvennost'* in the conclusion to Mandelstam's autobiographical prose collection *The Noise of Time:*

> The literature of the century was *well born*. Its house was a full cup. At the broad open table the guests sat with Walsingham [. . .] Around the table flew the request which, it seemed, was always being uttered for the last time—"Sing, Mary"—the anguished request of the final feast.
> [. . .]
> Looking back at the entire nineteenth century of Russian culture—shattered, finished, unrepeatable, [. . .] I see in it a unity of measureless cold which has welded the decades together into one day, one night, one profound winter, within which the terrible State glowed like a stove piping with ice.
> And in this wintry period of Russian history, literature, taken at large,

strikes me as something lordly [nechto barstvennoe], unsettling to me. ("In a Fur Coat above His Station," 1923) (II, 107–8, my emphasis)

Blok is the final invited guest at the nineteenth century's table. Mandelstam begins "In a Fur Coat above His Station" with a reference to Blok's "Night, street, street lamp, pharmacy" (Noch', ulitsa, fonar', apteka, 1912) ("So it was a quarter century ago. And today the raspberry globes of the pharmacies burn there in winter" [Tak bylo chetvert' veka nazad. I seichas goriat tam zimoi malinovye shary aptek] [II, 102]), and ends it with a reference to the nineteenth century's "measureless cold" [nepomernaia stuzha], borrowing Blok's phrase from "Steps of the Knight Commander."[19] Moreover, in "Badger Hole," Mandelstam directly associates Blok with *Feast in the Time of Plague* (Pir vo vremia chumy, 1830) and other works by Pushkin (II, 272). Finally, Blok's demeanor places him squarely among the invited guests, particularly in opposition to V. V. Gippius, the ostensible subject of the essay. Bely's first impressions of Blok were of surprise at his "properness, even 'good breeding' [korrektnost', dazhe 'svetskost''] [...] Could this young man, a Petersburger of entirely *good form* [vpolne *khoroshego tona*], really be the author of the mystical letters, the singer of the Eternal Feminine?"[20] Piast describes a habit Blok acquired in 1912 of strolling with a walking stick.[21] Sergei Solov'ev, who felt forever betrayed by Blok after their initial friendship, left the following unflattering lines, in the form of a memorial poem comparing Blok to James Steerforth from *David Copperfield:* "Noble and criminal, / Spoiled, imperious, proud— / You are with me inseparably, / Icy, magnificent lord" [Blagorodnyi i prestupnyi, / Izbalovan, vlasten, gord,— / Ty so mnoiu neotstupno, / Ledianoi, blestiashchii lord].[22] Perhaps, Mandelstam's depiction of Blok as English lord and "enlightened conservative" in "Badger Hole" was influenced by this poem. More likely, the two texts arise from a similar outward impression. Igor Severianin captured much the same cold, haughty aristocratism in his memorial verses: "Let him look with disdain through a lorgnette / At the Russian soul" [Pust' smotrit s prezren'em v lornet / Na russkuiu dushu].[23]

Blok's personal aloofness, if not outright anti-Semitism, was surely sensed by Mandelstam, who, in the early 1910s in particular, had quite a bit of personal contact with the poet.[24] Ronen, commenting on Blok's 22 October 1920 diary entry ("the 'little yid' hides, the artist is visible" ['zhidochek' priachetsia, viden artist]) calls Blok "fastidious to the point of prejudice in his racial attitudes."[25] Years later, in the 1930s, Mandelstam still took great offense at the "neutrality" of Blok's statement, in the introduction to his long poem *Retribution* (Vozmedie), regarding the Beilis affair, a provocation manufactured by the reactionary, anti-Semitic Black Hundreds: "In Kiev, there was the murder of Andrei Yushchinsky, and the question arose of Jews' use of Christian blood."[26]

Implicitly contrasted to the inbred aristocracy of Blok is the adopted manner of Vladimir Gippius. The latter is an outsider by nature, a *raznochinets*—that is, one without a distinctly defined social status—the usual social designation for the Russian intelligentsia. However, Gippius, as nineteenth-century Russian writer, has assimilated the century's lordliness, symbolized in his fur coat and his powerful call for a cab. Still, it is implied that Gippius is only a "witness" to literature—even if he is the most colorful of literature's "house servants" [domochadtsy] (II, 104). While Gippius is himself a poet and was close to the early Symbolists Ivan Konevskoi and Alexander Dobroliubov, his social status marks him and keeps him separate from the central stream of Russian nineteenth-century literature. He is close enough to know the anecdotes and even to live the life of the Russian Symbolist ("constantly in a state of militant and ardent death throws [agoniia]" [II, 107]). However, he will always remain a *"raznochinets littérateur* in a fur coat above his station"—hence his literary envy.

Formalist critic and prose author Victor Shklovsky, the antihero of Mandelstam's sketch "Fur Coat" (Shuba, 1922), is outwardly a *raznochinets* but at heart, by nature, a *barin* [lord]. While Mandelstam feels ill at ease in a fur coat, even a purchased one, Shklovsky, "like a true usurper, established himself by revolutionary order in the Eliseev's bedroom [the old master bedroom of what was now, in the winter of 1920–21, the House of Arts, S.G.], with a fireplace, a double bed, an icon-case and windows facing Nevsky Prospect. It was a pleasure to look at him [the implication being that he was exceedingly well-kept during that hungry winter, S.G.], and the ex-Eliseev servants respected and feared him" (IV, 508–9). At one point, he is called "master" [khoziain] (IV, 509). Ending his essay in the classic, civic tradition of mid-nineteenth-century Russian prose—with an expression of sympathy and shame before an old cook who was robbed of all her belongings on a train—Mandelstam makes clear his own organic link with, and loyalty to, the tradition of the *raznochintsy*.[27]

Mandelstam had no seat saved for him at Walsingham's table. Not only does Parnok, Mandelstam's double in his novella *The Egyptian Stamp* (Egipetskaia marka, 1927–28), explicitly lack a genealogy ("Just one trouble—he had no pedigree [rodoslovnaia]" [II, 37]), the narrator has family ties that specifically exclude him from "feast in the time of plague." If Pushkin's Walsingham sings, "And we *drink* the breath of a rosy girl— / Maybe...full of the Plague!" [I devy-rozy *p'em* dykhan'e,— / Byt' mozhet...polnoe Chumy!],[28] the narrator of *The Egyptian Stamp* intones: "My family, I propose to you a coat of arms: a glass of boiled water" (II, 5). In the novella, Petersburg surrounds the narrator with plague, infection, and disease. The narrator's ultimate act of creative freedom, his break with Parnok ("What pleasure for a narrator to switch from the third person to the first" [II, 41]) is compared to drinking "cold, unboiled water straight out of the faucet" (ibid.), in other words, to one small break from that caution through which he and his family protect themselves from the plague. His is a decidedly, even provocatively, small "abandon."

In the essay "Komissarzhevskaya," from *The Noise of Time*, Mandelstam relates with pride his own lack of an aristocratic genealogy:

> My desire is to speak not about myself but to track down the age, the noise and the germination of time. My memory is inimical to all that is personal [. . .] I was never able to understand the Tolstoys and Aksakovs, all those grandson Bagrovs, enamoured of family archives with their epic domestic memoirs. [. . .] A *raznochinets* needs no memory—it is enough for him to tell of the books he has read, and his biography is done. (II, 99)[29]

This passage is implicitly contrasted to Blok's *Retribution*, which can be seen as a foil to Mandelstam's autobiographical sketches. The shift in genre already says much: Mandelstam's elegant and flexible prose replaces Blok's uncharacteristically rigid poetry;[30] a varied cast of characters from all walks of life replaces Blok himself and Blok's family, whose history serves as the basis of the long poem's plot. The noble Aksakovs and Tolstoys with their epic familial memoirs are the Bloks of a happy and "naive" age (hence their Homeric hexameter ["Komissarzhevskaya"], rather than Blok's Archilochian iambs). However, Blok himself is no less self-obsessed. In depicting the approaching cataclysm that hangs over the head of the declining aristocracy, he glorifies his "Byronic" father and, in his unfinished plans, makes an imagined, illegitimate son the face of faceless, musical retribution.[31] At the same time, while Mandelstam's disagreements with Blok about the nature of the human actor in history can be fruitfully summed up in the contrast between Blok's Byronic family history (the content of the poem proper) and Mandelstam's own "tongue-tied" roots, the introduction to the poem displays the other side of Blok's historicism, his ability to hear the underground rumblings of history where others hear only a "syncopated pause" (II, 272). This exceptional quality remains for Mandelstam a model for his own sensitivity to the "noise of time."[32]

Mandelstam's understanding of *raznochinstvo* is revealed most fully in his theoretical masterpiece, "Conversation about Dante" (1933): "Dante is an inner *raznochinets* of old Roman blood" [vnutrennii raznochinets staroi rimskoi krovi] (II, 372). Outwardly, he is a product of the aristocracy, but his essence is that of the *raznochinets*: "What is for us a faultless hood and so-called aquiline profile was on the inside a painfully overcome awkwardness" (ibid.). This essence is manifested in a lack of manners appropriate to high society and in an isolation from, freedom from, and opposition to, power and the state. "Dante does not know how to behave himself" (ibid.) His inability to "apply his inner experience and objectivize it as etiquette" (ibid.) reflects his kinship to Mandelstam, who suffers from the same lack of acclimation to "society," judging both from the poet's own testimony and from the inexhaustible comments to this effect left by his contemporaries.[33]

Dante, an exile from his native city, even a "poor soul" [bedniak], participates in "a purely Pushkinian, chamber-man-like [kamer-iunkerskaia] struggle for social dignity and the societal station of the poet" (ibid.). The direct reference to Pushkin—who also had the equivalent, on one side of his family at least, of "old Roman blood"—makes the ultimate source of Mandelstam's concept of the "inner *raznochinets*" transparent: Pushkin's poem "My Genealogy" (Moia rodoslovnaia, 1830). In the face of accusations of literary "aristocracy," Pushkin stakes a claim to true nobility by separating himself from latecoming aristocrats, noble in name but not in character or deed—asserting with irony: "I am just a Russian burgher" [Ia prosto russkii meshchanin].[34] Pushkin had no doubts concerning his own, many-centuried noble pedigree, but his social isolation and struggle to maintain his inner freedom in the face of tsarist pressure and humiliation in the 1830s make him, for Mandelstam, the patron of Russia's "inner *raznochintsy*." This *raznochinstvo* paradoxically coexists with aristocratic birth and knowledge of society. Pushkin is the natural initiator of the nineteenth century's poetic feast—like Blok, a Walsingham. However, he is simultaneously, like Mandelstam, a Evgeny—i.e., the disenfranchised hero of Pushkin's *Bronze Horseman*, who in his futile challenge to the monument of Peter the Great would become the forefather of all of Russian literature's "little men."[35]

The tendency to view those cultural figures with whom he sympathizes and empathizes as "inner *raznochintsy*" extends to other declared precursors as well. André Chénier is both non-aristocratic and non-contemporary, "completely foreign to the Epicureanism of his century, the olympianism of grandees and *barins* [olimpiistvo vel'mozh i bar]" (II, 297). François Villon, whose marginal status within society and opposition to power are fundamental, is called by Mandelstam a "Paris clerk" (II, 306).[36] Another kindred spirit, the Charlie Chaplin of the screen, is also pointedly marginal and awkward.[37] Even archetypal poet King David, author of the psalms and hero of Mandelstam's "Canzone" [Kantsona, 1931]), is a shepherd-king.[38] Andrew Kahn places Bely, to whom Mandelstam became sympathetic in the 1930s, in the same context of *raznochinstvo* in connection with "Conversation about Dante."[39]

There is one prominent exception to this rule, though Mandelstam's enthusiasm here is from a much earlier period. Petr Chaadaev, the westernizing philosopher with whom Mandelstam strongly identified in 1914–15, is characterized by a towering intellectual and moral elitism.[40] Still, Chaadaev's aristocracy of spirit could never be confused with, and is, in fact, opposed to, Russian *barstvennost'*.

Blok, who was of modest noble origins but was also the grandson of the Rector of St. Petersburg University, son of a professor, and married to the daughter of the great chemist Dmitry Mendeleev, clearly associated himself more with the intelligentsia than with the nobility. He is, for Mandelstam, however, an "inner aristocrat." This is underscored in a series of implicit contrasts in Mandelstam's poetry between his own "lack of contemporariness" (*nesovremennost'*) and awkwardness and Blok's aristocratic behavior, "contemporariness" (to the nineteenth century), and *comme il faut*—the aristocrat's impeccable sense of social grace.

In "I was linked to the world of power in but a childish way" (S mirom derzhavnym ia byl lish' rebiacheski sviazan, 1931), Mandelstam writes:

С важностью глупой, насупившись, в митре бобровой
Я не стоял под египетским портиком банка,
И над лимонной Невою под хруст сторублевый
Мне никогда, никогда не плясала цыганка.

With ridiculous importance, frowning, in a raccoon mitre,
I did not stand under the Egyptian portico of a bank,
And above the lemon Neva to the crunch of hundred-ruble notes
A gypsy girl never, never danced for me.

Akhmatova saw in these lines an allusion to Blok.[41] Indeed, as Mandelstam wrote, Blok "caught up the gypsy song and made it the language of national passion" ("Badger Hole," II, 272). He flickers in the background here as the fallen aristocrat, who, in the mold of Dmitry Karamazov, plays at merchant debauchery.[42]

In "1 January 1924" (1 ianvaria 1924), cab imagery ("Spina izvozchika i sneg na pol-arshina: / Chego tebe eshche? Ne tronut, ne ub'iut" [The back of a cabby and a half-yard of snow: / What else do you need? They won't touch you or kill you]) implicitly contrasts Mandelstam-*raznochinets* to Blok-*barin*, who must literally watch his driver's back—in order to watch his own:

Сегодня ты на тройке звонкой
Летишь, богач, гусар, поэт,
И каждый, проходя сторонкой,
Завистливо посмотрит вслед...

Но жизнь — проезжая дорога,
Неладно, жутко на душе:
Здесь всякой праздной голи много
Остаться хочет в барыше...

Ямщик — будь он в поддевке темной
С пером павлиньим напоказ,
Будь он мечтой поэта скромной, —
Не упускай его из глаз...

Задремлешь — и тебя в дремоте
Он острым полоснет клинком

Today on a ringing troika you
Speed, rich man, hussar, poet,
And everyone, stepping aside,
Will watch with envy as you drive off.

But life is a through road,
Your soul's uneasy, horrified:
Here all sorts of idle paupers
Want to come out ahead . . .

The driver, be he in a dark caftan
With a peacock feather for show,
Be he the modest dream of a poet—
Don't let him out your sight . . .

If you doze off—in your sleep
He'll slash you with a sharp blade (III, 227)

Mandelstam's separation from the "world of power" is hinted at in the same poem, again with possible reference to Blok's counterexample:

> Я, рядовой седок, укрывшись рыбьим мехом,
> Все силюсь полость застегнуть.
> Мелькает улица, другая,
> И яблоком хрустит саней морозный звук,
> Не поддается петелька тугая,
> Все время валится из рук.

> I, a rank-and-file rider, having covered up with fish fur,
> Keep trying to fasten the lap robe.
> One street flashes past, another,
> And the frosty sound of the sleigh crunches like an apple,
> The taught loop won't cooperate,
> It is always slipping from my hands.

As Omry Ronen has noted, "This clumsy effort [to fasten the shabby lap robe of a hired sleigh] should be compared to the elegant facility with which 'the ritual of tucking in' used to be performed by a personage of Russian lyrical poetry a quarter of a century earlier: Ia chtu obriad: legko zapravit' | medvezh'iu polost' naletu [I honor the ritual: It's easy to tuck in the bearskin lap robe on the fly, S.G.] (Blok, 'Na ostrovakh' [On the Islands, 1909, S.G.])."[43] This metonym for the social dexterity in which Blok abounds, and which Mandelstam lacks, is combined with a lack of a fur coat (the speaker's "fish fur"), and later a reference to the poet's loyalty to the "fourth estate":[44]

> Ужели я предам позорному злословью —
> Вновь пахнет яблоком мороз —
> Присягу чудную четвертому сословью
> И клятвы крупные до слез?

> Can it be that I'd betray to shameful slander—
> When once again the frost smells of apple—
> The wondrous oath to the fourth estate
> And vows enormous to tears?

In tying the qualities of the *raznochinets*, unsoiled by association with power, to the poetic freedom of Dante, Mandelstam raises the personal, once again, to the level of poetry. Mandelstam's early discomfort with the charismatic, "messianic" nature of the Russian poet's stance, a result of both personality and his place as Jew and outsider attempting to enter an established and exclusionary poetic tradition (Freidin), is translated, in the 1920s, into class terms, finding its expression in a discomfort with *barstvennost'* and the relation to power that it represents.

In "Fourth Prose" (1930?), Mandelstam will reclaim his position as Jew and quintessential outsider (now with entirely positive implications). For the time being, the poet aligns himself with the intellectual "heritage" of the disenfranchised *raznochinets*, in opposition to the familial "inheritance" of the aristocratic Russian nineteenth century. Blok, as person and poet, is ultimately understood by Mandelstam as one of those who belong to the nineteenth century's poetic aristocracy, not as a result of his birth, but as a result of his being.

CHAPTER 13

CONCLUSION
Whence (and Whither) Authenticity?

As we have seen, the young Mandelstam's jettisoning of the Symbolist lyric hero, so powerfully realized in Blok's poetry, was integral to his adaptation of the myth-creation exercised by the younger Symbolists to a post-Symbolist poetics. After this first "triumph" in diffusing the source of Blok's charismatic power, Mandelstam's poetry betrayed not only parodic applications of Blok's imagery, but also a profound receptiveness to Blok's metaphorical poetics and embodiment in poetry of anachronistic modernist time structures. In the poet's second volume, *Tristia*, the key component of Blok's hero became for Mandelstam his theatricality, inevitably weighed against the older poet's tragic stance.

As I have demonstrated on the basis of "We shall gather anew in Petersburg," as late as November 1920, Mandelstam saw Blok as marginal and even antagonistic to the Pushkinian culture of the Word. And, in general, Mandelstam appears initially to have followed Annensky's lead in judging Blok's pose theatrical. However, this theatricality is ultimately transcended in the tragedy that emerged with Blok's early death in 1921, presciently foreshadowed only months earlier in his famous Pushkin speech, "On the Calling of the Poet."

The tragic Blok is subtly reflected in Mandelstam's "Concert at the Railway Station." And yet Mandelstam's autobiographical prose and essays of the early 1920s continue to reveal a substantial discomfort with Blok. Blok's *barstvennost'*, a matter of personality rather than genealogy, remains a defining characteristic of the poet for Mandelstam and ties him inexorably to the passing nineteenth century.

Blok's politics and his cultural anti-Semitism continued to rile Mandelstam in the 1930s, as reflected in the "pointed" and "venomous" marginalia (now lost) that he spiritedly entered in Emma Gershtein's mother's copy of "Retribution."[1] And Mandelstam continued, while remembering some poems fondly, to relate to Blok with what appears to have been a notable pique.[2] Blok's poetics and relation to tradition remained largely foreign, as reflected in the famous critical passage in "Conversation about Dante."[3] In general, we may conclude that Blok continued to engage Mandelstam's interest in the 1930s, but not, it seems, with anything close to the intensity that marked the years up to and surrounding the older poet's death.[4]

The issue of Blok's authenticity was clearly crucial for Mandelstam and in large part determined his developing relationship to the older poet. In fact, it would not be outrageous to assert that the most fundamental underlying difference between the two poets—that sea-change in poetics which, for Mandelstam and Akhmatova at least, heralds the inception of a truly "twentieth-century" literature—is a change in perception of the nature and source of authenticity and sincerity in the artwork. Is it not, above all else—including anti-Semitism—a failure to see the authenticity of Mandelstam's art that explains Blok's long indifference to his poetry?[5] For one who does not sense the authenticity of a piece will at best note its fireworks. And both Mandelstam and Blok set far higher demands on poetry.

For Mandelstam, authenticity in the abstract is a constant ("poetry is the consciousness of one's rightness" [II, 236]). However, the realization of poetic authenticity in time is dependent upon constant change:

> Poetic speech is a crossbred process, and it is composed of two sounds: the first of these sounds is the, to us, audible and palpable transformation of the very instruments of poetic speech, arising in motion, in the impulse; the second sound is speech itself, that is, the intonational and phonetic work executed by the above-mentioned instruments. [...]
>
> Poetic speech or thought can be said to sound only with a great degree

of conditionality, since we hear in it only the crossing of two lines, of which one, taken in and of itself, is absolutely mute; while the other, taken outside of instrumental metamorphosis, is bereft of any significance and any interest and can be paraphrased, which, in my opinion, is the surest sign of the absence of poetry [...] (II, 363–64)

The first of these two crossing lines, that which is mute, is the metamorphosis over time of the implements, the musculature of poetry.[6] Without this, verse, no matter how talented the author, will not be poetry. Only the constant metamorphosis of the tools of poetry, its inner generators, can assure the uniquely multi-semantic charge of the poetic image.[7]

The versifier's lines do not sound because his or her speech and worldview are constructed of clichés and associations already embedded in language and tradition and resurrected without interrogation. Nadson is "bad" [plokh], among other qualities, and *despite the reality of his personal tragedy*, because his "sincere" language and identity are bound by cliché. Herein lies the source of Mandelstam's criticism of the Symbolist rhymes so beloved of Vladimir Gippius: *kamen'-plamen'* (stone-flame), *plot'-Gospod'* (flesh-the Lord), *liubov'-krov'* (love-blood).[8] They imply a laziness of creative will; patterns of thought *given* in the superficial realities of the language are perpetuated. Moreover, in the case of *liubov'-krov'* especially, these linguistic realities inscribe, in both civic and decadent poetry, a simplistic and questionable ethics.[9] (In contrast, Mandelstam felt the strong compulsion to "*work* speech, not heeding, just the two of us" [*rabotat' rech', ne slushaias', sam-drug*].)[10]

Blok, unlike Nadson, is a poet. While he is a gatherer of the clichés of the nineteenth century, his ship has its own "build." His development as poet ("Letter on Russian Poetry") implies his own understanding of poetry as work and his active search for an authentic voice,[11] as too his discomfort with his own "mask" and the ossification of his image in the public eye.[12] Still, one senses that, for Blok, sincerity or authenticity is conceptualized as stable, and in any case not dependent upon an abstract need to transform the implements of poetry. Development, it seems, is driven instead by a changing worldview shaped by events and discourse.[13]

For Mandelstam and Blok, not only the constancy but also the constituents of the artwork's authenticity are differently understood. For Blok, a key locus of the artwork's authenticity is the person or persona of the artist. Blok's vision of the "person-artiste" [*chelovek-artist*] ("The Wreck of Humanism") demonstrates in no uncertain terms the importance for him of the artist as extraordinary individual (*lichnost'*). And it is no accident that he conceives his life's production of lyric poetry as a "'trilogy of being embodied as a human being'" ["trilogiia vochelovecheniia"] (*SS8*, VIII, 344).

The poet Ilya Sel'vinsky's maxim—"A talented poet is sincere; a major poet is candid"[14]—seems, when faced with Blok's poetry, quite plausible. Blok's poetry presents the image of an almost terrifying, brutal candor, which hinges upon a seeming violence toward the "interests" of the self (understood in conventional terms). This includes Blok's existential "heart pleads for death" [serdtse prosit gibeli],[15] his "betrayal" of his own social sphere, and his diary-like exposing of the poet's "falls" (*padeniia*). Unlike the "misdeeds" of a decadent like Briusov, for whom flirtation with the devil was a form of pure exhibitionism, positively valenced by the poet, Blok's "falls" retain their tragedy. His vices and offenses, however ecstatic, never lose their coloration as sin.

For Mandelstam, "candor" is not a relevant category. If anything, personal candor is perceived negatively, even if Mandelstam's assertion—"My memory is inimical to all that is personal" (II, 99)—must be taken as hyperbole. (Personal candor, however, must be understood as distinct from the charismatic and cathartic "directness" of "Fourth Prose"—which transgresses all bounds of social propriety—or of the poetry especially of first half of the 1930s.)[16]

Formal perfection clearly had meaning for Blok. Evidence of this, if it is needed, can be found in his remarks on his unsuccessful attempts to fix the technically imperfect poems of the first book.[17] Mandelstam—as is powerfully evidenced by his skepticism toward the older poet—sensed and thirsted for a grounding of art in life. And yet a simple juxtaposition of book reviews by the two poets illustrates well the depth of their differences.

In asking, in 1908 (i.e., toward the middle of his poetic path), why one is left cold by the often formally perfect poetry of Nikolai Minsky, Blok answers: "[. . .] the *incomplete sincerity* of the poet. I think that we no longer have any right to doubt that great works of art are chosen by history only from the number of those of a 'confessional' nature [. . .] only that creation where [the artist] burned himself to ash [. . .] can become great." He goes on to say that "If this [immolated] soul is vast it moves many generations, many peoples, many centuries." However, "Any *truth*, confession, be it paltry, ephemeral, parochial [. . .] we accept with open arms" (*SS8*, V, 278). In stark contrast, Mandelstam wrote, in reviewing Bely's prose in 1923, "The sincerity of Bely's book is a question lying beyond the bounds of literature [. . .] A bad book is always a literary and social crime, always a lie" (II, 422).

Another measure of the artwork's authenticity for Blok, inasmuch as he fits the mold of Ivanov's "realistic" Symbolism, is its relation to the transcendent Other. The Eternal Feminine will fade as that external truth against which the personal is weighed, that which must be intuited by the poet. However, the Other itself will remain in the form of the rumble of history (the poet's "ear to the ground") and the elemental "spirit of music." When this music ceases to be audible, the poet himself largely falls silent.

Mandelstam finds the measure of the artwork's authenticity not in a transcendent Other, but in the unique, pre-existing form of the poem itself, which the artist must divine and embody ("The Word and Culture"). And herein, unexpectedly, lies another most notable debt to mythopoetic Symbolism—a conception of the creative process as receptivity. Ivanov writes:

> We believe that the theurgic principle in art is the principle of least force and most receptiveness. Not to lay one's will on the surface of things—this is the highest precept of the artist, rather to discern and herald the hidden will of essences. As a midwife eases the process of birthing, so [the artist] ought to ease in things the emergence of beauty; with sensitive fingers he is called on to remove the film which hinders the birth of the word."[18]

For Ivanov, the artist, through anamnesis, seeks the Platonic ideal, the *realiora*. He rejects invention that is not supported by an intuition of this greater reality.[19] Mandelstam, just as vehemently, rejects (at least for himself) the artist's individualistic, purely imaginative creativity. The great poet, for Mandelstam, is not a writer, but a scribe:

> The secret of his capaciousness is in the fact that he does not introduce a single word of his own. He is moved by anything whatsoever, just not contrivance, just not invention. Dante and fantasy—but that is incompatible! Shame, French Romantics—you unfortunate *incroyables* in red vests who have maligned Aligheri! What fantasy? He writes from dictation, he's a copyist, he's a translator ... he's bent double in the pose of a scribe, glancing with fright at the illuminated original lent him from the library of the prior. [...]
>
> ... Here let me work a little more, and then I have to show the folio, doused with the tears of a bearded schoolboy, to most strict Beatrice, who radiates not only glory, but literacy. ("Conversation about Dante," II, 406–7)

Thus, it turns out that at the root of Mandelstam's memorable image of poetry as dictation lies Ivanov's concept of receptivity. Mandelstam seeks to recall not a metaphysical or spiritual ideal, but a pre-existing artistic prototype, a "resounding cast of form," for which he must listen, and which he must fill (II, 226). However, his "poet" too answers for his authenticity to a Fair Lady—a Fair Lady gifted with preternaturally impeccable literary taste.[20]

Candor, as stated, is not a valid category for Mandelstam, but sincerity is not equal to candor. In Mandelstam's poetry, the ironic is incorporated into the sincere. For Blok, by his own admission, the ironic voice is destructive and must be overcome. Blok's poetics functions on the assumption that sincerity is founded upon immediacy—immediacy of belief and immediacy of doubt, alike. Mandelstam's perception of sincerity is bound up in play with immediacy and distance, tension between irony and "hieratic" self-assuredness. The way in which these tensions and this play are realized in relation to the Symbolist heritage has been a major focus of this study. Mandelstam's Acmeism re-establishes boundaries and demarcates distance, but it does so for the potential energy that this discipline generates. The agitating, "mighty" curtains, which divide life and art, present and past, Symbolist and Acmeist poetics, can then emerge as featherweight sheets of onionskin paper, which may be raised and lowered at will, magical "Bergson's" fans collapsing spatial, temporal, and conceptual distance between phenomena.

On these pages, I have examined how a supremely gifted poet converted the material of potential anxiety into myriad strategies for uninhibited creation. The tradition of his birthright is, for Mandelstam, like the verbal source material of "Notre Dame," a "cruel weight" [tiazhest' nedobraia] that can be formed by the poet into "the sublime."

Ultimately, Mandelstam's interaction with mythopoetic Symbolism proceeds on two interconnected levels. On the one hand, mythopoetic Symbolism functions as a poetic *Weltanschauung* that can have a continuing attraction and meaning for the poet or his lyric persona. The "feminine," chaotic siren song of Symbolism remains ever the necessary complement of Apollonian, "masculine" cosmos, assuring the wholeness of the hermaphroditic lyric poet. On the other hand, mythopoetic Symbolism represents a historical stage in the development of Russian verse and of Mandelstam's own poetry, with its own characteristic set of motifs, *topoi*, and narrative structures, its own body of verse. If, in the former sense, Symbolism continues to provide the inner abyss of Mandelstam's poetry long after the watershed of 1911, in the latter, Symbolism, distanced through Mandelstam's own Acmeist "wanderings," can function as a distinct aesthetic realm, the bountiful source of ever new and generative play.

APPENDIX

Шаги Командора
В. А. Зоргенфрею

Тяжкий, плотный занавес у входа,
    За ночным окном — туман.
Что́ теперь твоя постылая свобода,
    Страх познавший Дон-Жуан?

Холодно и пусто в пышной спальне,
    Слуги спят, и ночь глуха.
Из страны блаженной, незнакомой, дальней
    Слышно пенье петуха.

Что изменнику блаженства звуки?
    Миги жизни сочтены.
Донна Анна спит, скрестив на сердце руки,
    Донна Анна видит сны...

Чьи черты жестокие застыли,
    В зеркалах отражены?
Анна, Анна, сладко ль спать в могиле?
    Сладко ль видеть неземные сны?

Жизнь пуста, безумна и бездонна!
    Выходи на битву, старый рок!
И в ответ — победно и влюбленно —
    В снежной мгле поет рожок...

Пролетает, брызнув в ночь огнями,
    Черный, тихий, как сова, мотор.
Тихими, тяжелыми шагами
    В дом вступает Командор...

Настежь дверь. Из непомерной стужи,
    Словно хриплый бой ночных часов —
Бой часов: «Ты звал меня на ужин.
    Я пришел. А ты готов?..»

На вопрос жестокий нет ответа,
    Нет ответа — тишина.
В пышной спальне страшно в час рассвета,
    Слуги спят, и ночь бледна.

В час рассвета холодно и странно,
    В час рассвета — ночь мутна.
Дева Света! Где ты, донна Анна?
    Анна! Анна! — Тишина.

Только в грозном утреннем тумане
    Бьют часы в последний раз:
Донна Анна в смертный час твой встанет.
    Анна встанет в смертный час.

Steps of the Knight Commander
V. A. Zorgenfrei

A heavy, dense curtain at the entrance,
    Beyond the night window—fog.
What now is your tired freedom,
    Don Juan, who has tasted fear?

The luxurious bedroom is cold and empty,
    The servants sleep, and the night is deep.
From a blessed, unfamiliar, distant country
    The singing of the cock is heard.

What are the sounds of paradise to a traitor?
    Life's moments are tallied up.
Donna Anna sleeps with hands crossed on her chest,
    Donna Anna sees dreams . . .

Whose cruel features have frozen,
    Are reflected in the mirrors?
Anna, Anna, is it sweet to sleep in the grave?
    Is it sweet to see unearthly dreams?

Life is empty, crazy and unfathomable!
    Come to battle, hoary fate!
And in answer—triumphant and enamored—
    A horn sings in the snowy gloom . . .

Having sprayed [its] lights into the night, flies by
    A black motorcar, silent as an owl.
With quiet, heavy steps
    The Knight Commander enters the house . . .

The door flung wide. From the inordinate cold,
    As if the hoarse striking of a night clock—
The striking of a clock: "You called me to dinner.
    I've come. But are you prepared? . . "

There is no answer to the cruel question,
    There is no answer—silence.
In the luxurious bedroom, it is frightening at the hour of dawn,
    The servants sleep, and the night is pale.

At the hour of dawn it is cold and queer,
    At the hour of dawn—the night is bleary.
Maiden of Light! Where are you, Donna Anna?
    Anna! Anna!—Silence.

But in the menacing morning fog
    The clock strikes for the final time:
Donna Anna will rise at your mortal hour.
    Anna will rise at the mortal hour.

1910–12

Blok, *Stikhotvoreniia*, III, 93–94

NOTES

ABBREVIATIONS

PSS	Polnoe sobranie sochinenii (except in relation to Mandelstam, in which case—Polnoe sobranie stikhotvorenii)
SS	Sobranie sochinenii
SS8	Sobranie sochinenii v *vos'mi* tomakh, etc.
IRLI	Institutut russkoi literatury (Pushkinskii Dom), St. Petersburg
GLM	Gosudarstvennyi Literaturnyi Muzei, Moscow
RNB	Rossiiskaia Natsional'naia Biblioteka, St. Petersburg
L.	Leningrad
M.	Moscow
Pb.	Petersburg
Pg.	Petrograd
SPb.	St. Petersburg

EDITIONS OF MANDELSTAM

Kamen' (1990)	Osip Mandel'shtam, *Kamen'*, ed. L. Ia. Ginzburg, A. G. Mets, S. V. Vasilenko and Iu. L. Freidin (L.: Nauka, 1990).
SS	O. E. Mandel'shtam, *Sobranie sochinenii v chetyrekh tomakh*, ed. G. P. Struve and B. A. Filippov [1967–81] (M.: Terra, 1991).

PSS   O. Mandel'shtam, *Polnoe sobranie stikhotvorenii*, ed. A. G. Mets (SPb.: Akademicheskii proekt, 1995).
SP   Osip Mandel'shtam, *Stikhotvoreniia. Proza*, comp. M. L. Gasparov (M.: AST, 2001).

When not otherwise indicated, poems written through 1915 are cited from *Kamen'* (1990), while poems written after 1915 are cited from *PSS*. References to Mandelstam's texts by volume and page number in parentheses are to *SS*. References to Blok's poetry by volume and page number without further clarification are to *Stikhotvoreniia* (SPb.: Severo-zapad, 1994), 3 vols., which is identical in textology to the analogous volumes of the 20-volume *Polnoe sobranie sochinenii* (M.: Nauka, 1997–).

This book is designed for both general reader and specialist. The casual reader should not feel obliged to refer to these endnotes, and the book is designed, as any good book should be, so that it may be read coherently without them. The reader who wishes to delve deeper will find here not only documentation, but, I hope, a wealth of other useful information, both filling out the picture developed in the main narrative and suggesting avenues for further exploration.

CHAPTER 1

1. "I did not hear the tales of Ossian" (Ia ne slykhal rasskazov Ossiana, 1914).
2. Blinov, "Ivanov i vozniknovenie akmeizma," 18. Blinov notes that, as late as December of that year, Mandelstam gave a talk at Ivanov's "academy" on Dionysiasm in Innokenty Annensky's works (ibid.).
3. *SS*, II, 227.
4. "Licenced thievery" is Cavanagh's formulation (*Modernist Creation*, 96).
5. This is not to say that Mandelstam could not, as a practical matter, pick and choose "gifts" from among the possibilities offered by the Symbolists' poetry. See, for instance, the poet's own catalog of what were for him the individual Symbolists' most lasting contributions in "Storm and Stress" (Buria i natisk, 1923).
6. I borrow the term from Hansen-Löve, who designates the second major phase of Russian Symbolism, most prominently practiced by the "younger" generation of Symbolist poets, including Alexander Blok, Andrei Bely, Viacheslav Ivanov and Sergei Solov'ev, "mythopoetic" (myth-creating), in opposition to the preceding "diabolic" Symbolism (introductions to *Rannii simvolizm* and *Mifopoeticheskii simvolizm*). Our usage is not, however, identical. (See below.)
7. See Freidin, "A Most Ineligible Bachelor" in *Coat*, 45–48.
8. Meijer, "Early Mandel'štam," 528.
9. The problem of Mandelstam and Symbolism has been considered from a number of different perspectives—primarily biographical and subtextual, but also on the level of poetics. See, especially, Taranovskii, "Pchely i osy," revised in his *Essays*, 83–114; Morozov, "Pis'ma"; Levinton, "Na kamennykh otrogakh"; Meijer, "Early Mandel'štam"; Ronen, *Approach*; Malmstad, "Mandelshtam's 'Silentium'"; Freidin, *Coat*; Venclova, "Ivanov and the Crisis," 206, 213; Averintsev, "Sud'ba i vest'"; Mikhail Gasparov, "Tri poetiki"; and his "Sonety Mandel'shtama"; Toddes, "Zametki"; Kling, "Latentnyi simvolizm"; Segal, *Mandel'shtam. Istoriia i poetika*; Goldberg, "Poetics of Return"; Lekmanov, *Kniga ob akmeizme*; Musatov, *Lirika*; Broitman, *Poetika*. My study brings to this discussion new ma-

terials and parallels (though this is not my primary goal), new conceptual analysis, new close readings. More importantly, a focus on the pragmatics of the text, the poet's play with distance and immediacy as the overarching strategy through which Mandelstam negotiates his relationship to Symbolism (see below) opens up fundamentally new perspectives on his works. Nor has anyone previously attempted to address the problem of Mandelstam and the younger Symbolists with similar scope and focus.

10. On "distanced reiteration" in Mandelstam's poetics, see Ronen's seminal "Leksicheskii povtor, podtekst i smysl."

11. See Cavanagh, *Modernist Creation*, 51; Mikhail Gasparov, "Poet i obshchestvo," 29–30. Note also the potential connection to one of Mandelstam's own most important Symbolist poems, "A body is given me—what shall I do with it" (Dano mne telo—chto mne delat' s nim, 1909) which, under the title "Breathing" (Dykhanie), opened the first edition of his first book, *Stone* (Kamen', 1913). As Musatov felicitously notes, "the poem as a whole is organized around the metaphor of the fragile, warmth-loving plant, which has grown in a greenhouse" (*Lirika*, 26). Mandelstam, in shattering the *serres chaudes* of Russian Symbolism, is also shattering the protective atmosphere of his own earliest poetry.

12. Nadezhda Mandel'shtam conveys the poet's own sentiment (*Vtoraia kniga*, 37).

13. Ronen, "Functional Technique," 119.

14. Cf. Harris on Mandelstam's attempt, in this period, to "assimilate discontinuity and change into his mythopoetic system" (*Osip Mandelstam*, 31); Mikhail Gasparov, "Tri poetiki," 28; Goldberg, "Poetics of Return," 142–44.

15. The scholarship on Mandelstam and Blok is spread over a large number of articles and books. Among the most informative, if one is to take the individual references in total, are Ronen's *An Approach to Mandel'štam* and Gregory Freidin's *A Coat of Many Colors*. Broitman submits several individual intertextual parallels to extensive analysis and considers Blok's influence on Mandelstam in his earliest poetry (articles collected in *Poetika*). Grishunin's article is largely documentary in approach ("Blok i Mandel'shtam"). For aspects of the influence of Blok's poetics on Mandelstam, see Zhirmunskii, "Poeziia Bloka," 123–24; Gromov, *A. Blok*, 357ff.; Broitman, "Venetseiskie strofy"; one should also mention the classic contrastive analysis of these two poetics in Ginzburg, *O lirike*. Several problems have been subjected to repeated analysis. These include, for instance, Mandelstam and Blok's Venice (Ivask, "Venetsiia"; Ronen, *Approach*, 353; Crone, "Blok's 'Venecija'"; Broitman, "Venetseiskie strofy") and Mandelstam's reaction to Blok's prose in the 1920s (most extensively, Margolina, *Mirovozzrenie*; Segal, *Mandel'shtam. Istoriia i poetika*); the resonance between Mandelstam's and Blok's sense of history; the Blokian subtextual layer of "Concert at the Railway Station" (Kontsert na vokzale, 1921?); the Blokian letters and diary entries (particularly the derisive "Mandelstamishness" [mandel'shtam'e] [*SS8*, VII, 100] and "A premium-grade Rubanovich" [Rubanovich luchshego sorta] [ibid., VIII, 344] and Blok's eventual recognition of Mandelstam [see chapter 9]); finally, Mandelstam's essay on Blok (see chapter 12). In addition, there are brief, but often invaluable, individual observations scattered throughout the scholarship on Mandelstam. This is a rich scholarly heritage that calls out for a more sustained, focused, synthesizing approach.

16. Annenskii, "O sovremennom lirizme," 7, noted in Freidin, *Coat*, 44.

17. Tynianov, "Blok i Geine," 240. Unless otherwise marked, italics convey author's emphasis.

18. Bukhshtab, "Poeziia Mandel'shtama," 147. Cf. Zhirmunskii, "O poezii klassicheskoi i romanticheskoi" and "Dva napravleniia sovremennoi liriki," in his *Voprosy teorii literatury*, 175–89.

19. Grishunin, "Blok i Mandel'shtam," 154–57. Regarding Blok's anti-Semitism, both as relates to Mandelstam and more broadly, see Brown, *Mandelstam*, 301n21; Nebol'sin, "Iskazhennyi i zapreshchennyi," 181–83; Cavanagh, *Modernist Creation*, 345n36; Timenchik and Kopel'man, "Viacheslav Ivanov i poeziia Bialika," 113–14n21; Bezrodnyi, "O 'Iudoboiazni,'" 101–2. Mandelstam was of course subject to repeated episodes of everyday (*bytovoi*) antisemitism, from the quota on Jews at St. Petersburg University to the moniker "Zinaida [Gippius'] little yid" [Zinaidin zhidenok] (N. Mandel'shtam, *Vtoraia kniga*, 33) to Sergei Gorodetsky's underhanded praise of Mandelstam—in print—for having "learned" Russian, "though no study can replace a native [prirodnoe] knowledge of the language" (excerpt from "Poeziia kak iskusstvo" [*Lukomor'e*, 30 April 1916], in Mandel'shtam, *Kamen'* [1990], 228). Memoirists too left any number of caricaturish portraits. Whether this social anti-Semitism presented an active psychological block to the young Mandelstam's *writing* is perhaps open to question, although his initial ambivalence toward his Jewishness and his reclaiming of the heritage of the Jewish outsider in the 1930s certainly imply that it did. Also of note is Mandelstam's letter to Yuri Tynianov of January 21, 1937: "Now it's already a quarter century that, mixing the serious with trifles, I stream onto Russian poetry; but soon my poetry will become one with it [sol'iutsia s nei], having changed something in its structure and composition" (*SS*, III, 281). Here, Mandelstam's *inorodnost'* ([ethnic] foreignness) to Russian poetry is presupposed. The power of his legacy is such that his "foreign" voice, having gradually infiltrated the tradition, will have qualitatively altered what *Russian* poetry is.

20. Blok, *SS*, VII, 78.

21. The Russian phrase "Vechnyi Zhid," neutral in itself, uses a word for Jew that, by the late nineteenth century, had become unequivocally demeaning.

22. Cf. Dmitry Merezhkovsky, "On the Reasons for the Decline of and New Currents in Contemporary Russian Literature" (O prichinakh upadka i o novykh techeniiakh sovremennoi russkoi literatury, 1892).

23. For a succinct semiotic analysis of the differences between these two waves of Russian Symbolism, see Smirnov, *Khudozhestvennyi smysl*, 53–59. The traditional distinction among "generations," however, can also give a false impression of strictly linear evolution and is overly dependent on the poets' own discourse. See, for instance, Z. G. Mints, "Ob evoliutsii russkogo simvolizma." For a more detailed overview of the movement, see Pyman, *History of Russian Symbolism*; Paperno and Grossman, eds., *Creating Life*; Matich, *Erotic Utopia*.

24. On the influence of Potebnia on the "culture of the Word" in Russia at the turn of the century, see esp. Seifrid, *Word Made Self*.

25. Myth-creation does not have to be collective in the present, however. In Ivanov's "Two Elements in Contemporary Symbolism" (Dve stikhii v sovremennom simvolizme, 1904), a veritable manifesto of myth-creation, the author notes that "myth, before it is lived through by all, must become "an event of inner experience, personal in its arena, suprapersonal in its content" (*Po zvezdam* [hereafter, *PZ*], 284).

26. In critiquing I. S. Prikhod'ko's use of the term "mythopoetic" to describe Blok and the Symbolists, Mikhail Gasparov writes that a "criterion for extracting 'myths' from the mass of other subtexts is structurality (strukturnost'): Myth is there, where discrete elements fuse into a whole, which underlies all of the work or the entire oeuvre of the poet and even the whole epoch." However, Gasparov finds that, for Prikhod'ko, the "Symbolist 'macro-myth'" instead amounts to an eclectic lumping together of heterogeneous mystic traditions, hardly a meaningful structural framework ("Otzyv," 8). Gasparov praises

Prikhod'ko precisely for her work in defining individual sources ("Otzyv," 6). It should be noted that Hansen-Löve, even more than Prikhod'ko, is concerned not with the individual sources of individual poets, but with parallels and sources, even if indirect, in a vast, eclectic range of mystic literature and classical mythologies (and even Jungian archetypes), sources to which the Symbolists *collectively* had potential access, and which can clarify the underlying valences of their imagery (*Mifopoeticheskii simvolizm*, 12–13). Hansen-Löve sees the overarching universal myth of Symbolism primarily synchronically, in terms of the nature of the symbol, the (Neoplatonic) relationship of world and text to ideal existence, and the poet's role in the revelation of this relationship, and defines the overarching plot-oriented autodescriptions and recyclizations of the Symbolists as a third stage in the development of Symbolism, closer to classical forms of mythology, which have rationalized their original mystical-symbolic content (ibid., 8–9, 52–55n60). However, it is precisely this overarching emphasis on *structure*, and, as a corollary, on emplotment, in the poet's life and work, which is a compelling characteristic of the mythopoetic Symbolists' work as a whole.

27. See Hansen-Löve, who reviews a broad range of scholarship contrasting mythological thinking and narrativity (ibid.). Robert Bird, in contrast, equates mythologizing and narrativizing (even "allegorizing") elements in lyric poetry (*Russian Prospero*).

28. Both Bely's and Blok's oeuvres can be seen as jigsaw puzzles (note the varying density of conceptual and structural information about the whole in individual poems), with interchangeable parts of shifting scale, due to the poets' recyclicization of their poetry; the poems as "details of a vast canvas" (as Vera Lur'e wrote about Bely in 1923). Lavrov cites Lur'e in "Ritm i smysl," 7, and notes the dramatically shifting nature of the relation of the individual pieces to each other and the whole, as a result of Bely's continual recyclicization (ibid., 8). On the similar dynamics of cyclicization in Blok, see Sloane, *Dynamics*, esp.118ff.

29. Gofman, *Poety simvolizma*, 301. On this narrative "prefiguring" in Blok's trilogy, see Sloane, *Dynamics*, 130. On Blok's "path" more generally, see esp. the first half of Maksimov's fundamental *Poeziia i proza Al. Bloka*; Mints, *Lirika Aleksandra Bloka*.

30. Briusov, that master of fully realized themes (cf. Mandel'shtam, SS, II, 342–43), presents a quite recognizable composite of this narrative in 1907 in "La belle dame sans merci." On the impact of the secularization of Christian history, which underpins this structure, in Western and especially English Romanticism, see Abrams, *Natural Supernaturalism*.

31. Cf. also Blok's self-reflexive "Instead of a Preface" (Vmesto predisloviia) to *Earth in Snow* (Zemlia v snegu, 1908); the poets' articles (Bely's "Green Meadow" (Lug zelennyi, 1905), Blok's "Stagnation/Evil Times" [Bezvremen'e, 1906]).

32. Ivanov's personal 'investment' does seem to grow in *Cor Ardens* with the revolution of 1905 and the death of his wife, Lidiia Zinov'eva-Annibal. See, for instance, Wachtel, *Symbolism and Literary Tradition*, 103.

33. For Ivanov, this falling away from the deity is already apparent in the Orphics' canonization of Dionysian orgiastic religion. See his "O Dionise orficheskom," 2nd pagination, 98.

34. Bird sees generative loss as a key trope in Ivanov's life and works and illuminates a series of narrative structures drawing in elements of vision, loss, searching, memory, and return (*Russian Prospero*). On the broader implications of "Maenad" as "an anthem that encapsulated Ivanov's complex social and metaphysical program in the wake of the 1905 revolution," see ibid., 59.

35. Human relations, as well, were subverted to mythopoetic emplotment by Bely's circle, the Argonauts, "becoming in many ways similar to artistic texts: they had their plot, their pragmatics, their system of stylistic definitions" (Lavrov, *Belyi v 1900-e gody,* 141).

36. Solov'ev, "Novye sborniki stikhov," 78.

37. Mikhail Gasparov, "Otzyv," 7; Mandel'shtam, *SS,* II, 273.

38. See Wachtel, *Russian Symbolism,* 97; Mandel'shtam, *SS,* II, 343.

39. See Freidin, *Coat,* 87–88; chapter 7 below.

40. Briusov, "Keys to the Secrets" (Kliuchi tain, 1904), *SS,* VI, 92. Pyman notes the tendency of Briusov, in his essays in *Libra* (Vesy), to aphoristically articulate the concensus in all manner of debates, rather than expressing his personal views (*History,* 176).

41. "The Legacy of Symbolism and Acmeism" (Nasledie simvolizma i akmeizm, 1913), in Gumilev, *SS4,* IV, 175.

42. Rubins, *Ecphrasis.*

43. These assaults are portended already in "The Morning of Acmeism" (Utro akmeizma)—"We do not fly, we climb only those towers which we ourselves can build" [II, 325]). Cf. Bely's "Symbolism as Worldview" (Simvolizm kak miroponimanie, 1904): "Others can answer [those who mourn for the setting sun], believing limitlesslessly in the miracle of flight" (*Arabeski,* 238).

44. Averintsev, "Sud'ba i vest'," 15.

45. For an overview of the problem, see Lekmanov, "Kontseptsiia," 216–19. See also Timenchik's fundamental "Zametki ob akmeizme." Such authors as Levin et al. ("Russkaia semanticheskaia poetika"); Taranovsky (*Essays*); Ronen (*Approach*) Freidin (*Coat*); Doherty (*Acmeist Movement*); Shindin ("Akmeisticheskii fragment"); Hansen-Löve ("Tekst-Tekstura-Arabeski"); and Lekmanov (*Kniga ob akmeizme*) present nuanced understandings of Mandelstam's Acmeist poetics unbounded by the tenets of the poet's often quite applicable, but not all-encompassing essays.

46. On the makeup of the Poets' Guild, see esp. Timenchik, "Zametki ob akmeizme" (1974), 33–39; cf. also his "Po povodu." On Lozinsky, see Segal, "Poeziia Mikhaila Lozinskogo."

47. Mandelstam's manifesto, "The Morning of Acmeism", was not printed at the time. On the dating of this essay, likely completed in its present form in 1914, see Mets, *Mandel'shtam i ego vremia,* 51–72. For excellent readings of "Notre Dame" and Gumilev's play *Acteon* respectively as artistic manifestos of early Acmeism, see Steiner, "Poem as Manifesto"; Basker, "Gumilyov's 'Akteon.'"

48. Zhirmunskii, "Preodolevshie simvolizm," 30.

49. On the influence of Ivanov's essays on Mandelstam, see especially Lekmanov, *Kniga ob akmeizme,* 119–28.

50. Cf. Gumilev, "Anatomy of a Poem" (Anatomiia stikhotvoreniia, 1921); Mandelstam, "On the Nature of the Word" (O prirode slova, 1922).

51. Nadezhda Mandel'shtam, *Vospominaniia,* 195; Ginzburg, "Kamen'," 266; Levin et al., "Russkaia semanticheskaia poetika." See also Tynianov's "Promezhutok" (1924), in his *Arkhaisty i novatory,* 570–73.

52. On the fundamental duality and "ambivalent antitheses" of Mandelstam's poetry, see, i.a., Segal, "O nekotorykh aspektakh"; Levin, et al. On semantic vectors, see Mandelstam's "Conversation about Dante" (Razgovor o Dante, 1933), *SS,* II, 374. For a provocative mapping of the writing-reading process as conveyed in this essay, see Glazov-Corrigan, *Mandelstam's Poetics,* 68–110.

53. Seifrid, *Word Made Self*, 99. Florensky wrote a fascinating apologia for the aporias of Orthodox dogma (*Stolp i utverzhdenie istiny*, 144ff.).

54. The nature of Mandelstam's poetics, his self-conscious citation and unparalleled "keyboard of references" [upominatel'naia klaviatura] (II, 368) make the recognition of subtext vital to any rounded reading of his works. The scholarly works of Taranovsky, Ronen and others present models for effective—even virtuosic—reading based on subtext. At the same time, subtextual criticism, in its arch-textual focus, can overlook other levels of meaning. Cf. Timenchik's broad theoretical approach to "the other's word" ("Tekst v tekste"). See also Mikhail Gasparov's admonitions regarding the attestation of subtexts in "Literaturnyi intertekst."

55. On the nature of Blok's allusion, in contrast to Acmeism, see Ronen, *Poetika*, 72–73.

56. Blok, "Ironiia," *SS*, V, 346ff.

57. Cf. Lavrov on Bely: "The lofty-mysterial is a recast into the humorous and grotesque without losing its essence and without any axiological recoding: the ironic element refracts in itself rays from the invisible center, making it possible to perceive the outlines of 'foggy Eternity' through the shroud of life's *realia*" ("Ritm i smysl," 23); Broitman on the "da" and "net," which are the inseparable components of the skeptical irony of Briusov (*Poetika*, 215).

58. Gumilev, *Sobranie sochinenii*, IV, 173. Cf. Timenchik, "Zametki ob akmeizme II" (1977), 184; Averinstev, "Sud'ba i vest'," 16–17. Karabchievskii writes of the "vertiginous height of Mandelstam's irony" ("Ulitsa Mandel'shtama" [1974], in *Voskresenie Maiakovskogo*, 197), while Lekmanov remarks on the "equilibrium between irony and metaphysical pathos" in Acmeism and notes that "The Acmeists gained the possibility to speak about the esoteric [sokrovennoe], without forcing their voice in the process, having looked at the outside world through the prism of irony" (*Kniga ob akmeizme*, 86, 78). Cavanagh explores the related phenomenon of Mandelstam's "powerful insignificance" in the poetry of the 1930s (*Modernist Creation*). Note also Zeeman, "Irony," in his *Later Poetry*, 89–125.

59. See, i.a., Levinton, "K voprosu" and "Akhmatovoi ukoly"; Parnis and Timenchik, "Programmy."

60. "О, годы! О, часы! О, бремя Иссуара! / Проточная вода в воронке писсуара! / В прорывы бытия брось лилию, Амбер! / Амбер! Кто вплел в твой герб позорный камамбер?" [*O, years! O, hours! O, burden of Issoire! / Running water in the funnel of a urinal! / Into the breaches of existence throw a lily, Ambert! / Ambert! Who has braided into your coat of arms disgraceful camembert?*] (*PSS*, 375)—"У меня остается одна лишь забота на свете: / Золотая забота, как времени бремя избыть. [. . .] В медленном водовороте тяжелые нежные розы, / Розы тяжесть и нежность в двойные венки заплела" [*One care remains for me in the world: / A golden care—how to cast off the burden of time. [. . .] In a slow whirlpool heavy, tender roses, / The roses heaviness and tenderness are braided into double wreaths*] (*PSS*, 149). So Mandelstam amuses himself, translating the results of a game of *bout-rimés* from Romains' novel. (The original reads: "Le temps! Le temps! Issoire, / Il coule et tourne et gire et vire et filtre en ta passoire, / Emmi l'absent décor lilial d'Ambert . . . / Issoire! Qui a dit que tu faisais des camemberts?" [Romains, *Les Copains*, 30]. A majority of the key words linking the translation to "Sisters," and even the image of the flower in the whirlpool, are Mandelstam's [as is of course the laying bare of the *pissoir* hiding in Romains' *passoire*].)

61. This was the basis, of course, for Bely's ongoing accusations that Blok had betrayed their common ideals. Magomedova presents an engaging and compelling argument that

Blok's insistence that through his inconstancy he was true is grounded in a Gnostic myth of the imprisonment of Divine Wisdom within the world (Magomedova, *Avtobiograficheskii mif,* 76ff.).

62. "The Slate Ode" (Grifel'naia oda, 1923).

63. See Ronen, "Sublation"—expanded as "Akmeizm" (2008)—a valiant attempt to present a concise, synthetic poetics of Acmeism (nonetheless, however, strongly focused around Akhmatova and Mandelstam).

64. Cf. Ronen, "Sublation," 320–22; "Akmeizm," 219–20. On Mandelstam's understanding of the nature of the word, see, i.a., Paperno, "O prirode poeticheskogo slova"; Seifrid, *Word Made Self,* 73–78; Rodnianskaia, "Svobodno bluzhdaiushchee slovo"; Kikhnei, "'Gieraticheskoe slovo.'"

65. I borrow the term "mystic presumption" from Averintsev ("Strakh, kak initsiatsiia," 18).

66. In Mandelstam's essay, this tradition begins with the great publicist Nikolai Novikov and civic poet Alexander Radishchev, reaches its peak in Pushkin and the Decembrists ("Feast in the Time of Plague" and conspiratorial punch) and Nikolai Nekrasov, fades in Afanasy Fet and Fedor Tiutchev (cf. their illnesses) and has its death-throws in Symbolism, whose early practitioners are "militant young monks" (II, 105) and evangelical abstractions are reeking, dead fish. Bethea has recently written about Pushkin and Joseph Brodsky as functional "bookends" for the "notion of romantic biography" in Russian poetry ("Brodsky and Pushkin Revisited" I, 101–2). Note, however, the way that this concept lives on in the works of Boris Ryzhii.

67. Private conversation, 2001.

68. The essay, in fact *The Noise of Time* in general, is full of often 'barometric' breachings of the boundary between literature or theory and life. To take just a couple examples, literature is like a "layman, rudely awakened and called, no, better, dragged by the hair to be a witness in the Byzantine trial of history," while "Life will burst into the most protected [teplichnaia], most sterile [vykipiachennaia] Russian school [. . .] A volume of *Libra* under the desk, and next to it, slag and steel shavings from the Obukhov factory" (II, 103, 86).

69. The word "afishi," which meant "playbill" in Mandelstam's day, as it does today, had meant "program books" up through the early nineteenth century. This is clearly the usage that is operative here, in all its appropriate obsolescence. See Fedosiuk, *Chto neponiatno,* 240.

70. The poet here does not outwardly accept the Symbolist syncretism of eras evinced, for instance, in Blok's "On Kulikovo Field" (Na pole kulikovom, 1908). Mandelstam's 1921 essay "The Word and Culture" (Slovo i kul'tura), which asserts that contemporary poets "In a sacred frenzy [. . .] speak in the language of all times, all cultures" (II, 227), demonstrates the renewed influence of Symbolist theory, specifically, Bely's "Emblematics of Sense" (Emblematika smysla, 1909; see Ronen, *Approach,* 134) and Ivanov's "Thou art" (Ty esi, 1907).

71. Freidin comments on the two antithetical forces dominating the poem, the "Apollonian 'heavy curtain' hiding that 'other world'" and the "Dionysian elimination of all boundaries." The poem is thus simultaneously "elegaically nostalgic and full of loss" and "ample and restorative" (*Coat,* 90–91). See also Zholkovskii, "Klavishnaia progulka," 177.

72. "Que ces vains ornements, que ces voiles me pèsent" (Racine, *Oeuvres,* 826, noted in Freidin, *Coat,* 90–91).

73. Note also the irony: Mandelstam's lyric "I" (supposedly) will not hear Phèdre's

line both because of his vividly imagined indifference as a member of the audience within Racine's theater and because of his historical distance from that very theater.

74. The transitive "agitating" [volnuia] is of course paranomastic play upon underlying "rippling" [volnuias'].

75. Freidin, "Poetry of Time," 180.

76. On this poem, see also, particularly, Etkind, "'Rassudochnaia propast'," 209-12; Terras, "Black Sun," 46-49.

77. In this sense, incest, which serves as the fundamental underlying paradigm for Mandelstam's mythology of self in Freidin's reading of *Tristia* in *Coat*, can be seen as one subset of transgressed (or non-transgressed) boundary.

78. Villon is described as "thieving angel" (angel voruiushchii) in Mandelstam's "So that, friend of wind and drops" (Chtob, priiatel' i vetra i kapel', 1937).

79. "*Takie* otritsaniia ravnotsenny polozhitel'noi uverennosti."

CHAPTER 2

1. The first critics to apply Bloom's theories to the context of Russian modernism were, it seems, Laferrière ("Mandel'shtam's 'Tristia'") and R. D. Timenchik ("Tekst v tekste," 68, 71). Note also Pratt's Bloom-inspired "Antithesis and Completion.'" More recently, Bethea, Pratt, Crone, and Reynolds have attempted to more broadly evaluate Bloom's potentialities and shortcomings as applied to the Russian context, with its traditionally permeable boundary between word and deed. See Bethea, *Realizing Metaphors* (esp. "Bloom: The Critic as Romantic Poet"); Pratt, "Garol'd Blum"; Crone, "Fraternity or Parricide?"; a number of studies by Reynolds, including "Burden of Memories" and "Return of the Dead."

2. Bloom, *Anxiety of Influence*.

3. Aspects of the argument I present below are open to accusations of reductiveness: first, in that I do not engage Bloom on the terms of his own *poetic* discourse on poetry, and, second, in that I choose to focus on one early, though of course seminal, work of Bloom's. However, there remains a fundamental irony. Bloom's *Anxiety of Influence*, which—adopting Bloom's own terms—is a self-begetting of the author as strong critic, is itself belated, and not only, as has been pointed out, in relation to the overshadowing Poetic tradition or to previous critics (Pratt, "Garol'd Blum," 8–10)—but also in relation to poets' own perceptions of the mechanisms of influence. In the Russian context, the most prominent critic in relation to whom Bloom can be seen as belated is Yuri Tynianov. See Zholkovsky, *Text counter Text*, 1.

4. Akhmatova, *Sochineniia* (1990), II, 172.

5. Nadezhda Mandel'shtam, *Vtoraia kniga*, 87. Livshits was a Futurist poet, friendly with Mandelstam in the mid-1910s, author of *The One-and-a-half-eyed Archer* (Polutoraglazyi strelets, 1933), a highly regarded memoir detailing the emergence of Russian Futurism.

6. Akhmatova, *Sochineniia* (1990), II, 162. The problem of Pushkin and Mandelstam has been explored extensively, specifically from a Bloomian perspective, by Andrew Reynolds. A recent attempt to broadly address Mandelstam's relationship to Pushkin is Surat, *Mandel'shtam i Pushkin*.

7. "But what is the Primal Scene, for a poet as poet? It is his Poetic Father's coitus with the Muse. There he was begotten? No—there they failed to beget him. He must be

self-begotten, he must engender himself upon the Muse his mother" (Bloom, *Anxiety of Influence*, 36–37). This passage is unusually straightforward. Typical of Bloom's playfully shifting logic is the fact that, in the next passage, it is the Son who begets the Father by defining him. The basic underlying features of Bloom's theory remain, however, clear.

8. On Ivanov's early influence, see, for instance, Morozov, "Pis'ma"; Freidin, *Coat*, 29 and elsewhere; Lekmanov, *Kniga ob akmeizme*, 119–20; Musatov, *Lirika*, 34–54ff., who goes on to contrast Ivanov with another important influence, Annensky.

9. Wachtel, *Russian Symbolism*, 4.

10. Belyi, "Fridrikh Nitsshe," in his *Arabeski*. Cf. Wachtel, *Russian Symbolism*, 210ff.; Lavrov, *Belyi v 1900-e gody*, 114.

11. Briusov, "Retsenziia," cited in Timenchik, "Tekst v tekste," 68.

12. "Perepiska Bloka s Solov'evym," 353.

13. Bloom, *Anxiety of Influence*, 16, 144.

14. Particularly striking in this regard is Fet's "You are all in lights. Your distant flashes" (Ty vsia v ogniakh. Tvoikh zarnits, 1886).

15. See, i.a., Taranovsky, *Essays*, 10–14; Ronen, *Approach*, 80–82; Reinolds [Reynolds], "Smert' avtora," 207.

16. The image of the biblical Joseph plays an important role in Freidin's analysis of Mandelstam's "mythologies of self-presentation" in *Coat*. However, the author does not discuss "The bread is poisoned," and his references to Joseph are directed quite differently from mine here.

17. The Bedouins can be seen as an analogue of Homeric naiveté in the modern world and are perhaps evoked as descendants of the actors hinted at in the first stanza (the "caravan of Ishmaelites coming from Gilead," Gen. 37:25).

18. Stars figure prominently in four other of Mandelstam's contemporary dialogues with the younger Symbolists: "I shudder from the cold" (Ia vzdragivaiu ot kholoda, 1912), "I hate the light of homogenous stars" (Ia nenavizhu svet odnoobraznykh zvezd, 1912), "Gold Ruble" (Zolotoi, 1912) and "The valor of northern maids" (Dev polunochnykh otvaga, 1913). On the significance of stars in Mandelstam's poetry and the influence of Ivanov on Mandelstam's conception of stars, see esp. Ronen, *Approach*, 63–74.

19. On Mandelstam's habit of reading with eyes closed, see, i.a., Brown, *Mandelstam*, 50.

20. "'[. . .] Now those were poets: what themes, what sweep [razmakh], what erudition! . . .' Lovers of Russian Symbolism are unaware that it is a giant many-tiered mushroom on the swamp of the 1890s, done-up, robed in many raiments" (*SS*, III, 32). The contrasting ethos of Acmeism is clearly visible in Akhmatova's "I have no use for odic hosts" (Mne ni k chemu odicheskie rati, 1940).

21. On the "infinitesimal" and the "'inner excess of space'—the internal realm that, contained in a small compass, has potential for infinite expansion," see Pollak's reading of Mandelstam's "Octaves" (*Mandelstam the Reader*, 49–79).

22. Cf. Bethea on Freud and literature: "there is a literalism (which at the same time can be completely reversible and hence a pure figuralism) about the Freudian mythos that makes it difficult to accept as continuously operative *in the present* of a creative personality and of his or her evolving biography" (*Realizing Metaphors*, 67).

23. Bloom, *Anxiety of Influence*, 78.

24. Cavanagh, *Modernist Creation*, 96.

25. Interesting, in this regard, is a comment Mandelstam made to Sergei Rudakov. The latter was downcast after the publication of Boris Pasternak's poems on Stalin in the

New Year's issue of *Izvestiia* in 1936, feeling that his own unpublished poetry would now be judged imitative of Pasternak's new work. Mandelstam commented, "Poetry never nullifies other poetry" ("Mandel'shtam v pis'makh Rudakova," 178).

26. Crone notes the Bloomian character of these lines ("Fraternity or Parricide?").

27. See Bethea, *Realizing Metaphors*, 70.

28. "The poem is alive through the inner image, that audible cast of form that anticipates the written poem. There is not yet one word, but the poem already sounds. It is the inner image that sounds; it is this that the hearing of the poet senses" (II, 226–27). On "the category of imperative" [kategoriia dolzhenstvovaniia], classical poetry as "that which ought to be," and not "that which already was," see "The Word and Culture" (Mandel'shtam, *SS*, II, 224).

29. "Not mine, not yours—but theirs" (Ne u menia, ne u tebia—u nikh, 1936). Note that, in this admittedly late poem, the use of the pronoun "they" excludes a reading under the aegis of a Romantic God figure/prophet relationship (while gesturing at, but not insisting on, the equally Romantic category of the folk). Pollak's *Mandelstam the Reader* contains a number of excellent passages on this poem.

30. Abrams, *Natural Supernaturalism*, 411.

31. A modified Bloomian approach is valuable precisely for presenting an alternative, in conceptualizing Mandelstam's interactions with other poets, to subtext (the reigning *modus operandi*). Bloom, however, too hastily rejects intertext as a meaningful indicator of influence. Practice in reading Mandelstam's poems shows that it is almost always one or more key subtexts (of the many which may be present in a poem), which direct the reader to the poet's key interlocutors, in the tension with whom the poem is generated.

32. Mandelstam refers here to Innokenty Annensky.

33. In general, in Acmeism, a valorization of the organic coexists with a sense of constructedness, craft with inspiration, as has been commented on, i.a., by Hansen-Löve ("Tekst-Tekstura-Arabeski") and Doherty (*Acmeist Movement*, 130ff.).

34. See Bethea, *Realizing Metaphors*, 67–88; Crone, "'Fraternity or Parricide?'"; Reynolds, "Burden of Memories" and "'Return of the Dead.'"

35. On Mandelstam's use of the leader as a monumental foil in his "Ode to Stalin," see Freidin, "Two Josephs," in *Coat*, 256ff. The concept of the shadowing wing is appropriately embodied in the Russian cultural context in the "demonic" sphere of History's iron nineteenth and twentieth centuries. Cf. Blok's "Vozmezdie": "The twentieth century . . . (Even blacker and more enormous / The shadow of Lucifer's wing)" [Dvadtsatyi vek . . . (Eshche chernee i ogromnei / Ten' Liutsiferova kryla)] (*SS8*, III, 305).

36. These mortal stakes were clearly apparent to Mandelstam, author of "Pushkin and Skriabin" (1916–17). See chapter 11, p. 190.

37. See Bethea, *Realizing Metaphors* and Reynolds, "'Return of the Dead.'"

38. Bloom, *Anxiety of Influence*, 152. Reynolds demonstrates how Mandelstam creates an in no way banal or incidental extratextual element to his ontological rhyme, which can be passed on by only one memoirist, Natasha Shtempel' ("'Return of the Dead'"). One can only be amazed at the poet's faith in literature's "house servants" ("In a Fur Coat beyond His Station") and literary providence! In *The Noise of Time* (1923), Mandelstam has not yet earned his seat as equal at Walsingham's table (an allusion to Pushkin's *Feast in the Time of Plague*) together with the writers of the Russian nineteenth century (II, 107–8).

39. Anna Akhmatova, *Sochineniia* (1990), II, 137.

40. See chapter 6.

CHAPTER 3

1. The extent to which composition plays a functional role in Mandelstam's books is addressed more fully in chapter 4, "The Pendulum at the Heart of *Stone*." For the literature on the composition of *Stone*, see chapter 4, note 8.

2. On "I am given a body" and its role in the composition of *Stone* (1913), see Lekmanov, *O trekh akmeisticheskikh knigakh*, 75–80; Musatov, *Lirika*, 25–26.

3. On "The sound, cautious and muffled" as a marker of the poet's genesis, see Pollak, "Mandel′štam's 'First' Poem"; Cavanagh, *Modernist Creation*, 34–36; Reynolds, "'Light Breathing,'" 118–20.

Mandelstam's first known poems—civic poems, published in the politically radical Tenishev School journal *Awakened Thought* (Probuzhdennaia mysl′)—date from 1906. (On *Awakened Thought*, see Mets, *Mandel′shtam i ego vremia*, 42–46.) Frolov, through an analysis of Mandelstam's prosody, presents powerful evidence that the three fragments opening *Stone* were composed later than 1908, and, more specifically, after the poet began attending Ivanov's "Academy" in spring of 1909 (Frolov, "Stikhi 1908 g.," 463–73). Mikhail Gasparov had similarly suggested in an unpublished encyclopedia article that "The sound, muffled and cautious," might have been composed later (related by Iu. L. Freidin). In any case, we can state with certainty that it was not the Mandelstam of 1908 who chose these four taught, iconic (Tsvetaeva, Pollak), "palpable" (Ronen) lines, from which, in true Acmeist fashion, sense spreads as if a sheaf, to be his "first poem" (Pollak).

4. The allusion to Pushkin is addressed by Ronen (*Approach*, 150), as well as Pollak, Reynolds and Frolov. On Tiutchev, see Khardzhiev, "Primechaniia," in Mandel′shtam, *Stikhotvoreniia* (1973), 255; on Sologub, see ibid.; Bel′skaia, "Tsitata," 13; Toddes, "Zametki," 288. Lekmanov sees an additional interwoven allusion to Tiutchev and Sologub in the first stanza of "In the forests" (*Kniga ob akmeizme*, 681); Broitman an interesting allusion to Blok in "To read only children's books" (*Poetika*, 282). See also Frolov, who adds to the list Verlaine, along with a number of other connections, some highly attenuated ("Stikhi 1908 g.," 474ff.); Bel′skaia, 12–14.

5. On Mandelstam's Symbolist poetry and early differentiations from Symbolism, see Toddes, "Mandel′shtam i Tiutchev" and "Zametki"; Morozov "Pis′ma"; Meijer, "Early Mandel′štam"; Malmstad "Mandelshtam's 'Silentium'"; Segal, "Stanovlenie"; Broitman, "Rannii Mandel′shtam i Sologub" and "Rannii Mandel′shtam i Blok," in *Poetika*, 268–98. Mandelstam's early period is also addressed in a series of monographs, including those by Brown, Freidin, Cavanagh, and Musatov, as well as in Ginzburg's *O lirike*. Frolov's *O rannikh stikhakh* focuses in detail on Mandelstam's earliest pre-Symbolist and Symbolist poetry with an eye particularly to periodization, prosody, and chronology.

6. Rhythmically, "Your vivacious tenderness" presents a mirror pattern of alternating three-beat and two-beat *dol′niks*, the scheme of which is 3–2–3–2–2–2 | 2–2–2–3–2–3. (*Dol′nik* is the term used in Russian prosody for meters usually with a regular number of *icti* but with an interval of *either* one or two unstressed syllables between stresses.). Mirroring is also intensified through the poem's tautological and semantically proximate (*glaza-sleza*) rhyme.

7. As M. Iu. Lotman notes, the rhyme scheme is additionally complicated by an initial impression of "two half-rhymed sestets: XaBxBa and aBxBaX." Lotman writes that "one can state with a great deal of certainty that the poet's goal here was far from contrivances with chains of rhyme, but rather an exit beyond the boundaries of temporal single-directedness" (*Mandel′shtam i Pasternak*, 73). Given Mandelstam's choice not to publish,

however, we might surmise that he himself felt that the poem's achievement as a lyric did not transcend its experimental character.

8. Mandel'shtam, *Kamen'* (1990), 334.
9. Mikhail Gasparov, "Lektsii Ivanova," 97
10. Panova, *Russkii Egipet*, II, 223–39.
11. On the discursive possibilities of the Sophiological tradition, see ibid., 224.
12. Even after Briusov's open disavowals, Blok continued to believe that his poetry was addressed to Sophia: "Briusov hides his knowledge of Her. In this he is sincere to the extreme" (Blok, *Zapisnye knizhki*, 65). Baudelaire's "À une passante" and its Russian offspring are engaged most directly in Mandel'shtam's works in "A thousand-streamed torrent" (Tysiachestruinyi potok, published in *The Hyperborean* in December 1912), with its passing stranger in mourning, but with frivolous black "voilette" (vualetta). A connection to Blok's "Stranger"—apt, but too narrow—is noted in Broitman, *Poetika*, 284.
13. Cf. "Her porch is as if a parvis" [Kryl'tso Ee, slovno papert']: *rumianets-tanets, rumiantsa-tantsa* (I, 314); "O, what to me is the flush of sunset" [O, chto mne zakatnyi rumianets] (II, 313).
14. See Mandel'shtam, II, 243–44, 363.
15. Cf. Fridlender, "'Trilogiia vochelovecheniia,'" 96–97.
16. Cf. Panova: "Despite the fact that about ten Russian poets contributed to the Sophiological canon, Sophia is associated with only two of them, and so firmly that their brethren in the guild made these poets the heroes and antiheroes of her cult" (*Russkii Egipet*, 225). On Gorodetsky and Briusov's negotiation of issues of poetic propriety and struggle with Blok's too firm ensconcement in the role of Bridegroom, see my article "Your Mistress or Mine: Three Symbolist Claims on Blok's Muse" (in preparation).
17. "She, She, everywhere She [Ona, Ona, vezde Ona]" (Zinaida Gippius, quoted in Blok, *SS12*, I, 333, my emphasis).
18. Tynianov wrote, "[Blok] prefers traditional, even trite images (commonplace truths), since in them is preserved old emotion; slightly updated, it is stronger and deeper than the emotion of a new image" ("Blok i Geine," 245–46). Note also the possible, but distant, association with Blok's "The Inevitable" (Neizbezhnoe, 1907) from "The Snow Mask" (Snezhnaia maska): "Inevitably and calmly / [My] gaze fell into her eyes" [Neizbezhno i spokoino / Vzor upal v ee glaza] (II, 277). Blok's poem begins, "She led me quietly from the rooms, / Shut the door" [Tikho vyvela iz komnat, / Zatvorila dver'], i.e., with a situation roughly akin to the lovers' exit in "From the half-lit room," which can be seen as introducing "More tender than tender" in *Stone* (1916).
19. Blok's image is of course constructed on the conflict between the image of the prostitute/Stranger and the icon with which she is openly and blasphemously conflated in the introduction to his second book, *Unexpected Joy* (Nechaiannaia Radost', 1907, the name, also, of the famous icon). On this icon, reflecting the intercession of the Mother of God for a terrible sinner, who, however, has always been loyal in his love for Her, see Blok, *SS12*, II, 5.
20. Segal, "Stanovlenie," 482. Interestingly, Segal notes, in regard to her "antithetical" nature, that the heroine's "other characteristics force one, apparently, to assume that her fingers will be *cold*, cooling [ostyvaiushchimi]. But this is not so. In other words, *tender* [nezhnoe], *white, distant* associates with *cold*, but here this association is broken" (ibid.). It seems curious, however, that tenderness should be associated with cold, were not these both characteristic elements of the implicit prototype, *Blok's* maiden: "Rose-colored, tender / Morning wakes the world. [. . .] The Maiden in snowy hoarfrost / I will meet in the

waking world" [Rozovoe, nezhnoe / Utro budit svet [. . .] Deva v snezhnom inee / Vstrechu naiavu] (I, 149). Cf. also "Before you—like a flower—I am tender [Pred toboi—kak tsvetok—ia nezhna] (I, 330); "The Snow Maiden" (Snezhnaia deva, 1907).

21. See Ronen, *Approach*, xiii–xv; Cavanagh, *Modernist Creation*, 39–41.

22. Gorodetskii, "Idolotvorchestvo," 96.

23. Gorodetsky praises in his article precisely this image of Blok's hero: "The receptive soul of the youth, lighting candles at the altar, tending the incense flame [. . .] was in communion with the mystery" (ibid., 99). On the liturgical function of sunsets for the Argonauts, see, for instance, Lavrov, *Belyi v 1900–e gody*, 135.

24. Perhaps also "Vsegda vostorzhennuiu tish'" [Always ecstatic stillness] recalls Romantic poet Vladimir Lensky's "Vsegda vostorzhennuiu rech'" [Always ecstatic speech] (*SS*, V, 39) in Pushkin's *Eugene Onegin*, in effect confirming the directedness of Mandelstam's lines toward a clichéd, overly Romantic poetry—like that of the Symbolists. I thank an OSU Press reviewer for pointing out this connection.

25. Cf. what may be a retrospective nod at the image of poets as idols in *The Noise of Time*. I restore the second sentence, elided by Ronen, who was uninterested in the Symbolist aspect but cites this passage to much the same purpose (*Approach*, xiv): "The intellectual erects a temple of literature with immobile idols [istukany]. For instance, [the Symbolist novelist Vladimir] Korolenko, it seems to me, wrote so much about the Komi [zyriane], that he himself turned into a Komi god [zyrianskii bozhok]. V. V. [Gippius] taught [us] to construct literature not like a temple, but like a clan [rod]" (II, 106).

26. Broitman, "Rannii Mandel'shtam i Sologub," 33.

27. Belyi, *Stikhotvoreniia i poemy*, I, 206.

28. Gorodetskii, "Idolotvorchestvo," 97.

29. Belyi, *Stikhotvoreniia i poemy*, I, 79; Ivanov, *Stikhotvoreniia*, I, 84.

30. Cf. Mandelstam's later reflections on the Symbolists: "abuse of big themes and abstract concepts, poorly imprinted in the word" (II, 342); "absence of a sense of measure, characteristic of all Symbolists" (II, 341).

31. Blok: "And your eyes shine for me / In reality or a dream?" [I tvoi mne svetiat ochi / Naiavu ili vo sne?] (II, 279); "(Or is this but a dream?)" [(Il' eto tol'ko snitsia mne?)]" (II, 212); "not dream, nor waking" [ni son, ni iav'] (III, 32).

32. "What is Chénier's poetics? Maybe he has not one poetics, but several in different periods, or, rather, minutes of poetic consciousness?" (Mandel'shtam, II, 299).

CHAPTER 4

1. On the history of *Works and Days*, see Lavrov, "'Trudy i dni,'" in his *Russkie simvolisty*, 499–514. Ivanov, and Bely—until his fascination with anthroposophy—used the journal as a mouthpiece for orthodox recastings of theurgic, "realistic" Symbolism. Blok noted in his diary at the time that "for authentic 'life-creation' (the 'mode' of *Works and Days*) [. . .] 'one must become embodied, show one's sorrowful human face, and not the pseudo-face of a non-existing school'" (ibid., 508; Blok, *SS8*, VII, 140).

2. On the artistic design of *Hallelujah*, see Beletskii, *Narbut*, 64–65. On *Wild Porphyry* and *Hallelujah*, see Lekmanov, *O trekh akmeisticheskikh knigakh*.

3. Public discussion of the movement, including reactions in print, began after Gorodetsky's lecture, "Symbolism and Acmeism," presented at the Stray Dog cabaret, 19 December 1912. See Stepanov, "Nikolai Gumilev. Khronika," 378.

4. "Preodolevshie simvolizm," *Russkaia mysl'* 12 (1916). This term, in Zhirmunsky's own usage, is richer than it might seem at first glance, implying Hegelian synthesis rather than simple opposition (Ronen, "Zhirmunskii i problema 'preodoleniia,'" 57).

5. Lekmanov, *Zhizn'*, 48-49. Cf. also the tone of Narbut's review of Ivanov's *Cor Ardens* in *Novyi zhurnal dlia vsekh* 9 (1912), reprinted in Lekmanov, ed., *Kritika*, 222-23.

6. See, for instance, Akhmatova, *Sochineniia* (1990), II, 154; Nadezhda Mandel'shtam, "Fal'shivye kreditory," in *Vtoraia kniga*, 407-15.

7. Lekmanov, *Kniga ob akmeizme*, 29ff. Cf., however, Panova's recent revoicing of the opposite claim, about the Acmeists' attachment to the earth (*"Mir," "prostranstvo," "vremia"* [hereafter, *MPV*], 124ff.).

8. *Kamen'* (1990), 281-82. On the composition of the various editions of *Stone*, see also Mets, "O sostave i kompozitsii"; Lekmanov, *O pervom "Kamne"* and *Kniga ob akmeizme*, 76-77; Nerler, "O kompozitsionnykh printsipakh," 328; Margolina, *Mirovozzrenie*, 25-27ff.; and Frolov, *O rannikh stikhakh*, 149-83.

9. "Let, in the stuffy room, where there are clumps of gray cotton" (Pust' v dushnoi komnate, gde kloch'ia seroi vaty), "Barrel Organ" (Sharmanka), "When [the clock] shows eight" (Kogda pokazyvaiut vosem') and "A thousand-streamed torrent" (Tysiachestruinyi potok).

10. The single instance in which the author *openly* violates chronology, placing "When blow meets blows" (Kogda udar s udarami vstrechaetsia)—marked "1910"—amidst poems marked "1909," can be seen as a subtle tip-off that the collection is compiled in conditional, rather than absolute, chronological order.

11. Mandel'shtam, *Kamen'* (1916), 30-35.

12. Averintsev, "Khorei," 43-44.

13. In his notes to the edition of Mandelstam in the *Novaia biblioteka poeta* series, Mets writes of a growing tendency toward exact chronological order in the placement of poems in Mandelstam's books and argues that violations of this order, as a rule, can be explained through lapses of memory on the part of the poet (Mandel'shtam, *PSS*, 517, 521). The key document supporting this point of view is a copy of the third edition of *Stone* (1923), found by Mets in the rare book fund of the State Literary Museum (GLM). Indeed, based on Mandelstam's markings in this collection, it is possible to suppose with a great deal of likelihood that the poet re-examined the chronology of the poems in *Stone* while preparing his collection *Poems* (Stikhotvoreniia) in 1927, and that, at that time, he could not remember the precise dating of all the poems. However, firstly, it is the correct year for each poem that Mandelstam attempts to recall, and, secondly, this fact does not at all annul the poet's work on the composition of the collection, which is based also on the omission and addition of poems and on the choice of position within any given year for those poems that are relocated. For instance, during the final stage of compilation of *Poems*, Mandelstam inserted two poems, "Like the shadow of sudden clouds" (Kak ten' vnezapnykh oblakov) and "From an evil and miry pool" (Iz omuta zlogo i viazkogo) between the the relatively weakly linked "Hearing tenses its sensitive sail" (Slukh chutkii parus napriagaet) and "In the giant pool it is transparent and dark" (V ogromnom omute prozrachno i temno), creating, in this way, two additional clearly palpable facing pairs of poems (reflected in IRLI, f. 124, op. 1, ed. khr. 208, l. 94 [table of contents of the proofs]; RNB, f. 474, al'bom 2, ll. 375-76). In addition, the bulk of the work on the composition of *Stone* was completed in 1915, and afterwards much simply did not change. It is entirely likely that the poet followed more strict chronological principles in compiling the other portions of his collection in 1927-28. (Still, "mountains . . . of Siena" [*sienskie . . . gory*] in

the single retained stanza of "What steepness in the crystal pool!" [V khrustal'nom omute kakaia krutizna!], with the marked date—*1919* [also a late addition to the collection], follow "*Venetian* life" [*Venitseiskoi* zhizni] among the poems of *1920*, possibly to distract attention from this stanza's real calling—to be a marker for the entire absent Christian thematic layer of *Tristia*.) There are also, in *Poems*, instances of apparent "disinformation," beyond the placement of "We shall gather anew in Petersburg" (V Peterburge my soidemsia snova), which, as is well known, was moved to the beginning of the collection for censorship reasons. See my article, "The Shade of Gumilev." Mets does not provide supporting evidence for his assertion that the more chronologically flexible composition of the third edition of *Kamen'* is not the author's (*PSS*, 521).

14. See Introduction, note 52. On Mandelstam's *dvoichatki*, see also Nadezhda Mandel'shtam, *Vospominaniia*, 206–12.

15. This irony is palpable, for instance, in an echo of Blok's *The Fair Booth* (Balaganchik, 1906). Subtext noted by Ronen, *Approach*, 69.

16. The poet's thought, antagonistic to the empty heavens, is also perceived in "I hate the light" as an arrow and a gothic spire. However, Toddes correctly notes that Blok's "Siena" (1909), which utilizes similar imagery, was published too late to have influenced Mandelstam's poem. To the potential sources that he demonstrates from Briusov ("Nabliudeniia," 327*n*5) and that Ronen attests from Gogol and Chaadaev ("Leksicheskii povtor," 368–69), as well as Pindar's "Second Olympian Ode" (*Approach*, 188–89), we might certainly add Verlaine's "L'Angoisse": "Je ris [...] des tours en spirales / Qu'étirent dans le ciel vide les cathédrales" (Verlaine, *Oeuvres*, 65); in Sologub's translation: "Mne smeshno [...] i khram i bashni vekovoi / Stremlen'e gordoe v nebesnyi svod pustoi" [I find humorous [...] also a church, and the haughty striving of an age-old tower into the empty heavenly vault] (Verlen, *Izbrannye stikhotvoreniia* [1912], 21). Nor, indeed, should we ignore Blok's deeply consonant 1904 poem "Vse otoshli, shumite sosny" (All have left, rustle, pines, 1904), in which the projectile of the poet's thought meets no resistance from a seemingly empty and implacable heavens: "Mechty pronzitel'nyi oskolok / Svobodno primet sineva" [The blue will *freely* accept / The piercing shard of a dream] (II, 72, emphasis mine). The last two lines of Mandelstam's poem, with their Symbolist coordinates ("There—I could not love, / Here—I fear to love ..." [Tam—ia liubit' ne mog, / Zdes'—ia liubit' boius' ...]), are quite possibly in dialogue with Harlequin's accusations in *The Fair Booth:* "Here, no one knows how to love ... [Zdes' nikto liubit' ne umeet ...]" (*SS6*, III, 18).

17. Stratanovskii points out the influence of Bely in "I shudder from the cold," and particularly of Bely's images of dancing gold and dancing worlds, images that Bely himself borrows from Nietzsche's *Thus Spoke Zarathustra* ("Tvorchestvo i bolezn'," 215). However, Mandelstam's 'dancing' *dol'nik* shows little rhythmical variation. Perhaps, here, we can already see an attraction to the stricter rhythmic organization of logaoedic verse.

18. Paperno, "O prirode poeticheskogo slova," 31–32.

19. On the relation between Acmeism and Symbolism in this poem, see Ginzburg, *O lirike*, 358–59; Baevskii, "Ne luna, a tsiferblat," 314–22; Lekmanov, *O pervom "Kamne*," 12; and his *Kniga ob akmeizme*, 57–61; Toddes, "Nabliudeniia," 292–94.

20. Brown, *Mandelstam*, 179–80.

21. See Lekmanov, *Kniga ob akmeizme*, 463–67. Gasparov writes that this poem is "consummately Acmeistic" ("Sonety," 156).

22. It is possible that Mandelstam himself ultimately found this juxtaposition of "Falling" and "Tsarskoe selo" too jarring. In the third edition of *Stone* (1923), this set of

poems is absent. (Clearly, censorship or self-censorship impacted the decision to drop "Tsarskoe selo," which would have seemed ironic-nostalgic from the point of view of 1923. Note, though, that the poems are dropped as a pair.) The composition of the author's manuscript of *Poems* (1928)—without "Falling" and transposing "Tsarskoe selo" and "Gold Ruble"—goes about the task of achieving a pendulum construction differently, but with similar results (IRLI, f. 124, op. 1, ed. khr. 208, ll. 1, 31–33). "Gold Ruble" again falls on the conventionally Symbolist pole, but is paired with the quintessentially Acmeist "Tsarskoe selo," while the three "confessional" poems, all securely Acmeist in their poetics, naturally form a mini-cycle.

23. Mikhail Gasparov finds the poem more akin to Symbolism than "Pedestrian" ("Sonety," 158). To *prove* that "Falling" is *stylistically* still under the sway of Symbolism would demand a separate and entirely different kind of study. Purely intuitively, however, I will note that the poems in *Stone* on the Symbolist pole of the pendulum "catch up" stylistically to the Acmeist poetics of "Casino" only in "Gold Ruble." By this time, however, we have already read "Tsarskoe Selo," a poem absolutely free of any characteristic of Symbolism whatsoever. (Poems like "Casino" and "Gold Ruble" retain Symbolism as a crucial point of reference.)

24. See Lekmanov, *Kniga ob akmeizme*, 480–84. On Symbolist aspects of "Gold Ruble," see also Kling, "'Latentnyi' simvolizm," 30–31. Edmond's "From Pathos to Parody" is problematic in both its textology and its readings.

25. Steiner, "Poem as Manifesto." The cycle of three Christian confessions, noted by Brown, and the sonnet series noted by Lekmanov (introduced by "No, not the moon") function as counterpoints to this binary organization (Brown, *Mandelstam*, 189; Lekmanov, *O pervom "Kamne*," 32).

26. This phenomenon can be observed on a wider scale in Mandelstam's poetry: ". . . every poem turns out to be tied to another through the mediation of semantic oppositions" (Levin et al., "Russkaia semanticheskaia poetika," 58).

27. *Kamen'* (1990), 216.

28. Ibid., 222.

29. On the second wave of influence of Symbolism in *Tristia*, the approach of which is visible already in "Ode to Beethoven" (Oda Betkhovenu, 1914), see, i.a., Mikhail Gasparov, "Tri poetiki," 15; Segal, *Mandel'shtam. Istoriia i poetika*, 331–38; and chapter 7 below.

CHAPTER 5

1. Averintsev, "Sud'ba i vest'," 25.

2. In this sense, Mandelstam's late-Symbolist "Your image," while differing in tone, bears comparison on a semiotic plane to that stage of Symbolism, which Hansen-Löve labels SIII: "For the grotesque image of the world of SIII, it is characteristic that, here, simultaneously and in equal measure, both models [i.e., art as ersatz of religion, SI, diabolic Symbolism, and art as ersatz-religion, SII, mythopoetic Symbolism) are realized as alternating poles of some vertical hierarchy of values [. . .] in one text, within the boundaries of one pragmatic situation" (*Mifopoeticheskii simvolizm*, 10).

3. Paperno, "O prirode poeticheskogo slova," 30–32.

4. Seifrid, *Word Made Flesh*, 112.

5. Losev, "Imiaslavie," 8.

6. Paperno, "O prirode poeticheskogo slova," 30.

7. Ibid., 31.

8. Ronen, *Approach*, 91.

9. A typewritten manuscript of "You passed through a cloud of fog" was found in Lozinsky's archive among papers relating to the first issue of *The Hyperborean*, in which "Your image" was first published (Mets, "Primechaniia," in *PSS*, 642). The connection to Blok in this latter poem had been even stronger in one of the drafts: "You walked past, *queen* of the fog" [Ty proshla *tsaritseiu* tumana] (*PSS*, 507, emphasis mine).

10. In the first stanza, the reality of the impending vision is subtly undermined in the "*flickering* of red lamps" [*mertsan'(e)* krasnykh lampad]; in the third stanza, through the racing of "fairytales and dreams" (I, 240).

11. Ibid.

12. Mandelstam's transposition of Blok's play with icon and essence to the realm of the word mirrors the analogy in theological terms between the doctrine of the living word and the problem of the ontology of icons. See, for instance, Losev, "Imiaslavie"; Paperno, "O prirode," 30; Seifrid (who presents Sergei Bulgakov's exposition), *Word Made Self*, 128.

13. "Nochnye dushi" [night souls] is clearly paranomastic play on "nashi dushi" [our souls], the two concepts being essentially equivalent in Blok's metaphysics.

14. Belyi, *Sochineniia*, I, 294.

15. The connection is perhaps not entirely absent, however. Cf. Kudeiarov's birdlike incantations: "'Staridon, karion, kokire—stado [herd]: stridado . . .' Dry shards of curses, prayers, incantations and shouts *cluck* death-like in his very throat: are spit out with a cough; this whole motley *herd*, spit out by the carpenter, now chased after Matrena" (ibid., I, 574, my emphasis). Cf. also the final lines of Blok's "Incantation by Fire and Darkness" (Zakliatie ognem i mrakom, 1908): "The *living name* of the Snow Maiden / Will still *fly* from [my] tongue . . ." [*Zhivoe imia* Devy Snezhnoi / Eshche *sletaet* s iazyka . . .] (II, 318–19, emphasis mine) The poet's heart is compared to a bird earlier in the cycle.

16. Note the use of the same device in the opening line of "You passed through a cloud of fog."

17. The folk colorings are strongly reinforced in the meter, which borrows from a long tradition of folk imitations. The first poem of the cycle, for instance, is made up entirely of highly characteristic pentasyllabic feet with stress on the third syllable. Kliuev, though, combines this folk rhythm with rhyme.

18. *Giperborei* 1 (1912), 19.

19. The question of Kliuev's own double-voicedness can be posed in the light of Khodasevich's memoirs (*Nekropol'*, 124–25).

20. Bely notes, with reference to Nietzsche, that an author's "attitude toward the content of expressed opinions, this accompaniment of the soul to words, is what is most important in the sage" (*Arabeski*, 229). While tone does not lend itself to quantification, Averintsev's similar interpretation of the multiple shifts between seriousness and irony in the poem (without specific reference to Symbolism) serves as powerful confirmation of my reading, which was initially formulated without consideration of his model. See Averintsev, "Konfessional'nye tipy," 288–89.

21. In contrast, Blok could find it difficult to use the words "zdes'" [here] and "tam" [there] *without* invoking their Symbolist connotations. See Ronen, *Approach*, 175.

22. These two lines "in the reader's perception may easily approach the boundary of the comical" (Averintsev, "Konfessional'nye tipy," 289). Cf. Victor Shklovsky, referring to Mandelstam's poetry of 1920: "And all this seems almost a joke, so loaded is it with proper nouns and Slavonicisms. As if it were written by [the nineteenth-century fictional deadpan

comic poet] Koz'ma Prutkov. These poems are written on the boundary of the comical" (*Mandel'shtam i ego vremia*, 109).

23. Averintsev calls it "not more than an exclamation," but "simultaneously a substitute for the most important, unspeakable Biblical name of God" ("Konfessional'nye tipy," 289).

24. This "serious irony" is itself inherited, in a less radical form, from the Symbolists. See Introduction, note 57.

25. Cf. Sergei Gorodetsky: "Both [Georgii Chulkov and Viacheslav Ivanov] are characteristic in that the heretics turned out to be the Symbolists themselves; heresy was initiated [zavodilas'] in the center" (*Ot simvolizma do "Oktiabria,"* 91); and Paperno on "Your image": "A scion of Symbolism, not having refused its inheritance, Mandelstam seeks new paths, giving himself up to (from the point of view of Symbolism) 'heresy' and 'Protestantism'" ("O prirode," 32).

26. Solov'ev, *SS*, IV, 30.

27. Ibid., 35.

28. Kornblatt, "Spiritual Nationhood," 161, 158. On Solov'ev's influence on the Russian Symbolists, see, for instance, Pyman, *History*, chapter 8.

29. Ivanov, *SS*, II, 613.

30. Ibid., 619.

31. Ibid., 621.

32. Solov'ev, *SS*, IV, 42–43.

33. Ibid., 36–38.

34. Ibid., 42–43.

35. Babayan, *Mystics, Monarchs & Messiahs*, xvi.

36. See ibid., xv, xxivff.

37. Cited in OED, s.v. "Pedestrian."

38. Cf., for instance, Taranovsky on the sources of the connection of the swallow with the underworld in Mandelstam's later poetry (*Essays*, 158).

39. Gorodetsky, in his review of the first edition of *Stone*, noted: "Mandelstam doesn't embellish or exaggerate his experience" (*Kamen'* [1990], 216).

40. Ivanov, "Zavety simvolizma," *SS*, II, 591.

41. Cf. Lekmanov, *Kniga ob akmeizme*, 465.

42. Rusinko remarks on "Nietzsche's recognition of the practical impossibility of purely Dionysian music": "Such pure music would be shattering in its evocation of primordial universality and its unbearable representation of suffering and pain, which is the Dionysian truth about the world" ("Nietzsche's influence," 98).

43. Ivanov, "Zavety simvolizma," *SS*, II, 591, my emphasis.

44. Segal, "Poeziia Mikhaila Lozinskogo," 403; Lekmanov, *Kniga ob akmeizme*, 36.

45. Mikhail Gasparov calls the parallels with Lozinsky "too distant" ("Sonety," 155). In addition, it seems that "Wayfarer"—anything but a programmatic poem and written in relatively distant 1908—is unlikely to have served as a basis for dialogue between these two poets who grew close in 1912. Note that none of the poems included by Lozinsky in his first publications (in *Giperborei* 2 [1912] and 6 and 9/10 [1913]) had been written earlier than 1910.

46. One might suppose, following Ronen (*Poetika*, 193–94), that Mandelstam dedicated his poem to Lozinsky not right away, but in answer to the latter's poetic response. (The 1913 edition of *Stone* does not include the dedication.)

47. Shileiko's poem "His love struggled overmuch" (Ego liubov' pereborolas', 1914),

which references Lozinsky's "At the river's edge" (U potoka, 1913), reads "But in him alone can I find / All that is antiquated, all that is beloved" [No v nem odnom mogu naiti / Vsë, chto starinno, chto liubimo] (Shileiko, *Pometki*, 10; cited in Segal, "Poeziia Mikhaila Lozinskogo," 358). See also a Latin inscription of February 1916 (A. G. Mets and I. G. Kravtsova, "Predislovie," in Shileiko, *Pometki*, 6)

48. See Ronen, *Poetika*, 195–96.

49. On the contemporary reception of *Brand*, see Eroshkina and Khalizev, "Spektakl' i p'iesa."

50. Somewhat muddled lines from an impromptu sonnet-acrostic by Vladimir Piast (who was sure to have shared it with Mandelstam) serve as evidence that contemporaries saw Bely as a "walker" (*khodok*). The original version, differing somewhat from that printed in Piast's memoirs, is reproduced in "Trankhops." Ronen's mention of Pavel Batiushkov is likely motivated by the figure of the bridge in the latter's idiolect, and perhaps also by a scholarly pun: early nineteenth-century poet Konstantin Batiushkov has long been considered a potential prototype here (see *Kamen'* [1990], 294).

51. Lekmanov, *Kniga ob akmeizme*, 449. Such criticism does not of course encompass the full scope of Mandelstam's attitude toward Bely even at this time (during the 1920s). Cf. *SS*, II, 327, 343, 423. On Mandelstam and Bely, see, i.a., Cooke, "'Abundant is My Sorrow'"; Kahn, "Belyi, Dante and 'Golubye glaza'"; Lekmanov, *Kniga ob akmeizme*, 448–50, 480–84, *Zhizn'*, 163–65, and "'Legkost' neobyknovennaia'"; Pavlov, *Shok pamiati*, 126–36.

52. Belyi, *Stikhotvoreniia i poemy*, I, 301–2, emphasis mine.

53. *Arabeski*, 231–32, emphasis mine.

54. Ibid., 343, emphasis mine.

55. Walter Kauffmann's translation (*Portable Nietzsche*, 410), fifth line altered to conform to alliteration and tautological rhyme of original. On Nietzsche and Mandelstam, see Cavanagh, "Mandelstam, Nietzsche"; Rusinko, "Nietzsche's influence"; and Ronen, who links Mandelstam's early Nietzscheanism to Bely's *Arabesques* ("Functional Technique," 118, 120).

56. Stratanovskii sees "Pedestrian" as a polemic against Ibsen as much as Bely (a challenge to whom he sees, in general terms, on the basis of Bely's desire to efface "the boundary between life and art") ("Tvorchestvo i bolezn'," 216). However, a rejection of the path of Ibsen's heroes on a personal plane is combined in Mandelstam with an acceptance of Ibsen's posing of the questions that confront them. A careful reader of Ibsen, not blinded by the epoch's infatuation with moral maximalists like Brand—i.e., someone like Mandelstam or, indeed, Annensky ("Brand-Ibsen," 1907), could not help seeing that, in *Brand*, the righteousness of the hero's convictions and his approach to life are put to question. Bely felt that Brand perished because of a moment of doubt (*Arabeski*, 34–35), i.e., that he was not strong enough! The clear implication of the play's ending, however, is that Brand has misconceived the nature of God, who indeed *is not* the God of comfortable bourgeois morality, but *is* "Deus Caritatis"—caring, merciful. One can also see in the deaths of Brand and Rubek (on whom, see also Ronen, *Poetika*, 195) inevitable retribution for *attempting* the heights of spiritual ascension, for treading forbidden ground. In this sense, we can see Mandelstam as saying that he believes in the fate of Ibsen's heroes, who perish in the quest to ascend spiritual heights, not the sanguine claims of Bely's lyric hero, who watches from his perch on the mountaintop as the avalanche rolls by into the abyss. Mandelstam's *personal* choice, however, is to reverse (not just reject), the developmental trajectory of Ibsen's heroes. As Bely put it (in a passage that Stratanovskii quotes): "Rubek sat at a restaurant table and suddenly stepped into a new heaven, onto a new earth. True, he didn't make it

across [ne pereshagnul], he fell to his death" (*Arabeski*, 33). As Mandelstam moves from "Pedestrian" to the quatrains and then tercets of "Casino" on the facing page, he passes from an immediate sensation of the true danger of the real abyss to contemplation of an abstract, metaphorical one and, finally, finds himself back at the restaurant table—though not "stonefaced," as Bely describes Rubek (ibid.), but enamored of the simple pleasures of life.

57. Margolina's analysis betrays a dogmatic faithfulness to the allegorical sense of Father Pavel Florensky's writings which is out of place when applied to to Mandelstam's poetry (*Mirovozzrenie*, 39–42). Ronen has returned repeatedly to the Biblical subtexts of "Falling," most recently in *Poetika*, 196; on these, see also Margolina, *Mirovozzrenie*, 22–24; Gasparov, "Sonety," 151–52. Broadly, on the crisis of faith in Mandelstam's early poetry, see, for instance, Musatov, *Lirika*, 45–50.

58. *Kamen'* (1990), 204.

59. Ibid.

60. On the potential motives for Mandelstam's conversion, see esp. Averintsev, "Konfessional'nye tipy," 291–92; Mikelis, "K voprosu o kreshchenii."

61. On these poems, see Ronen, "Mandelshtam, Osip Emilyevich" (1973); Taranovsky, *Essays*, 51–54; Freidin, *Coat*, 48–54.

62. Cf. Alexandre Benois: "At the present time, Catholicism, one might say, hangs on aestheticism, and beauty is its last (but how powerful!) bastion" ("Khudozhestvennye eresi" [1906], 86).

63. On this reversal, see Averintsev, "Konfessional'nye tipy," 289. Ronen and Ospovat present a detailed analysis of the semantics and subtextual underpinnings of Tiutchev's "kamen' very," particularly in relation to Mandelstam's works, in "Kamen' very." To their observations, I will add that the appearance in "A black crucifix" of the word "sviatynia" (a sanctuary; a relic; or generally something held sacred), rather unexpected from the point of view of usage (hence my unusual translation), implies that Mandelstam was thinking here of the source of the image of the stumbling block in Isaiah 8:14: "And he will be a sanctuary; but for both houses of Israel he will be a stone that causes men to stumble and a rock that makes them fall. And for the people of Jerusalem he will be a trap and a snare." (Cf. the Synodal translation: "I budet On osviashcheniem i kamnem pretknoveniia, i skaloiu soblazna dlia oboikh domov Izrailia" and the French, "Et il sera un *sanctuaire*, Mais aussi une pierre d'achoppement, Un *rocher* de scandale pour les deux maisons d'Israël." Note that the image of shipwreck is potentially present in this passage (in the Russian and French), and that the promised fall specifically threatens the houses of Israel. The call to Christian faith, for Mandelstam, represents a special danger—because of his Jewish roots.

64. Cf. Shershenevich: ". . . precision and fluidity of verse are undermined by striking tastelessness. He doesn't shy from setting down in verse such maxims [the first two lines of "Falling" are quoted, S.G.]" (cited in *Kamen'* [1990], 220).

65. Cf. Ronen, *Poetika*, 196. The punctuation in the 1916 edition stresses the potential for such an intonational break: "Kto kamni k nam brosaet s vysoty— / I kamen' otritsaet igo prakha? (Mandel'shtam, *Kamen'* [1916], 33).

66. On 1 Peter in this context, see Ronen, *Approach*, 204–5. Note that I do not wish to impute a linearity of development to the poet, but rather to explore the implicit logic of intersecting texts that form a progression when viewed in hindsight.

67. The allusion to Tiutchev's stone from "Problème" has been commented on numerous times, starting with Toddes, "Mandel'shtam i Tiutchev," 77ff. Toddes calls the

reference to Tiutchev in "The Morning of Acmeism" "significantly more unexpected from both a literary-historical and a logical point of view than the Symbolists' statements about Tiutchev" ("Mandelstam i Tiutchev," 78). On chapter 2 of Daniel as foundation for Tiutchev's "Problème" and Mandelstam's semantics of the stone in "The Morning of Acmeism" and related poems, see Ronen, "Mandelshtam (1891–1938)," 1634–35. Mandelstam himself realizes the allusion to Daniel retrospectively, when in "On the Nature of the Word" (1922), he calls the Symbolism of the poets of *Libra* a "colossal structure, even if on clay feet" (II, 255). The implication of course is that Acmeism, armed with Tiutchev's stone, has destroyed this idol of pseudo-Symbolism (*lzhesimvolizm*).

68. Gogol', "Ob arkhitekture nyneshnego vremeni," *PSS*, VIII, 57. Ronen notes the influence of this essay on Mandelstam's poetry ("Leksicheskii povtor," 368–69).

69. Cf. Bely's "In the Church" (Vo khrame, 1903): "And once more I pray, tormented with doubts. / From the walls saints threaten with a shriveled finger" [I snova ia molius', somnen'iami tomim. / Ugodniki so sten groziat perstom sukhim] (*Stikhotvoreniia i poemy*, I, 94).

70. One might conjecture that the poet had in mind such figures as his older friend, the deeply religious S. P. Kablukov, secretary of the Religious-Philosophical Society, when he penned that line. Cf. his unfinished "I remember the ancient shore" (Ia pomniu bereg vekovoi, 1910), dedicated to Kablukov (*Kamen'* [1990], 242).

71. *Kamen'* (1990), 206, emphasis mine.

72. See Dal', *Tolkovyi slovar'*, s.vv. "morok," "obmorochit'." Cf. Gogol's defense of the colossal scale of Gothic architecture: "Magnificence [velikolepie] casts the simpleton into some sort of dumbfoundedness [onemenie] . . ." ("Ob arkhitekture nyneshnego vremeni," *PSS*, VIII, 66); Bely on Ivanov: "he will not rest until he captivates [plenit]" (*O Bloke*, 353); Blok's epistle to Ivanov: "Many enchantments, and many songs, / And the beauty of ancient visages . . . / Your world, indeed, is wondrous! / But you are autocratic tsar." [I mnogo char, i mnogo pesen, / I drevnikh likov krasoty . . . / Tvoi mir, poistine, chudesen! / Da, tsar' samoderzhavnyi—ty] (III, 166).

73. Cf. Blok's "The distance is blind" (Dali slepy, 1904), the poem that closed his collection *Poems about the Fair Lady* (1905): "There will be springs in an eternal chain / And the yoke of fallings" [Budut vesny v vechnoi smene / I padenii gnet] (II, 337). Falling is also, of course, a key topos for the *decadent* older generation. See Hansen-Löve, *Russkii simvolizm*, 122–125 and elsewhere.

74. Bely on Blok: "Symbols, like roses, hide the sense and wholeness of the dramas lived through; lift up this garland; a funnel [proval; cf. *provalit'sia*—to fall through] into emptiness will look back at you" (*Arabeski*, 464).

75. The connection with Nadson, posited by Lekmanov (*Kniga ob akmeizme*, 474–76), would not exclude this circle of associations. See chapter 6, pp. 95–96.

76. Fantasies about the cowl perhaps reach an apogee in Sergei Solov'ev's "Sergii Radonezhskii," in which a youthful casting of the famous monk serves as a mask for the lyric "I." Solov'ev, it should be noted, made good on this monastic imagery, entering the priesthood in life.

77. Blok, "Monk" (Inok, 1907), II, 320.

78. "From the crystal fog" (Iz khrustal'nogo tumana, 1909), III, 12. Cf. Mandelstam on the Symbolists in "Letter on Russian Poetry": "[. . .] the lovers of the grand style sigh [. . .]: 'Now those were poets; what themes, what sweep [razmakh]'" (III, 32). Ronen sees the poet in this stanza addressing François Villon, who envisions his impending hanging (*Poetika*, 197–99). While I read this stanza differently, it is worth noting that Villon is, for

Mandelstam, the prototype of the poet who can smash the hothouse of allegorical poetry, thus the spiritual father, in my reading, of this poem's "So, be damned."

79. Cf. Mandelstam: "You can't light a fire because what it could mean you yourself will regret" (II, 255); Briusov: "May your virtue be— / A readiness to ascend the pyre" [Da budet tvoia dobrodetel'— / Gotovnost' vzoiti na koster] (SS, I, 447).

80. Hansen-Löve, *Russkii simvolizm*, 266.

81. Lekmanov, *Kniga ob akmeizme*, 477–78.

82. Mandel'shtam, *Kamen'* (1990), 204. Cf. Ronen on "Gumilev's philosophy of artistic creativity: the latter's formula 'to be annihilated as unity and to blossom out as plurality'" ("Mandelshtam [1891-1938]," 1629). Lozinsky, who, despite his close connections to the Acmeists, retained a Symbolist outlook, wrote in a poem dedicated to Gumilev: "You worked to create multifarious ravings, / Splitting and distorting the ray of Eden" [Ty sozidal mnogoobraznyi bred, / Edemskii luch drobia i iskazhaia] ("Stones" [Kamen'ia], *Gornyi kliuch*, 41).

83. Cavanagh, *Modernist Creation*, 72–81.

84. Mikhail Gasparov, "Poet i obshchestvo," 27.

85. A revision to the poem introduced by Gumilev, but not reflected in the publication in *Apollo*, seems calculated to eliminate this "Symbolist" accent ("I bogomol'tsev gulkoe rydane [And the resonant wailing of pilgrims]). On the textual history, see Mets, "Primechaniia," *PSS*, 531.

86. Cf. Cavanagh on similar dynamics in "Notre Dame" ("Mandelstam, Nietzsche," 347–49); Rubins, *Ecphrasis*, 193–94.

CHAPTER 6

1. The source of this image is the Futurists' manifesto, "A Slap in the Face of Public Taste" (Dec. 1912): "What coward would fear to yank the paper armor off the black tuxedo of warrior Briusov?" (*Literaturnye manifesty*, 142).

2. On "akme" understood as *ostrie*—"edge, tip, point"—in the writings of Acmeists and contemporaries, see Timenchik, "Zametki ob akmeizme" (1974), 39ff.; specifically in Mandelstam, see Ronen, "Leksicheskii povtor," 368–69.

3. On the role of charisma in Russian poetry, see Freidin, "Sidia na saniakh" and *Coat*, 1–19 and elsewhere. On the Symbolist lyric hero, Freidin writes: "In fact, these aspects of the lyric [. . .] constituted a specific 'confessional' mode, a matter of tradition and choice, which put a high premium on the poet's 'sincerity' of expression—a mode that Blok practiced with consummate skill" (ibid., 47).

4. The word *toska* lacks a compelling equivalent in English. It combines connotations of world-weariness, longing, sorrow, and mental anguish and might be described as a feeling of palpable absence or emptiness.

5. See Brown, *Mandelstam*, 179–80.

6. *Slovar' sovremennogo russkogo literaturnogo iazyka*, s.v. "Gigantskii [gigantskie shagi]." I would like to thank Prof. R. D. Timenchik for first bringing this definition to my attention.

7. Ushakov, ed., *Tolkovyi slovar'*; s.v. "Gigantskii [gigantskie shagi]."

8. Cf. Mikhail Gasparov, "Sonety," 149.

9. Private conversation, spring 2006.

10. An additional impetus for the equation of clock and steps may have come from

Émile Verhaeren's "Les horloges": "Les horloges / . . . / Pareilles aux vieilles servantes / Tapant de leurs sabots ou glissant sur leurs bas" (*Poèmes,* 203). Cf. also Briusov's translation, in which an open connection is made to illness: "Chasy! / . . . / Vy stuchite nogami sluzhanok v bol'shikh bashmakakh, / Vy skol'zite *shagami bol'nichnykh sidelok*" [Clocks! / . . . / You knock with servants' feet in great shoes, / You glide with the steps of hospital nurses] (Verkharn, *Stikhi o sovremennosti* [1906], reprinted in *Stikhotvoreniia,* 67, my emphasis).

11. Mikhail Gasparov, "Sonety," 149.

12. Zhukovskii, *PSS12,* X, 59, 60–61, 58, 61.

13. Lerner, "Smert' i pokhorony Pushkina," 133. That Mandelstam personally reacted to this date is hinted by the fact that he may have begun to wear his sideburns in 1912. See Karpovich, "Moe znakomstvo," 260–61.

14. The leap from "Quiet, *heavy* steps" [Tikhimi, *tiazhelymi* shagami] to "Giant steps" [*Gigantskie* shagi] is assisted by the Pushkinian subtext ("What a *giant* he is made here!" [Kakim on zdes' predstavlen *ispolinom*!] ["Kamennyi gost'," *SS10,* V, 390, emphasis mine]).

15. *Kamen'* (1990), 367; Blok, letter to Piast of 22 April 1912 ("Perepiska s Piastom," 214).

16. Blok, *SS,* VII, 141.

17. "Like Ovid in Pushkin's *The Gypsies* [Tsygany], Alexander Blok had the gift not only of poetic invention, but of the embodiment of his creations in the material of audible speech [real'no zvuchashchaia rech']. In articles dedicated to the memory of Blok [. . .] invariably we encounter references to the 'surprising mastery' with which he pronounced his poems, to the individuality of his manner of declamation, to his 'voice, indelible in memory'" (Bernshtein, "Golos Bloka," 458–59). See also Piast, "Dva slova."

18. Should we mere mortals doubt Mandelstam's ability to meaningfully allude to "Steps of the Knight Commander" after a single hearing, let us consider the testimony of Sergei Rudakov, who wrote his wife on 16 May 1935, after reading to the poet his elegy on the death of Konstantin Vaginov, "I was witness to an unbelievable [neveroiatnoe] physical phenomenon: he listened one time—[then] repeated the whole poem, declaiming it like his own poetry (on account of which it sounded even better)" ("Mandel'shtam v pis'makh Rudakova," 50).

19. Mandelstam may also possibly be overlaying "Steps of the Knight Commander" upon Blok's translation of Verhaeren's "Les pas" (published in the New Year's issue of *Niva* for 1907). This translation, entitled "Steps" (Shagi), appears to have influenced "Steps of the Knight Commander" and contains several images evocative of "Let, in the stuffy room": phantoms, a brain burning with exhaustion, "steps heard in childhood" [shagi, uslyshannye v detstve] that are "like news of a terrible vengeance" [kak vesti groznoi mesti], as well as a loop [petlia] and dull straps (Blok, *SS8,* II, 344–45).

20. "∞" is, of course, the mathematical symbol for infinity.

21. Annenskii, *Stikhotvoreniia i tragedii,* 55, emphasis mine.

22. Blok, *SS8,* V, 82.

23. *Kamen'* (1990), 195. Cf. also, from "Petr Chaadaev" (1914): "'progress,' and not history, the mechanical movement of a clock-hand, and not the sacred connection and succession of events" (ibid., 191).

24. On the image of the rooster in Akhmatova, Blok, Mandelstam, and others, see Toporov, *Akhmatova i Blok,* 26, 107–8n64.

25. "[. . .] the 'antithesis' begins, the 'changing of aspect,' which was anticipated already in the very beginning of the 'thesis'" (Blok, *SS,* V, 428); "But I fear: You will change Your appearance" [No strashno mne: izmenish' oblik Ty] (I, 99).

26. Belyi, "To Bal'mont" (Bal'montu, 1903), *Stikhotvoreniia i poemy*, I, 79.

27. Merezhkovskii, *PSS*, XV, 7. On the influence of this poem on Blok, see Toporov, *Akhmatova i Blok*, 108n64.

28. I thank G. A. Levinton for this observation.

29. Fet, *Polnoe sobranie stikhotvorenii*, 260.

30. Dal', *Tolkovyi slovar'*, s.v. "Ves [*Vesy*]." My thanks to Nikolai Bogomolov, who pointed out the connection to *Libra*, and the fact that Libra was a *September* sign before the revolution.

31. Coincidentally, September also marks the "hatching" of Symbolism (or at least the naming of the movement) through the publication of Jean Moréas's manifesto, "Le Symbolisme" (*Le Figaro*, 18 September 1886).

32. Cf. Fet, "Organ Grinder" (Sharmanshchik, 1854): "And—the old song!—with melancholy / We tenderly coddle the past" [I—staraia pesnia!—s toskoi / My proshloe nezhno leleem] (*Polnoe sobranie stikhotvorenii*, 464). Mandelstam's generally Symbolist barrel organ is also tinted with specifically Blokian references. The most characteristic comes in the first stanza: "viscous arias" [tiaguchi(e) ari(i)]. "Barrel Organ" is dated 16 June 1912, three days after Mandelstam saw Blok at Vladimir Piast's apartment (Blok, *SS*, VII, 150). At the time, Blok was working on *Rose and Cross* [Roza i krest], and June 1912 falls in the interlude during which Blok considered this work an opera libretto (ibid., IV, 583–85). Blok's diary entry displays more direct points of contact with "Barrel Organ": "During the day, I wander aimlessly—heat, stench, melancholy. The city reeks" [Dnem shliaius'—znoi, von', toska. Gorod provonial] (ibid., VII, 150). Cf. "I wander like a shadow" [brozhu kak ten']; "the *laziness* of *stagnant* waters" [vod stoiachikh len'] (emphasis mine); the barrel organ itself, with which *toska* is a recurrent association ("Barrel organ, barrel organ, melancholy and melancholy! [Sharmanka, sharmanka, toska i toska!]," Gorodetskii, "Sharmanka," in *Poety simvolizma* [1908], 355). In addition, a barrel organ plays a crucial role in the "poet's" genesis in Blok's "Conceived in the night, in the night I was born" (Zachatyi v noch', ia v noch' rozhden, 1907).

33. On the biographical plane, Piast notes that Blok, in the winter and early spring of 1912, was obsessed with rollercoasters and sledding down ice hills (Piast, "Vospominaniia," 384–85).

34. Cf. "In the poetry of Russian Symbolism repetition found its embodiment particularly in 'rotational' [krugovaia] symbolics—of the 'circle,' 'swings,' 'carousels'" (Panova, *MPV*, 359). Iurgis Baltrushaitis's "Carousel" (Karusel'), from his book *Mountain Path* (Gornaia tropa), reviewed in the inaugural issue of *The Hyperborean* (Oct. 1912), brings together several of these images, which unite Mandelstam's sonnets: carousel, barrel organ, mechanistic circular motion, falling: "And from this monotonous song / Often, often, in a tiresome hour, / The knight falls from [his] horse . . ." [I ot pesni odnozvuchnoi / Chasto-chasto, v chas dokuchnyi, / Rytsar' valitsia s konia . . .] (Baltrushaitis, *Derevo v ogne*, 131).

35. "The highest accusation against contemporary bourgeois civilization is the accusation of its non-musicality [bezmuzykal'nost']" (Mints, "Blok i russkii simvolizm," 505).

36. In fact, in Church Slavonic, the word rooster appears, besides *alektor*, as *pĕtel'* and *pĕtel''*, in both cases with the anticipated nominative plural *pĕtli*.

37. On these three realizations of Pushkin's statuary myth, see Jakobson, "Statue," 321–29.

38. Nadson, *Polnoe sobranie stikhotvorenii*, 245–46. Lekmanov is convinced that at this time Mandelstam was reading Nadson's diaries and letters, newly published in con-

nection with the fiftieth anniversary of his birth (*Kniga ob akmeizme,* 474). On Nadson's cult in the 1880s, see Mandelstam's "Bookcase" (Knizhnyi shkap), *SS,* II, 59–61.

39. *Nadsonovshchina* is a derisive collective designation for poetry in imitation of or influenced by the immensely popular, politically engaged poet, Semyon Nadson, who, for the generation of Modernists, became a shibboleth for second-rate poetry.

40. Mikhail Gasparov, "Sonety," 150. The date (Gasparov gives 1910) is taken from Mets, *Mandel'shtam i ego vremia,* 37. While the exact date of Sinani's death is not known, Mets relates in private correspondence that a relative communicated to him that Sinani died in May.

41. Mikhail Gasparov, "Sonety," 150.

42. "On Drama" (O drame, 1907), Blok, *SS,* V, 186–93.

43. Pushkin's death came to play a central role in Mandelstam's art and thought. Cf. Mandelstam's "Pushkin and Skriabin": "Twice the death of an artist has gathered the Russian people and lit above them a sun. They showed an example of communal, Russian death, died a full death, as people live a full life. Their person, in dying, expanded to become a symbol of the whole people, and the sun-heart of he who was dying was forever halted in the zenith of suffering and glory [. . .] It seems to me that the death of an artist should not be removed from the chain of his creative accomplishments but should be looked at as the last, concluding link [. . .] They buried Pushkin at night [. . .] at night they laid the sun in a coffin" (II, 313). See chapter 11, note 11.

44. Akhmatova called Blok "the epoch's tragic tenor" ("And having groped around in black memory, you will find" [I v pamiati chernoi poshariv, naidesh'], 1960). Cf. Blok's own statement, recorded by Akhmatova in her short memoir about Blok: "Anna Andreevna, we are not tenors" (Akhmatova, *Sochineniia* [1990], I, 365; II, 136).

45. Blok, "Ironiia," *SS,* V, 345–49.

46. It may be particularly appropriate to speak of the poem as a talisman, given Mandelstam's use of that word in line seven. *Pushkin* appears to be anagrammatically encoded in the first half of the opening line: "PUst' v dUSHnoi KomNate." In general, the poem brims with understated sound play: STKkliANKI—GIgANTSKIe; pETLI—verTELIs'; GRUZno—KaRUSel'; and the exquisite mirroring in "V TUMAnnoi pAMiati VIden'ia ozhIVUT." On the place of incantation, shamanism and talismans in Mandelstam's poetry, see Ronen, "An Introduction"; and Freidin, *Coat,* 5ff., 180–81, 284–85n65. Ronen mentions "Let, in the stuffy room" among Mandelstam's poems that openly used the word "talisman."

47. See also S. N. Broitman, who presents a compendium of Blokian subtexts—sometimes too laxly attributed—in Mandelstam's earliest poetry ("Rannii Mandel'shtam i Blok," in *Poetika,* esp. 282–84).

48. Mets, "'Kamen,'" 283–84.

CHAPTER 7

1. See, however, Panova's intruiging "Uvorovannaia Solominka," 134–43; and Gorelik, "'Tainstvennoe stikhotvorenie "Telefon',"' 49–52, both of which tie Mandelstam texts of this interim period to "Steps of the Knight Commander."

2. "Thus we struggle within the walls of the old jail, in which paganism struggled [. . .] The reason for our illness is our *forgetting of Christianity* [zabvenie khristianstva]. Humanity forgot that which was already revealed in Christianity" (*PZ,* 420, my emphasis;

noted by Mets in "Mandel'shtam. 'Skriabin i khristianstvo,'" 77). Mandelstam announces this myth in "Pushkin and Skriabin": "We demand a chorus, we are bored with the grumbling of the thinking reed. For a long, long time we played with music, unsuspecting of the danger which is hidden within it, and for now—maybe from boredom—we thought up a myth, in order to beautify our existence, music cast us a myth—not invented, but born, foam-born, mantle-born, of royal descent, the legitimate heir of the myths of antiquity—the myth of forgotten Christianity" (II, 317).

3. Panova, *MPV*, 359-60.

4. Briusov, in his introduction to a volume of translations of Verlaine's poetry, described the poet's final years thus: "So, over the course of more than 10 years, the greatest lyric poet of late-19th-century France led a piteous existence, alternately revoltingly drunk, shouting curses with bloodshot eyes, or a pitiful, infirm old man, jotting down verse [. . .] At times religious moods once again seized Verlaine, and then this 'dualistic person,' who had spent the night in a tavern, went to church, fell on his knees, cried, prayed . . . and at the doors of the church he was awaited by one of his lovers [. . .] or her pimp" (Verlen, *Izbrannye stikhotvoreniia*, 16).

5. Mikhail Gasparov notes that the resemblance of Verlaine and Socrates was a commonplace ("Komentarii," in *SP,* 617).

6. Amelin and Morderer, *Miry,* 72. On Kul'bin, see, for instance, Livshits, *Polutoraglazyi strelets,* 359-61.

7. This is said only on the way to establishing their own thesis, that "the hero of 'Old Man' is the word, and, more than that, precisely the comic word," embodied in the multivalent, wandering morpheme "mot" and its paranomastic and semantic echoes (Amelin and Morderer, *Miry,* 74). This layer of the poem, however, if indeed it exists, remains, at best, secondary.

8. Blok radically broadens the usage of the verb "tsvesti" (to bloom), which becomes a marker of the female addressee of his poetry or her influence: "To blossom with your azure" [Tvoei lazur'iu protsvesti] (I, 103), "Lips will blossom with new strength" [Novoi siloi rastsvetut usta] (I, 166), "Your features blossomed" [Rastsveli cherty tvoi] (II, 288).

9. Shindin, "Tret'i mezhdunarodnye Mandel'shtamovskie chteniia," 337. Shkuropat also connects the "grotesque" in Mandelstam's urban poems of the early Acmeist period to the Petersburg of the Symbolists, particularly Blok's 'terrible world,' which becomes a "parodic underworld" ("Grotesk," 92-93).

10. Blok's revisits this image, with a clearly negative valence, in "Irony" (*SS8*, V, 346).

11. The subtext is noted by A. D. Mikhailov and P. M. Nerler ("Kommentarii," in Mandel'shtam, *Sochineniia,* I, 462-63). Its implications, however, have not been explored.

12. Tynianov, *Arkhaisty i novatory,* 433.

13. Zhirmunskii, "Poeziia Bloka," 123-24.

14. See Introduction, note 15. See also Broitman, "Simvolizm i postsimvolizm," 25-26; Mikhail Gasparov, "Antinomichnost'," 259-60.

15. This phrase, heralding back to Orthodox theology and the writings of Solov'ev, is used by Blok in his foreword to *Vozmezdie,* where it refers to "art, life and politics" (*SS8*, III, 296). Broitman traces its history and usage in *Poetika,* 147-57.

16. Panova conducts an extensive and rigorous grammatical analysis of time structures as they relate to competing models of time in Mandelstam's poetry (*MPV,* 340-477). In her analysis, the conceptual collapsing of time inherent in Bergson's fan can correlate to cyclical and spiral models of time, as well as "synchronization of events." The markers of these time structures in Mandelstam's poetry include, firstly, the phenomenon of repeti-

tion in culture (427), propagated particularly through choice of narratives, arrangement of events, organization of classical plots and subtexts (440) and the overlaying of classical plots on the personal (453–55; Panova draws here upon research by Ginzburg and Mikhail Gasparov); secondly, dynamic shifts in tense (for instance, "narrativity, opening the poem, establishing temporal distance, and then superseded by present tenses, which cancel this distance" [455]), present tenses of description and generalization, as well as the "usual" (uzual'noe) present tense (reflecting the world as it is and ought to be, reality conceptualized through adherence to natural laws [zakonomernosti] [426]); finally, lexical markers of eternal return and synchronization. Interesting in this regard is the decrease in markers of subjectivity in *Tristia* (428). This seems logical, as the syncretism of eras, in order to be compelling, must be perceived as an objective reality (the actuality of time's shape), not the impressionistic fruit of the poet's imagination.

17. Translation, Harris and Link, in Mandelstam, *Collected Critical Prose*, 117. It seems that Harris was first to establish that this passage is a misreading of Bergson ("Mandelstamian zlost'," 116, 130). Recent scholarship on the influence of Bergson on Mandelstam includes Panova, *MPV*, 343–56, 444; Lachmann, "Cultural Memory," 369–70; Pak, "Problema."

18. See Panova, *MPV*, 425–26, 432–33.

19. Ibid., 439.

20. See chapter 6, pp. 89–90. In any case, Blok published his poem that fall in *Russkaia mysl'*, no. 11.

21. Consummate Modernist Valerii Briusov was taken aback by "Don Juan's 'motorcar'" (*SS8*, III, 520).

22. See Ronen on this Blokian subtext (*Poetika*, 76–77).

23. *Kamen'* (1990), 298.

24. Broitman, "Venetseiskie strofy," 93–94.

25. Regardless of the wealth of interpretive possibilities opened up through the poet's suggestive evocation of Hippolytus (see esp. Freidin, *Coat*) and third-person depiction the young Levite ("Among the priests a young Levite" [Sredi sviashchennikov levitom molodym, 1917]), the texts in which they appear do not insist upon a relation of "inseparability and unfusedness" between these heroes and a poetic "I." "For not being able to keep hold of your hands" (Za to, chto ia ruki tvoi ne sumel uderzhat', 1920) is most similar in character in this regard to "On a straw-covered sledge." On "We shall gather anew in Petersburg," see chapter 10.

26. Nietzsche, *Birth of Tragedy*, 121.

27. Ibid., 109ff.

28. Ibid., 59, 67, 74.

29. "Vagner i dionisovo deistvo," *PZ*, 67.

30. "Religiia Dionisa" (hereafter, RD), *Voprosy zhizni* 7 (1905), 140.

31. Ibid.

32. Cf. "Nitsshe i Dionis," *PZ*, 19.

33. Cf. ibid., 10–11, 14.

34. RD, *Voprosy Zhizni* 7 (1905), 133–34, 142–43, and elsewhere.

35. RD, *Voprosy Zhizni* 7 (1905), 136, 142ff. In this influential and expansive early comparative mythological and anthropological study in two parts, "The Hellenic Religion of the Suffering God (Ellinskaia religiia stradaiushchego boga) and "The Religion of Dionysus" (Religiia Dionisa), Ivanov traces the history of the religion of the Greek god. According to Ivanov's study (which relies heavily in this argument upon Frazer's *The Golden*

Bough), the cult of Dionysus arose from cannibalistic and orgiastic funeral feasts, particularly in Asia Minor, in which a ritual victim took on the role first of a deceased hero, then later of the dying god, periodically resurrected (RD, *Voprosy zhizni* 6 [1905], 185-220). This chthonic cult gradually took on features of the Greek Dionysian myths. In Greece, the new religion quickly gained ground, absorbing many local cults until its expansion was finally halted through a truce with the religion of Apollo, in which each god adopted many of the other's features and emblems (RD, *Voprosy zhizni* 7 [1905], 122-33). The "barbarian" religion of Dionysus emerged from this synthesis "illuminated" (ibid., 124), and from the Dionysian-Apollonian synthesis, the art of ancient Greek tragedy was born (ibid., 130.). Through the Hellenic thought of the Alexandrian period, the central ideas and symbols of the Dionysian religion prepared the ground for widespread acceptance of Christianity in the post-Hellenic world (ibid., 133-34). For other contemporary sources on the development of tragedy and the sources of Dionysian religion, see Levinton, "'Na kamennykh otrogakh,'" 208-9.

36. Nadezhda Mandel'shtam, *Vtoraia kniga*, 114.

37. Freidin considers the "myth of forgotten Christianity," as do I, central to Mandelstam's poetry of this period (Freidin, *Coat*, 77-78, 87-88; Freidin, "Sidia," 25). However, our understanding of the sense of this myth differs radically: while Freidin sees the poet taking the role of prophet among forgetful contemporaries, I see *Tristia* as the poet's own willed act of forgetting and remembering over time. In addition, Freidin's achronological analysis of the poet's use of analogical "masks" contrasts with my focus on this myth as narrative. Finally, while Freidin chooses the term prolepsis (anticipation) to describe the relation of *Tristia* to Mandelstam's later works in which his "Dichtung and Wahrheit" become "mutually transparent" (Freidin, *Coat*, 221), he nonetheless sees the poet's artistic career, as projected within "Pushkin i Skriabin" and *Tristia*, as possessing the "capacity to redeem a collectivity that had fallen into sin" (ibid., 73). In contrast, I see the poet's art as inherently and necessarily distanced, as play, from extraliterary redemption, taking the poet himself at his word (see below, pp. 127-28).

On the mythopoetics of *Tristia* generally, see also, i.a., Levin, "Zametki"; Myers "'Hellenism' and 'Barbarism'"; Hansen-Löve "Thanatopoetics"; Terras "Black Sun"; Kovaleva, "Psikheia u Persefony."

38. Cf. Nadezhda Mandelstam's understanding of the organic nature of a true poetic book (*Vtoraia kniga*, 395). Freidin's compelling apology for the reading of *Tristia* as book (*Coat*, 84-88) is at the foundation of my own.

39. On the controversy surrounding *Tristia* (1922) and the poet's rejection of the volume, see Lekmanov, *Kniga ob akmeizme*, 490; *Zhizn'*, 102; Levinton, "Eshche raz," 230. Levinton argues for an undercurrent of playful literary malice (directed against Mikhail Kuzmin) in the poet's perhaps too vociferous note for posterity ("This book is compiled without me against my will by illiterates from a pile of randomly pulled pages"). It is all too easy, however, to imagine his indignation at the volume's mangled composition and terrible distortions ("Solominka, when you sleep . . ." in a poem about insomnia; "from the blessed, singing den of sin [priton]"). In any case, what Mandelstam rejects is not the concept of his second book, but its realization.

40. Freidin, *Coat*, 87. On *Vtoraia kniga* as a unified poetic book, see also Rudneva, "Metriko-semanticheskoe edinstvo."

41. See Freidin, *Coat*, 87-88.

42. Aeschylus, *Seven Against Thebes*, 293. This specifically ritual dirge is contrasted by the chorus to the personal lament of Antigone and Ismene.

43. On Ivanov's influence in "Ode to Beethoven," see Freidin, *Coat*, 366n66; Margolina, *Mirovozzrenie*, 30–31; Segal, *Mandel'shtam. Istoriia i poetika*, 331–38; Mets, in Mandel'shtam, *PSS*, 537; Dobritsyn, "Slovo-logos," 39–40.

44. See Przybylski, *God's Grateful Guest*, 92-93; Mikhail Gasparov, "Tri poetiki," 15. This poem is properly seen as a synchronic anticipation of Mandelstam's diachronic challenge to Ivanov and Nietzsche in *Tristia*.

45. Roman numerals I and II reflect the publication in *Tristia*.

46. Ivanov, "Ellinskaia religiia stradaiushchego boga," *Novyi put'* 1 (1904), 127.

47. Taranovsky relates this passage to the 1917 poem "Still far is of the asphodels" (Eshche daleko asfodelei) in *Essays*, 157.

48. Lattimore, "Introduction," 30.

49. Ibid., 130.

50. A copy of Athena-Minerva's statue stood in the Admiralty (Svin'in, *Dostopamiatnosti*, 384).

51. Cf. Ivanov's "dithyramb" "The Firebearers" (Ognenostsy), from *Cor Ardens*: "Unstable and new / Are the Olympian thrones, / Ancient chaos in the dungeon is more sacred" (*SS*, II, 239). Ivanov is, however, in this poem, unequivocally sympathetic to the rebellion of these chthonic forces, which are for him allied with Prometheus and Dionysus and, through them, oppressed humanity. Mandelstam clearly has a more ambivalent attitude toward Tiutchev's "ancient chaos."

52. The Dionysian context is strongly reinforced through an echo of Verhaeren's *Hélène de Sparte* in Briusov's translation (first publ., *Vesy* 8-12 [1908], separately 1909): "Bacchante: We glorify Dionysus. Our body / Burns; you, Helen, we thirst for! / The dark enebriates us, like black wine. / The woods quake from our night dances" [Vakkhanka: Diónisa my slavim. Nashe telo / Pylaet; my tebia, Elena, zhazhdem! / T'ma nas p'ianit, kak chernoe vino. / Ot nashikh pliask nochnykh drozhat lesa] (Verkharn, *Elena Spartanskaia*, 81).

53. Cf. Mikhail Gasparov on the unusual density of references to the current press in the poems of winter 1917, summer 1918 ("Tri poetiki," 20).

54. The poems most obviously "out of character" in this regard are the frightening and retrograde "Return to the incestuous womb" (Vernis' v smesitel'noe lono, 1920) and the incantatory "I want just like the others" (Ia naravne s drugimi, 1920).

55. For readings of "On the rocky spurs," see Taranovsky, *Essays*, 83–98; Nadezhda Mandel'shtam, *Vtoraia kniga*, 36–37, 120; Levinton, "'Na kamennykh'"; Przybylski, *God's Grateful Guest*, 166–89; Segal, *Mandel'shtam. Istoriia i poetika*, 562–78. Despite the vast comparative, subtextual, and structural material gathered in these studies, the underlying semantic structure of the poem, which connects its images, has not been described in its richness and simplicity.

56. On this occasion, see Nadezhda Mandel'shtam, *Vtoraia kniga*, 120.

57. In spite of Taranovsky's assertion that this feature is a synecdoche for the muses (*Essays*, 153n12), the primary referent here is Sappho, the human "tenth muse." (See Levinton, "'Na kamennykh,'" 136; Terras, "Classical Motives," 261.) The expression "tenth muse" is also repeated in Ivanov's introduction to *Alkei i Safo*, 17. Inasmuch as this same feature also evokes, in a more general way, the Muses and Nadezhda Mandelstam, the poem's addressee (see Taranovsky, *Essays*, 153n11), it can also be seen to hint at three sources of the poet's inspiration.

58. The tone of these is tender, and the thematics relevant. Cf. particularly fragment XLV; see Taranovsky, *Essays*, 86; Levinton, "'Na kamennykh,'" 129.

59. Ivanov concludes the introduction to his translation of Sappho and Alkeus with Sappho's own words: "Trust that, with time, someone / Us too will remember" [Vspomnit so vremenem / Kto-nibud', ver', i nas] (*Alkei i Safo*, 27).

60. See Taranovsky, *Essays*, 87–92.

61. On the paronomasia, see Hansen-Löve, "Thanatopoetics," 142. Levinton's claim, that "cherepakha-lira" is a "compression" of the literal "cherapakha" used in Ivanov's translation of Sappho's fragment about her lyre and the explanatory "lira" found in Veresaev's translation, is unfounded ("'Na kamennykh,'" 125). "Cherepakha-lira" is simply a calque from the Greek "chelys-lyra," the full name of the ancient instrument. On death as the penalty for poetic creation in Mandelstam's poetry, see Taranovsky, *Essays*, 78, 81, 160n23.

62. The *chelys-lyra* even resembles a forehead when seen from the back. The effect is accentuated as the bars (sometimes antelope horns), which hold the cross-bar to which the strings are attached, are reminiscent of horns emerging from this forehead.

63. *Alkei i Safo*, 95, emphasis mine.

64. *Hesiod, Homeric Hymns*, 111.

65. "Why does the turtle-lyre await Terpander and not Mercury?" Irina Odoevtseva purportedly asked Mandelstam after he read "On the rocky spurs" for the first time. "Because Terpander was really born, lived on Lesbos and really made a lyre," Mandelstam replied (Odoevsteva, *Izbrannoe*, 336). On this incident, see Levinton, "Germes, Terpandr."

66. Taranovsky, *Essays*, 94; cf. also Terras, "Classical Motives," 261; Gasparov in Mandel'shtam, *SP*, 635.

67. Note that, in "The Shell" (Rakovina, 1911), the poet is not simply an empty vessel; his "shell" lacks a pearl, but there is something within it—be it only a lie—that the night will come to love.

68. See Nancy Pollak on the image of the skull-cupola and the "inner excess" of salient figures in Mandelstam's poetry of the 1930s (*Mandelstam the Reader*, 21, 35, and passim).

69. "Bare-headed grass rustles" [*Prostovolosaia shumit trava*] implies mourning or loss (cf. Mandelstam's "Tristia" [1918]; see below), and "Lungwort wafts to the delight of wasps" is, here, unsettling, while the Ukranian-intoned *krinitsa* [spring] localizes the stanza, at the same time that it betrays its inner Greek heritage (κρηνων) (see Levinton, "'Na kamennykh,'" 125, 135–36, 148–49). In this sense, my reading contrasts with both Przybylski, who sees in these lines "the Arcadian image of the land of inspiration" (*God's Grateful Guest*, 186) and Taranovsky, who sees "absolutely no reason to tear these lines away from the central two stanzas" (*Essays*, 96). I see in these lines a sharp break that returns us to the poetic present and, tonally, prepares the wistful call of the final lines.

Note that while wasps are often positively encoded by Mandelstam, resemanticization of the image occurs constantly in Mandelstam's poetry within the context of individual works. Bukhshtab, for instance, contrasts Mandelstam and Blok on the basis of the tendency of Blok's vocabulary to accrue persistent and cumulative symbolic meaning based upon prior contexts ("Poeziia Mandel'shtama," 137–38, 146). In this poem, ancient poets are compared to bees. They and the metaphorical honey (*med*) of their verse give way to literal wasps and *medunitsa* of the present.

There is no controversy surrounding the heartfelt longing that must have provoked Mandelstam's idyllic outpouring during times of bloodshed. See Przybylski, *God's Grateful Guest*, 189; Taranovsky, *Essays*, 98; Segal, *Mandel'shtam. Istoriia i poetika*, 567.

70. Schiller, *Werke*, I, 123; Reed, *Schubert Song Companion*, 217–18, line breaks added.

71. I thank the anonymous reviewer at The Ohio State University Press, who sug-

gested this subtext, as well as my colleague, Bettina Cothran, for her translations and her advice on the cultural context of Schiller's poem.

72. Schiller, *Werke*, II, Part 1, 366; Reed, *Schubert Song Companion*, 164, line breaks added. Mandelstam simultaneously alludes to the idyll embedded in Roman poet Tibullus's third elegy from the first book in Batiushkov's "free translation" (Elegiia iz Tibulla. Vol'nyi perevod, 1814?). "Zachem my ne zhivem v zlatye vremena?" [Why do we not live in the golden age?], asked Tibullus (and with him Batiushkov), in earlier, but no less real, or war-filled, times (Batiushkov, *Opyty*, 207).

73. Schiller, *Werke*, II, Part 1, 367.

74. Saito, "Poetika izgnaniia," 48. "Tristia" is also meaningfully mapped onto Tibullus's separation from and reuniting with Delia in Elegy I, 3, mentioned above (Bukhshtab, "Poeziia Mandel'shtama," 143–44; Saito, "Poetika izgnaniia," 66). The competing set of associations for loose hair, with sexuality—as, indeed, in the finale of Tibullus's elegy—is not, however, activated in the closing stanza of "On the rocky spurs." Note that both the verb "shumit'" [lit., make noise] and the adjective "prostovolosyi" are far closer to Mandelstam's own usage in the opening of "Tristia" than to the finale of the elegy.

75. Schiller, *Werke*, II, Part 1, 366; Fet, *Vechernie ogni*, 106.

76. My thanks to the anonymous reviewer who suggested this potent connection between the broken bread and forgotten Christianity. Cf. the following description of a scene symbolizing the Eucharist from the early Christian Catacombs of St. Callixtus: "Both sides of the composition, right and left, are coordinated semantically through the inclusion in one and the other of the foregrounded lamb [agnets] and its metaphor—the broken [nadlomlennyi] bread, which reminds us of the liturgical bread" (Vorob'eva, "Tema trapezy," 21).

77. See Mikhail Gasparov in Mandel'shtam, *SP*, 635; Brown, *New Companion*, 120 (s.v. "libation"). Here too, Mandelstam subtly, and paradoxically, inscribes death into his poem. Fet's translation of the sixth stanza of Schiller's poem reinforces the contrast specifically between Christian and pagan rites: "Strogii chin s pechal'nym vozderzhan'em / Byly chuzhdy zhertvennomu dniu" [The severe rite and sorrowful temperance / Were foreign to the day of sacrifice] (*Vechernie ogni*, 104). "Chin" describes specifically a Church rite, as, among others, *chin Prichashcheniia* (the rite of Communion).

78. The allusion to Schiller's "Gods of Greece," with its image of the passing of the old gods, perhaps also pulls within the associative range of the collection Plutarch's resonant myth of the death of Pan—patron of idylls—during the reign of Tiberius. This myth signaled for Christian writers the death of the old gods at the instant of Christianity's birth.

79. See chapter 9, note 27.

80. Ronen notes how the four "Lethean" poems in *Tristia*—"Still far is of the asphodels," "When Psyche-life descends to the shades" (Kogda Psikheia-zhizn' spuskaetsia k teniam, 1920), "I have forgotten the word," and "I into the circle dance of shades, trampling a tender meadow" (Ia v khorovod tenei, toptavshikh nezhnyi lug, 1920)—"i.a., through a montage of numerous classical and modern motifs, [produced] an extremely complex and emotionally and semantically charged quasi-mythological plot, in which the reality, soul, poetic word, and name appeared as protagonists in four interrelated texts [. . .] describing the act of recollection in terms of the Orphic or Eleusinian *katabasis* [i.e., descent to the underworld, S.G.]" (Ronen, "Dry River," 177).

81. Blok, *SS8*, V, 8. Cf. Mandelstam, influenced by Ivanov: "Hellenism fertilized by death *is* Christianity" (II, 318).

82. It may reasonably be asked how *Tristia* evinces the myth of forgotten Christianity while including Christian poems. "Behold the pyx, like a golden sun" (Vot daronositsa, kak solntse zolotoe, 1915) was among the tail end of the transplants from the period of *Stone*, none of which were included in later editions of *Tristia/Vtoraia kniga*. It is this Eucharist that must be forgotten to initiate the collection. "In the crystal pool," while celebratory in tone, has as much to do with Palestrina's Christian music as with Christianity *per se*, and "In the cacophony of the maiden choir" (V raznogolositse devicheskogo khora, 1916) to an even greater extent deals with cathedrals only as a medium for talking about architecture, art and the symbiosis between Russian and Italian culture. "Among the priests a young Levite" (Sredi sviashchennikov, levitom molodym, 1917) is manifestly a poem of retrovert time and *forgotten* Christianity. The phrase "*uzh nad Evfratom noch'*" [*already* over the *Euphrates* it is night]—during the morning watch—implies, from the perspective of Jerusalem, not so much a portentous eclipse (Nadezhda Mandelstam), as the unnatural regress of time. In addition, a Sabbath *mentioned* by the elders cannot be Christ, whether we understand these elders as memory-laden Judean Jews or as amnesia-stricken Russian Christians, and in any case, their "heavy menorah [semisveshchnik]," can only be seen as a most iconic reference to Judaism (cf. Mandel'shtam, *SS*, II, 65). Musatov's reading (*Lirika*, 160–65) notes aspects of this retrograde time but persists in equating the Sabbath with Christ. On "O, etot vozdukh, smutoi p'ianyi" (O this air, drunk with trouble, 1916), see below.

83. Translation of first and final stanza, Freidin, *Coat*, 106.

84. See *Zhiv Bog*, 328.

85. See, for instance, Ivanov's "The Calling of Bacchus" (Vyzyvanie Vakkha), as well as "Trial of Fire" (Sud ognia), which retells what is, for Ivanov, quite possibly the quintessential Dionysian myth, that of Eurypylos (*Stikhotvoreniia*, I, 319, 232–35).

86. Ivanov, *PZ*, 7, 10; Zelinskii, *Drevne-grecheskaia religiia*, 35.

87. Ivanov, *SS*, III, 188. This, Alexander Skriabin's final, synthetic and synaesthetic composition, of which he completed only the poetry and some musical sketches for a "Preliminary Act" (Predvaritel'noe deistvo) before his sudden death in 1915, was intended, in completion, to be literally transfigurative.

88. Cf. "Dionysus, 'igniter of ecstasies' [zazhigatel' poryvov] [. . .] Dionysus is dangerous in Russia: he can easily appear among us as a deadly force, a violence only destructive" (Ivanov, "Sporady," *PZ*, 356, 360).

89. Mandelstam preferred to efface the too-obvious symbolism of the opening lines as cited here. The *Tristia* version of "St. Isaac's" is, it seems, an early version, as the first five lines, replaced in a 1922 journal publication, are crossed out in the State Literary Museum *Tristia*. Mandelstam wrote next to these lines "iskazheno" [distorted]. However, it stretches the imagination to believe that these five lines, functionally similar to, though weaker than the journal version, were composed by Kuzmin or another of the editors.

A Eucharist is also implied subtly in the form of the poem, with its "semantic" anaphora in the key central stanza:

Соборы...
Амбары...
Зернохранилища...
И риги...

Cathedrals . . .

> Storehouses . . .
> Granaries . . .
> And threshing barns . . .

Anafora is the central section of the Orthodox liturgy containing those prayers of thanksgiving from which the Eucharist derives its name and during which the priest holds aloft the Gifts (*Zhiv Bog*, 319ff.).

90. *Tristia* version, *PSS*, 512, 415.

91. See E. Toddes, "Poeticheskaia ideologiia," 38; Mandel'shtam, *PSS*, 652; chapter 11, p. 189.

92. *Zhiv Bog*, 309–10.

93. See Przybylski, *God's Grateful Guest*, 94. In an autograph from RGALI [photocopy, GLM, f. 352-k], Mandelstam wrote in and then crossed out a *title* to the stanza in which he directly addresses Beethoven as Dionysus: "Kniaz' vinograda" [Prince of Grapes]!

94. The Dionysian coloring of the passages on Skriabin, the analysis of music (the Phrygian mode, Beethoven), the call for the chorus, the mention of the night sun (in conjunction with the sun-heart [solntse-serdtse]), and references to anamnesis (once more, appearing next to the name Dionysus) point directly to Ivanov. On Ivanov in "Pushkin and Skriabin," see Freidin, *Coat*, 70–73, 310*n*66; Mets, introduction, and Mets et al., notes to "Mandel'shtam. 'Skriabin i khristianstvo,'" 68, 76–77; Lekmanov, *Kniga ob akmeizme*, 125–26; Musatov, *Lirika*, 137–41; Terras, "Black Sun," 52.

According to Nadezhda Mandelstam, the poet said of this only partially preserved essay, "the most important [thing I have] written . . . is lost . . . I'm unlucky" (*Vospominaniia*, 183). Nadezhda Mandelstam herself calls the article "a true companion to *Tristia*, beginning from Phaedra and ending with the poem about the granaries, where the 'grain of deep, full faith' was preserved" (*Vtoraia kniga*, 114).

95. Freidin's statement, referring to the Christian artist's death in Mandelstam's essay, that "More important, such a death, imitating Christ's passion, had the power of an innocent's self-sacrifice, that is, the power of 'extrapersonal' redemption" (*Coat*, 73) is clearly contradicted by this passage.

96. Geertz, "Deep Play: Notes on the Balinese Cockfight." For Geertz, these layers of meaning include masculinity and the surrogate self, animality, and social hierarchies and rivalries. Cf. Mandelstam's description of poetry as "monstrously compacted reality" in "The Morning of Acmeism" (II, 320).

97. It is worth noting that, in *Tristia*, a book thoroughly suffused with images of death and the underworld and written during the World War, revolutions, and Civil War, no individual contemporary's death is ever addressed. After the loss of Blok and Gumilev, death takes on a qualitatively different immediacy.

98. Ivanov's *Cor Ardens*, the long, opening section of the eponymous two-volume collection, like *Tristia*, follows a path, loosely speaking, from the Dionysian to the Christian. While Dionysian and Christian imagery is greatly mixed throughout—sometimes conflated within a single poem, sometimes dispersed among various poems—the first poem of the "book" is the Dionysian "Maenad" (which Mandelstam remarks on positively [II, 343]), while the last depicts a universal Eucharist: "Look: at the rim of the deep chalice / The yellow honey of sunset radiances has mingled / With the dim poppy, that blossomed, a moon, in the pastures of the ether. / And the beneficence of dark waters / Produces the wine of divine freedoms, / A communion at the vespers of the world . . ." [Гляди: в краях глубокого потира / Закатных зорь смесился желтый мед / И тусклый мак, что в

пажитях эфира расцвел луной. / И благость темных вод / Творит вино божественных свобод / Причастием на повечерии мира . . .] (Ivanov, *SS*, II, 281–82). This is also roughly the path of Ivanov's own evolution as a religious thinker.

99. Cf. "A sense of the past as the future makes [Ivanov] akin to Khlebnikov" (II, 343). A comparison of Mandelstam's analyses of each of these two poets in this essay, "Storm and Stress," demonstrates the depth of the similarities he sees in them.

100. "There is an unshakable scale of values" (Est' tsennostei nezyblemaia skala, 1914).

CHAPTER 8

1. The most expansive analysis of theatrical motifs in Mandelstam can be found in Segal, "Fragment." See also, i.a., Broyde, *Mandel'štam and His Age*, 76–102; "Opernyi teatr," in Mandel'shtam, *SS*, III, 401–4; Malmstad, "Note"; Myers, "'Hellenism' and 'Barbarism,'" 89ff.

2. Meierkhol'd, *O teatre*, 145.

3. By and large, analyses of Alexander Blok and theater break down into three categories: Blok's dramaturgy, essays, and theatrical productions and their role in the development of Russian theater (e.g., Westphalen, *Lyric Incarnate*; Borisova, *Na izlomakh traditsii*); the biographical aspect of Blok's theatrical relationships and the reflections of these relationships in his poetry; and Blok's professional involvements in the post-Revolutionary Russian theater. Analyses of the theater poems are sometimes included in works on Blok and theater (e.g., Volkov, *Blok i teatr*), and the interconnectedness of Blok's lyrics and dramas is broadly acknowledged (cf. Rodina, *Blok i russkii teatr*, 14). Gromov is particularly sensitive to the "theatricality" of Blok's lyrics [cf. *Blok*, 111–12]). However, to the best of my knowledge, there has been no significant inquiry into the impact of Blok's theatrical sense on the structuring of space in his theatrical poems. There have been excellent analyses of spatiality in Blok's poetry more generally (Bowlt, "Question of Space"; Mints, "Struktura 'khudozhestvennogo prostranstva' v lirike Al. Bloka" [1970], in her *Poetika*: 444–531).

4. Lotman, "Teatr i teatral'nost'," 618.

5. On Symbolist life-creation and its parallels and sources in Romanticism (referring specifically to Ivanov and Novalis), see Wachtel, *Russian Symbolism*, 143–56. More broadly, on the phenomenon of life-creation among the Symbolists, see, for instance, Khodasevich, *Nekropol'*, esp. "Konets Renaty," 19–29; Paperno and Grossman, eds., *Creating Life*; Broitman, "Tvorchestvo zhizni ('zhiznestroenie')," in his *Poetika*, 194–201.

6. Belyi, "Shtempelevannaia kalosha," 49–52.

7. See Bakhtin, *Rabelais*, 7. Bakhtin refers to carnival, but describes it in precisely these terms.

8. Cf. Viacheslav Ivanov: "Dionysus accepts and, together, rejects any predicate; in his understanding, A is not A" (*PZ*, 8). As Oleg Lekmanov has noted (*Kniga ob akmeizme*, 121), Mandelstam attacks this postulate when he proposes, "A=A: what a wonderful poetic theme" ("Utro akmeizma," II, 324).

9. "Through the sanctuaries of Greece leads the path to the Mysterium, which transforms the crowds who have gathered to the spectacle into true communicants of the Mystery [Deistvo], a living Dionysian body" (Ivanov, *PZ*, 67).

10. On the "homology" between these two artistic systems, see Khanzen-Lëve, *Rannii simvolizm*, 15.

11. These formulations on the nature of theater and the *rampa* have been greatly aided by Lotman's articles, "Semiotika stseny" and "Teatr i teatral'nost' v stroe kul'tury nachala xix veka."

12. "Teatr dlia sebia" was Nikolai Evreinov's slogan and the title of a theoretical work (1915-17) in which he called for "the creation of theater in everyday life." See Clark, *Petersburg*, 105-6.

13. Ginzburg, *O lirike*, 283, emphasis mine.

14. Cited in Pyman, *Life*, I, 273. V. I. Verigina, Volokhova's friend and another actress of Kommissarzhevskaya's theater recognized this poeticized existence, in hindsight, as precisely masquerade: "Our life of the period also went on in some unreal plane, in play [. . .] we did not guess that the spell of Blok's poetry almost deprived us of our real essence, having turned us into bauttas [Venetian half-masks]" (Verigina, "Vospominaniia," 437-38). Verigina's memoirs contain interesting insights into the psychology of masquerade, from the initial awkwardness of using the familiar "you" at the first masked ball to the manner in which the atmosphere and mood of "The Snow Mask" built gradually before coming to fruition (ibid., 428, 424).

15. Theater as a framework is prominent only in the opening poems of "Faina," which I will be discussing below, although similar dynamics are revealed in other poems as well (see note 21 below). As the cycle took form only in 1916 (the poems had been included previously in various other groupings in *Earth in Snow* [Zemlia v snegu, 1908] and *Collected Poems* [Sobranie stikhotvorenii, 1911-12]), I am less concerned with its structure or the full development of the heroine as realized in some of the later poems than in the theatrical poems themselves, which present a contemporaneous alternative to the masquerade aesthetics of "The Snow Mask." As the dating of the poems demonstrates, it would be wrong to see in Blok a linear evolution from Symbolist masquerade to post-Symbolist theater, despite the impression clearly created by Blok himself in the final cyclization of his poems in the second book: from the masquerade of "The Snow Mask" to the theater poems and the prosaic conclusion of "Faina," and then to the "Realism" and blank verse of "Free Thoughts" (Vol'nye mysli, 1907). On Blok's structuring of his poetic path through the final arrangement of these cycles, see Maksimov, *Poeziia i proza*, 92-94; Mints, *Lirika*, 152, 167-68; Sloane, *Dynamics*, 251-52.

16. Blok, *SS8*, VI, 273.

17. Bowlt remarks on the absence, in Blok's poetry, of a middle ground that would connect the foreground (conventionally viewed spatiality) and the background, a "space beyond space," in the viewing of which "perspective, proportion, ratio, chiaroscuro assume unorthodox, 'unreal' values" ("Question of Space," 63). I would argue that the footlights, in the theater poems, serve, in spatial terms, to replace the middle ground, not only separating, but connecting—idiosyncratically and according to the laws of theater, as Blok understands them—foreground and background, here and there.

18. Cf. Blok's letter to Fedor Sologub and Anastasia Chebotarevskaya (22 January 1909): "If you insist, it means that you love not me but my mask, which always brings *me* suffering" (*SS8*, VIII, 271).

19. Note that in an open field the sun sets at the horizon, lighting the world from below.

20. The veil as mask presents a shifted dynamic between the visible and the actual. The eyes of a mask, generally, can provide an outlet to the real (cf. the eyes of an icon), producing play between the wittingly posed and a reality, which, stripped of social determinacy and conventions, is, in a sense, more real than could be achieved without shielding the

face. The veil is an arch-Blokian mask: it gives an imperfect and shifting (or shimmering) vision of the reality it hides.

21. This same fundamental structure (unattainable heroine/well-defined boundary/ reception by the hero of a "draught" of her essence) is also repeated in "non-theatrical" poems from "Faina." In "The Snow Maiden" (Snezhnaia deva, 1907), it is armor that functions as the boundary, but snow, the heroine's element, rushes into the hero's spirit. In "Monk" (Inok, 1907), the boundary is formed by the river and the monastery wall, while the heroine's "blossoming hop" [tsvetushchii khmel'] strikes the hero (II, 320–21).

22. "I entered the lower world" seems, intuitively, to carry an inordinate semantic weight within the cycle. It is interesting to note that at the time of its appearance (before the body of "The Snow Mask"), it "garnered exceptional attention since it appeared as the resolution of Blok's agitated mental state" (Verigina, "Vospominaniia," 415). Note, however, that, at the time this poem is written, Faina has yet to take shape in the socially concrete form developed in the play or later poems of the cycle, which do not exist even in outline yet.

23. The vertical hierarchy of space is also suggested by the Heroine's cosmic quality ("I am the star . . . You burn, my slender belt, / The Milky Path!").

24. Alexandre Benois and Igor Stravinsky's ballet *Petrouchka* is a prominent contemporary example of exploitation of the topos of tragic hero as puppet. Moreover, in Blok's "On the Contemporary State of Russian Symbolism" (O sovremennom sostoianii russkogo simvolizma, 1910), the poet depicts himself, in his poetic "antithesis," as the demiurgic director of a puppet theater, who also takes a role on stage. On this essay, see Masing-Delic's close reading ("Symbolist Crisis," 216–22); and Bogomolov's contextualization within current occult trends (*Russkaia literatura i okkul'tizm*, 186–202).

25. Cf. the use of this *topos* in *Eugene Onegin* (Pushkin, *PSS10*, V, 18).

26. It is possible to envision the hero on a stage, it is true, looking up at the heroine's box, though this demands the larger leap of faith, given the transition from "I was embarrassed and joyous" and the darkness of the "theater," which would seem to imply that the play *on stage* has not yet begun. More importantly, however, the lower level of the theater presents one unified space within the poem. It is ultimately irrelevant whether the hero finds himself on stage or in the orchestra seats because, on a metaphysical plane, he is on stage even in the audience, and the performance has begun as soon as the Heroine's footlight-eyes light up in the lower world.

27. Ginzburg, *O lirike*, 290.
28. Etkind, "'Karmen,'" 65.
29. Mints, "Struktura," 526–27.
30. Etkind, "'Karmen,'" 67.
31. Ibid., 68.
32. Blok, *Zapisnye knizhki*, 211–12.
33. Ibid., 211.
34. The potential for a "one-sided," erotically charged meeting with the heroine is reinforced in Blok's poetry through his famous "Stranger" (Neznakomka, 1906).
35. Mints, "Struktura," 526–30.
36. Duality in unity (*dvuedinstvo*), as the underlying quality of Godmanhood (*bogochelovechestvo*), played a central role in the theology of Vladimir Solov'ev. "Del'mas," consubstantial to both life and art and, therefore, providing the lyric hero access to an inner or other realm of music, displays a semi-secularized duality in unity.
37. These lines are part of the cycle's repeated allusions to Pushkin's poems to Amalia

Riznich, "Under the blue sky of her native land" (Pod nebom golubym strany svoei rodnoi, 1826) and "For the shores of a distant homeland" (Dlia beregov otchizny dal'nei, 1830).

38. On the place of music in Blok's worldview and its relation to the "World Soul," see Maksimov, *Poeziia i proza*, 361–64; Mints calls music the "main criterion of value" in Blok's third book (Mints, "Blok i russkii simvolizm," 505). It is noteworthy that music figures in Blok's vision of the *rampa* in "I was embarrassed and joyous": "And music transfigured / And burnt your face "[I muzyka preobrazila / I obozhgla tvoe litso].

39. Cf. "do uzhasa znakoma" [familiar to the point of horror]. Mints interprets this remembering in a different, but ultimately complementary key, through the prism of Blok's "first love" (*Lirika*, 326), which is also directed beyond this world and the confines of his experience.

40. The development of the sixth quatrain in the manuscript is interesting in this regard. The first variant (written in pencil) ends: "I ne blesnet mne riad zhemchuzhnyi" [And the pearl row will not flash to me]. (The stanza remains incomplete, without a fourth line.) Possibly under the influence of "The snowy spring rages" (Bushuet snezhnaia vesna, 1914), where the lyric hero is transported by a similar flash of Carmen's teeth (occurring in the novella), Blok initially conflates his hero with the opera's Jose. However, this is in clear conflict with the line "A tam, pod krugloi lampoi, tam" [But there, under the round lamp, there] above. The second variant (changes in pen) reads: "I ne blesnet uzh riad zhemchuzhnyi / Zubov stradal'tsu moemu." [And the pearl row of teeth / Will not flash for my sufferer.]. While no longer conflating himself with Jose, the lyric hero still expresses an "Onegin-like" closeness to the hero on stage. It is only in the final version (in which "stradal'tsu moemu." is crossed out, also in pen, with "neschastnomu tomu . . ." [that unfortunate . . .] written in) that Blok differentiates himself completely from the actor on stage, reaffirming the dynamics of contrast between stage and hall, real and the false theater, that I have been discussing (Blok, signed draft [*chernovik-avtograf*] of "Serdityi vzor bestsvetnykh glaz," IRLI [Pushkinskii dom], f. 654, op. 1, no. 72).

41. Or inasmuch as the hero himself is an artist: "I am the same, *Carmen*" [ia sam takoi, *Karmen*] (III, 272).

CHAPTER 9

1. Gumilev, *SS*, IV, 169.
2. Ronen was first to note the influence of *Images of Italy* on the poem (*Approach*, 353). Muratov describes the dissolute life of eighteenth-century Venice in connection with its representation in Pietro Longhi's paintings just pages after a discussion of Tintoretto and a full-page reproduction of "The Bathing Susanna" with the caption "Susanna i startsy" [Susanna and the Elders] (*Obrazy Italii*, vol. 2). See also Panova, *MPV*, 447–49.
3. The concept of "ambivalent antitheses" is applied extensively in relation to "Venetian life" by Segal in his thorough structuralist reading ("Fragment," 61–86, and elsewhere; see also his *Mandel'shtam. Istoriia i poetika*, 607–8ff.). Margolina writes that the "'lyric hero' of ['Venetian life'] . . . is antinomy" (*Mirovozzrenie*, 84–85). See also Freidin, *Coat*, 150 (on the partial resolution of antagonistic essences); Gasparov and Ronen, "O 'Venitseiskoi zhizni . . .'" 197.
4. Crone, "Blok's 'Venecija,'" 80. "Venetian life" has been much studied in connection with Blok's "Venetsiia" cycle. See Ivask, "Venetsiia"; Ronen, *Approach*, 353; Crone, "Blok's 'Venecija'"; Broitman, "Venetseiskie strofy."

5. Matich, *Erotic Utopia*, 152.
6. Blok, *SS8*, III, 302.
7. Matich, *Erotic Utopia*, 302–3n43, 49; Segal, *Mandel'shtam. Istoriia i poetika*, 625.
8. See Segal, "Fragment," 72.
9. *Veche* refers to the popular assembly of pre-Muscovite Russian cities. On the unusual usage, see Ivask, "Venetsiia," 114.
10. Margolina and Segal attribute the voice that speaks these lines to the "poet" (*Mirovozzrenie*, 86; "Fragment," 81–82). Indeed, the words "Green Adriatic, farewell!" may be understood as the speaker's own play at "Venetian death." However, the following lines, "Why are you silent, do tell, veneziana / How can one escape this festive death?" do not at all indicate that the farewell to the Adriatic *cannot* be pronounced by the veneziana, who presumably, at this point, would be either dead or playing dead.
11. Subtext noted in Crone, "Blok's 'Venecija,'" 79–80.
12. Blok himself conceived of melodrama as a desirable, popular influence, which could infuse fresh blood into the worn out Russian theater ("On Theater" [O teatre, 1908], *SS8*, V, 272–73).
13. Full text restored according to Mandel'shtam, *Sochineniia*, I, 488. The editors, Mikhailov and Nerler, cite Grishunin as the researcher who conveyed to them the complete text.
14. Segal, *Mandel'shtam. Istoriia i poetika*, 615. Cf. also Freidin, *Coat*, 341n86.
15. Note the tone with which Nadezhda Mandelstam conveys this: "Blok alone [among the Symbolists] vascillated a bit, but *still* [vse zhe] wrote in his diary about the yid and the artist" (*Vtoraia kniga*, 344, emphasis mine).
16. Taranovsky, *Essays*, 1.
17. The relation of the poem's images to Venetian *art*, almost certainly perceived by Blok, to judge by his diary entry, and noted specifically already by Ivask ("Venetsiia," 116), has received much attention.
18. On the displacement of paranomastic associations for *Venetsiia* in the poem: Vesper for *Venera* (Venus), the phial for *venena* (Lat. poisons, from Blok's "Dances of Death" [Pliaski smerti, 1912]), Saturn's ring—for *svinets* (lead, his element), etc., see Freidin, *Coat*, 150–51; Gasparov and Ronen, "O 'Venitseiskoi zhizni,'" 197, 200–201. In the iconic composition of the opening, there lurks, potentially, yet another Venus.
19. See, for instance, Hadeln, "Veronese's Venus," 115; Goodman-Soellner, "Poetic Interpretations"; Santore, "Tools of Venus." Curiously, these last two articles interpret the tradition of the "Lady at Her Toilet" as, on the one hand, a visual analogue of Petrarchian love poetry, on the other, visual representations of Venetian courtesans. Our reading is only strengthened by the traditional poetic references to Venice as queen of the sea, gazing into the looking glass of her canals. See subtexts from Karolina Pavlova and Apollon Grigor'ev, noted in Poliakova, *"Oleinikov"*, 74; Gasparov and Ronen, "O 'Venitseiskoi zhizni,'" 199–200.
20. Cf. Blok's note to the 1912 publication of "The Girl from Spoleto" (Devushka iz Spoleto, 1909): "The artists of the Renaissance loved to depict themselves on their own paintings as witnesses or participants. Some of them watch wantonly from behind a curtain, like the elders the bathing Susanna [. . .]" (III, 339).
21. The influence of Tintoretto's painting is noted in Ivask, "Venetsiia," 116; Ronen, *Approach*, 353; Crone, "Blok's 'Venecija,'" 74, 84.
22. *Meierkhol'd v teatral'noi kritike*, 234.
23. The unexpected imagery of this line finds its explanation in Arbenin's description

of the crowd in Lermontov's *Masquerade* (Maskarad, 1835): "*Pestreet i zhuzhzhit* tolpa peredo mnoi . . ." [The crowd is *mottled and buzzes* before me . . .] (Lermontov, *SS,* III, 271). *Masquerade* was another of Meyerhold and Golovin's famed productions (Alexandrinsky Theater, 1917) and a production in which Olga Arbenina, to whom "The spectral stage" is dedicated, participated.

24. Segal, "Fragment," 88ff.; Broyde, *Mandel'shtam and His Age,* 82–84; Averintsev, "'Chut' mertsaet,'" 116.

25. Ginzburg was first to point out the connection to the death of the Italian singer Angiolina Bosio, related in Nikolai Nekrasov's "On Weather" (O pogode, 1858–65) (*O lirike,* 384–85).

26. "I kromeshna nochi t'ma" [And the darkness of the night is infernal] (*PSS,* 462).

27. See Mandel'shtam, *SS,* III, 402–4; Nadezhda Mandel'shtam, *Vospominaniia,* 148; Broyde, *Mandel'shtam and His Age,* 83ff.; Malmstad, "Note," 193ff. Even Alexandre Benois, set designer of Diaghilev's *Petrouchka* (1911) and the lone critical voice who generally disapproved of the production, noted that the transition to Elysium was among "the most magical moments I have ever seen" (*Meierkhol'd v teatral'noi kritike,* 244).

28. In this, Meyerhold and Golovin hoped to emulate Gluck's own skilful accommodation of the "real and conventional" in one plane (Meierkhol'd, *O teatre,* 204).

29. *Meierkhol'd i khudozhniki,* 114.

30. Mandel'shtam, *PSS,* 462.

31. Notably, Kommissarzhevskaya's Theater is, for Mandelstam, like Gluck's Elysium and the Elysium of his own "Lethean poems," a "disembodied, transparent little world" (II, 101). The house curtain was painted by Lev Bakst, and the center portion, a study for which can be seen on the cover of this book, even depicted an "Elysium." Mandelstam refers to Blok in a negative sense in his essay on Kommissarzhevskaya—Blok's wickedly metatheatrical *The Fair Booth* (Balaganchik, 1906, dir. Meyerhold) destroys the fragile "theatrical wonder" of Kommissarzhevskaya's theater. However, he was likely influenced in his definition of "theatrical wonder" by Blok's own essay on Kommis—sarzhevskaya and the "chudo" (miracle) of her production of Maurice Maeterlinck's *Sister Beatrice* ("The Dramatic Theater of V. F. Kommissarzhevskaya [A Letter from Petersburg]" [Dramaticheskii teatr V. F. Kommissarzhevskoi (Pis'mo iz Peterburga), 1906]).

32. Meierkhol'd, *O teatre,* 205.

33. In "I have forgotten the word," the "poet" is an Orphic figure who strives to retrieve the lost word from the underworld, and, for his labors, retains but "the memory of a Stygian ringing" on his lips (and his poem). See Taranovsky on the underworld associations of the swallow (*Essays,* 158*n*18). Kikhnei notes an interesting and well-developed parallel between "I have forgotten the word" and Blok's "Artist" (Khudozhnik, 1913) (Kikhnei, "'Gieraticheskoe slovo,'" 189–91).

34. Cf. Segal, "Fragment," 96–97.

35. Toddes, "Mandel'shtam i Tiutchev," 83–84. Gasparov and Ronen see here a subtext ("Pokhorony solntsa," 219).

36. Segal recalls Mandelstam's "Eucharist" in connection with the motifs of this final stanza ("Fragment," 96).

37. Averintsev, "'Chut' mertsaet,'" 121. Viacheslav Vs. Ivanov had previously commented on the influence of the meter (and also to some extent imagery and rhythm) of "Steps of the Knight Commander" on "Venetian life," "The spectral stage," and "We shall gather anew in Petersburg" (V Peterburge my soidemsia snova, 1920) ("K issledovaniiu," 175–76).

38. Nadezhda Mandel'shtam, *Vtoraia kniga*, 37. (See also ibid., 119.)
39. Taranovsky's analysis can be found in *Essays*, 83–98.
40. The allusion is noted in Freidin, *Coat*, 211.
41. Pushkin, *PSS10*, V, 19. Subtext noted in Malmstad, "Note," 194–95.
42. This passage is compared to "The spectral stage" in Poliakova, *"Oleinikov"*, 106.
43. In this regard, cf. Averintsev, "Sud'ba i vest'," 43.
44. Poliakova notes that the plural is not used to convey a simple, physical reality ("onto the snow") (*"Oleinikov"*, 112).
45. Ibid., 104.
46. Broyde, *Mandel'štam and His Age*, 86.

CHAPTER 10

1. See chapter 9, note 37.
2. Broitman, "'V Peterburge,'" 145. In "Letter on Russian Poetry" (Pis'mo o russkoi poezii, 1922), which Mandelstam did not include in his collection *On Poetry*, the poet writes: "We measured the past with Blok as a land surveyor parcels with a fine net the boundless fields. Through Blok we saw Pushkin and Goethe and Baratynsky and Novalis, but in a new order, for they all stood before us as tributaries of Russian poetry, flowing into the distance, unitary and undiminishing, in eternal motion" (*SP,* 526). Note, however, the geographical and temporal limitations of this vision when juxtaposed with the full range of Western culture accessible to and accessed by Mandelstam. The overarching thrust of Mandelstam's essays will be precisely to highlight Blok's myopia in this regard. (See chapter 12.)
3. Both of these subtexts are noted by Khardzhiev ("Primechaniia," in Mandel'shtam, *Stikhotvoreniia*, 279).
4. Private collection of A. A. Ivich (I. I. Bernshtein), photocopy, Gosudarstvennyi Literaturnyi Muzei (GLM), Moscow, f. 352-k. *Tristia* has one additional significant change, "tsvetut" (bloom) in line 8, where the autograph has "zhivut" (live).
5. In a more general sense, Mandelstam did indeed see in the Petersburg of 1920 a "half-Venice, half-theater" (Akhmatova, *Sochineniia* [1986], II, 206). On post-revolutionary mass theater, see, for instance, Clark, *Petersburg*, 122–34. Viacheslav Ivanov's role in the development of the Soviet ideology of mass performance implies the deep potential kinship between these two modes of theater (mass enactments and *mysterium*). See Bird, "Massovye prazdnestva." On the semiotics of masquerade and mysterium in the context of Lotman and Bakhtin's theoretical writings, see chapter 8.
6. Mikhail Gasparov and Ronen provide an extensive bibliography of the literature on "We shall gather anew" through 2003 ("Pokhorony," 208). See especially van der Eng-Liedmeier, "Mandel'štam's Poem"; Broyde, *Mandel'štam and His Age*, 86–102; Ivask, "Mandel'štam's 'We Shall Gather'"; Malmstad, "Note"; Crone, "Plight," 91–93; Freidin, *Coat*, 180ff.; Segal, "Fragment," 106–7, and his *Mandel'shtam. Istoriia i poetika*, 620–24, Musatov, *Lirika*, 200–206; Broitman, "'V Peterburge'"; Gasparov and Ronen, "Pokhorony," 207–14; and Gillespie, "Between Myth and History."
7. Mandel'shtam, *PSS*, 154, with original, *Tristia* version of lines 25–28 restored per ibid., 461.
8. On the orphic in Mandelstam and its roots in Viacheslav Ivanov, see especially Ronen, *Approach*, 198–99; Terras, "Black Sun"; cf. also Freidin, *Coat*, 155–58; 183–86.

Expanding our frame of reference to include the Dionysian in Mandelstam or the night and black sun in general yields a very large body of literature. We would be remiss, however, not to mention "Chernoe solntse," in Mandel'shtam, *SS*, III, 404–11.

9. Milestones in the scholarship on Blok in "We shall gather anew," in addition to Khardzhiev and Viach. Vs. Ivanov's observations (see chapter 9, note 37), include Toddes, "K teme," 97–98; Broitman, "'V Peterburge,'" 145–49; and Gasparov and Ronen, "Pokhorony," 213–14.

10. Nadezhda Mandelstam and Kiril Taranovsky each challenged the association with love poetry (*Vtoraia kniga*, 65; Taranovsky, *Essays*, 164n26). Gasparov and Ronen defend a reading growing out of these thematics ("Pokhorony," 210–11). For a summation of the controversy, see ibid.

11. See, for instance, Freidin, *Coat*, 182.

12. Blok, *SS8*, VII, 371, emphasis mine.

13. "We, with a funeral song [. . .] will appease the black sun of wild and sleepless passion" [My zhe, pesn'iu pokhoronnoi, / [. . .] / Strasti dikoi i bessonnoi / Solntse chernoe uimem]. Cf. "But the golden-haired luminary / Becomes well again" [No svetilo zlatokudroe / Vyzdoravlivaet vnov'], from a variant recorded in S. P. Kablukov's copy of *Stone* (*PSS*, 453). The phrase "I will pray in the Soviet night / For the blessed, senseless word" [Za blazhennoe, bessmyslennoe slovo / Ia v nochi sovetskoi pomolius'] retains two equally valid meanings: prayer to heal or protect the Word and prayer to obtain the Word as a protective and curative talisman in the Soviet night. On this latter sense, see Ronen, *Approach*, 5–7; Freidin, *Coat*, 181–83.

14. The logic of the entire circle of ideas, particularly apparent in Mandelstam's essay "Pushkin and Skriabin," is as follows: the night sun is a sun of redemption, which has been banished to the underworld, while the black sun of guilt is that which ascends to replace it in moments of retrograde historical movement. Russia, in placing its faith in the retrograde and Christ-/redemption-forgetting Skriabin (who functions as antithetical hypostasis of the Pushkinian sun), raises from the depths the black sun of guilt and banishes (buries) the sun of Christian culture, represented by Pushkin (about whom Vladimir Gippius had written as Christian artist par excellence in "Pushkin and Christianity" [Pushkin i khristianstvo, 1915]). Note, however, that in "Pushkin and Skriabin" and "This night is irreparable" (Eta noch' nepopravima, 1916), *the terms* (night sun vs. black sun) *are reversed* in comparison with "How these coverings" and "We shall gather anew in Petersburg." On the influence of Gippius's book on Mandelstam, see Freidin, *Coat*, 69–70.

15. Compare the Gnostic understanding of Judas as favored apostle, since his betrayal has a direct role in executing divine salvation. See Averintsev, "Iuda Iskariot"; John Noble Wilford and Laurie Goodstein, "In Ancient Document, Judas, Minus the Betrayal," *New York Times*, April 7, 2006. Compare also Blok: "What are the sounds of paradise to the *traitor*" [Chto *izmenniku* blazhenstva zvuki] (Blok, *Stikhotvoreniia*, III, 93, my emphasis).

16. "On Kulikovo Field" (Na pole Kulikovom, 1908). Note Blok's gloss in "The People and the Intelligentsia" (Narod i intelligentsiia, 1908): "[. . .] Gorky's intellect [. . .] 'deifies'; Gorky's heart, however, is troubled and loves, without deifying, severely and demandingly, in the way of the people [narod], as one may love a mother, a sister and a wife in the single person of the motherland—Russia" (Blok, *Rossiia i intelligentsiia*, 12).

17. Blok, Foreword to "Retribution" (Vozmezdie, publ. 1921), *SS8*, III, 298.

18. Freidin points out the incongruence, for 1920, of a "capital" called "Petersburg" (*Coat*, 182); cf. also Eng-Liedmeier, "Mandel'štam's Poem," 185, 193–94. While it should be noted that roughly half of the books published in this city in 1920 were imprinted

"Peterburg," rather than "Petrograd," still it is significant that the poem's draft is dated "24 noiabria 1920. *Peterburg"'* (24 November 1920. *Petersburg*—with a hard sign!). A hard sign, it seems, also graces the poet's rather blotchy signature. These are the sole instances of the use of the hard sign in the draft and would seem to convey graphically that vital connection between past, present, and future which is developed thematically in the poem.

19. Blok, "Bezvremen'e" (Stagnation/Evil Times, 1906).

20. Cf. Mandelstam's "Where night drops its anchors" (Gde noch' brosaet iakoria, 1920), in which "Remote constellations of the zodiac" (Glukhie sozvezdiia zodiaka) is clearly code for epochs not bordering (or equivalent to) a utopic Age of Aquarius.

21. Syntactically, the expression is then akin to "noch' bezlunna" [the night is moonless], morphologically to "mnogotonnyi" (from "to*nn*a" [ton]). Compare also Sergei Gorodetsky's resemanticizing of the Church term "Nenevestnaia" [Virgin/Unbridal] in the poem "Nevesta" (Bride, publ. *Niva* 43 [24 October 1909], 737). Gorodetsky, with some bitterness, depicts his muse, Rus, spirited away and defiled—hence, *no longer* "nevestnaia" [of bridal quality]—by a "bridegroom" transparently representing Blok's lyric hero. In the hero's *perception,* Anna is nowhere to be found: "Maiden of Light! Where are you, Donna Anna? / Anna! Anna!—Silence."

22. On the connection to *Eugene Onegin,* see Malmstad, "Note," 194–97.

23. Note also the presence of the patrol, which Segal not unreasonably connects to Blok's "The Twelve" (*Mandel'shtam. Istoriia i poetika,* 623). Elsewhere, he unconvincingly links Mandelstam's "word" through Gumilev's Word to Christ as Word in the Gospel of John and thus to Blok's finale (ibid., 123–24).

24. "Afishi," in Pushkin's time, meant program books. See Introduction, note 69. Clearly it is these, and not playbills, that drift down from the gallery.

25. See, i.a., Brown, *Mandelstam,* 231–33; Broyde, *Osip Mandel'štam,* 90–92; cf. Akhmatova, *Sochineniia* (1990), II, 162.

26. Blok, "Bez bozhestva, bez vdokhnoven'ia (Tsekh akmeistov)," *SS8,* VI, 178; *Stikhotvoreniia,* III, 71. "Courageously sober" is a quote from Gumilev's Acmeist manifesto, but Blok asserts, not entirely without cause, that the concept was stolen from his essay, "On the Contemporary State of Russian Symbolism." On the influence of Gnosticism on Blok, see especially Magomedova, *Avtobiograficheskii mif,* 70–83.

27. Kremlin (*kreml'*) is the old Russian word for a city fortress, and such kremlins can still be found in many Russian cities today (Novgorod, Pskov, Suzdal, Kazan). The Moscow Kremlin, with its venerated cathedrals and icons, indeed came under destructive fire during the October Revolution.

28. See Blok, "Intelligentsiia i revoliutsiia," in his *Rossiia i intelligentsiia,* 37.

29. Note, however, that in Orphic fashion, these positively charged phenomena draw their vitality from the surrounding night and death. Cf. Terras, "Black Sun," 57. See also Ivask, "Mandel'štam's 'We Shall Gather,'" 255; Gillespie, "Between Myth and History," 364.

30. Gasparov and Ronen, "Pokhorony," 210.

31. In contrast, in "Venetian life, morbid and barren," fear and love are equal counterweights on the Saturnian wheel of existence.

32. Perhaps the "wind-up doll of an officer" in the *Tristia* version of these lines also arose from a set of Blokian associations. As Gillespie notes, the sense of the phrase is ambiguous. She ties it to Blok's deflations of the Fair Lady ("Between Myth and History," 379). In addition, if we understand the officer as the wind-up doll itself, Blok is a possible model. One of the anonymous reviewers at OSU Press submits the following intruiging summary: "Blok [. . .] struck many as a man of military bearing and he was actually an officer

(provisions) in the first world war and also lived on 'Officer Street' [. . .] Furthermore, by this time Blok was already a person with medical and psychological problems, and his movements could have appeared to be those of a 'wound-up doll.'" Of course, this equation would place Blok himself inside the sanctum of the theater, even if he is represented in a most ambiguous light. At the same time, Gumilev, a rival for Arbenina's affections, was also an officer of notably stiff comportment; Shubinskii sees him here ("Neuiazvimyi," 472).

33. Through careful analysis of the handwriting of the draft, I have been able to demonstrate that the reading given in Mandel'shtam, *PSS*, 462, implying denial of "communion" with the night sun ("ne prigubish' ty" [you won't partake of]), is in error. "Pogubish'" (you will not destroy) has now been accepted by the editor, A. G. Mets, and is given in the just published Osip Mandelstam, *Polnoe sobranie sochinenii i pisem v trekh tomakh* (Moscow, 2009–11), 1:459.

34. Cf. Gasparov and Ronen, "Pokhorony," 210.

35. Pushkin, "To Krivtsov," *PSS10*, I, 326.

36. Broitman, "V Peterburge," 154; Blok, "On the Snow Pyre," II, 284.

37. Toddes, "K teme," 97; Boris Gasparov, "Tridsatye gody." Note that in editions of Pushkin's works through at least 1887 "To Krivtsov" was incorrectly dated 1819 (Gaevskii, "Pushkin i Krivtsov," 456).

38. This profound imitation of Pushkin is echoed superficially in Mandelstam's appearance at the masquerade ball at the Zubov mansion (11 January 1921) dressed as Pushkin (Musatov, *Lirika*, 201). On Mandelstam's extensive *imitatio* Pushkin in the 1930s, see especially Boris Gasparov, "Tridtsatye gody"; Reynolds, "Smert' avtora" and "Return of the Dead"; Surat, *Mandel'shtam i Pushkin*.

39. "As is visible from later hints, Krivtsov 'tried to corrupt' [razvrashchal] his young friend, especially through his disbelief, more precisely—superficial materialism," Gershenzon, *Dekabrist Krivtsov*, 93. Gaevskii, however, describes Krivtsov as "always merry and joyous" (Gaevskii, "Pushkin i Krivtsov," 456), an assertion seemingly well supported by the biography he provides.

40. Pushkin, *PSS10*, I, 326.

41. Mandelstam's line, "*Chasovykh ia ne boius'*" (*I do not fear the watchmen*), recalls the forboding of the striking clock in "Steps of the Knight Commander." On the choice of "chasovykh" (watchmen), rather than the reported early variant "militsionerov" (militiamen), as an abstracting marker of "time itself," see Gillespie, "Between Myth and History," 368.

42. See, however, Lindeberg, "Vospominaniia Vl. Gippiusa," 255.

43. [Gippius], *Noch' v zvezdakh*, 113. Cf. also "And walk in darkness, as in the light!" [I vo mrake idi, kak v svetu!], from his *Vozvrashchenie*, 37. Curiously, one of the copies of *Vozvrashchenie* held by the Russian National Library (under call no. 37.35.5.14) features what appears to be a dark sun, hand-drawn in ink and painstakingly centered in the bottom third of the cover above the lower line of text (the only image on the usually unadorned cover).

44. *Giperborei. Ezhemesiachnik stikhov i kritiki* 2 (1912), 3.

45. Ibid., 4. Cf. also Blok's "When I first gained insight" (Kogda ia prozreval vpervye, 1909), in which the day is actually a voiceless night: "The daytime night is mute" [Nemotsvuet dnevnaia noch'] (III, 84).

46. Gippius himself notes that Blok, though he never answered this "lengthiest homily" (Gippius's expression), replied instead through an inscription on his *Collected Works*

(Gracheva, "Istoriia tvorcheskoi polemiki," 247–48). The inscription was a quatrain taken from Gippius's *Vozvrashchenie*. Gracheva, who relates this episode in Gippius' words, is mistaken, however, in concluding that "Blok's inscription attested to the poet's desire to end the polemics on a conciliatory note" (ibid., 248) The inscription, when read carefully, appears intended to say that Gippius himself understands deep down that Blok is right. After all, he let slip out:

И *усыпительно и сладко*
Поет незвучная вода, —
Что сон ночной, что сумрак краткий —
Не навсегда, не навсегда...

And *soporifically and sweetly*
Sings the hushed water—
That the nightly slumber, that the brief gloom—
Is not forever, not forever . . . (ibid., emphasis mine.)

In terms of their image structure and the nature of their irony (possibly unintended by Gippius?), these lines could have come straight from a poem by Blok. The outer message of the water, that the dark, unconscious night is soon to end, is but a sweet siren lulling the feckless poet back to sleep, and preventing the clear vision and actively willed struggle that Blok himself espouses.

47. Blok, *Stikhotvoreniia*, III, 72. Subtext noted in Ronen, *Approach*, 125.

48. Akhmatova, *Sochineniia* (1990), II, 151. Sergei Borisovich Rudakov remarks in a letter to his wife (21 July 1935): "I berated Os'ka for Blok (for flipping out [psikhovan'e] etc.)" ("Mandel'shtam v pis'makh Rudakova," 77).

49. See, in this regard, Broyde, *Mandel'štam and His Age*, 101; Eng-Liedmeier, "Mandel'štam's Poem," 199. See also Ivask's rich interpretation of this line ("Mandel'štam's 'We Shall Gather,'" 258).

50. "Voice from the Chorus" was the only poem printed out of chronological order. Its function in setting the collection's tone was thus clearly emphasized. The perceptive reader would also have noted, however, that the volume closes with "You assert that I am cold, remote, and dry" (Ty tverdish', chto ia kholoden, zamknut i sukh, 1916), a poem that presents a distinct counterpoint to "Voice from the Chorus" (though still positing light from *outside* the world).

51. This subtext is first noted in Gasparov and Ronen, "Pokhorony," 213–14, and, though it is not explored by the authors, its implications are, it seems, quite apparent. One particularly suggestive source for the image of the snuffed out candles in "We shall gather anew in Petersburg" is Leonid Andreev's "Darkness" (T'ma, 1907): "If we can't light all the darkness with our lanterns [fonariki], then let's douse all the lights and all creep into the dark [. . .] Let's drink, girls, to all the lights going out [chtoby vse ogni pogasli]" (Andreev, *SS*, II, 298; my thanks to Alexander Zholkovsky for suggesting this connection). Blok liked and wrote about Andreev, whom Mandelstam disliked, and "Darkness" had a particularly strong resonance for him (see ibid., 536). The story's continuing importance is attested by a letter to the poet's cousin, S. N. Tutolmina (16 January 1916), in which Blok specifically refers to "Darkness" (though not by name) and writes: "sometimes even these individual bright spots seem a sacrilegious dissonance because the night which surrounds us is too black, and, in its blackness, majestic" (*SS8*, VIII, 454).

52. One may see lines 29–31 as an inversion of the theatrical imagery that initiates and frames "Steps of the Knight Commander" ("A weighty, dense curtain at the entrance" [Tiazhkii plotnyi zanaves u vkhoda]). Cf. Broitman, "V Peterburge," 146–47; Dmitrienko, "O problematike," 50–51. In Mandelstam's conception (expressed in his essay "Iakhontov" [1927]), a *"complete"* theater includes "the square and the frosty night" outside (*SS*, 3:113). Poliakova juxtaposes this passage with "The spectral stage" and "Valkyries fly" in *"Oleinikov"*, 106.

53. Cf. Blok: "The excited theater was extinguished/went dark" [Teatr vzvolnovannyi pogas] (II, 290). Historically, of course, in the period through the mid-nineteenth century, when theaters were actually illuminated by candles, these were not extinguished during the action. Cf. Mandelstam's own "I will not see the celebrated *Phèdre*."

54. Blok's half-participation in the circle of culture in Mandelstam's eyes should also be seen in light of the cultural situation in Petersburg in 1920. Mandelstam appears to have participated in a project, possibly initiated in a narrow sense by Gumilev, but clearly tapping into broader artistic sentiments then current, to rejuvenate and redefine, to see and greet anew the Word. One important reflection of this labor was the almanac, *The Dragon* (Drakon, publ. Feb. 1921), which included such manifestos of the new poetics of the Word as Gumilev's "The Word" [Slovo, 1919] and "Poem of the Beginning. Book One. The Dragon" [Poema nachala. Kniga pervaia. Drakon, 1918–19?], Andrei Bely's "Excerpts from Glossolalia (A Poem about Sound)" (Otryvki iz Glossolalii [Poemy o zvuke], 1917) and Mandelstam's own "The Word and Culture." Blok, in his contribution, "The Sphinx" (Sfinks, 1902 [sic!]) intoned: "I will grasp the forgotten word Love, / In a forgotten, living language! ..." [Ia postignu zabytoe slovo Liubov', / Na zabytom zhyvom iazyke! ...] (*Drakon. Al'manakh stikhov* [Peterburg, 1921], 4). As Georgii Ivanov rightly noted in a review, Blok's submission, though good, did little to expand anyone's conception of the author ("O novykh stikhakh," 97). It should also be noted that Blok's version of the myth of the Word is executed in a deeply personal key. Rather than the mythologizing abstractions of Gumilev, Bely, or Mandelstam, Blok's claims relate to his own "I." Moreover, the word that he will recall lies at the heart of his own personal poetic mythology: "Liubov'" (Love/Lyubov), the name of his forgotten Heroine (cf. "Those Who Have Forgotten You" [Zabyvshie Tebia, 1908]). On the antagonism between Blok and Gumilev and their struggle for leadership of literary organizations in 1920–21 Petersburg, see, for instance, Khodasevich, "Blok i Gumilev," in his *Nekropol'*, 87–91.

CHAPTER 11

1. "There is an unshakable scale of values" (1914).

2. These names clearly include that of Blok, as Annensky devotes several passages to the poet in his essay.

3. Annenskii, "O sovremennom lirizme," 6–7, my emphasis. According to Mandelstam, Annensky's reticence was "fed by a consciousness of the impossibility of tragedy in contemporary Russian art, thanks to the absence of a synthetic national consciousness, indisputable and absolute." "Born to be a Russian Euripides," Annensky instead "bore with dignity his lot of withdrawal—renunciation [otrechenie]" (Osip Mandel'shtam, *SP*, 527–28).

4. Bely's "fall," however, itself smacks of tragedy: "to laugh at Bely is unwelcome and a sin: he wrote Petersburg" (II, 423).

5. Cf.: "The apothecary from Christiania [i.e., Ibsen] succeeded in luring a thunderstorm into the professorial chicken coop and raising the ominously courteous squabbling of Hedda and Brack to the heights of tragedy" (II, 101).

6. This text correctly reproduces the first edition, while Filippov and Struve have a distorting error in the final line of the essay.

7. Eikhenbaum, "Sud'ba Bloka," 59.

8. Ibid., 44-46, 45. Similarly, Sergei Solov'ev wrote to Bely under the fresh impression of Blok's death: "We did not believe in the sincerity of his 'snow pyres,' but now he has proven that the theme of death was not, for him, 'literariness'" (cited in Gaidenko, "Soblazn," 109).

9. On this eighty-fourth Pushkin anniversary, see Khodasevich, *Nekropol'*, 85-87; Hughes, "Pushkin in Petrograd."

10. See Mets, "Primechaniia," in Mandel'shtam, *PSS*, 652; and Surat, *Mandel'shtam i Pushkin*, 34-35, who cites Nadezhda Pavlovich's description and adds a telling detail—that Pushkin had similarly ordered a memorial service for Byron on the anniversary of his death.

11. See Freidin, "Sidia na saniakh"; Boris Gasparov, "Tridtsatye gody," 151, 153; Reinolds, "Smert' avtora," 200-214, especially 212-13; and "'Return of the Dead'"; Surat, *Mandel'shtam i Pushkin*, 16-46. On the phenomenon of projection onto Pushkin's biography in general during the "Silver Age," see Paperno, "Pushkin v zhizni," 36 and elsewhere. On Pushkin's death as part of a tragedy ultimately shaped by the poet, see Iu. M. Lotman, *Pushkin*, 180ff.; Bethea, *Realizing Metaphors*, 44, 137ff.

12. Strangely, it seems that the obvious subtext of "We shall gather anew" in this regard, which would seem to underly the understanding of Ivask and others, has not been noted: "*Ugas,* kak *svetoch, divnyi genii*" [The wondrous genius *went out* like a *torch*] (Lermontov, "The Poet's Death" [Smert' poeta, 1837], *SS*, I, 372). Note also Vasily Surikov's painting "Morning of the Execution of the Streltsy" (Utro streletskoi kazni, 1881), in which the *strel'tsy* hold burning candles, and one of Peter the Great's soldiers is seen blowing out a candle.

13. "Blok died over the course of several months, before everyone's eyes; he was treated by doctors—and no one named or was able to name his illness" (Khodasevich, *Nekropol'*, 93). On Blok's illness, see Shcherba and Baturina, "Istoriia bolezni" and Matich's retort (*Erotic Utopia,* 106-11).

14. Naturally, we are not speaking here of any simple linearity, but rather of a complexly signifying relationship. In "Pushkin and Skriabin," the artist's death is part of his Christ-like *play*. However, this play is fraught with meaning. See chapter 7, pp. 127-28. Similarly, in "Conversation about Dante," the poet describes prison as a "resonator" for the "cello-like voice of Ugolino" (II, 398).

15. On "Concert at the Railway Station," see esp. Ginzburg, *O lirike,* 372-74; Taranovsky, *Essays,* 7-17; Ronen, *Approach,* xvii-xx; Freidin, *Coat,* 187-94; Boris Gasparov, "Eshche raz"; Faryno, "Arkheopoetika"; Purin, *Vospominaniia o Evterpe,* 72-79; Musatov, *Lirika,* 231-40; Surat, *Mandel'shtam i Pushkin,* 37-39, 266. On Blokian echoes, see below, note 24. Surat's discussion happens to concur on certain important points with my 2001 Ph.D. dissertation. These include Blok's Pushkin speech (first noted by Musatov ["Mifologema," 284]) and Pushkin's last words as subtext to line 1; the passage on Skriabin from *The Noise of Time* as subtext for the third stanza (Surat cites Morozov's commentary [2002]); and the memorial service for Pushkin as the primary reference for the funeral feast here.

16. A similar, radical revision of the poet's response to a contemporary can be observed in connection with Mayakovsky's suicide in 1930. As Lekmanov demonstrates, Mandelstam's understanding of Mayakovsky as a "well-healed Soviet writer" was overturned in an instant by, as the poet himself put it, the "'oceanic tidings of Mayakovsky's death.'" Mandelstam praised Mayakovsky effusively, hyperbolically at a reading in 1932 (Lekmanov, "Mandel'shtam i Maiakovskii," 223).

17. See esp. Khodasevich, *Nekropol'*, 83ff.

18. Gasparov, "Eshche raz," 176.

19. Cited as per *SP*, 86, but with date as printed in *Stikhotvoreniia* (1928). Angle brackets mark a line omitted in *Stikhotvoreniia*.

20. This seemingly idiosyncratic reading, overriding conventional logic, is suggested by the cadence of the lines and underscores the way in which disharmony is synthesized within the music of this final concert. A more neutral translation would be "And once again, the violin-filled air, torn by the whistles of steam-engines, is fused."

21. Taranovsky, *Essays*, 15–17; *O poezii*, 30, 38.

22. Ronen, *Approach*, xvii; Gasparov, "Eshche raz," 171–72, 178–80.

23. Mandelstam wrote, with the hindsight of the Pushkin speech, in which Blok had revised his concept of stagnant civilization and dynamic, but destructive culture: "Poetic culture arises from a striving to stave off catastrophe, to make it dependent on the central sun of the entire system, be that love, about which Dante spoke, or music, to which, in the end, came Blok" (II, 275). Blok's repentance of his former views can be observed directly in his letter to N. A. Nolle-Kogan of 8 January 1921 (*SS6*, VI, 300).

24. Ronen, *Approach*, xviii–xx; Freidin, *Coat*, 191–92. These include passages from "Gogol's Child" (Ditia Gogolia, 1909), "Irony," "The Wreck of Humanism" (Krushenie gumanizma, 1919 [publ. 1921]), "Intelligentsia and Revolution" and "Lightning Flashes of Art" (Molnii iskusstva, 1909; publ. 1923). On Blok in "Concert at the Railway Station," see also Gasparov, "Eshche raz," 172–73; Purin, *Vospominaniia*, 74–78; and Surat, *Mandel'shtam i Pushkin*, 37–39. Purin, assuming that his disquisition on Blok is meant to imply a similar conception on Mandelstam's part, comes to an understanding of Mandelstam's relation to Blok before and after his death diametrically opposed to my own, i.e., that Blok's performance is initially believed, but with the loss of his physical presence unravels, leaving only "a foggy phantom—the eternal companion of undiscriminating youth" (76). Purin's argument in this regard is based not on an analysis of Mandelstam's writings, but on misrepresentation of Tynianov's "Blok and Heine" (1921) and a late-twentieth-century perspective on Blok. Moreover, as far as this reader can see, Mandelstam demonstrated such youthful indiscriminacy in regard to Blok in only one place, the poem "Dark bonds of worldly imprisonment" [Temnykh uz zemnogo zatocheniia, 1910?], assuming, as likely is the case, that there is no irony implied in his donning there of Blok's masks.

25. See chapter 2, note 15.

26. Subtext noted by Ronen (*Approach*, xix).

27. Cf., in his letters, "it's hard to breathe" [trudno dyshat'] (to his mother, 4 June 1921, *SS8*, VIII, 539); "I'm constantly short of breath" [postoianno zadykhaius'] (to N. A. Nolle-Kogan, 2 July 1921, *SS6*, VI, 306). Here, perhaps, is a secondary source of the talk that Blok "suffocated," talk that Khodasevich derives, not of course without cause, from the Pushkin speech (*Nekropol'*, 92–93). See also Surat, *Mandel'shtam i Pushkin*, 37–38.

28. Musatov, "Mifologema," 287.

29. "Here the cupola writhing with worms turns into the vault of a sepulchre (this

image is reinforced, of course, in such details as 'the scent of roses in rotting hothouses')" (Boris Gasparov, "Eshche raz," 166).

30. See Pavlovich, "Vospominaniia," 63–64. Cf. Boris Gasparov on "The wild beginning of the night chorus," with its potential reminiscence of the chorus of furies from *Orpheus and Eurydice* ("Eshche raz," 180).

31. The image of the station perhaps reflects the underground hall of Blok's "Canto of Hell" (Pesn' ada, 1909), lines 22–33. Compare the following passages:

[. . .] *здесь умерли слова;*
[. . .]
Все к пропасти стремятся безнадежной,
И я вослед. Но вот, в прорыве скал,
Над пеною потока белоснежной,

Передо мною *бесконечный зал.*
Сеть кактусов и *роз благоуханье,*
Обрывки мрака в *глубине зеркал;*
[. . .]
И *душное спирается дыханье.*

Мне этот зал напомнил *страшный мир,*
Где я бродил *слепой,* как в дикой сказке,
И где застиг меня последний пир.

И ни одна звезда не говорит,

И мнится мне: *весь в музыке и пене,*

И я вхожу в *стеклянный лес вокзала,*
И *запах роз* в гниющих парниках —

Нельзя дышать [. . .]

Я опоздал. Мне *страшно.* Это *сон.*
Горячий пар зрачки смычков *слепит.*
Куда же ты? На *тризне милой тени*
В последний раз нам музыка звучит!
(III, 15–16, my emphasis)

[. . .] here words have died;
[. . .]
All rush toward the hope-bereft precipice,
And I behind. But there, in the breach of the cliffs,
Above the *foam* of the snow-white torrent,

Before me is an *endless hall*

A grid of cactuses and the *scent of roses,*

Shards of darkness in the depth of *mirrors;*
[. . .]
And stuffy breath comes up short.
This hall reminded me of a *frightening world,*

And not a single star speaks,

And it seems to me: all in music and in *foam,*

And I enter the *glass forest* of the *station* [Vaux*hall*]
And the *scent of roses* in rotting hothouses—

One cannot breathe [. . .]
I'm late. I'm *frightened.* This is a dream.

Where I wandered *blind,* as in a savage fairytale,	Hot steam *blinds* the pupils of the violin bows.
And where the final feast overtook me.	Where are you off to? At the *funeral feast* of a dear shade
	Music sounds for us for the final time!

32. On line 3 as polemic against Lermontov, see Taranovsky, *Essays,* 15; *O poezii,* 27–28, 31.

33. On Blok's violins, see, for instance, Magomedova, "O Briusovskom istochnike," 65–66.

34. This is all not to say that Skriabin is the "native shade" of this stanza (a possibility Przybylski toys with [*God's Grateful Guest,* 99]), although this possibility cannot be excluded. (*Native* is then taken in the sense that he is native, akin, close to the nineteenth century and music—hence to the station—rather than to the speaker, and in comparison with those who only pass through.) In general, we might allow for Skriabin as "native shade" and Pushkin as "dear shade" (since it was his "funeral feast" that was being celebrated in 1921 just before Blok and Gumilev prematurely left the "station"). Note also that these two artists are two hypostases of the same sun for Mandelstam, the "sun of redemption" and "sun of guilt" ("Pushkin and Skriabin"). The question of Annensky, raised by Purin (*Vospominaniia,* 73–74, 78–79), is quite interesting, though Purin ultimately accords him an altogether outsized role in the poem.

35. Ronen, *Approach,* xviii.

36. See Ginzburg, *O lirike,* 373; Purin, *Vospominaniia,* 72. On the ontology of the text, see, for instance, Faryno, "Arkheopoetika," 183–84.

37. See, i.a., Ginzburg, *O lirike,* 374; Averintsev, "Sud'ba i vest'," 44, 64.

38. On the influence of Gumilev's "Wayward Tram" on Mandelstam's poem, see Freidin, *Coat,* 193; Boris Gasparov, "Eshche raz," 173–75. On the relevance of the date 1837 and the opening of the train line, see Boris Gasparov, "Eshche raz," 171. The Pavlovsk portion of the line opened in 1838.

39. See Boris Gasparov, "Eshche raz," 171, 175–76; Purin, *Vospominaniia,* 72–73.

40. Purin, *Vospominaniia,* 73.

41. "'Trankhops.'"

42. Boris Gasparov, "Eshche raz," 168ff. The most powerful textual evidence Gasparov presents is the connection to the "dear shade" [milaia ten'] of "I into the circle dance of shades" (1920), a poem permeated with clear subtextual references to Pushkin. Hughes notes the presence of Kuzmin's "Pushkin" as a subtext in the final stanza of "Kontsert na vokzale," strenghtening Gasparov's already convincing argument ("Pushkin in Petrograd," 211*n*5).

43. Given the paradoxes noted above, a glass entrance compartment is not too off-putting.

44. Musatov, *Lirika,* 235–36. Musatov is also strangely reductive in his insistence that the poem represents specifically the Pavlovsk Station of the 1890s (ibid., 233–34, 236).

45. "Blok is a most complicated manifestation of literary eclecticism—he is the gatherer of Russian verse [sobiratel' russkogo stikha], scattered and lost by the historically fragmented nineteenth century. The tremendous labor of the gathering of Russian verse completed by Blok is still not clear to his contemporaries and is only felt instinctively by them as melodic power [pevuchaia sila]" (Mandel'shtam, *SS,* II, 347–48). See also chapter 12, pp. 200–202.

46. See Pyman, *Life,* II, 365–66. We are speaking here of a relative silence, but a silence Blok's contemporaries and the poet himself acknowledged as a psychological reality: "All the sounds have gone silent. Can't you hear that there aren't any sounds any more?"; "It would be blasphemous and false to try by any rational process to recall sounds in soundless space" (ibid.). See Lotman on Pushkin's remarkably resilient creativity during his difficult final years (*Pushkin,* 167ff.).

47. Elements of polemic vis-à-vis Blok's conception of the nineteenth century, pointed out by Ronen (who sees Mandelstam allying with Gogol *Approach,* xix–xx), seem ultimately secondary to the integration of Blok within Mandelstam's composite image of the musical nineteenth century.

CHAPTER 12

1. *Barstvennost'* means "lordliness," particularly in that sense of lordly that is conveyed in the OED by the words "haughty, imperious, lofty, disdainful."

2. "A. Blok: 7 August 1921–7 August 1922" was published in *Rossiia* 1 (1922).

3. On the composition of *O poezii,* see Iu. L. Freidin, "Avtorizovannyi nabrosok."

4. Mandelstam's references to Blok's conservatism are touched upon in Musatov, *Lirika,* 11–12, who cites the two passages quoted immediately below, as well as Gurvich, "Tip teksta," 36. More broadly speaking, Gurvich's polemical article unfortunately relies on a combination of omissions of the best scholarship and straw-man fallacies in an attempt to discredit *en masse* the entire compelling corpus of semantic readings of Mandelstam.

5. Cf. Ivanov-Razumnik's "Blok i revoliutsiia," *Znamia* (1921), which sets forth the thesis that "Blok is the bearer of the 'great truth' of the revolution" ("Blok v kritike sovremennikov," 809). Mandelstam talks about the "swamp vapors" [bolotnye ispareniia], the "poisonous fog" of Ivanov-Razumnik and others' criticism after Blok's death (II, 270). Cf. also Mandelstam's reference to "idle talk" about the meaning of "The Twelve" (II, 274).

6. See Musatov, *Lirika,* 11, who refers to S. P. Kablukov's diary entry on Mandelstam's "Sobiralis' elliny voinoiu" (The Hellenes gathered for war, 1916). Kablukov noted the poet's "antipathy, mistrust and lack of respect for England, which he considers a haughty, proud, self-assured and, in a bourgeois way, self-satisfied island nation, foreign in spirit and even antagonistic to (continental) Europe" (Mandel'shtam, *PSS,* 545).

7. I have adopted several phrases from Harris and Link's translation in Mandelstam, *Collected Critical Prose,* 177.

8. Mandelstam clearly sympathizes here with Khlebnikov, as is apparent from his poem "No, never was I anyone's contemporary" (Net, nikogda nichei ia ne byl sovremennik, 1924). On Mandelstam's shift to a positive conception of the "contemporary" in the early 1930s, see, for instance, Ronen, *Approach,* 335–36.

9. Brown, trans., *Prose of Mandelstam,* 124, with slight modifications.

10. Regarding Blok's knowledge of antiquity, see Magomedova, *Avtobiograficheskii mif,* 60–83.

11. Cf. Lekmanov on Blok's bilious final essay, "'Without a god, without inspiration' (The Acmeists' Guild" ('Bez bozhestva, bez vdokhnoven'ia' [Tsekh akmeistov]), 1921): "The snickering comparison of Nikolai Gumilev to a foreigner runs like a crimson thread through Blok's article" ("O stat'e 'Bez bozhestva,'" 215). While the article did not appear, as planned, in *Dom iskusstv* 2 (1921), its general thrust was likely known to Mandelstam, and perhaps here Mandelstam repays Blok.

12. See Mikhail Gasparov, *Zapisi i vypiski*, 8.

13. "The poetic fate of Blok was tied in the closest way to Russian poetry's nineteenth century" ("Storm and Stress," II, 341). On Mandelstam's "one-sided" understanding of Blok in this regard, see Gromov, *Blok*, 359.

14. Sloane, *Dynamics*, 328. Note that the passage to which Sloane refers, about "all contemporary Russian poetry" emerging "from the native womb of Symbolism," is connected specifically, by name, with Viacheslav Ivanov (II, 230).

15. Cf. Akhmatova: "Calendar dates have no meaning. Undoubtedly, Symbolism was a phenomenon of the 19th century. Our revolt against Symbolism was entirely natural, since we felt ourselves people of the 20th century and did not wish to remain in the preceding one . . ." (cited in Timenchik, "Zametki ob akmeizme" [1974], 46).

16. Mandel'shtam, *SP*, 526.

17. Struve and Filippov give "measure" and "see" [III, 33]), citing *Molot* (Rostov-na-Donu), 1922, and making no mention of a section on the Imaginists. Russian editions, starting with *Slovo i kul'tura* (1987), reproduce the text cited here, giving the source as *Sovetskii iug* (Rostov-na-Donu), 21 January 1922. There, Mandelstam first published several articles in early 1922.

18. Mandel'shtam, *SP*, 527.

19. "Live yet another quarter century— / It'll all be the same. No escape" [Zhivi eshche khot' chetvert' veka— / Vse budet tak. Iskhoda net] (Blok, III, 42). See Segal, "Fragment," 118; Ronen, *Approach*, 77, 297–98. In addition, *The Noise of Time* as a whole begins with an allusion (or retort) to Blok: "I remember well the lost years [glukhie gody] of Russia— the [18]90s" (II, 45). The reference is to "Those born in the lost years" (Rozhdennye v goda glukhie, 1914): "Those born in the lost years / Do not remember their way" [Rozhdennye v goda glukhie / Puti ne pomniat svoego] (III, 319), and also the introduction to the second chapter of *Retribution*. As early as 1925, D. Sviatopolk-Mirskii noted that Mandelstam's book begins with a "semiquotation" from Blok (cited in Mandel'shtam, *Sochineniia*, II, 384).

20. Mochul'skii, *Blok*, 93.

21. Piast, *Stikhotvoreniia. Vospominaniia*, 260.

22. "Blok v poezii sovremennikov," 585–86.

23. Ibid., 584.

24. As noted in the Introduction, the two shared a common friend, Vladimir Piast. Piast, incidentally, caused a stir with a December 1913 lecture in which he contrasted Blok and Mandelstam, such that "'it was clear that Piast considers Mandelstam a much greater poet [poet gorazado krupneishii] than Blok'" (I. V. Evdokimov, cited in Lekmanov, "Dva poeta," 286). On Blok's anti-Semitism, see Introduction, p. 7 and note 19.

25. Ronen, *Approach*, 308.

26. Blok, *SS8*, III, 296. The editors note that Blok, at the time of the incident, signed an appeal aimed at exposing the fabrication (ibid., 615). On Mandelstam's reaction to the Beilis reference in *Vozmezdie*, see Gershtein, *Memuary*, 27.

27. It is likely that some version of "Shuba" was seen by Shklovsky, who, in his memoirs the following year, seems to answer Mandelstam's vignette quite in the mode of "literary malice": "Mandelstam loved sweets to the point of hysteria. Living in very difficult conditions, without boots, in the cold, he managed to remain spoiled" (*Mandel'shtam i ego vremia*, 109). Shklovsky is also the prototype for the following lines from *The Egyptian Stamp* (1927–28), which continue the exchange: "No one ever particularly spoiled them, but they are dissolute, as if their whole life they received an academic ration with

sardines and chocolate. These are bunglers, who know only chess moves [cf. Shklovsky's *Knight's Move* (Khod konia, 1923), S.G.], but nonetheless clamber into the fray, to see how it will turn out" (II, 13–14). Ronen's recent article "Poedinki" relates a similar "sharp, but well-meaning" exchange between Mandelstam and Shklovsky (220–21). For a radically contrasting, positive reading of the image of Shklovsky in "Fur Coat," see Toddes, "OPOIAZovskaia filosofiia," 81–82.

28. Pushkin, *PSS10*, V, 419.

29. Brown's translation with slight modifications (Mandelstam, *Prose*, 122–23). This passage regarding the biography of a *raznochinets* betrays the direct influence of Vladimir Gippius (subject of the following essay), who wrote his own biography as a series of sonnets chronicling his reading (*Tomlenie dukha*, sonnets LIII–LXX).

30. Mandelstam told Semen Lipkin that *Retribution* did not work because the rhythmic structure is "slavishly borrowed from Pushkin [. . .] Schoolboy iambs [Gimnazicheskii iamb]!" (in contrast to the development of iambic tetrameter in Tiutchev, Nekrasov, and Blok himself, later in the century) (*Mandel'shtam i ego vremia*, 304).

31. For a description of Blok's father, Alexander L'vovich, see Pyman, *Life*, 12.

32. Harris, in Mandelstam, *Collected Critical Prose*, 621n7.

33. Cf., for instance, Ginzburg, "Iz starykh zapisei," in *Mandel'shtam i ego vremia*, 275–76.

34. Pushkin, *PSS10*, III, 208.

35. This association arises from Mandelstam's "Petersburg Strophes": "The eccentric Evgeny—is ashamed of his poverty, / Breathes gas fumes, and curses his fate!" [Chudak Evgenii—bednosti styditsia, / Benzin vdykhaet i sud'bu klianet!].

36. Villon is also "le pauvre Villon" (II, 303)—cf. Dante as "poor soul," and in a late poem, "Brazen schoolboy and pilfering angel" [Naglyi shkol'nik i angel voruiushchii] and "Advocate of carefree dust" [Bezzabotnogo prakha istets] ("So that, friend of wind and raindrops"). Konstantin Batiushkov, despite his "cold hand in a light-colored glove" is, in a highly sympathetic poem, "city-dweller and friend of city-dwellers" [gorozhanin i drug gorozhan] ("Batiushkov," 1932). I thank G. A. Levinton for suggesting Villon and Batiushkov in this regard. On Villon and Mandelstam's *raznochinstvo*, see also Mikhail Gasparov, "Dve gotiki," 29–30.

37. On the lowbrow Chaplin as Mandelstam final double, see Cavanagh, *Modernist Creation*, 286–303.

38. Cf. *Fourth Prose* (Chetvertaia proza, 1930): "My blood, weighed down with the inheritance of sheep herders, patriarchs and kings, rebels against the thievish gypsyism of the writers' brood" (II, 187).

39. Kahn, "Belyi, Dante." Kahn is clearly correct that Mandelstam in the 1930s identified with Bely as *raznochinets*. Less convincing is his assertion that the Dante of the "Conversation" is drawn from the older poet. It should be noted that, while Bely the artist Mandelstam was able to capture in his memorial poems with deft precision (as Kahn illustrates), Bely the person he deeply misread (as demonstrated on the basis of Bely's letters and contemporary memoirs by Lekmanov [*Zhizn'*, 163–65]).

40. Cf. the following phrases from Mandelstam's essay, underscoring Chaadaev's independence and elitism: "private person"; "absolute freedom"; "the structure of chosen minds" [stroi izbrannykh umov]; "'proud' mind"; "sovereign individual" [suverennaia lichnost']; "hieratic pomp" [gieraticheskaia torzhestvennost'] (II, 284–91).

41. *Zapisnye knizhki Akhmatovoi*, 301, cited in Lekmanov, *Kniga ob akmeizme*, 447. Cf. also Taborisskaia, "Peterburg," 516.

42. "[...] 'aristocratic behavior' as a system not only allowed for, but presupposed certain exceptions to the norm [...] The striving of the nobleman to take part in another lifestyle for short periods—the life of the backstage, the [Gypsy] encampment, the folk festival [narodnoe gulian'e]" (Iu. M. Lotman, "Teatr i teatral'nost'," 628). Cf. Masing-Delic on Blok's self-fashioning as a Dmitry Karamazov in "On the Contemporary State of Russian Symbolism" ("Symbolist Crisis," 220). Joseph Brodsky has a fine, sensitive reading of these lines making reference only to the "merchant class" ("'S mirom derzhavnym,'" 12–13).

43. Ronen, *Approach*, 286.

44. Cf. also the "embarrassment, heartbreak and grief" [smushen'(e), nadsad(a) i gor(e)]" Mandelstam reaps from the tender "European" beauties of the Crimea in "I was linked with the world of power" and Blok's habitualized and effective romantic skills: "And, having wrapped an arm round a slender frame, be sly" [I, tonkii stan obniav, luka-vit'] (III, 22); "And there remained [but] a brow shifted with a smile, / A taught mouth and the unfortunate power / To rile up insatiable female blood, / Igniting animal passion . . ." [I ostalos'—ulybkoi svedennaia brov', / Szhatyi rot i pechal'naia vlast' / Buntovat' nenasyt-nuiu zhenskuiu krov', / Zazhigaia zverinuiu strast'] (III, 182). On the "Fourth Estate," see esp. Ronen, *Approach*, 314–18. On Mandelstam's *raznochinstvo*, see also Nadezhda Mandelstam, *Vospominaniia*, 183–84.

CONCLUSION

1. Gershtein, *Memuary*, 27.

2. For examples, see Gershtein, *Memuary*, 30; "Mandel'shtam v pis'makh Rudakova," 126, 77.

3. "The cult of Dantean mysticism spread luxuriously [...] In our Russia the victim of such salacious philistinism on the part of Dante's rapt adepts, who do not read Dante, was none other than Blok: 'The shade of Dante with aquiline profile / Sings to me of the New Life . . .' [Ten' Danta c profilem orlinym / O Novoi Zhizni mne poet . . .]. The internal illumination of Dantean space, derived only from structural elements, interested decidely no one" (II, 378). On Blok in "Conversation about Dante," see Grishunin, who cites the draft version, "A Dantean effigy from the nineteenth century" (Mandel'shtam, *SS*, II, 181; Grishunin, "Blok i Mandel'shtam," 157–58); Pinskii, *Magistral'nyi siuzhet*, 391–96. During his exile in Voronezh, Mandelstam also prepared a radio show about Blok, though we do not know the contents (Mikhailov and Nerler, "Kommentarii," in Mandel'shtam, *Sochineniia*, I, 442).

4. This does not exclude, of course, individual echoes and reactions. For instance, Ronen analyzes Mandelstam's negotiation of the "Russian voice" on the backdrop of Blok's poetry in "Preserve my speech for all time for the aftertaste of misfortune and smoke" (Sokhrani moiu rech' navsegda za privkus neschast'ia i dyma, 1931) (*Poetika*, 51–52); Zholkovskii (following a suggestion by Magomedova) traces the source of the image of "limpid anguish" [iasnaia toska] from "Don't compare: the living is incomparable" (Ne sravnivai: zhivushchii nesravnim, 1937) to a note by Blok regarding Dante ("Klavishnye progulki," 174, 182*n*20).

5. Cf., in this regard, Gromov's spot-on contextualization of Blok's quip, "a premium-grade Rubanovich (by the name of Mandelstam)" (*Blok*, 357–58).

6. A rough draft of "Conversation about Dante" seems to confirm this understanding: "[Dante] is the instrument itself in the metamorphosis of collapsing and unfolding

literary time, which we have ceased to *hear*, but study both here and in the West as a paraphrase of so-called 'cultural formations'" (II, 181).

7. Tynianov's vision regarding the necessity of poetry to continuously transform itself is largely cognate with Mandelstam's: "I speak about that novelty of interaction of all aspects of poetry [stikh, a word with technical/stylistic connotations], which gives birth to new poetic sense [novyi stikhovoi smysl]" ("Promezhutok," in *Arkhaisty i novatory*, 549).

8. Ronen gives a likely source of this image in Gippius's poetry (*Approach*, 293). His characterization of Mandelstam's own practice is somewhat misleading, however: "M. himself has used the three favorite rhymes of Gippius 'vigorously and happily'" (ibid.). "Energichno i schastlivo" implies a lack of reflection or tension in usage and, likely, repetition. Mandelstam indeed uses all three rhymes, but *plot'-Gospod'* only in two early Symbolist poems, while *plamen'-kamen'* appears in one poem, in which the semantics of ardor-inertness his criticism presumably implies are not reproduced, and in another very early unpublished poem. In 1906, Mandelstam rhymed *liubov'-krov'* quite vigorously and happily in the Nadsonian civic style. This rhyme will be repeated only twice more, however, once in an early love poem never published and a second time, retaining its traditional semantics, in a poem that is clearly part of his main corpus—"I just like the others" (1920). Surely, this rare usage should not be compared to the reflexiveness that Mandelstam criticizes.

9. Nadson rhymes *krov'-liubov'* and *zakhlebnetsia v krovi—k bezzavetnoi liubvi* (will choke with blood—to selfless love) in "My friend, my brother, [my] weary, suffering brother" (Drug moi, brat moi, ustalyi, stradaiushchii brat, 1880), a poem of known significance to Mandelstam. "And innocent blood flows— / Believe: a time will come—and Baal will perish, / and love will return to the Earth" [I struitsia nevinnaia krov',— / Ver': nastanet pora—i pogibnet Vaal, / I vernetsia ne zemliu liubov'] (*Polnoe sobranie stikhotvorenii*, 110). Cf. Blok (with a variation on the rhyme scheme): "Spring will pass—above this virgin soil, / Watered with your blood, / Will ripen a new love" [Proidet vesna—nad etoi nov'iu, / Vspoennaia tvoeiu krov'iu, / Sozreet novaia liubov'] (III, 102). In general, Blok is not at all averse to this traditional rhyme. (Cf., among many examples, the finale of "Gem Ring-Suffering" [Persten'-Stradan'e, 1905].)

10. "Stanzas" (Stansy, 1935), emphasis mine. While not contesting—and in fact affirming—the "organicity" of Mandelstam's "worldview" [tselostnost' miroponimaniia], I fail to see any indication that Mandelstam himself saw in this, as Nadezhda Mandelstam indicates, "the measure of the authenticity of the poet." She is, however, unquestionably correct when she connects authenticity with the concepts of *pravota* (rightness) and *priamizna* (straightness, directness). These are precisely the terms Mandelstam himself engages: "Where is the straightness of speech // Tangled like honest zigzags" [Gde priamizna rechei, // Zaputannykh kak chestnye zigzagi] ("10 January 1934" [10 ianvaria 1934]). (Straightness and propulsion—the comparison as it develops is to a speed skater—here emerge in a synthesis of seemingly antagonistic vectors.) The poet's widow is likewise on the mark when she further connects the poet's authenticity to his or her role as "unsettler of sense" [kolebatel' smysla] ("Conversation about Dante") and rejection of pre-existing "proposition-formulas" [suzhdeniia-formuly] ("Chitatel' odnoi knigi," in *Vospominaniia*).

11. Blok's maturation, however, is implicitly cast by Mandelstam as an *outgrowing of Romanticism* after Pushkin's model (*SP,* 526).

12. This discomfort is conveyed quited powerfully, for instance, in Khodasevich, *Nekropol'*, 91-92. One must wonder how well Blok must have liked Mandelstam's brilliant

impromptu of 1911: "Блок / Король / И маг порока. // Рок / И боль / Венчают Блока" [Blok / Is king / And magus of vice. // Fate / And pain / Crown Blok] (*PSS*, 367).

13. Mandelstam too, of course, reacts to a—rapidly and radically—changing world. Again, the difference is of emphasis, the "specific gravity" so to speak within their respective poetics of these types of change. Cf. Blok: "I find it painful [. . .] when [Ivanov] crows about κάθαρσις with the same tone in 1912 as [he did] in 1905" (*SS8*, VIII, 386); Mandelstam: "[Pushkin], the author of *Boris Godunov*, even if he wanted to could not repeat the lyceum verse, just like nowadays no one will write a Derzhavin ode. Who likes what better is another thing" (II, 244).

14. See Mikhail Gasparov, *Zapisi i vypiski*, 245.

15. "Doomed" (Obrechennyi, 1907).

16. Building upon the observations of Zhitenev ("'Oskorblennyi i oskorbitel'"), we can say that, through the communicative strategies of "scandal" in "Fourth Prose," Mandelstam achieves in deed the exit beyond the bounds of "civilized" literature that Blok espouses in his essays, and, with it, an authenticity in the mode of Trilling (*Sincerity and Authenticity*, 11) and Blok himself.

17. Blok, *Stikhotvoreniia*, I, 343. This evidence is an important corollary to Blok's more Romantic statements: "In light of such a consciousness, artists' works themselves become secondary, since to present they are all imperfect creations, fragments of concepts far grander" (Blok, *SS8*, VI, 109). At the same time, when Blok asks, "why are we moved by Andreev's *Life of Man*, which is distant from art [. . .]?" (*SS8*, V, 278), he both demonstrates that he recognizes artistry and its absence and makes a compromise unimaginable for Mandelstam.

18. Ivanov, *PZ*, 250.

19. On receptivity in Ivanov's aesthetics, see Wachtel, *Russian Symbolism*, 64–65.

20. This shift has significant consequences. If sincerity is located in the poet (or if the anointedness of the poet is assumed), then the ethics of the work are not essential to its validity (as opposed to the precision with which it conveys the poet's privileged vision). For Blok, individual poems patently "erroneous" in their outlook retain their validity as genuine stages of his poetic path. Their truth is specific to the poet. In contrast, if the authenticity of the poem is external to the poet and the mark of sincerity is the "audible" veracity of the artwork itself, then ethics—conscience, as an active and searching faculty—arises as a key element within the individual poem.

SELECTED BIBLIOGRAPHY

Abrams, M. H. *Natural Supernaturalism: Tradition and Revolution in Romantic Literature.* New York: W. W. Norton & Co., 1971.
Aeschylus. *Seven Against Thebes.* Trans. David Grene. In *The Complete Greek Tragedies.* Vol. 1. *Aeschylus.* Chicago: U of Chicago P, 1959. 259–302.
Akhmatova, Anna. *Sochineniia v dvukh tomakh.* M.: Khud. Lit., 1986.
———. *Sochineniia v dvukh tomakh.* M.: Pravda, 1990.
———. *Zapisnye knizhki Anny Akhmatovoi: 1958–1966.* M.: Rossiiskii gos. arkhiv litry i iskusstva, 1996.
Amelin, G. G. and V. Ia. Morderer. *Miry i stolknoveniia Osipa Mandel'shtama.* M.: Iazyki russkoi kul'tury, 2000.
Andreev, Leonid. *Sobranie sochinenii v shesti tomakh.* M.: Khud. Lit., 1990.
Annenskii, Innokentii. "O sovremennom lirizme. 2. 'Oni.'" *Apollon* 2 (1909): 3–29.
———. *Stikhotvoreniia i tragedii.* L.: Sovetskii pisatel', 1990.
Averintsev, Sergei. "Iuda Iskariot." In E. M. Meletinskii, ed. *Mifologicheskii slovar'.* M.: Sov. entsiklopediia, 1990. 257–58.
———. "Sud'ba i vest' Osipa Mandel'shtama." In O. Mandel'shtam. *Sochineniia v dvukh tomakh.* 5–64.
———. "Konfessional'nye tipy khristianstva u rannego Mandel'shtama." In *Slovo i sud'ba. Osip Mandel'shtam. Materialy i issledovaniia.* M.: Nauka, 1991. 287–98.
———. "'Chut' mertsaet prizrachnaia stsena . . .': Podstupy k smyslu." In *Otdai menia Voronezh . . .": tret'i mezhdunarodnye mandel'shtamovskie chteniia.* Voronezh: Izd-vo Voronezhskogo univ., 1995. 116–22.
———. "Khorei u Mandel'shtama." *Sokhrani moiu rech'* 3/1 (2000): 42–54.
———. "Strakh, kak initsiatsiia: odna tematicheskaia konstanta poezii Mandel'shtama." *Smert' i bessmertie poeta. Materialy mezhdunarodnoi nauchnoi konferentsii,*

posviashchennoi 60-letiiu so dnia gibeli O. E. Mandel'shtama (*Moskva, 28–29 dekabria 1998 g.*). M.: RGGU, 2001. 17–23.

Babayan, Kathryn. *Mystics, Monarchs & Messiahs: Cultural Landscapes of Early Modern Iran.* Cambridge, MA: Harvard UP, 2002.

Baltrushaitis, Iurgis. *Derevo v ogne.* Vilnius: VAGA, 1983.

Baevskii, V. S. "Ne luna, a tsiferblat (Iz nabliudenii nad poetikoi O. Mandel'shtama)." In *Zhizn' i tvorchestvo O. E. Mandel'shtama.* Voronezh: Izd. Voronezhskogo univ., 1990. 314–22.

Bakhtin, Mikhail. *Rabelais and His World.* Trans. Helene Iswolsky. Bloomington: Indiana UP, 1984.

Basker, Michael. "Gumilyov's 'Akteon': A Forgotten Manifesto of Acmeism." *Slavonic and East European Review* 63.4 (1985): 498–517.

Batiushkov, K. N. *Opyty v stikhakh i proze.* M.: Nauka, 1978.

Beletskii, Platon. *Georgii Ivanovich Narbut.* L.: Iskusstvo, 1985.

Bel'skaia, L. L. "Tsitata ili 'tsikada'?" *Russkaia rech'* 1 (1991): 10–15.

Belyi, Andrei. *Arabeski. Kniga statei.* M.: Musaget, 1911.

———. *Sochineniia v dvukh tomakh.* M.: Khud. lit., 1990.

———. *O Bloke. Vospominaniia. Stat'i. Dnevniki. Rechi.* M.: Avtograf, 1997.

———. *Stikhotvoreniia i poemy.* 2 vols. SPb.: Akademicheskii proekt, 2006.

Benois, Alexandre [Aleksandr Benua]. "Khudozhestvennye eresi." *Zolotoe Runo* 2 (1906): 80–88.

Bernshtein, S. I. "Golos Bloka." 1921–25. Publ. A. Ivich and G. Superfin. *Blokovskii sbornik II. Trudy Vtoroi nauchnoi konferentsii, posviashchennoi izucheniiu zhizni i tvorchestva A. A. Bloka.* Tartu: Tartuskii GU, 1972. 454–525.

Bethea, David M. *Realizing Metaphors: Alexander Pushkin and the Life of the Poet.* Madison: U of Wisconsin P, 1998.

———. "Brodsky and Pushkin Revisited: The Dangers of the Sculpted Life." In *The Real Life of Pierre Delaland: Studies in Russian and Comparative Literature to Honor Alexander Dolinin.* Stanford Slavic Studies, v. 33. Oakland: Berkeley Slavic Specialties, 2007. I, 100–119.

Bezrodnyi, Mikhail. "O 'Iudoboiazni' Andreia Belogo." *Novoe literaturnoe obozrenie* 28 (1997): 100–125.

Bird, Robert. *The Russian Prospero: The Creative Universe of Viacheslav Ivanov.* Madison: U of Wisconsin P, 2006.

———. "Viach. Ivanov i massovye prazdnestva rannei sovetskoi epokhi." *Russkaia literatura* 2 (2006): 174–97.

Blinov, Valerii. "Viacheslav Ivanov i vozniknovenie akmeizma." In *Cultura e memoria: atti del terzo simposio internazionale dedicato a Vjaceslav Ivanov.* Florence: La Nuova Italia, 1988. 13–25.

Blok, Aleksandr. *Rossiia i intelligentsia (1907–1918).* M.: Revoliutsionnyi sotsializm, 1918.

———. *Sedoe utro.* Pb.: Alkonost, 1920.

———. *Sobranie sochinenii v vos'mi tomakh.* M.: Gos. izd-vo khudozh. lit-ry, 1960–63.

———. *Zapisnye knizhki.* M.: Khud. lit., 1965.

———. "Perepiska Bloka s S. M. Solov'evym (1896–1915)." Ed., intro. and comm. N. V. Kotrelev and A. V. Lavrov. *Literaturnoe nasledstvo* 92/1. M.: Nauka, 1980. 308–413.

———. "Perepiska s A. A. i S. M. Gorodetskimi." Ed. and intro. V. P. Enisherlov, comm. V. P. Enisherlov and R. D. Timenchik. *Literaturnoe nasledstvo* 92/2. M.: Nauka, 1981. 5–62.

———. "Perepiska s Vl. Piastom." Ed., intro. and comm. Z. G. Mints. *Literaturnoe nasledstvo* 92/2. M.: Nauka, 1981. 175–228.

———. *Sobranie sochinenii v shesti tomakh.* M.: Khud. lit., 1982.

———. *Stikhotvoreniia.* 3 vols. SPb.: Severo-zapad, 1994.

———. *Sobranie sochinenii v dvenadtsati tomakh.* M.: Litera, 1995–.

"Blok v kritike sovremennikov (Annotirovannaia bibliograficheskaia khronika. 1902–1921)." Comp. V. I. Iakubovich. *Literaturnoe nasledstvo* 92/5 (1993): 633–826.

"Blok v poezii ego sovremennikov." Intro. and comp. Iu. M. Gel'perin. *Literaturnoe nasledstvo* 92/3 (1982): 540-97.
Bloom, Harold. *The Anxiety of Influence: A Theory of Poetry*. 1973. New York: Oxford UP, 1997.
Bobrov, Sergei. "Osip Mandel'shtam. Tristia." *Pechat' i revoliutsiia* 4 (1923): 259-62.
Bogomolov, N. A. *Russkaia literatura xx veka i okkul'tizm. Issledovaniia i materialy*. M.: NLO, 1999.
Borisova, L. M. *Na izlomakh traditsii. Dramaturgiia russkogo simvolizma i simvolistskaia teoriia zhiznetvorchestva*. Simferopol': Tavricheskii natsional'nyi universitet, 2000.
Bowlt, John. "Here and There: The Question of Space in Blok's Poetry." In *Aleksandr Blok Centennial Conference*. Columbus, OH: Slavica, 1984. 61-71.
Briusov, V. Ia. *Sobranie sochinenii v semi tomakh*. M.: Khud. lit., 1973.
———. "Retsenziia na rukopis' B. V. Tomashevskogo 'Pushkin i frantsuzskie poety.'" *Literaturnoe nasledstvo* 85 (1976): 243-44.
Brodskii, Iosif. "'S mirom derzhavnym ia byl lish' rebiacheskii sviazan . . .'" In *Stoletie Mandel'shtama. Materialy Simpoziuma*. Tenafly, NJ: Hermitage, 1994. 9-17.
Broitman, S. N. "Venitseiskie strofy Mandel'shtama, Bloka i Pushkina (k voprosu o klassicheskom i neklassicheskom tipe khudozhestvennoi tselostnosti v poezii)." In *Tvorchestvo Mandel'shtama i voprosy istoricheskoi poetiki. Mezhvuzovskii sbornik nauchnykh trudov*. Kemerovo: Kemerovskii GU, 1990. 81-96.
———. "Simvolizm i postsimvolizm (k probleme vnutrennei mery russkoi neklassicheskoi poezii)." In *Postsimvolizm kak iavlenie kul'tury*. M.: RGGU, 1995.
———. "Rannii O. Mandel'shtam i F. Sologub." *Izvestiia akademii nauk. Seriia literatury i iazyka* 55/2 (1996): 27-35.
———. "Rannii O. Mandel'shtam i Blok." In his *Poetika russkoi klassicheskoi i neklassicheskoi liriki*. 281-98.
———. *Poetika russkoi klassicheskoi i neklassicheskoi liriki*. M.: RGGU, 2008.
Brown, Clarence. *Mandelstam*. Cambridge, Cambridge UP, 1973.
Brown, Andrew. *A New Companion to Greek Tragedy*. London: Croom Helm, 1983.
Broyde, Steven. *Osip Mandel'štam and His Age: A Commentary on the Themes of War and Revolution in the Poetry, 1913-1923*. Cambridge, MA: Harvard UP, 1975.
Bukhshtab, Boris. "Poeziia Mandel'shtama." *Voprosy literatury* 1 (1989): 123-48.
Cavanagh, Clare. "Mandelstam, Nietzsche, and the conscious creation of history." In *Nietzsche and Soviet Culture: Ally and Adversary*. Cambridge: Cambridge UP, 1994. 338-66.
———. *Osip Mandelstam and the Modernist Creation of Tradition*. Princeton: Princeton UP, 1995.
Clark, Katerina. *Petersburg, Crucible of Cultural Revolution*. Cambridge, MA: Harvard UP, 1995.
Cooke, Olga Muller. "'Abundant Is My Sorrow': Osip Mandel'stam's Requiem to Andrei Belyi and Himself." In *Symbolism and After: Essays on Russian Poetry in Honour of Georgette Donchin*. London: Bristol Classical, 1992. 70-84.
Crone, Anna Lisa. "Blok's 'Venecija' and *Molnii iskusstva* as Inspiration to Mandel'štam: Parallels in the Italian Materials." In *Aleksandr Blok Centennial Conference*. Columbus, OH: Slavica, 1984. 74-88.
———. "Petersburg and the Plight of Russian Beauty: The Case of Mandel'štam's *Tristia*." In *New Studies in Russian Language and Literature*. Columbus: Slavica, 1986. 73-95.
———. "Fraternity or Parricide? The Uses and Abuses of Harold Bloom in the Study of Russian Poetry" (unpublished keynote address). Slavic Forum, April 17-18, 1998, University of Chicago.
Dal', V. I. *Tolkovyi slovar' zhivogo velikorusskogo iazyka*. 2nd ed. 1880. M.: Rus. iaz., 1989.
Dmitrienko, S. F. "O problematike stikhotvoreniia A. A. Bloka 'Shagi Komandora.'" In Musatov and Igosheva, eds. *Aleksandr Blok i mirovaia kul'tura*. 48-62.

Dobrytsyn, A. A. "Slovo-logos v poezii Mandel'shtama ('beloe plamia' i 'sukhaia krov')." In *Quinquagenario Alexandri Il'ušini: oblata*. M.: MGU Fil. fak., 1990. 39–44.

Doherty, Justin. *The Acmeist Movement in Russian Poetry: Culture and the Word*. Oxford: Clarendon Press, 1995.

Drakon. Al'manakh stikhov. Pb.: 15-ia Gosud. tipografiia, 1921.

Edmond, Jacob B. P. "From Pathos to Parody: Ambivalent Antithesis and Echoes of 'Vykhožu odin ja na dorogu' in 'Obraz tvoj mučitel'nyj i zybkij' and 'Zolotoj' from Osip Mandel'štam's *Kamen*'." *Russian Literature* 58 (2005): 357–73.

Eikhenbaum, Boris. "Sud'ba Bloka." In *Ob Aleksandre Bloke*. 39–63.

Eng-Liedmeier, Jeanne van der. "Mandel'štam's Poem 'V Peterburge my sojdemsia snova.'" *Russian Literature* 7/8 (1974): 182–201.

Epshtein, Mikhail. "Khasid i talmudist: Sravnitel'nyi opyt o Pasternake i Mandel'shtame." *Zvezda* 4 (2000): 82–96.

Eroshkina, E. V. and V. E. Khalizev. "Spektakl' i p'esa (Drama G. Ibsena 'Brand' na stsene Khudozhestvennogo teatra)." *Izvestiia RAN. Seriia literatury i iazyka* 66/4 (2007): 54–58.

Etkind, Efim. "'Rassudochnaia propast'": O mandel'shtamovskoi 'Fedre.'" In his *Tam, vnutri*. 197–212.

———. "'Karmen'. Liricheskaia poema kak antiroman." In his *Tam, vnutri*. 60–81.

———. *Tam, vnutri. O russkoi poezii xx veka*. Ocherki. SPb.: Maksima, 1997.

Faryno, Erzhi [Jerzy]. "Arkheopoetika Mandel'shtama (Na primere 'Kontserta na vokzale')." In *Stoletie Mandel'shtama. Materialy simpoziuma*. Tenafly, NJ: Ermitazh, 1994. 183–204.

Fedorov, A. V. *Teatr A. Bloka i dramaturgiia ego vremeni*. L.: Izdatel'stvo Leningradskogo univ., 1972.

Fedosiuk, Iu. A. *Chto neponiatno u klassikov, ili Entsiklopediia russkogo byta XIX veka*. M.: Flinta, 1998.

Fet, A. A. *Polnoe sobranie stikhotvorenii*. L.: Sovetskii pisatel', 1959.

———. *Vechernie ogni*. M.: Nauka, 1971.

Florenskii, Pavel. *Stolp i utverzhdenie istiny*. 1914. M.: Pravda, 1990.

Freidin, Gregory. "Osip Mandelstam: The Poetry of Time (1908–1916)." *California Slavic Studies* 11. Berkeley: U of California P, 1980. 141–86.

———. *A Coat of Many Colors: Osip Mandelstam and His Mythologies of Self-Presentation*. Berkeley: U of California P, 1987.

Freidin, Grigorii. "Sidia na saniakh: Osip Mandel'shtam i kharizmaticheskaia traditsiia russkogo modernizma." *Voprosy literatury* (Jan. 1991): 9–31.

Freidin, Iu. L. "Avtorizovannyi nabrosok plana i kompozitsii knigi statei Mandel'shtama *O poezii*." *Russian Literature* 42.2 (1997): 153–70.

Fridlender, G. M. "'Trilogiia vochelovecheniia' (A. Blok i sovremennye spory o nem)." *Russkaia literatura* 4 (1995): 94–116.

Frolov, Dmitrii. "Stikhi 1908 g. v 'Kamne' (1916)." *Sokhrani moiu rech'* 4/2 (2008): 463–86.

———. *O rannikh stikhakh Osipa Mandel'shtama*. M.: Iazyki slavianskikh kul'tur, 2009.

Gaevskii, V. "Pushkin i Krivtsov. Po neizdannym materialam." *Vestnik Evropy* 6 (December, 1887): 453–63.

Gaidenko, P. "Soblazn 'sviatoi ploti' (Sergei Solov'ev i russkii serebrianyi vek)." *Voprosy literatury* (July–Aug. 2006): 72–127.

Gasparov, Boris. "Tridtsatye gody—zheleznyi vek (k analizu motivov stoletnego vozvrashcheniia Mandel'shtama." In Boris Gasparov, Hughes, and Paperno, eds. *Cultural Mythologies of Russian Modernism*. 150–79.

———. "Eshche raz o funktsii podteksta v poeticheskom tekste ('Kontsert na vokzale')." In his *Literaturnye leitmotivy. Ocherki po russkoi literature XX veka*. M.: Nauka, 1993. 162–86.

Gasparov, Boris, Robert P. Hughes, and Irina Paperno, eds. *Cultural Mythologies of Russian Modernism: From the Golden Age to the Silver Age*. Berkeley: U of California P, 1992.

Gasparov, Mikhail. "Antinomichnost' poetiki russkogo modernizma." In *Sviaz' vremen. Problemy preemstvennosti v russkoi literature kontsa XIX-nachala XX v.* M.: Nasledie, 1992. 244–64.
———. "Lektsii Viach. Ivanova o stikhe v poeticheskoi akademii 1909 g." *Novoe literaturnoe obozrenie* 10 (1994): 89–105.
———. "Poet i kul'tura: Tri poetiki Osipa Mandel'shtama." In Mandel'shtam. *Polnoe sobranie stikhotvorenii*. 5–64.
———. "Otzyv ofitsial'nogo opponenta o doktorskoi dissertatsii I. S. Prikhod'ko 'Mifopoetika Aleksandra Bloka' (VGU, 1996)." *Filologicheskie zapiski. Vestnik literaturovedeniia i iazykoznaniia* 8 (1997): 6–12.
———. "Sonety Mandel'shtama 1912 g.: ot simvolizma k akmeizmu." *Europa Orientalis* 1 (1999): 147–58.
———. "Poet i obshchestvo: Dve gotiki i dva Egipta v poezii O. Mandel'shtama." In *Sokhrani moiu rech'* 3/1 (2000): 25–41.
———. *Zapisi i vypiski*. M.: NLO, 2001.
———. "Literaturnyi intertekst i iazykovoi intertekst." *Izvestiia Akademii Nauk. Seriia literatury i iazyka* 61.4 (2002): 3–9.
Gasparov, Mikhail and Omri Ronen. "O 'Venitseiskoi zhizni . . .' O. Mandel'shtama. Opyt kommentariia." *Zvezda* 2 (2002): 193–202.
———. "Pokhorony solntsa v Peterburge: O dvukh teatral'nykh stikhotvoreniiakh Mandel'shtama." *Zvezda* 5 (2003): 207–19.
Geertz, Clifford. "Deep Play: Notes on the Balinese Cockfight." *Daedalus* 101 (Winter, 1972): 1–38.
Gershenzon, M. *Dekabrist Krivtsov i ego brat'ia*. M.: M. and S. Sabashnikov, 1914.
Gershtein, Emma. *Memuary*. SPb.: Inapress, 1998.
Gillespie, Alyssa Dinega. "Between Myth and History: An Interpretation of Osip Mandel'štam's Poem 'V Peterburge my sojdemsja snova.'" *Russian Literature* 56 (2004): 363–95.
Ginzburg, Lidiia. *O lirike*. L.: Sovetskii pisatel', 1974.
———. "Kamen'." In *Osip Mandel'shtam. Kamen'*. 1990. 261–76.
Gippius, Vladimir [Vl. Bestuzhev, pseud.]. *Vozvrashchenie. Stikhotvoreniia Vl. Bestuzheva*. SPb.: Tsekh poetov, 1912.
———. *Noch' v zvezdakh. Stikhotvoreniia Vl. Bestuzheva*. Petrograd: R. Golike i A. Vil'borg, 1915.
———. [Vl. Neledinskii, pseud.]. *Tomlenie dukha. Vol'nye sonety*. Petrograd: Sirius, 1916.
Glazov-Corrigan, Elena. *Mandelstam's Poetics: A Challenge to Postmodernism*. Toronto: Toronto UP, 2000.
Goodman-Soellner, Elise. "Poetic Interpretations of the 'Lady at Her Toilette' Theme in Sixteenth-Century Painting." *The Sixteenth Century Journal* 14.4 (1983): 426–42.
Gofman, Modest. *Poety simvolizma (Kniga o russkikh poetakh poslednego desiatiletiia)*. 1908. Munich: Wilhelm Fink, 1970.
Gogol', N. V. *Polnoe sobranie sochinenii*. M.: Izd-vo Akademii Nauk SSSR, 1937–52.
Goldberg, Stuart. "The Poetics of Return in Osip Mandel'štam's 'Solominka.'" *Russian Literature* XLV-II (1999): 131–47.
———. "Bedside with the Symbolist Hero: Blok in Mandel'shtam's 'Pust' v dushnoi komnate.'" *Slavic Review* 63.1 (Spring 2004): 26–42.
———. "The Shade of Gumilev in Mandelstam's *Kamen'* (*Stikhotvoreniia* [1928])." *Slavonic and East European Review* 87.1 (2009): 39–52.
———. "Sootnoshenie iskrennosti-podlinnosti (authenticity) v poetike Mandel'shtama i Bloka." *Miry Osipa Mandel'shtama. IV Mandel'shtamovskie chteniia: materialy mezhdunarodnogo nauchnogo seminara*. Perm: PGPU, 2009. 271–85.
Gorodetskii, Sergei. "Idolotvorchestvo." *Zolotoe runo* 1 (1909): 93–101.
Gorelik, L. L. "'Tainstvennoe stikhotvorenie "Telefon"' O. Mandel'shtama." *Izvestiia RAN. Seriia literatury i iazyka* 65.2 (2006): 49–54.

Gracheva, A. M. "Istoriia tvorcheskoi polemiki A. Bloka i Vl. Gippiusa." In Musatov and Igosheva, eds. *Aleksandr Blok i mirovaia kul'tura.* 242–50.

Grishunin, A. L. "Blok i Mandel'shtam." In *Slovo i sud'ba. Osip Mandel'shtam. Materialy i issledovaniia.* M.: Nauka, 1991. 152–60.

Gromov, Pavel. *A. Blok, ego predshestvenniki i sovremenniki: Monografiia.* 2nd ed. L.: Sovetskii pisatel', 1986.

Gumilev, Nikolai. *Sobranie sochinenii v chetyrekh tomakh.* 1962–68. M.: Terra, 1991.

———. *Sobranie sochinenii v trekh tomakh.* M.: Khud. lit., 1991.

Gurvich, I. "Mandel'shtam: Tip teksta i tip prochteniia." *Izvestiia RAN. Seriia literatury i iazyka* 60.5 (2001): 34–41.

Hadeln, Detlev Baron von. "Veronese's Venus at Her Toilet." *The Burlington Magazine for Connoisseurs* 54/312 (1929): 115–17.

Hansen-Löve, Aage A. "Mandel'shtam's Thanatopoetics." In *Readings in Russian Modernism.* M.: Nauka, 1993. 121–57.

Khanzen-Lëve [Hansen-Löve], A. *Russkii simvolizm. Sistema poeticheskikh motivov. Rannii simvolizm.* 1989. SPb.: Akademicheskii proekt, 1999.

———. "Tekst-Tekstura-Arabeski. Razvertyvanie metafory tkani v poetike O. Mandel'shtama." *Tynianovskii sbornik. Vyp. 10. Shestye-sed'mye-vos'mye Tynianovskie chteniia.* M.: n.p., 1998. 241–69.

———. *Russkii simvolizm. Sistema poeticheskikh motivov. Mifopoeticheskii simvolizm nachala veka. Kosmicheskaia simvolika.* 1998. SPb.: Akademicheskii proekt, 2003.

Harris, Jane Gary. "Mandelstamian *Zlost'*, Bergson, and a New Acmeist Esthetic?" *Ulbandus Review* 2 (1982): 112–30.

———. *Osip Mandelstam.* Boston: Twayne Publishers, 1988.

Hesiod, The Homeric Hymns, and Homerica. Trans. Hugh G. Evelyn-White. Stilwell, KS: Digireads.com, 2008.

Hoover, Marjorie L. *Meyerhold and His Set Designers.* New York: Peter Lang, 1988.

Hughes, Robert P. "Pushkin in Petrograd, Februrary 1921." In Boris Gasparov, Hughes, and Paperno, eds. *Cultural Mythologies of Russian Modernism.* 204–13.

Pak, Sun Iun. "Problema bytiia—nebytiia v rannem tvorchestve O. Mandel'shtama." *Russkaia literatura* 3 (2007): 181–86.

Ibsen, Genrik [Henrik]. *Brand. Polnoe sobranie sochinenii Genrika Ibsena.* Vol. 1. SPb.: A. F. Marks, 1909. 93–245.

Ivanov, Georgii. "O novykh stikhakh." *Dom iskusstv* 2 (1921): 96–99.

Ivanov, Viacheslav. "Ellinskaia religiia stradaiushchego boga." *Novyi put'* 1–3, 5, 8–9 (1904).

———. "Religiia Dionisa." *Voprosy zhizni* 6–7 (1905).

———. *Po zvezdam.* SPb.: Ory, 1909.

———. "O Dionise orficheskom." *Russkaia mysl'* 11 (1913): 2nd pagination, 70–98.

———. *Sobranie sochinenii.* 4 vols. Brussels: Foyer Oriental Chrétien, 1971–86.

———. *Stikhotvoreniia. Poemy. Tragedii.* SPb.: Akademicheskii proekt, 1995.

Ivanov, Viacheslav, trans. *Alkei i Safo. Sobranie pesen i liricheskikh otryvkov v perevode razmerami podlinnikov Viacheslava Ivanova so vstupitel'nym ocherkom ego-zhe.* M.: M. and S. Sabashnikov, 1914.

Ivanov, Viach. Vs. "K issledovaniiu poetiki Bloka ('Shagi komandora')." In *Russian Poetics. Proceedings of the International Colloquium at UCLA, September 22–26, 1975.* Columbus, OH: Slavica, 1983. 169–94.

Ivask, George. "Osip Mandel'štam's 'We Shall Gather Again in Petersburg,'" *Slavic and East European Journal* 20.3 (1976): 253–60.

Ivask, Iurii. "Venetsiia Mandel'shtama i Bloka." *Novyi zhurnal* 122 (1976): 113–26.

Jakobson, Roman. "The Statue in Puškin's Poetic Mythology." In his *Language in Literature.* Cambridge, MA: Belknap Press, 1987. 318–67.

Kahn, Andrew. "Andrei Belyi, Dante and 'Golubye glaza i goriashchaia lobnaia kost'": Mandel'shtam's Later Poetics and the Image of the *Raznochinets*." *Russian Review* 53 (January 1994): 22-35.
Karabchievskii, Iu. A. *Voskresenie Maiakovskogo*. M.: Russkie slovari, 2000.
Karpovich, M. "Moe znakomstvo s Mandel'shtamom." *Novyi Zhurnal* 49 (1957): 258-61.
Kikhnei, L. G. "'Gieraticheskoe slovo' v akmeisticheskoi traditsii (Mandel'shtam—Gumilev—Tarkovskii)." In *Pamiati professora V. P. Skobeleva: Problemy poetiki i istorii russkoi literatury xix-xx vekov*. Samara: Samarskii univ., 2005. 187-91.
Khodasevich, Vladislav. *Nekropol': Vospominaniia. Literatura i vlast'. Pis'ma B. A. Sadovskomu*. M.: CC, 1996.
Kling, O. A. "Latentnyi simvolizm v 'Kamne' (I) (1913 g.) O. Mandel'shtama." *Filologicheskie nauki* 2 (1998): 24-32.
Kornblatt, Judith Deutsch. "Vladimir Solov'ev on Spiritual Nationhood, Russia and the Jews." *Russian Review* 56.2 (1997): 157-77.
Kovaleva, Irina. "Psikheia u Persefony: Ob istokakh odnogo anitichnogo motiva u Mandel'shtama." *Novoe literaturnoe obozrenie* 73 (2005): 203-11.
Kupchenko, V. "Osip Mandel'shtam v Kimmerii (Materialy k tvorcheskoi biografii)." *Voprosy literatury* 7 (1987): 186-203.
Lachmann, R. "Cultural Memory and the Role of Literature." In *Kontrapunkt. Kniga statei pamiati Galiny Andreevny Beloi*. M.: RGGU, 2005.
Laferrière, Daniel. "Mandel'shtam's 'Tristia': A Study of the Purpose of Subtexts." In his *Five Russian Poems: Exercises in a Theory of Poetry*. Englewood, NJ: Transworld, 1977. 117-32.
Lavrov, A. V. *Andrei Belyi v 1900-e gody: zhizn' i literaturnaia deiatel'nost'*. M.: NLO, 1995.
———. "Ritm i smysl: Zametki o poeticheskom tvorchestve Andreia Belogo." In Belyi. *Stikhotvoreniia i poemy*. Vol. 1. 5-40.
———. *Russkie simvolisty: Etiudy i razyskaniia*. M.: Progress-Pleiada, 2007.
Lattimore, Richmond. "Introduction to the Oresteia." In *The Complete Greek Tragedies*. Vol. 1. Aeschylus. Chicago: U of Chicago P, 1959. 1-31.
Lekmanov, Oleg. *O pervom "Kamne" Mandel'shtama*. M.: Moskovskii kul'turologicheskii litsei no. 1310, 1994.
———. "Dva poeta (iz nabroskov k biografii Mandelshtama)." *Tynianovskii sbornik. Vyp. 10. Shestye-sed'mye-vos'mye Tynianovskie chteniia*. M.: n.p., 1998. 284-91.
———. *Kniga ob akmeizme i drugie raboty*. Tomsk: Vodolei, 2000.
———. "Mandel'shtam i Maiakovskii: Vzaimnye otsenki, pereklichki, epokha." *Sokhrani moiu rech'* 3/1 (2000): 215-28.
———. "Kontseptsiia 'Serebrianogo veka' i akmeizma v zapisnykh knizhkakh A. Akhmatovoi." *Novoe literaturnoe obozrenie* 46 (2000): 216-30.
———. *Zhizn' Osipa Mandel'shtama. Dokumental'noe povestvovanie*. SPb.: Zvezda, 2003. Expanded and revised edition: *Osip Mandel'shtam: Zhizn' poeta*. M.: Molodaia gvardiia, 2009.
———. "'Legkost' neobyknovennaia v mysliakh': Andrei Belyi i O. Mandel'shtam." *Voprosy literatury* 6 (2004): 262-67.
———. *O trekh akmeisticheskikh knigakh: M. Zenkevich, V. Narbut, O. Mandel'shtam*. M.: Intrada, 2006.
———. "'Pust' oni teper' slushaiut . . .': O stat'e Al. Bloka 'Bez bozhestva, bez vdokhnoven'ia' (Tsekh akmeistov)." *NLO* 87 (2007): 214-27.
Lekmanov, Oleg, ed. *Kritika russkogo postsimvolizma*. M.: AST, 2002.
Lermontov, M. Iu. *Sobranie sochinenii v 4-kh tomakh*. L.: Nauka, 1979-80.
Lerner, N. "Smert' i pokhorony Pushkina." *Niva* 7 (1912): 133-34.
Levin, Iu. I. "Zametki o krymsko-ellinskikh stikhakh O. Mandel'shtama." *Russian Literature* 10/11 (1975): 5-31.
Levin, Iu. I., D. M. Segal, R. D. Timenchik, V. N. Toporov, and T. V. Tsiv'ian. "Russkaia seman-

ticheskaia poetika kak potentsial'naia kul'turnaia paradigma." *Russian Literature* 7/8 (1974): 46-82.

Levinton, G. A. "'Na kamennykh otrogakh Pierii' Mandel'shtama. Materialy k analizu." *Russian Literature* 5/2 (April 1977): 123-70 and 5/3 (July 1977): 201-37.

———. "K voprosu o statuse 'literaturnoi shutki' u Akhmatovoi i Mandel'shtama" and "Akhmatovoi ukoly." In *Anna Akhmatova i russkaia kul'tura nachala xx veka. Tezisy konferentsii.* M.: Sovet po istorii mirovoi kul'tury AN SSSR, 1989. 40-47.

———. "Germes, Terpandr i Alesha Popovich (Epizod iz otnoshenii Gumileva i Mandel'shtama?)." In *Nikolai Gumilev. Issledovaniia i materialy. Bibliografiia.* SPb.: Nauka, 1994. 563-70.

———. "Eshche raz o literaturnoi shutke (sobranie epigrafov)." In *Shipovnik. Istoriko-filologicheskii sbornik k 60-letiiu R. D. Timenchika.* M.: Vodolei, 2005. 229-39.

Lindeberg, O. A. "Vospominaniia Vl. Gippiusa ob A. Bloke (po arkhivnym materialam)." In Musatov and Igosheva, eds. *Aleksandr Blok i mirovaia kul'tura.* 250-58.

Literaturnye manifesty ot simvolizma do nashikh dnei. M.: XXI vek—soglasie, 2000.

Liubimova, O. E. "Blok i sektantstvo: 'Pesnia sud'by', 'Roza i krest.'" In *Aleksandr Blok. Issledovaniia i materialy.* SPb.: Institut russkoi literatury (Pushkinskii Dom) RAN, 1998. 69-89.

Livshits, Benedikt. *Polutoraglazyi strelets.* L.: Sovetskii pisatel', 1989.

Losev, A. F. "Imiaslavie." In *Imia. Izbrannye raboty, perevody, besedy, issledovaniia, arkhivnye materialy.* SPb.: Aleteia, 1997. 7-17.

Lotman, Iu. M. *Aleksandr Sergeevich Pushkin. Biografiia pisatelia.* In *Pushkin. Biografiia pisatelia. Stat'i i zametki. 1960-1990. "Evgenii Onegin". Kommentarii.* SPb.: Iskusstvo-SPB, 1995.

———. "Semiotika stseny." In his *Ob iskusstve.* 583-603.

———. "Teatr i teatral'nost' v stroe kul'tury nachala xix veka." In *Ob iskusstve.* 617-36.

———. *Ob iskusstve.* SPb.: Iskusstvo-SPB, 1998.

Lotman, M. Iu. *Mandel'shtam i Pasternak (popytka kontrastivnoi poetiki).* N.p.: Aleksandra, n.d. [1996?].

Lozinskii, Mikhail. *Gornyi kliuch. Stikhi.* Petrograd: Al'tsiona, 1916.

Magomedova, D. M. *Avtobiograficheskii mif v tvorchestve A. Bloka.* M.: Martin, 1997.

———. "K istochniku imeni Faina u Bloka." In Musatov and Igosheva, eds. *Aleksandr Blok i mirovaia kul'tura.* 41-47.

———. "O Briusovskom istochnike nazvaniia tsikla A. Bloka 'Arfy i skripki.'" In *V. Ia. Briusov i russkii modernizm. Sbornik statei.* M.: IMLI RAN, 2004. 65-73.

Maksimov, D. E. *Poeziia i proza Al. Bloka.* L.: Sovetskii pisatel', 1975.

Malmstad, John. "A Note on Mandel'štam's 'V Peterburge my soidemsia snova.'" *Russian Literature* V-2 (April 1977): 193-99.

———. "Mandelshtam's 'Silentium': A Poet's Response to Ivanov." In *Vyacheslav Ivanov: Poet, Critic and Philosopher.* New Haven: Yale Center for International Area Studies, 1986. 236-52.

Mandel'shtam, Nadezhda. *Vospominaniia.* New York: Izd. im. Chekhova, 1970.

———. *Vtoraia kniga.* M.: Soglasie, 1999.

Mandel'shtam, Osip. *Kamen'. Stikhi.* SPb.: Akme, 1913.

———. *Kamen'. Stikhi.* Petrograd: Giperborei, 1916.

———. *Tristia.* Pb.-Berlin: Petropolis, 1922.

———. *Vtoraia kniga.* M.-Pb.: Krug, 1923

———. *Kamen'. Pervaia kniga stikhov.* M.-Petrograd.: Gos. Izdatel'stvo, 1923.

———. *Shum vremeni.* L.: Vremia, 1925.

———. *Stikhotvoreniia.* M.-L.: Gos. izdatel'stvo, 1928.

———. *Stikhotvoreniia.* L.: Sovetskii pisatel', 1973.

———. *Kamen'.* L.: Nauka, 1990.

———. *Sochineniia v dvukh tomakh.* M.: Khud. lit., 1990.

———. *Sobranie sochinenii v chetyrekh tomakh.* 1967-81. M.: Terra, 1991.

———. "O. Mandel'shtam. 'Skriabin i khristianstvo.'" Intro. A. G. Mets, comm. A. G. Mets, S. V. Vasilenko, Iu. L. Freidin, and V. A. Nikitin. *Russkaia literatura* 1 (1991): 64–78.
———. *Polnoe sobranie stikhotvorenii.* SPb.: Akademicheskii proekt, 1995.
———. *Stikhotvoreniia. Proza.* M.: AST, 2001.
Mandelstam, Osip. *The Prose of Osip Mandelstam: The Noise of Time, Theodosia, The Egyptian stamp.* Trans. Clarence Brown. Princeton: Princeton UP, 1965.
———. *The Collected Critical Prose and Letters.* 1979. Ed. Jane Gary Harris. Trans. Jane Gary Harris and Constance Link. London: Collins Harvill, 1991.
"O. E. Mandel'shtam v pis'makh S. B. Rudakova k zhene (1935–1936)." Intro. E. A. Toddes and A. G. Mets, ed. L. N. Ivanova and A. G. Mets, comm. A. G. Mets, E. A. Toddes and O.A. Lekmanov. In *Ezhegodnik rukopisnogo otdela Pushkinskogo Doma na 1993 god. Materialy ob O. E. Mandel'shtame.* SPb.: Akademicheskii proekt, 1997. 7–185.
Margolina, Sof'ia M. *Mirovozzrenie Osipa Mandel'shtama.* Marburg: Blau Hörner Verlag, 1989.
Masing-Delic, Irene. "'Peredonov's Little Tear'—Why is it shed? (The Sufferings of a Tormentor)." *Scando-Slavica* 24 (1978): 107–24.
———. "The Symbolist Crisis Revisited: Blok's View." *Issues in Russian Literature Before 1917. Selected Papers of the Third World Congress for Soviet and East European Studies.* Columbus, OH: Slavica, 1989. 216–27.
Matich, Olga. *Erotic Utopia: The Decadent Imagination in Russia's Fin de Siècle.* Madison, WI: U of Wisconsin P, 2005.
Meierkhol'd i khudozhniki: Al'bom. M.: Galart, 1995.
Meierkhol'd v russkoi teatral'noi kritike: 1892–1918. M.: Artist. Rezhysser. Teatr, 1997.
Meierkhol'd, Vsevolod. *O teatre.* SPb.: Prosveshchenie, 1912[?].
Meijer, Jan M. "The Early Mandel'štam and Symbolism." *Russian Literature* VII (1979): 521–36.
Merezhkovskii, D. S. *Polnoe sobranie sochinenii.* Vol. 15. SPb.: M. O. Vol'f, 1912.
Mets, A. G. "O sostave i kompozitsii pervoi knigi stikhov O. E. Mandel'shtama 'Kamen'.'" *Russkaia literatura* 3 (1988): 179–82.
———."'Kamen'' (k tvorcheskoi istorii knigi)." In *Kamen'* (1990). 277–85.
———. *Osip Mandel'shtam i ego vremia. Analiz tekstov.* SPb.: Giperion, 2005.
Mikelis, Ch. Dzh. de [Cesare G. de Michelis]. "K voprosu o kreshchenii Osipa Mandel'shtama." *Sokhrani moiu rech'* 4/2 (2008): 370–76.
Mints, Z. G. *Lirika Aleksandra Bloka.* 1965–75. In her *Poetika Aleksandra Bloka.* SPb.: Iskusstvo-SPB, 1999. 12–332.
———. "K genezisu komicheskogo u Bloka (Vl. Solov'ev i A. Blok)." 1971. In *Aleksandr Blok i russkie pisateli.* SPb.: Iskusstvo-SPB, 2000. 389–442.
———. "Blok i russkii simvolizm." 1980. In her *Aleksandr Blok i russkie pisateli.* 456–536.
———. "Ob evoliutsii russkogo simvolizma (K postanovke voprosa: tezisy)." In *A. Blok i osnovnye tendentsii razvitiia literatury nachala XX veka. Blokovskii sbornik VII* [*Uchen. zap. Tartuskogo gos. univ.* 735]. Tartu: Tartuskii gos. univ., 1986. 7–24.
Mochul'skii, K. *Aleksandr Blok.* Paris: YMCA-Press, 1948.
Morozov, A. A. "Pis'ma O. E. Mandel'shtama k V. I. Ivanovu." *Gosudarstvennaia publichnaia biblioteka SSSR im. V. I. Lenina. Zapiski otdela rukopisei* 34 (Moscow, 1975): 258–74.
Musatov, Vladimir. "Mifologema 'Smerti poeta' v stikhotvorenii Osipa Mandel'shtama 'Kontsert na vokzale.'" In *Pushkin i drugie. Sbornik statei k 60-letiiu professora Sergeia Aleksandrovicha Fomicheva.* Novgorod: Novgorodskii GU, 1997. 284–92.
———. *Lirika Osipa Mandel'shtama.* Kiev: El'ga-L, 2000.
Musatov, V. V. and T. V. Igosheva, eds. *Aleksandr Blok i mirovaia kul'tura. Materialy nauchnoi konferentsii 14–17 marta 2000 goda.* Novgorod: NovGU, 2000.
Myers, Diana. "'Hellenism' and 'Barbarism' in Mandel'shtam." In *Symbolism and After: Essays on Russian Poetry in Honour of Georgette Donchin.* London: Bristol Classical, 1992. 85–101.

Nadson, S. Ia. *Polnoe sobranie stikhotvorenii*. M: Sovetskii pisatel', 1962.
Nebol'sin, Sergei. "Iskazhennyi i zapreshchennyi Aleksandr Blok." *Nash sovremennik* 8 (1991): 176-84.
Nerler, Pavel. "O kompozitsionnykh printsipakh pozdnego Mandel'shtama." *Stoletie Mandel'shtama. Materialy simpoziuma*. Tenafly, NJ: Hermitage, 1994. 326-41.
Nietzsche, Friedrich. *The Birth of Tragedy and The Case of Wagner*. Trans. Walter Kaufmann. New York: Vintage Books, 1967.
———. *The Portable Nietzsche*. Trans. Walter Kauffmann. New York: The Viking Press, 1968.
Ob Aleksandre Bloke. Peterburg: Kartonnyi domik, 1921.
Muratov, Pavel. *Obrazy Italii*. 2nd ed. Vol. 2. M.: Nauchnoe slovo, 1912.
Odoevtseva, Irina. *Izbrannoe*. M.: Soglasie, 1998.
Osip Mandel'shtam i ego vremia. M.: L'age d'Homme—nash dom, 1995.
Ot simvolizma do "Oktiabria." Comp. N. L. Brodskii and N. P. Sidorov. M.: Novaia Moskva, 1924.
Panova, Lada. *"Mir," "prostranstvo," "vremia" v poezii Osipa Mandel'shtama*. M.: Iazyki slavianskoi kul'tury, 2003.
———. *Russkii Egipet: Aleksandriiskaia poetika Mikhaila Kuzmina*. 2 Vols. M.: Vodolei, 2006.
———. "Uvorovannaia Solominka: k literaturnym prototipam liubovnoi liriki Osipa Mandel'shtama." *Voprosy literatury* 5 (2009): 111-51.
Paperno, Irina. "O prirode poeticheskogo slova. Bogoslovskie istochniki spora Mandel'shtama s simvolizmom." *Literaturnoe obozrenie* 1 (1991): 29-36.
———. "Pushkin v zhizni cheloveka serebrianogo veka." In Boris Gasparov, Hughes, and Paperno, eds. *Cultural Mythologies of Russian Modernism*. 19-51.
Paperno, Irina and Joan Delaney Grossman, eds. *Creating Life: The Aesthetic Utopia of Russian Modernism*. Stanford: Stanford UP, 1994.
Parnis, A. and R. Timenchik. "Programmy 'Brodiachei sobaki.'" In *Pamiatniki kul'tury. Novye otkrytiia. Ezhegodnik. 1983*. L.: Nauka, 1985. 160-257.
Pavlov, Evgenii. *Shok pamiati. Avtograficheskaia poetika Val'tera Ben'iamina i Osipa Mandel'shtama*. M.: NLO, 2005.
Pavlovich, Nadezhda. "Vospominaniia." In *Osip Mandel'shtam i ego vremia*. 63-64.
Piast, Vladimir. "Dva slova o chtenii Blokom stikhov." In *Ob Aleksandre Bloke*. 327-36.
———. "Vospominaniia o Bloke." In *Aleksandr Blok v vospominaniiakh sovremennikov*. 2 vols. M.: Khudozhestvennaia literatura, 1980. Vol. 1. 364-97.
———. *Stikhotvoreniia. Vospominaniia*. Tomsk: Vodolei, 1997.
Pinskii, L. *Magistral'nyi siuzhet. F. Viion, V. Shekspir, B. Grasian, V. Skott*. M.: Sovetskii pisatel', 1989.
Poliakova, S. V. *"Oleinikov i ob Oleinikove" i drugie raboty po russkoi literature*. N.p.: Inapress, 1997.
Pollak, Nancy. "Mandel'štam's 'First' Poem," *Slavic and East European Journal* 32.1 (1988): 98-108.
———. *Mandelstam the Reader*. Baltimore: Johns Hopkins UP, 1995.
Pratt, Sarah. "'Antithesis and Completion': Zabolotskij Responds to Tjutčev." *Slavic and East European Journal* 27.2 (1983): 211-27.
———. "Garol'd Blum i 'Strakh vliianiia.'" *Novoe literaturnoe obozrenie* 20 (1996): 5-16.
Przybylski, Ryszard. *Wdzięczny gość Bogu: Esej o poezji Osipa Mandelsztama*. 1980. Republished as *God's Grateful Guest. An Essay on the Poetry of Osip Mandelstam*. Ann Arbor: Ardis, 1987.
Purin, Aleksei. *Vospominaniia o Evterpe*. SPb.: Zvezda, 1996.
Pushkin, A. S. *Polnoe sobranie sochinenii v 10-i tomakh*. M.: Akad. nauk SSSR, 1956-58.
Pushkin. Dostoevskii. Pb.: Izdanie Doma Literatorov, 1921.
Pyman, Avril. *The Life of Aleksandr Blok*. 2 vols. Oxford: Oxford UP, 1979-80.
———. *A History of Russian Symbolism*. Cambridge, Cambridge UP, 1994.
Racine, Jean. *Oeuvres completes. I. Théâtre. Poésie*. Paris: Gallimard, 1999.

Reed, John. *The Schubert Song Companion.* Manchester: Mandolin, 1997.
Reynolds, A[ndrew] W. M. "The Burden of Memories: Toward a Bloomian Analysis of Influence in Osip Mandelstam's Voronezh Notebooks." D. Phil. Dissertation. Oxford, 1996.
———. "'Light Breathing': Osip Mandelstam's 'First' Poems, Pushkin and the Poetics of Influence." *Pushkin Review* 10 (2007): 103-27.
———. "'The Return of the Dead'": Alexander Pushkin, Osip Mandelstam's 'K pustoi zemle nevol'no pripadia', and the Poetics of Influence." *Pushkin Review* (forthcoming).
Reinolds, Endriu [Andrew Reynolds]. "Smert' avtora ili smert' poeta? Intertekstual'nost' v stikhotvorenii 'Kuda mne det'sia v etom ianvare? . . .'" In *"Otdai menia Voronezh . . .": Tret'i mezhdunarodnye mandel'shtamovskie chteniia.* Voronezh: Izd-vo Voronezhskogo univ., 1995. 200-214.
Rodnianskaia, I. B. "Svobodno bluzhdaiushchee slovo (K filosofii i poetike semanticheskogo sdviga)." In *"Literaturovedenie kak literatura": sbornik v chest' S. G. Bocharova.* M.: Iazyki slavianskoi kul'tury, 2004. 183-96.
Rodina, T. M. *A. Blok i russkii teatr nachala XX veka.* M.: Nauka, 1972.
Romains, Jules. *Les Copains.* Paris: Le rayon d'or, 1952.
Ronen, Omry. "Mandelshtam, Osip Emilyevich (1891-1938?)." *Encyclopedia Judaica: Year Book 1973.* Jerusalem, 1973. 294-96.
———. "Leksicheskii povtor, podtekst i smysl v poetike Osipa Mandel'shtama." In *Slavic Poetics: Essays in Honor of Kiril Taranovsky.* The Hague: Mouton, 1973. 367-87.
———. "The Dry River and the Black Ice: Anamnesis and Amnesia in Mandel'štam's Poem 'Ja slovo pozabyl, čto ja xotel skazat'." *Slavica Hierosolymitana* 1 (1977): 177-84.
———. *An Approach to Mandel'štam.* Jerusalem: Magnes Press, 1983.
———. "A Functional Technique of Myth Transformation in Twentieth-Century Russian Lyrical Poetry." In *Myth in Literature.* Columbus, OH: Slavica, 1985. 110-23.
———. "Osip Mandelshtam (1891-1938)." In *European Writers. The Twentieth Century.* Vol. 10. New York: Scribner, 1990. 1619-49.
———. "Sublation [*Aufhebung*] in the Poetics of Acmeism." *Elementa* 2 (1996): 319-29.
———. *Poetika Osipa Mandel'shtama.* SPb.: Giperion, 2002.
———. "V. M. Zhirmunskii i problema 'preodoleniia' v smene stilei i techenii." In *Acta linguistica petropolitana. Trudy Instituta lingvisticheskikh issledovanii* 1, Part 1. SPb.: Nauka, 2003. 55-62.
———. "Akmeizm." *Zvezda* 7 (2008): 217-26.
———. "Poedinki." *Zvezda* 9 (2008): 216-22.
Ronen, Omri and Aleksandr Ospovat. "Kamen' very (Tiutchev, Gogol', i Mandel'shtam)." In Ronen, *Poetika.* 119-26.
Rubins, Maria. *Crossroad of Arts, Crossroad of Cultures: Ecphrasis in Russian and French Poetry.* New York: Palgrave, 2000.
Rudneva, E. P. "Metriko-semanticheskoe edinstvo 'Vtoroi knigi' stikhov Osipa Mandel'shtama." In *Studia Metrica et poetica. Sbornik statei pamiati P. A. Rudneva.* SPb.: Akademicheskii proekt, 1999. 131-47.
Rusinko, Elaine. "Apollonianism and Christian Art: Nietzsche's Influence on Acmeism." In *Nietzsche and Soviet Culture: Ally and Adversary.* Cambridge: Cambridge UP, 1994.
Saito, Takeshi. "Poetika izgnaniia v sbornikakh O. Mandel'shtama 'Kamen'' i 'Tristia.'" *Acta Slavica Iaponica* 21 (2004): 47-66.
Santore, Cathy. "The Tools of Venus." *Renaissance Studies* 11/3 (1997): 179-207.
Schiller, Friedrich. *Werke. Nationalausgabe.* Weimar: Hermann Böhlaus Nachfolger, 1983.
Segal, D. M. "O nekotorykh aspektakh smyslovoi struktury 'Grifel'noi ody' O. E. Mandel'shtama." *Russian Literature* 2 (1972): 48-102.
———. "Fragment semanticheskoi poetiki O. E. Mandel'shtama." *Russian Literature* 10/11 (1975): 59-146.

———. "Poeziia Mikhaila Lozinskogo: simvolizm i akmeizm." *Russian Literature* 13/4 (1983): 333–414.
———. "Istoriia i poetika u Mandel'shtama. A. Stanovlenie poeticheskogo mira." *Cahiers du Monde russe et soviétique* 33.4 (oct.–dec. 1992): 447–96.
———. *Osip Mandel'shtam. Istoriia i poetika*. Berkeley: Slavica Hierosolymitana, 1998.
Seifrid, Thomas. *The Word Made Self: Russian Writings on Language, 1860–1930*. Ithaca: Cornell UP, 2005.
Shcherba, M. M. and L. A. Baturina. "Istoriia bolezni Bloka." *Literaturnoe nasledstvo* 92/4: 729–35.
Shindin, S. G. "Tret'i mezhdunarodnye Mandel'shtamovskie chteniia." *Novoe literaturnoe obozrenie* 9 (1994): 334–48.
———. "Akmeisticheskii fragment khudozhestvennogo mira Mandel'shtama: Metatekstual'nyi aspekt." *Russian Literature* 42 (1997): 211–58.
Shileiko, V. K. *Pometki na poliakh. Stikhi*. SPb.: Limbakh, 1999.
Shkuropat, I. I. "Grotesk v stikhotvoreniiakh O. Mandel'shtama 1912–1913 gg. K probleme klassicheskogo i neklassicheskogo obraza mira v poezii." In *Mandel'shtamovskie dni v Voronezhe. Materialy*. Voronezh: Izd. Voronezhskogo univ., 1994. 92–93.
Shubinskii, V. "Neuiazvimyi." *Novoe literaturnoe obozrenie* 82 (2006): 465–74.
Sloane, David A. *Alexander Blok and the Dynamics of the Lyric Cycle*. Columbus, OH: Slavica, 1987.
Slovar' sovremennogo russkogo literaturnogo iazyka v 20-i tomakh. 2nd ed. M.: Russkii iazyk, 1992–.
Smirnov, I. P. *Khudozhestvennyi smysl i evoliutsiia poeticheskikh system*. M.: Nauka, 1977.
Solov'ev, Sergei. "Novye sborniki stikhov." *Vesy* 5 (1909): 76–81.
Solov'ev, Vladimir Sergeevich. *Sobranie sochinenii*. Vol. 4. SPb.: Obshchestvennaia pol'za, 1901.
Steiner, Peter. "Poem as Manifesto: Mandelstam's 'Notre Dame.'" *Russian Literature* 5/3 (1977): 239–56.
Stepanov, E. "Nikolai Gumilev. Khronika." In Gumilev, *Sobranie sochinenii v trekh tomakh*. Vol. 3. 344–429.
Stratanovskii, Sergei. "Tvorchestvo i bolezn': O rannem Mandel'shtame." *Zvezda* 2 (2004): 210–21.
Surat, Irina. *Mandel'shtam i Pushkin*. M.: IMLI RAN, 2009.
Svin'in, P. P. *Dostopamiatnosti Sankt-Peterburga i ego okrestnostei. Kniga piataia*. 1828. SPb.: Liga Plius, 1997.
Taborisskaia, E. M. "Peterburg v lirike Mandel'shtama." In *Zhizn' i tvorchestvo O. E. Mandel'shtama*. Voronezh: Izd. Voronezhskogo univ., 1990. 512–28.
Taranovskii, K. F. "Pchely i osy v poezii Mandel'shtama." In *To Honor Roman Jakobson: Essays on the Occasion of His Seventieth Birthday*. Mouton: The Hague, 1966. 1973–95.
———. *O poezii i poetike*. M.: Iazyki russkoi kul'tury: 2000.
Taranovsky, Kiril. *Essays on Mandel'štam*. Cambridge: Harvard UP, 1976.
Terras, Victor. "Classical Motives in the Poetry of Mandel'štam." *Slavic and East European Journal* 10.3 (1966): 251–67.
———. "The Black Sun: Orphic Imagery in the Poetry of Osip Mandelstam." *Slavic and East European Journal* 45.1 (2001): 45–60.
Timenchik, R. D. "Zametki ob akmeizme." *Russian Literature* 7/8 (1974): 23–46; V-3 (1977): 281–300; IX-II (1981): 175–89.
———. "Po povodu *Antologii peterburgskoi poezii epokhi akmeizma*." *Russian Literature* V-4 (1977): 315–23.
———. "Tekst v tekste u akmeistov." *Trudy po znakovym sistemam* 14 [*Uchen. zap. Tartuskogo gos. univ*. 567] (1981): 65–75.

Timenchik, Roman and Zoia Kopel'man. "Viacheslav Ivanov i poeziia Kh. N. Bialika." *Novoe literaturnoe obozrenie* 14 (1995): 102-18.
Tiutchev, F. I. *Lirika*. 2 Vols. M.: Nauka, 1965.
Toddes, E. A. "Mandel'shtam i Tiutchev." *International Journal of Slavic Linguistics and Poetics* 17 (1974): 59-86.
———. "Mandel'shtam i OPOIAZovskaia filosofiia." In *Tynianovksii sbornik. Vtorye tynianovskie chteniia*. Riga: Zinatne, 1986. 78-102.
———. "Poeticheskaia ideologiia." *Literaturnoe obozrenie* 3 (1991): 30-43.
———. "Zametki o rannei poezii Mandel'shtama." In *Themes and Variations: In Honor of Lazar Fleishman*. Stanford: Stanford Slavic Studies, 1994. 283-92.
———. "K teme: Mandel'shtam i Pushkin." *Philologia: Rizhskii filologicheskii sbornik* 1 (1994): 74-109.
———. "Nabliudeniia nad tekstami Mandel'shtama." *Tynianovksii sbornik*. Vyp. 10. *Shestye-sed'mye-vos'mye Tynianovskie chteniia*. M.: n.p., 1998. 292-334.
Toporov, V. N. *Akhmatova i Blok (k probleme postroeniia poeticheskogo dialoga: "blokovskii" text Akhmatovoi*. Berkeley: Berkeley Slavic Specialties, 1981.
Toporov, V. N. and T. V. Tsiv'ian. "Nervalianskii sloi u Akhmatovoi i Mandel'shtama (Ob odnom podtekste akmeizma)." In *Novo-Basmannaia, 19*. M.: Khud. lit., 1990. 420-47.
"'Trankhops' i okolo (po arkhivu M. L. Lozinskogo). Chast' II." Publ. of I. V. Platonova-Lozinskaia. Ed., accompanying text and annot. A. G. Mets. In *Gabrieliada. K 65-letiiu G. Superfina*. http://www.ruthenia.ru/document/545494.html.
Trilling, Lionel. *Sincerity and Authenticity*. Cambridge, MA: Harvard UP, 1973.
Tynianov, Iu. N. "Blok i Geine." In *Ob Aleksandre Bloke*. 235-64.
———. *Arkhaisty i novatory*. L.: Priboi, 1929.
Ushakov, D. N., ed. *Tolkovyi slovar' russkogo iazyka*. M.: Sovetskaia entsiklopediia, 1935-40.
Venclova, Tomas. "Viacheslav Ivanov and the Crisis of Russian Symbolism." In *Issues in Russian Literature Before 1917. Selected Papers of the Third Wold Congress for Soviet and East European Studies*. Columbus, OH: Slavica, 1989. 205-15.
Verhaeren, Émile. *Poèmes: Les Flamandes.—Les moines.—Les bords de la route*. Paris: Mercure de France, 1927.
———. [Verkharn, Emil']. *Elena Spartanskaia*. Trans. Valerii Briusov. M.: Skorpion, 1909.
———. *Stikhotvoreniia. Zori. Moris Meterlink. P'esy*. M.: Khud. lit., 1972.
Verigina, V. I. "Vospominaniia ob Aleksandre Bloke." In *Aleksandr Blok v vospominaniiakh sovremennikov*. 2 vols. M.: Khud. lit., 1980. Vol. 1. 410-88.
Verlaine, Paul. *Oeuvres poétiques completes*. [Paris]: Gallimard, 1973.
——— [Verlen, Pol']. *Izbrannye stikhotvoreniia*. 1912. M.: Pol'za, 1915.
Volkov, N. V. *Aleksandr Blok i teatr*. M.: n.p., 1926.
Vorob'eva, Tat'iana Iur'evna. "Tema trapezy v zhivopisi rannekhristianskikh katakomb. Semantika. Istoriko-kul'turnyi kontekst." Avtoreferat dissertatsii na soiskanie uchenoi stepeni kandidata iskusstvovedniia. MGU, 2009.
Wachtel, Michael. *Russian Symbolism and Literary Tradition: Goethe, Novalis, and the Poetics of Vyacheslav Ivanov*. Madison: U of Wisconsin P, 1994.
Westphalen, Timothy C. *Lyric Incarnate: The Dramas of Aleksandr Blok*. Amsterdam: Harwood Academic Publishers, 1998.
Zelinskii, F. F. *Drevne-grecheskaia religiia*. Petrograd: Ogni, 1918.
Zhirmunskii, V. M. "Preodolevshie simvolizm." *Russkaia mysl'* 12 (1916): 25-56.
———. "Poeziia Bloka." In *Ob Aleksandre Bloke*. 65-165.
———. *Voprosy teorii literatury*. 1928. 'S-Gravenhage: Mouton, 1962.
Zeeman, Peter. *The Later Poetry of Osip Mandelstam: Text and Context*. Amsterdam: Rodopi, 1988.

Zhiv Bog, semeinyi katekhizis, sostavlen gruppoi pravoslavnykh khristian. London: Overseas Publications Interchange, Ltd., 1988.

Zhitenev, A. "'Oskorblennyi i oskorbitel": estetika vyzova v proze O. Mandel'shtama." *Miry Osipa Mandel'shtama. IV Mandel'shtamovskie chteniia: materialy mezhdunarodnogo nauchnogo seminara*. Perm: PGPU, 2009. 258–70.

Zholkovsky, Alexander. *Text counter Text: Rereadings in Russian Literary History*. Stanford: Stanford UP, 1994.

Zholkovksii, A. "Klavishnye progulki bez podorozhnoi: 'Ne sravnivai: zhivushchii nesravnim.'" *Sokhrani moiu rech'* 3/1 (2000): 160–84.

Zhukovskii, V. A. *Polnoe sobranie sochinenii v dvenadtsati tomakh*. Vol. 10. SPb.: Izd. A. F. Marksa, 1902.

INDEX OF WORKS BY MANDELSTAM AND BLOK

WORKS BY MANDELSTAM

Poetry:

"1 ianvaria 1924" (1 January 1924), 207–9
"10 ianvaria 1934" (10 January 1934), 275n10
"Abbat" (Abbot), 52
"Admiralteistvo" (The Admiralty), 108
"Aiia-Sofiia" (Hagia-Sophia), 50–51, 54, 57, **79–81**, 106, 107
"Amerikan bar" (American Bar), 101
"Amerikanka" (American Girl), 101
"Bakh" (Bach), 52, 112
"Batiushkov," 273n36
"Besshumnoe vereteno" (The noiseless spindle), 38
"Chut' mertsaet prizrachnaia stsena" (The spectral stage barely glimmers), 5, **153–64**, 167
"Chtob, priiatel' i vetra kapel'" (So that, friend of wind and drops), 119, 273n36
"Dano mne telo, chto mne delat' s nim" (A body is given me, what shall I do with it), 35, 223n11
"Dev polunochnykh otvaga" (The valor of northern maids), 230n18
"Dombi i syn" (Dombey and Son), 101
"Esche daleko asfodelei" (Still far is of the asphodels), 250n47, 252n80
"Est' tselomudrennye chary" (There are chaste charms), **43–47**
"Est' tsennostei nezyblemaia skala" (There is an unshakable scale of values), 186, 255n100
"Eta noch' nepopravima" (This night is irreparable), 262n14
"Evkharistiia" (Eucharist). *See* "Vot daronositsa"
"Evropa" (Europe), 52
"Gde noch' brosaet iakoria" (Where night drops its anchors), 263n20
"Gde sviazannyi i prigvozhdennyi ston?" (Where is the bound and crucified moan?), 186
"I ponyne na Afone" (And to this day at Mount Athos), 61–62

291

"Ia naravne s drugimi" (I want just like the others), 250n5, 275n8

"Ia ne slykhal rasskazov Ossiana" (I have not heard the tales of Ossian), 26–27, 200

"Ia ne uvizhu znamenitoi 'Fedry'" (I will not see the celebrated *Phèdre*), **16–19**, 111, 266n53

"Ia nenavizhu svet odnoobraznykh zvezd" (I hate the light of the monotonous stars), 51–52, 54, 230n18

"Ia slovo pozabyl, chto ia khotel skazat'" (I have forgotten the word), 193, 252n80, 260n33

"Ia v khorovod tenei, toptavshikh nezhnyi lug" (I into the circle dance of shades, trampling a tender meadow), 160–61, 252n80, 270n42

"Ia vzdragivaiu ot kholoda" (I shudder from the cold), 51–52, 54, 85, 230n18

"Isakii pod fatoi molochnoi belizny" (St. Isaac's under a veil of milky white), 123, **125–27**

"Iz omuta zlogo i viazkogo" (From an evil and miry pool), 235n13

"Iz polutemnoi zaly, vdrug" (From the half-lit hall, suddenly), 36–37, 233n18

"Kak etikh pokryval i etogo ubora" (How these coverings), 19, **111–12**, 171

"Kak ten' vnezapnykh oblakov" (Like the shadow of sudden clouds), 235n13

"Kantsona" (Canzone), 207

"Kassandre" (To Cassandra), 115

"Kazino" (Casino), 51, 53–54, 68, 87, 240n56

"Kinematograf" (Cinema), 100

"K pustoi zemle nevol'no pripadaia" (To the empty earth), 30

"Kogda b ia ugol' vzial dlia vysshei pokhvaly" (Ode to Stalin), 231n

"Kogda mozaik niknut travy" (When the grasses of the mosaics droop), 73

"Kogda pokazyvaiut vosem'" (When [the clock] shows eight), 235n9

"Kogda Psikheia-zhizn' spuskaetsia k teniam" (When Psyche-life descends to the shades), 252n80

"Kogda udar s udarami vstrechaetsia" (When blow meets blows), 235n10

"Kogda ukor kolokolov" (When the bells' reproach), 73

"Kontsert na vokzale" (Concert at the Railway Station), **190–96**, 212

"Letaiut val'kirii, poiut smychki" (Valkyries fly, bows sing), 174, 266n52

"Liuteranin" (Lutheran), 51, 53, 66

"Mne kholodno. Prozrachnaya vesna" (I am cold. Transparent spring), **112–15**

"Na kammenykh otrogakh Pierii" (On the rocky spurs of Pieria), **116–22**, 160

"Na perlamutrovyi chelnok" (Onto the mother-of-pearl shuttle), 52

"Na rozval'niakh, ulozhennykh solomoi" (On a straw-covered sledge), 108–9

"Ne sravnivai: zhivushchii nesravnim" (Don't compare: the living is incomparable), 274n4

"Ne u menia, ne u tebia—u nikh" (Not mine, not yours—but theirs), 28

"Net, ne luna, a svetlyi tsiferblat" (No, not the moon, but a radiant clock face), 51–54, 87

"Net, nikogda nichei ia ne byl sovremennik" (No, never was I anyone's contemporary), 271n8

"Nevyrazimaia pechal'" (Inexpressible sadness), 52

"Nezhnee nezhnogo" (More tender than tender), **37–43**

"Notre Dame," 50–51, 54–55, 71, 81, 106, 107, 216, 243n86

"O, gody! O, chasy! O, bremia Issuara" (O, years! O, hours! O, burden of Issoire), 14, **227n60**

"O, etot vozdukh, smutoi p'ianyi" (O, this air, drunk with trouble), 125, 253n82

"Obraz tvoi, muchitel'nyi i zybkii" (Your image, agonizing and unstable), 51–54, 56, **57–64**, 85, 237n2, 238n9

"Oda Betkhovenu" (Ode to Beethoven), 15, 112, 237n29, 254n93

"Otravlen khleb i vozdukh vypit" (The bread is poisoned and the air drunk up), **24–26**

"Paden'e—neizmennyi sputnik strakha" (Falling is the constant companion of fear), 51, 53–54, 56, **71–79**, 94

"Peshekhod" (Pedestrian), 51, 53–54, 56, **64–71**, 78–79, 87

"Peterburgskie strofy" (Petersburg Strophes), 95, 107, 273n35

"Pust' v dushnoi komnate, gde kloch'ia seroi vaty" (Let, in the stuffy room where there are clumps of gray cotton), **85–99**, 235n9

"Rakovina" (Seashell), 119
"S mirom derzhavnym ia byl lish' rebiacheski sviazan" (I was linked to the world of power in but a childish way), 207, 274n44
"Sestry—tiazhest' i nezhnost'" (Sisters—heaviness and tenderness), 14
"Sharmanka" (Barrel Organ), 85, 94, **235n9**
"Skudnyi luch, kholodnoi meroiu" (A meager beam, with chill measure), **47–48**
"Slukh chutkii parus napriagaet" (Hearing tenses its sensitive sail), 235n13
"Sobiralis' elliny voinoiu" (The Hellenes mustered for war), 52, 271n6
"Sokhrani moiu rech' navsegda za privkus neschast'ia i dyma" (Preserve my speech for all time for the aftertaste of misfortune and smoke), 274n4
"Sredi sviashchennikov levitom moldym" (Among the priests a young Levite), 115, 248n25, 253n82
"Starik" (Old Man), **101–5**, 107
"Stikhi o neizvestnom soldate" (Verses on the unknown soldier), 119–20
"Sumerki svobody" (The Twilight of Freedom), 115
"Susal'nym zolotom goriat" (In the forests Christmas trees), 36–37, 232n3
"Synov'ia Aimona" (Aymon's Sons), 52
"Temnykh uz zemnogo zatocheniia" (Dark bonds of worldly imprisonment), 268n24
"Tennis" (Tennis), 100
"Tol'ko detskie knigi chitat'" (To read only children's books), 36, 232n3
"Tristia," 122
"Tsarskoe selo," 51, 53–54
"Tvoia veselaia nezhnost'" (Your vivacious tenderness), **38–39**, 43
"Ty proshla skvoz' oblako tumana" (You passed through a cloud of fog), **41–42**, 59, 238n16
"Tysiachestruinyi potok" (A thousand-streamed torrent"), 233n12, 235n9
"Vernis' v smesitel'noe lono" (Return to the incestuous womb), 250n54
"V ogromnom omute prozrachno i temno" (In the giant pool it is transparent and dark), 235n13
"V tot vecher ne gudel strel'chatyi les organa" (That evening the lancet forest of the organ did not hum), 52, **115**, **250n52**
"V khrustal'nom omute kakaia krutizna!" (What steepness in the crystal pool!), 236n13, 253n82
"V Peterburge my soidemsia snova" (We shall gather anew in Petersburg), **167–84**, 188, 190, 211, 236n13
"V raznogolositse devicheskogo khora" (In the cacophony of the maiden choir), 253n82
"Venitseiskoi zhizni, mrachnoi i besplodnoi" (Venetian life, morbid and barren), 5, **148–53**, 164, 167, 236n13, 263n31
"Vot daronositsa" (Behold the pyx), 123, 253n82, 260n36
"Za to, chto ia ruki tvoi ne sumel uderzhat'" (For not being able to keep hold of your hands), 248n25
"Zolotoi" (Gold Ruble), 51, 53–54, 230n18
"Zvuk ostorozhnyi i glukhoi" (The sound, cautious and muffled), 36–37

Essays:

"A. Blok: 7 August 1921–7 August 1922," 189, 197, 200. *See also* "Barsuch'ia nora"
"Barsuch'ia nora" (Badger Hole), 167, **197–203**, 207
"Buria i natisk" (Storm and Stress), 98, 199, 202, 222n5, 255n99
"Deviatnadtsatyi vek" (The Nineteenth Century), 114, 148
"Fransua Villon" (François Villon), 4, 20, 40, 71, 75, 103, 147–48
"Gumanizm i sovremennost'" (Humanism and Modernity), 182
"Iakhontov," 162, 266n52
"Krovavaia misteriia 9-go ianvaria" (The Bloody Mystery Play of the 9th of January), 169
"O prirode slova" (On the Nature of the Word), 15, 106, 199, 226n50
"Petr Chaadaev," 244n23
"Pis'mo o russkoi poezii" (A Letter about Russian Poetry), 187, 201, 213, 242n78
"Pushkin i Skriabin" (Pushkin and Skriabin), 11, 19, 115, 118, 126–27, 129, 175, 189–90, 194, 231n36, 245n43, 247n2, 262n14

INDEX OF WORKS BY MANDELSTAM AND BLOK

"Razgovor o Dante" (Conversation about Dante), 120, 168, 206, 207, 212, 267n14, 275n10
"Slovo i kul'tura" (The Word and Culture), 198, 215, 231n28, 228n70, 266n54
"Utro akmeizma" (The Morning of Acmeism), 71, 75, 78, 226nn43, 47

Prose:

Chetvertaia proza (Fourth Prose), 210, 214, 273n38
Egipetskaia marka (The Egyptian Stamp), 187, 204–5, 272n27
"Shuba" (Fur Coat), 204, 272n27
Shum vremeni (The Noise of Time), 172, 195, 197, 205, 228n68, 272n78
  "Sem'ia Sinani" (The Sinani Family), 95, 97
  "Komissarzhevskaya," 187–88, 202, 205
  "V ne po chinu barstvennoi shube" (In a Fur Coat above His Station), **15–16**, 79, 98, 148, 202–3, 231n38, 234n25

Books:

O poezii (On Poetry), 20, 197–98
Kamen' (Stone), 29, 31, 106, 112
  Stone (1913), 35, 98, 47, 50, 54, 223n11, 239n46
  Stone (1916), 16, 35, 37, **49–55**, 98–99, 233n18
  Stone (1923), 36, 51–52, 235n13, 236n22
  Stone (1928, in *Poems*), 36, 51, 235n13, 237n22
Tristia, 11, 15, 19, 29, 100, **109–29**, 130, 168, 211, 236n13
Vtoraia kniga (Second Book), 110, 118
Stikhotvoreniia (Poems), 110

Radio program:

"Iunost' Gete" (Goethe's Youth), 151

WORKS BY BLOK

Poetry:

"Balaganchik" (The Fair Booth), 134, 188–89

"Bushuet snezhnaya vesna" (The snowy spring rages), 258n40
"Dali slepy" (The distance is blind), 242n73
"Devushka iz Spoleto" (The Girl from Spoleto), 259n20
"Ee pesni" (Her Songs), 94
"Golos iz khora" (Voice from the Chorus), 171, 265n50
"Ia byl smushchennyi i veselyi" (I was embarrassed and joyous), **135–36**, 139
"Ia, otrok, zazhigaiu svechi" (A youth, I light the candles), 45
"Ia v dol'nii mir voshla, kak v lozhu" (I entered the lower world as a theater box), **136–39**, 144, 145
"Ia zhdu prizyva, ishchu otveta" (I await a call, I seek an answer), 60–61, 63
"Inok" (Monk), 257n21
"Iz khrustal'nogo tumana" (From the crystal fog), 242n78
"Khozhu, brozhu ponuryi" (I pace, I wander downcast), 92
"Khudozhnik" (Artist), 260n33
"Kogda ia prozreval vpervye" (When I first gained insight), 264n45
"Kryl'tso Ee, slovno papert'" (Her porch is as if a parvis), 233n13
"Moei materi" (To My Mother, 1905), 91–92, 98
"Na ostrovakh" (On the islands), 209
"Neizbezhnoe" (The Inevitable), 233n18
"Net, nikogda moei, i ty nichei ne budesh'" (No, never mine, nor anyone's will you be), 145
"Neznakomka" (The Stranger), 42–43, 104, 145, 233n12, 257n34
"Na pole kulikovom" (On Kulikovo Field), 106, 228n70, 262n16
"Na smert' Kommissarzhevskoi" (On the death of Kommissarzhevskaya), 159–60
"Na snezhnom kostre" (On the Snow Pyre), 171
"Neznakomka" (Stranger), 257n34
"Noch', ulitsa, fonar', apteka" (Night, street, street lamp, pharmacy), 203
"Persten'-Stradan'e" (Gem Ring-Suffering), 275n9
"Pesn' ada" (Canto of Hell), 269n31
"Predchuvstvuiu Tebia. Goda prokhodiat mimo" (I feel Your approach. The years go by), 9–10, 53

"Rozhdennye v goda glukhie" (Those born in the lost years), 272n19
"Serdityi vzor bestsvetnykh glaz" (The angry gaze of colorless eyes), **140–45**, 171, 177
"Sfinks" (Sphinx), 266n54
"Shagi" (Steps, translation from Verhaeren), 244n19
"Shagi Komandora" (Steps of the Knight Commander), 89–90, 93–95, 99, 106, 107, 159, 167–68, 171, **172–74**, 188, 197, 201, 203, 217–19, 244n19, 246n1, 260n37, 264n41, 266n52
"Siena," 236n16
"Snezhnaia deva" (The Snow Maiden), 257n21
"Tri poslaniia" (Three Missives), 171
"Ty, kak otzvuk zabytogo gimna" (You are like the echo of a forgotten hymn), 159
"Ty tverdish', chto ia kholoden, zamknut i sukh" (You assert that I am cold, remote and dry), 265n50
"V chas, kogda p'ianeiut nartsissy" (At the hour when the daffodils become intoxicated), 133–34, 139
"Venetsiia" (Venice), 108, 150, 151–52, 171
"Vkozhu ia v temnye khramy" (I enter dark churches), 59–60
"Vl. Bestuzhevu. Otvet" (To Vl. Bestuzhev. Reply), 181
"Vot iavilas'. Zaslonila" (She appeared. She overshadowed), 134–35, 136
"Vse na zemle umret—i mat', i mladost'" (All on Earth will die—both mother and youth), 180
"Vse otoshli, shumite sosny" (All have left, rustle, pines), 236n16
"Zachatyi v noch', ia v noch' rozhden" (Conceived in the night, in the night I was born), 245n32

Long poems:

"Dvenadtsat'" (The Twelve), 173, 263n23, 271n5
"Vozmezdie" (Retribution), 150–51, 203, 205, 212, 231n35, 247n15, 272n19

Cycles:

"Arfy i skripki" (Harps and Violins), 193

"Faina," **133–39**, 145
"Strashnyi mir" (Frightening World), 193
"Karmen" (Carmen), 133, **140–45**, 159
"Nepodvizhnost'" (Motionlessness), 59
"Pliaski smerti" (Dances of death), 259n19
"Pod znakom Devy" (Under the Sign of Virgo/the Virgin), 94
"Snezhnaia maska" (The Snow Mask), 10, 94, 132–35, 140, 233n18
"Stikhi o Prekrasnoi dame" (Poems about the Fair Lady), 59–61
"Zakliatie ognem i mrakom" (Incantation by Fire and Darkness), 238n15
"Vol'nye mysli" (Free Thoughts), 256n15

Plays:

Balaganchik (The Fair Booth), 95, 132, 188–89, 236nn15–16, 260n31
Neznakomka (The Stranger), 104–5
Pesnia sud'by (Song of Fate), 91
Roza i krest (Rose and Cross), 245n32

Prose and essays:

"Bez bozhestva, bez vdokhnoven'ia (Tsekh akmeistov)" (Without a god, without inspiration [The Acmeists' Guild]), 271n11
"Bezvremen'e" (Stagnation/Evil Times), 90–91, 225n31
"Ditia Gogolia" (Gogol's Child), 268n24
"Dramaticheskii teatr V.F. Kommissarzhevskoi (Pis'mo iz Peterburga)" (The Dramatic Theater of V. F. Kommissarzhevskaya [A Letter from Petersburg]), 260n31
"Intelligentsiia i revoliutsiia" (Intelligentsia and Revolution), 173, 175, 263n28, 268n24
"Ironiia" (Irony), 98, 247n10, 268n24
"Krushenie gumanizma" (The Wreck of Humanism), 213, 268n24
"Molnii iskusstva" (Lightning Flashes of Art), 268n24
"Narod i intelligentsiia" (The People and the Intelligentsia), 262n16
"O sovremennom sostoianii russkogo simvolizma" (On the Current State of Russian Symbolism), 10, 257n8, 263n26

"Pis'mo o teatre" (Letter on the Theater), 133

Books:

Sedoe utro (Gray Morning), 183
Sobranie stikhotvorenii (Collected Works), 256n15, 264n46
Stikhi o Prekrasnoi Dame (Poems about the Fair Lady), 41–42, 59, 103–4, 242n73
Nechaiannaia Radost' (Unexpected Joy), 233n19
Zemlia v snegu (Earth in Snow), 225n31, 256n15

Speech:

"O naznachenii poeta" (On the Calling of the Poet), 182, 184, 189–90, 193, 211, 268n23

SUBJECT INDEX

For reasons of space, names of scholars have been indexed only when appearing in the main text.

Acmeism, 6, 26, 44, 53–55, 57, 61, 65, 68, 71, 75, 78, 81–82, 85, 99, 100, 112, 167, 171, 216, 221n33, 241n67; definition of, 12–13; organicity and constructedness in, 29; overview of, 12–15; piety of artist-builder in, 12; rationality and mysticism in, 12; respect for boundaries in, 12; semantic poetics of, 13–14; struggle in vs. conversion, 50, 54–55; sublation in, 14–15; subtextual poetics of, 14; synthesis with Symbolism in *Tristia*, 100, 129; and taste, 13; year 1912 in, 49–50
Acmeists: as "younger Symbolists," 50
Aeschylus: *The Eumenides*, 115; *The Libation Bearers*, 114; *Seven Against Thebes*, 112
Akhmatova, Anna, 13, 22, 30, 49–50, 182, 195, 202, 207, 212, 246n44; *Evening* (Vecher), 49; "I have no use for odic hosts" (Mne ni k chemu odicheskie rati), 230n20

Alexandrian age, 110, 114–16, 122–23
"ambivalent antitheses," 14
ambivalent irony, 57–64
Amelin, G. G., 103
anamnesis, 111, 123, 125, 145, 215, 254n94
Anaxagoras. *See* Pushkin, "To Krivtsov"
Andreev, Leonid: "Darkness" (T'ma), 265n51; *Life of a Man* (Zhizn' cheloveka), 97
Annensky, Innokenty, 185–86, 195, 211, 230n8, 231n32; "The Dying Turgenev" (Umiraiushchii Turgenev), 85; "∞," 90; Mandelstam on Dionysiasm in, 222n2
anti-Semitism, 7, 152, 203–4, 212, 224n19
anxiety of influence. *See* Bloom, Harold; creative anxieties
Aphrodite, 175, 177–79
Apollo (Apollon), 49, 50, 243n85
Apollonian and Dionysian, 5, 9, 13–15, 68, 71, 109–10, 129, 216

297

SUBJECT INDEX

apophrades (Bloom), 24, 29
Arbenina, Olga, 176–77, 260n23, 264n32
Argonauts (Bely's circle), 45, 226n35
aristocracy, 78, 199, 201–5, 206–7
Athena, 114–15
authenticity, 11, 16, 211–16; skepticism as to Symbolist, 66–67, 69–71, 131–32, 185–88
Averintsev, Sergei, 12, 51, 159
Awakened Thought (Probuzhdennaia mysl'), 232n3
Azov, Vladimir, 153

Bakhtin, Mikhail, 255n7
Bakst, Lev, 260n31
Bal'mont, Konstantin, 8, 85
Baltrushaitis, Iurgis: "Carousel" (Karusel'), 245n34
Baratynsky, Evgenii, 201
barbarism, 129
barstvennost', 7, 16, 201–5, 207, 210
Batiushkov, Konstantin, 273n36, 240n50; "Elegy from Tibullus. Free Translation" (Elegiia iz Tibulla. Vol'nyi perevod), 252n72
Batiushkov, Pavel, 69, 240n50
Baudelaire, Charles, 39, 41; "À une passant," 233n12
Bedouins, 25–26
Bely, Andrei, 9, 23, 38, 49, 58, 69–70, 93, 187, 203, 207, 214, 225n28, 227n61, 236n17
  Works: *Arabesques*, 70; *The Beginning of the Century* (Nachalo veka), 69; "Emblematics of Sense" (Emblematika smysla), 228n70; "Excerpts from Glossolalia (A Poem about Sound)" (Otryvki iz Glossolalii [Poemy o zvuke]), 266n54; "F. Nietzsche" (F. Nitsshe), 70; *Gold in the Azure* (Zoloto v lazuri), 46, 95; "Green Meadow" (Lug zelenyi), 225n31; "Images" (cycle, Obrazy), 95; "In the Church" (Vo khrame), 242n69; "Meeting" (Vstrecha), 69–70; *Northern Symphony* (Severnaia simfoniia), 95; *Notes of an Eccentric* (Zapiski chudaka), 69; *Petersburg*, 266n11; *The Silver Dove* (Serebrianyi golub'), 61; "Stamped Galosh" (Shtempelevannaia kalosha), 70; "Symbolism as Worldview" (Simvolizm kak miroponimanie), 70, 226n43; "To Briusov" (Briusovu), 69; *Urn* (Urna), 10, 69; "The Wilderness" (Pustynia), 46; "World Soul" (Dusha mira), 41
Benois, Alexandre, 241n62, 260n27
Benthamites (Utilitarianism), 128
Bergson, Henri, 106
Bethea, David, 8, 29–30
bezvremen'e, 90–91, 92, 173
Black Hundreds, 204
black sun, 19, 111–12, 126, 171. *See also* night sun
Blok, Alexander, 123, 130–46, 225nn28–29, 266n2; and anti-Semitism, 7, 203–4, 212; aristocracy (*barstvennost'*) of, 7, 199, 201–5, 207–8, 212; as badger, 199–200; and Briusov, 233n16; charisma of, 30–31, 85–86, 198, 211; conservatism, 198–99, 201, 203; creative anxieties of, 23–24, 34; death of, 6–7, 16, 105, 167, 187, 190, 192–93, 196, 197, 211, 254n97; and Fet, 24; and Vladimir Gippius, 180–81; attitude toward formal perfection, 214; and Gnosticism, 175, 227–228n61, 262n15; and Gorodetsky, 233n16; Heroine, 41–43, 46, 53, 103, 130, 134–39, 144, 263n32 (*see also* Ideal); irony in works and worldview of, 6, 14, 98, 185, 189, 265n46; "living and dangerous," 6–8; lyric hero, 7, 31, 53, 85–86, 98, 104–5, 108–9, 139, 211, 263n21; Mandelstam and, 6–8, 11, 16, 22, 24, 29–31, 41–43, 47–48, 50, 58–61, 63, 77, 85–86, 88–98, 100–101, 103–9, 148, 150–52, 159–60, 167–68, 171–84, 185, 187–90, 192–93, 195–96, 197–210, 211–14, 216; 232n3; maximalism of, 7, 99, 188; and melodrama, 259n12; metaphorical poetics of, 100, 105–6, 211; and modernist time structures, 100, 106–9; myth-making of, 11, 197; and music, 94, 145, 192–93, 271n45; and *nadsonovshchina*, 95–96; and Pushkin, 97–98, 177–79, 182, 184, 189–90, 195–96, 206, 273n30; Romantic persona, 6–7; semioticization of traditional imagery in, 42; theater poems of, 130–46; theatricality of, 7, 96, 130, 151, 167, 184, 185, 188, 196, 211; tragic-prophetic stance of, 6–7, 31, 89–90, 94, 98, 172–73, 183, 188–89, 199–200, 211; and Vladimir Solov'ev,

24, 64; wornness of *topoi* of, 63. *See also* Index of Works, Blok
Bloom, Harold, 8, 21–24, 26–31; *The Anxiety of Influence*, 21; and Freudian "Family Romance," 22, 26; and subtextual criticism, 231n31
bogochelovechestvo (Godmanhood), 64, 257n36
Bosio, Angiolina, 260n25
boundaries: between art and life, 5–6, 15–16, 140, 147–48, 151–53, 156, 161, 163–64, 228n68; clock face representing temporal, 90; footlights as, 18, 131–46; incest as transgression of, 229n77; ontological, 12; play with, 5–6, 12, 15–19, 140, 144–46, 163–64; between religion and life, 69; between self and world, 187; between spatial realms, 174–75; between Symbolism and Acmeism, 6, 19–20, 55; Symbolist transgressing of, 5, 12, 65–66, 131; between this and other world, 5, 46, 60, 65; between time frames, 18–19, 106–9; between tragedy and theatricality, 7, 185–89
Briusov, Valery, 8, 12, 23, 38, 42, 50, 214, 236n16, 243n1, 247n4; and Blok, 233n16
  Works: *All Melodies* (Vse napevy), 10–11; "La belle dame sans merci," 225n30; "Star" (Zvezda), 11; "To Her, Close at Heart" (K Blizkoi), 41; *Urbi et Orbi*, 23
Brodsky, Joseph, 228n66
Broitman, S. N., 46, 106, 108, 168
Brown, Clarence, 53
Broyde, Steven, 163
Bukhshtab, Boris, 7
Bulgakov, Sergei, 238n12

candor, 214, 216
Carmen, 11, 140–43, 188, 202
Catullus, 27
Cavanagh, Clare, 27, 44, 46, 80–81
Chaadaev, Petr, 207, 236n16
Chaplin, Charlie, 207
charisma, 30–31, 86, 198, 211, 243n3
Chebotarevskaya, Anastasia, 50
chelys-lyra, 251nn61–62
Chénier, André, 197, 206
chorus, 192, 194; of antiquity, 19, 111–12, 126, 171; operatic, 122, 154, 156; rebirth of, 110–11, 247n2, 254n94

Christianity, 8, 57, 62, 66, 72–76, 122–29; and artist, 127–28; religion of Dionysus and, 110, 112, 124–25, 127; and heresies, 64–66; myth of forgotten, 11, 109–29 62, 66, 73, 239n25
circular motion: of clock hands, 87, 91; of *gigantskie shagi*, 87, 94; of horseman (Blok, "Bezvremen'e"), 90–91; sentimental song of barrel organ, 94; of weathervanes, 92. *See also* eternal return
Classicism, theater of, 131
clinamen (Bloom), 28
composition: and censorship, 236n13, 237n22; chronology in, 235n13; use of facing pages in, 51–53; of *Stone* (1913), 50, 54; of *Stone* (1916), 49–55, 98–99; of *Stone* (various editions); 35–37, 235n8; of *Tristia*, 110–11
Constantinople: Hagia Sophia, 126–27
Craig, Gordon, 151
creative anxieties, 6, 8, 21–31; extra-poetic, 29–30; among younger Symbolists, 23–24
creative freedom, 4, 25–26, 29, 127, 190, 193, 197, 205, 209
Crone, Anna Lisa, 29
Cubo-Futurism. *See* Futurism
curtain and onionskin. *See* distance and immediacy

Dal', Vladimir, 88
danger, acceptance of/flirtation with, 16, 29, 67–68, 73–75, 95, 112, 118–19, 125, 127–28, 182–83
Dante, 42, 206, 209
d'Anthès, George, 88
David, King, 207
David Copperfield (Dickens), 203
death, 61, 120, 190; of the artist, 16, 118; of the poet, competing models of, 86, 88, 90, 94–98, 189–90, 194; theatrical, 150–52
Del'mas, Liubov', 140, 143–46, 176
Dionysian, 68, 110, 112, 115; and Apollonian, 5, 9, 13, 15, 109; and boundaries in Mandelstam, 228n70; Christianity and, 110, 112, 124–25, 127; religion, 110–11
Dionysus, theater of, 111
distance: in Acmeism, 12; imposed from

mythopoetic Symbolism, 45; necessary for aesthetic tension, 4
distance and immediacy: curtain and onion-skin as representation of, 6, 15–20; play with, 3–6, 15–20, 55, 150–153, 163–64, 216
distanced reiteration, 4, 28–29
Divine Feminine. *See* Ideal
Dobroliubov, Alexander, 77, 204
Don Juan, 11, 89–90, 172–74
Donna Anna. *See* Ideal
Dragon, The (Drakon), 266n54

Ego-Futurism, 49
Eikhenbaum, Boris: "Blok's Fate" (Sud'ba Bloka), 185, 188–89
epigones, 4, 12, 57, 70, 131
Epirus, 119
Eternal Feminine, 41, 42, 45, 59, 93, 104, 173–74, 215. *See also* Ideal
eternal return, 90, 102, 106–7, 173
Etkind, Efim, 140
Eucharist, 122–25, 127, 254n98, 264n33
eunomia, 114
Euripides, 19
Evreinov, Nikolai, 151, 256n12
exaggeration, Symbolist/Romantic, 66–67, 71, 99
excesses: artistic and epistemological of Symbolism, 46

Fair Lady. *See* Ideal
Fet, Afanasy, 42, 122, 228n66; influence on Blok, 24, 93
    Works: "Convalescent" (Bol'noi), 93; "Organ Grinder" (Sharmanshchik), 245n32, "You are all in lights. Your distant flashes" (Ty vsia v ogniakh. Tvoikh zarnits), 230n14
Field, The (Niva), 88
Finland, 97
Florensky, Pavel, 14, 241n57
footlights: as boundary, 18–19, 131–46; false vs. real, 138
footpaths of mystery, 19, 115, 128
France, 19
Frazer, James: *The Golden Bough*, 248n35
Freidin, Gregory, 4, 18, 30–31, 111, 192, 210, 249n37
French Revolution, 114, 148
Furies, 114–16, 123
Futurism, 6, 13, 49

Gasparov, Boris, 179, 190, 192, 195–96
Gasparov, Mikhail, 11, 88, 96, 106, 176
Geertz, Clifford, 128
Gershtein, Emma, 212
gigantskie shagi (yard game), 87, 96–97
Ginzburg, Lydia, 132–33, 140
Gippius, Vladimir, 3, 16, 73, 78–79, 179–81, 203, 204, 213; and Blok, 180–81
    Works: "To Alexander Blok" (Aleksandru Bloku), 180–81; "I was overtaken by ecstasy in the steppe" (Menia vostorg v stepi nastig), 180; "Pushkin and Christianity" (Pushkin i khristianstvo), 262n14; *Return* (Vozvrashchenie), 264n43, 265n46; *Starry Night* (Noch' v zvezdakh), 180
Gippius, Zinaida, 8
Gluck, Christoph Willibald: *Orpheus and Eurydice*, 122–23, 156–57, 163, 269n30
Goethe, J. W. von, 42, 201
Gofman, Modest, 9
Gogol, Nikolai, 69, 76, 242n68, 242n72, 271n47; "Overcoat" (Shinel'), 107, 236n16
Golovin, Alexander, 122, 156, 260n23
Gorodetsky, Sergei, 12–13, 49–50, 224n19, 234n3, 239n25, 239n39; and Blok, 233n16
    Works: "Bride" (Nevesta), 263n21; "Idol-creation" (Idolotvorchestvo), 44–46
Gothic, 71, 76
Great War, 5
Greece, ancient, 19, 119. *See also* Aeschylus, Athena, chorus (of antiquity), etc.
Grene, David, 112
Grishunin, A. L., 7
Gromov, Pavel, 106, 108
Gumilev, Nikolai, 12, 13, 49, 50, 195, 243n82, 243n85, 264n32; death of, 16, 190, 192–93, 196; reviews of *Stone* (1913) and (1916), 54–55; theory of the word, 171, 263n11
    Works: "Anatomy of a Poem" (Anatomiia stikhotvoreniia), 226n50; "The Life of Verse" (Zhizn' stikha), 147; "Poem of the Beginning. Book One. The Drag-

on" (Poema nachala. Kniga pervaia. Drakon), 266n54; "Wayward Tram" (Zabludivshiisia tramvai), 194; "The Word" (Slovo), 266n54

heresiography, 56; Christian, 64–65; Islamic, 65–66
Homer, 27
Homeric Hymn to Hermes, 118
homoiousia vs. *homoousia*, 65
Hyperborean, The (Giperborei), 13, 49, 59, 62, 85, 98, 179, 233n12, 238n9, 245n34

Ibsen, Henrik, 200; *Brand*, 68–69, 240n56
Ideal (or ideal realm), 4, 6, 9, 14, 41, 41–42, 90, 92, 93–94, 103, 139, 215; and idols, 45–46; location of, 175; and poetic image, 44–45. *See also* Eternal Feminine; Blok (Heroine)
Iran, 65
irony, 6, 9, 12, 14, 20, 47, 52–53, 88, 98, 161, 164, 189, 216, 265n46; ambivalent, 20, 56–64; in Symbolism and Acmeism, 14, 98, 227nn57–58; "luminous," 14
Islam, 65–66
Ivanov, Georgii, 266n54
Ivanov, Viacheslav, 10–11, 29, 38, 49–50, 58, 67–68, 76, 100, 109–12, 114, 118, 123–25, 127–29, 159–60, 171, 186, 215, 250n55, 251n59, 255n8, 260n37, 261n5, 272n14; dithyrambs, 112, 250n51; early influence on Mandelstam, 22; and heresy, 65; lectures on versification (Academy), 3, 7, 40, 232n3; realistic and idealistic Symbolism, 15, 44, 214; and receptivity in poetry, 215; religious experimentation and syncretism, 110
Works: *Alkei i Safo*, 250n57; *By the Stars* (Po zvezdam), 26, 76–77, 81; "The Calling of Bacchus" (Vyzyvanie Vakkha), 253n85; *Cor Ardens*, 225n32, 254n98; "The Firebearers" (Ognenostsy), 250n51; "The Hellenic Religion of the Suffering God" (Ellinskaia religiia stradaiushchego boga), 248–49n35; "Exit Cor Ardens," 254–55n98; "Maenad" (Menada), 10, 254n98; "On Sect and on Dogma" (O sekte i o dogmate), 65; *Pilot Stars* (Kormchie zvezdy), 26; "The Religion of Dionysus" (Religiia Dionisa), 248–49n35; "Sporady," 253n88; "Thou art" (Ty esi), 228n70; "Trial of Fire" (Sud ognia), 253n85, "Artistic Creation" (Tvorchestvo), 46; "Two Elements in Contemporary Symbolism" (Dve stikhii v sovremennom simvolizme), 224n25
Ivanov-Razumnik (Razumnik Ivanov), 271n5
Ivich collection, 168

Joseph (biblical), 25–26
Judaism, 4, 7, 73, 210, 224n19, 241n63, 253n82
Judas (Gnostic), 262n5

Kablukov, S. V., 242n70, 271n6
Kahn, Andrew, 207
kenosis (Bloom), 31
Khardzhiev, Nikolai, 50
Khayyam, Omar, 139
Khazina, Nadezhda. *See* Mandelstam, Nadezhda
Khlebnikov, Velimir, 199; death of, 16
Khodasevich, Vladislav, 238n19, 268n27, 276n12
Kliuev, Nikolai: "Woodsong" (Lesnaia), 62–63
Kochanowski, Jan, 139
Kommissarzhevskaya, Vera, 134, 151, 156, 159, 200
Konevskoi, Ivan, 77, 204
Krivtsov, Nikolai Ivanovich, 179
Kul'bin, Nikolai, 103
Kuzmin, Mikhail, 249n39, 253n89; "Pushkin," 189, 270n42
Kvisisana (restaurant), 7

Lattimore, Richmond, 114
Lebedev, L. V., 195
Lekmanov, Oleg, 68–69, 78; *Kniga ob akmeizme*, 12–13, 50
Lermontov, Mikhail, 192–93; *Masquerade* (Maskarad), 148, 260n23; "The Poet's Death" (Smert' poeta), 267n12
Lerner, Nikolai, 88
Levinton, Georgii, 87
Libra (Vesy), 93, 226n40, 228n68, 241n67

Libra (zodiacal sign), 93–94
life-creation, 9, 12, 64, 97, 131, 234n1
"literary malice," 98
lived life of the poet, 8, 16
Livshits, Benedikt, 22, 30; *The One-and-a-half-eyed Archer* (Polutoraglazyi strelets), 229n5
Logos, 13, 15, 78, 171, 184, 190
Longhi, Pietro, 148, 258n2
Lotman, Yuri, 131
Lozinsky, Mikhail, 13, 70, 195; "At the river's edge" (U potoka), 239n47; "Stones" (Kamen'ia), 243n82; "There is in the world a music of windless heights" (Est' v mire muzyka bezvetrennykh vysot), 68; "Wayfarer" (Putnik), 68
lyric hero, Symbolist. *See* Blok (lyric hero)
lzhe-simvolizm (pseudo-Symbolism), 132

Maeterlinck, Maurice, 200; *Sister Beatrice*, 260n31
Mandelstam, Osip. *See* Index of Works, Mandelstam
Mandelstam, Nadezhda, 22, 50, 118, 160, 249n38, 250n57, 254n94, 259n15, 275n10
Margolina, Sof'ia, 72
mask, 133, 135, 185, 256–57n20
masquerade, 131–35, 140, 148–53; and *mysterium*, 132, 169
materialism, 110, 179
Matich, Olga, 151
Mayakovsky, Vladimir, 106; "Down the Cobblestones" (Po mostovoi), 41; suicide of, 268n16
Medusa, 114–15
Melpomene, 18, 154, 156, 158
Mendeleev, Dmitry, 207
Mendeleeva, Lyubov', 134, 152
Merezhkovsky, Dmitry, 8; "Children of the Night" (Deti nochi), 93; "On the Reasons for the Decline of and New Currents in Contemporary Russian Literature" (O prichinakh upadka i o novykh techeniiakh sovremennoi russkoi literatury), 224n22
metatheatricality, 145, 187
meter: dol'nik, 52, 232n6; hexameter, 205; logaoedic, 52; pentasyllabic, 238n17; in Mandelstam's poetry, 18–19, 39, 52, 93, 163, 167, 232n6; of "Steps of the Knight Commander," 167, 260n37. *See also* stanzaic structure
Mets, A. G., 50, 195
Meyerhold, Vsevolod, 130, 156, 187, 260n23
Milky Way, 139
Minsky, Nikolai, 214
Mints, Z. G., 140, 143–44
misprision (Bloom), 22–23
modernist time poetics, 105–9
Moréas, Jean: "Le Symbolisme," 245n31
Morderer, V. Ia., 103
Morozov, A. A., 96
Moscow Art Theater, 151
Mount Athos, Orthodox monks of, 57
Muratov, Pavel: *Images of Italy* (Obrazy Italii), 148
Musatov, Vladimir, 196
mysterium, 132, 169
myth-creation (mifotvorchestvo), 9, 11, 211
"myth of forgotten Christianity," 11, 100, 109–29
mythopoetic Symbolism: boundary crossings in, 5, 12, 65–69, 70–71, 131–33, 135, 140; *mysterium* and, 132, 169; and myth, 9, 11; narrative structures in, 5, 9–12, 38–39, 56, 59–62, 103, 109, 171, 225n28, 226n35; overview of, 8–12; receptivity in, 215; and religion, 8–12, 41–42, 44–46, 56–81, 109–11, 124–25, 132, 214–15; term, 222n6; and theatricality, 7, 96, 98, 130, 132–33, 151–52, 184, 185–89; influence on structure of *Tristia*, 109–29

Nadson, Semyon, 98, 213, 242n75; "I dreamed I was ill, that my brain burned" (Snilos' mne, chto ia bolen, chto mozg moi gorit), 95–96; "My friend, my brother, [my] weary, suffering brother" (Drug moi, brat moi, ustalyi, stradaiushchii brat), 275n9
nadsonovshchina, 95
Narbut, Vladimir, 13; *Hallelujah* (Alliluiia), 49; review of *Cor Ardens*, 235n5
Nekrasov, Nikolai, 98, 202; "On Weather" (O pogode), 260n25
Neoplatonism, 8–9, 44
Nietzsche, Friedrich, 8, 28, 69, 102, 109, 110, 115, 116, 122, 173, 238n20; *The Birth of*

SUBJECT INDEX | 303

Tragedy, 109, 116, 156; *Thus Spoke Zarathustra*, 23, 64, 70, 236n17
night sun, 97, 126, 168, 171, 173, 175, 177, 179, 182, 184, 254n94, 262n14. *See also* black sun
nominalism, 15
Northern Flowers (Severnye tsvety), 59
Novalis, 201
Novikov, Nikolai, 228n66

Odoevtseva, Irina, 251n65
"ontological rhymes," 30
opera, 116, 122–23, 140, 151, 156–58, 163, 245n32
Orpheus and Eurydice (Gluck), 122–23, 156–57, 163, 269n30
Orthodoxy, Russian, 8, 57, 125–27, 227n53, 247n15. *See also* Christianity
Other. *See* Ideal
"overcoming" of Symbolism, 6, 50, 56, 87
Ovid, 27, 122

pairing of poems, compositional, 51–54
Panova, Lada, 41, 102, 106–7, 247n16
Paperno, Irina, 57–58
parody, 100–105
Pascal, Blaise, 28
Pasternak, Boris, 230n25
Pavlovich, Nadezhda, 267n10
Pavlovsk, 194–95
pendulum: Mandelstam's poems of 1912 organized as, 49–55
Peter's Academy (Petrovskoe uchilishche), 89
Petersburg, 3, 7, 49, 114, 145, 153, 156, 163, 168–69, 184, 195, 205, 262–63n18, 266n54; myth, 107; Symbolists, 70
Petrarch, 42
Petrouchka (Benois and Stravinsky), 257n24
Piast, Vladimir, 7, 203, 240n50, 245n33, 272n24
Pindar, 236n16
play: aesthetic, 6, 55; with boundaries, 12, 132–33, 140, 144–46, 163–64; with boundaries of Sophiological tradition, 41–42; Christian art as, 19, 128; with immediacy and distance, 6–5, 216; poetry as deep, 128; with pragmatics of text, 19–20; realm of within artwork, 45–46
Plutarch: myth of the death of Pan, 252n78

Poe, Edgar Allan: "The Fall of the House of Usher," 78
Poets' Guild, 12, 49
positivism, 8
Potebnia, Alexander, 8
pragmatics of text, 5, 19, 46, 131, 164
Prekrasnaia Dama. *See* Ideal
priority (poetic): and Mandelstam, 27–28
Prometheus, 186, 250n51
propriety (poetic): and Mandelstam, 27
Proserpina, 113–15
Protestantism, 62, 66, 73, 239n25
Prutkov, Koz'ma, 238–39n22
Pushkin, Alexander, 27, 30, 37, 89, 126, 175–76, 184, 195–96, 201, 204, 206, 228n66, 262n14; anniversaries, 88, 184, 189, 192; and Blok, 97–98, 177–79, 182, 184, 189–90, 195–96, 206, 273n30; death of, 88, 97, 184, 189–90, 193–94, 246n43; imitation of, 179; Mandelstam's "superhuman chastity" before, 22
Works: "The Bronze Horseman" (Mednyi vsadnik), 95, 107, 206; *Eugene Onegin* (Evgenii Onegin), 107, 174, 234n24, 257n25; *Feast in the Time of Plague*, 203, 231n38; "For the shores of a distant homeland" (Dlia beregov otchizny dal'nei), 257n37; "Gabrieliade" (Gavriiliada), 160–61; "My Geneaology" (Moia rodoslovnaia), 206; "Prophet" (Prorok), 62; "Remembrance" (Vospominanie), 88; *The Stone Guest* (Kamennyi gost'), 95; Stone Island cycle, 196; "Tale of the Golden Cockerel" (Skazka o zolotom petushke), 95; "To Krivtsov" (Krivtsovu), 168, 177–79, 182; "Under the blue sky of her native land" (Pod nebom golubym strany svoei rodnoi), 257n37

Racine, Jean: *Phèdre*, 18–19, 119
Radishchev, Alexander, 228n66
rampa. See footlights
rationalism, 15, 110
raznochinstvo, 204–10
Realism, 8; theater of, 131
realism (medieval philosophical), 15
receptiveness, vs. independent creativity, 24, 28, 45, 215–16

revolution, 28-29, 114, 122, 125, 148, 168-69, 174-75, 197-99
Reynolds, Andrew, 8, 29
Romains, Jules: *Les Copains*, 14
Romanticism, 6, 8, 10, 23, 79, 105, 115, 131, 161, 172-73, 186; as precursor of Bloom and Symbolism, 28-29, 31; theater of, 131
Rome: St. Peter's Cathedral, 126-27
Ronen, Omry, 4, 14, 44, 46, 59, 68-69, 72, 176, 192, 196, 203, 208
Rudakov, Sergei, 230n25, 244n18, 265n48
Russian civil war, 118, 122
Russian Orthodoxy. *See* Orthodoxy, Russian; Christianity
Russian Riches (Russkoe bogatstvo), 95
Russian Thought (Russkaia mysl'), 89, 94
Ryzhii, Boris, 228n66

St. Petersburg. *See* Petersburg
St. Petersburg University, 224n19
Sappho, 118-20, 160
Schiller, Friedrich, 122; "Elysium," 120-21; "Die Götter Griechenlands" (The Gods of Greece), 121-22
Schubert, Franz: *Lieder*, 115, 121
Scorpio: publishing house, 93; zodiacal sign, 93
Segal, Dimitrii, 68, 151-52
Sel'vinsky, Ilya, 214
semiotics, 131-32, 145-46, 148, 161-62
Severianin, Igor, 49
Shakespeare, William, 139, 200
Shashina, Elizaveta, 193
Shileiko, Vladimir, 68; "His love struggled overmuch" (Ego liubov' pereborolas'), 239n47
Shklovsky, Victor, 204, 238-39n22; *The Knight's Move* (Khod konia), 272n27
Shkuropat, I. I., 103
Shtempel', Natasha, 231n38
Sinani, Boris, 95-97, 172
Skriabin, Alexander, 125, 190, 262n14; Mysterium, 125; "Preliminary Act" (Predvaritel'noe deistvo), 253n87; *Prometheus*, 193-94
Slap in the Face of Public Taste (Poshchechina obshchestvennomu vkusu), 49, 243n1
Sloane, David A., 201
"smysloviki" (senseworkers), 13

Socialist-Revolutionaries, 96-97
Socrates, 102-4
Sologub, Fedor, 8, 37, 42, 50, 185, 236n16
Solov'ev, Sergei, 23, 203, 267n8; "Korolevna," 23; review of *All Melodies* (Briusov), 10-11; "Sergii Radonezhskii," 242n76
Solov'ev, Vladimir, 8, 39, 42, 81, 93, 236n16, 257n36; influence on Blok, 24; theology of, 64-65
Sophia, divine, 8, 81, 103
Sophiological poetry, 41-42
spatial issues in theater, 131-46
spring (Symbolist), 93
Stalin, Iosif, 230n25, 231n35
stanzaic structure, 18, 35, 38-41, 162-63; sonnet, 53, 85, 87. *See also* meter
State Literary Museum, 125, 235n13
Stray Dog cabaret, 49, 103
subtextual criticism/poetics, 13, 29, 44, 150; and Bloom, 231n31
Surikov, Vasily: "Morning of the Execution of the Streltsy" (Utro streletskoi kazni), 267n12
Symbolism: crisis of, 12; early Russian, 8, 11, 42, 77-78, 132, 242n73; European, 8, 42; rhymes, 41, 79, 159, 213; theater of, 131. *See also* mythopoetic Symbolism
syncretism, temporal. *See* modernist time poetics

Taranovsky, Kiril, 114, 160, 192
Tenishev School, 3, 232n3
Terpander, 118-19
theater: Blok's poems of the, 130-46; definition of, 132-33; Mandelstam and, 151, 153-64, 167; vs. masquerade, 131-35
theatricality, 130-46, 148, 151-52, 167, 184; tragedy and, 7, 96, 98, 185-96
theatrical wonder, 153-64
theurgy, 9, 12, 31, 46, 64, 111, 171, 179
Tibullus, 252nn72 and 74
time poetics, modernist, 105-9, 247n16
Tintoretto: "Susanna and the Elders," 153, 258n2
Tiutchev, Fedor, 37, 68, 73-74, 79, 158, 192, 228n66, 250n51; "Problème," 75-76
Toddes, Evgenii, 158, 179
Tolstoy, Lev, 30; *Anna Karenina*, 196
tone: ambivalence of, 5, 43, 45-47, 58, 63,

74; structural cues to, 5; subtleties of, 37–38, 41, 43; unity of, characteristic of Symbolism, 47–48
tragedy: Greek, 109–12, 115, 156; and theatricality, 7, 96, 98, 185–96
Tsarskoe selo, 195
Tynianov, Yuri, 7, 105, 224n19, 229n1, 233n18, 275n7; "Blok and Heine," 268n24

Unexpected Joy (Nechaiannaia radost'; icon), 233n19

Vaginov, Konstantin, 244n18
Verhaeren, Émile: *Hélène de Sparte*, 250n52; "Les horloges," 243n10; "Les pas," 244n19
Verigina, V. I., 256n14
Verlaine, Paul, 4, 77, 102–3, 105, 232n3; "L'Angoisse," 236n16; *Parallèlement*, 51
"verses to *you*," 37, 41–42
Villon, François, 4, 77, 206, 242n78; rhyme in, 40
Virgo (zodiacal sign), 93–94
Volokhova, Natalya, 133, 134

Wachtel, Michael, 22–23
Wandering Jew, 7
Warsaw, 3
Wilde, Oscar: *Salome*, 151
Word, the. *See* Logos
Works and Days (Trudy i dni), 49
World Soul. *See* Ideal

Yakhontov, Vladimir, 162
younger Symbolists. *See* mythopoetic Symbolism

Zenkevich, Mikhail, 13; *Wild Porphyry* (Dikaia porfira), 49
Zhirmunskii, Viktor, 162; "The Poetry of Alexander Blok" (Poeziia Aleksandra Bloka), 105–6, 189; "They Who Have Overcome Symbolism" (Preodolevshie simvolizm), 13, 50
zhiznetvorchestvo. *See* life-creation
Zhukovsky, Vasily: "Pushkin's Last Minutes" (Poslednie minuty Pushkina), 88–89
Zinov'eva-Annibal, Lidiia, 225n32
zodiacal signs, in Symbolism, 93–94

www.ingramcontent.com/pod-product-compliance
Lightning Source LLC
Chambersburg PA
CBHW030107010526
44116CB00005B/129